Essay Index

DATE

93

75-6-76

THE ERA OF
GERMAN EXPRESSIONISM

THE ERA OF
GERMAN EXPRESSIONISM

Edited and annotated by Paul Raabe

Translated by J. M. Ritchie

THE OVERLOOK PRESS
Woodstock, New York

CONTENTS

The Early Years 1910-14

CONTENTS

During and After the War 1915-20

Page

GENERAL REFLECTIONS IN RETROSPECT

APPENDIX

TRANSLATOR'S NOTE

Some of the items included in the present volume of documentation are written in "difficult" prose styles, for which there are no adequate English equivalents. Fortunately, however, the vast majority of the passages are straightforward attempts to recapture the excitement of an age of cultural revolution. Responses to this revolution ranged from the ecstatic to the sarcastic. Diversity is in fact the key-note of this volume, which unfolds the impact of an artistic movement on places as far apart as Hamburg and Prague.

Clearly there have been difficulties in translating this book. However, I have been able to call on the help of Annabel Brown, Rex Last and David Turner, all of whom share my enthusiasm for everything concerned with Expressionism. I also had the extreme good fortune to have my entire translation checked by Agnes Rook who suggested many improvements and corrections. The faults and shortcomings that remain are entirely my own.

J. M. R.

PREFACE

The first decade of the twentieth century still has no name in histories of literature. It was quite simply the "end of Modernism" (S. Lublinski, 1909). Naturalist and impressionist trends were exhausted, *art nouveau* (*Jugendstil*) turned into a neo-classicism: the great literary revolution which had arisen in Germany between 1880 and 1890 had disintegrated into an apparently almost endless series of separate reform movements. And yet, beneath appearance, the roots and seeds of a new artistic explosion were beginning to stir and would bear fruit through the will and passion of a young generation. In the years immediately preceding the First World War, from 1910 to 1914, this generation set itself new goals. Looking back Johannes R. Becher wrote of this generation: "We were possessed. In cafés, in the streets and squares, in artists' studios, we were 'on the march' day and night, we drove ourselves to fathom the unfathomable, and, as poet, painter and composer in one, to create the incomparable 'Art of the Century', a timeless art which would surpass all art forms of preceding centuries." But the will to live and work was not unmixed with premonitions of disaster. Unwittingly this generation bore the mark of Cain: war and death came like a visitation upon mankind, and the words of those writers who survived formed themselves into a scream of revolt, desperation and hatred. Yet something of the old European heritage survived in the passionate hope and faith in the future. In poems and dramas, in declarations and manifestoes, a song of praise to humanity was sung, along with the swan-song of the nineteenth century. For a short period after the war Expressionist literature was supreme in the cultural life of Germany. Then it all faded away. Idealism was finished. The sceptics and cynics took over. Expressionism was dead and there was a turning back to New Objectivity. Gottfried Benn summed up: "As a generation it was ridiculed, despised, and rejected politically as decadent; as a generation, it was abrupt, flashing suddenly like lightning, plunging down, stricken by accidents and wars, doomed to a short life."

What remains is a series of works, poetry and some prose. A number have survived, but many have disappeared without a trace. What is left is the memory of a seething, agitated age in the literary life of the country. Doubt and dilemma have been the lot of those who came after. What was Expressionism? The term has been exhausted of all meaning by the strife of the historians and ideologues. Once the phenomena of the movement have been more closely examined it is no longer possible to assume any unity of style.

Yet with any attempt to describe what it was really like the colourful image of Expressionism rises like a phoenix from the ashes. Expressionism was atmosphere, movement, vivacity. To define the concept it must be concrete. So we let the contemporaries tell the story, the ones who played an active part in it: authors and publishers, wives of the poets and friends of the writers, painters, and impresarios. Each gives his own picture of the age, his own experiences, his own individuality. These memories—many written ten, twenty years ago, some only in the last few years—are subjective backward glances, varied in intention and attitude, varied in form and content. Many wrote from the more detached viewpoint of old age; many are still caught up in the unforgotten experiences of their youth; some are unjust in their evaluation and biased in their judgement, while others strive for objectivity and historical justice. But all the witnesses and contempories represented here are participants in an imaginary discussion about the nature of Expressionism.

All that remained for us to do was to collect these scattered accounts and place them in the appropriate relationship to each other. Many of the contributions have been printed before, although often in inaccessible places; some we have extracted from memoirs. Half a dozen are published here for the first time, some were written specially for this book. The chronological arrangement makes some kind of historical survey possible. At the same time overlapping could not altogether be avoided. But the real intention of this book was not only to capture the atmosphere of a period. What was more important was to let the testimonies of those who were themselves involved communicate as much as possible the names, works and events relating to Expressionism, that is to say the facts. The Expressionist movement took place in the big cities, so it seemed the obvious thing to arrange the accounts according to local centres within the particular time sequence. Expressionistic "Big City" literature originated in Berlin, its natural home. Hence Berlin is evoked the most, although smaller German centres are not neglected.

These accounts fit together to create a whole, and yet this whole remains a fragment. How could anyone succeed in capturing historical life in all its aspects and ramifications? Perhaps the theatre has not been dealt with exhaustively enough: in view of the complexity of Expressionistic drama this is a question of limited space. In the case of Dadaism too we have restricted ourselves to hints and pointers. The parts included here must be considered as representative for the whole. Much additional and related material is given in the appendix. This seemed to be the most sensible way: to mirror a literary epoch in constant succession of new surfaces, and on different planes. It should be pointed out that the editor felt it important to do more than merely present documentary evidence and has added something by way of explanatory commentary in the appendix. In the same way the bibliography and the indexes are intended to make the book a more valuable tool for the further study of Expressionism.

Without the personal view presented by contemporaries, history remains colourless. Their accounts are indispensable for any examination of Expressionism. It is our hope that many more of those who played an active part in these years will follow this example and record their memoirs before it is too late, for what is forgotten is lost for ever.

Paul Raabe

THE EARLY YEARS
1910-14

BERLIN

Heinrich Eduard Jacob
Pre-war writing and the atmosphere in Berlin

Novalis and the Schlegels would probably have been very surprised if someone had approached them in the street, tapped
them on the shoulder and told them they were Early Romantics.
Moreover the man who first popularized the term Romanticism,
namely Wieland (who in his *Oberon* had saddled the hippogryph
for a "ride into the old Romantic land") was certainly no Romantic himself but the very opposite.

By 1920 everybody knew what an Expressionist was. But in
1910 when Expressionism began nobody really knew it as such
... The Expressionists themselves least of all! The painters knew,
because they were consciously anti-Impressionists. But being a
painter didn't count. Contact and connection between the
extremes of literature and the extremes of painting did not exist
until the war. Or rather they became far more frequent then.
Long before he had mounted his great Van Gogh Exhibition[1]
(which, it must be added, was acclaimed by all and sundry and
not merely by art-lovers), the art dealer Paul Cassirer once asked
me crossly why writers hardly ever came to his shows. I felt
entitled to answer because it was too easy to use gimmicks in
painting, the kind of thing we writers detested. It was more
difficult to be gimmicky in writing. (A remarkable answer which
I should certainly never have given at the time of writing this
in 1961.)

Be that as it may: until 1914 progressive Berlin, Expressionist
Berlin was clearly in a state of war between word and image—
between, for example, the painters' journal, Herwarth Walden's
Sturm and Franz Pfemfert's *Aktion*. The *Aktion* was the journal
of the word of action, or at least of the word aspiring to action,
and certainly of the politically loaded word. (The fact that it
also displayed exceptionally good woodcuts was in the nature of

a bonus.) And the *Sturm*—although Else Lasker-Schüler's poems, glosses and verbal quips appeared in it—was really the trail blazer for the painters. They were mutually exclusive! Harden and Kerr, who were at that time at the pinnacle of their polemical notoriety, never, as far as I can remember, commented on a picture . . . That the non-political Walden should later die a political death—he was liquidated as a refugee somewhere in Siberia—is part of his own personal tragedy, just as it was to be the ironic fate of Franz Pfemfert, who had lived so dangerously, not to die at Hitler's hands but to survive the horrors and live out his life in far-away Mexico.

The intellectual climate of the *Aktion* is unforgettable to all who ever worked for it. If you opened the first issue for the year 1912 there was a poem by U. Gaday.[2] The name was Russian and meant: Who am I? There were Russians on the editorial staff who, like Alexandra Ramm, the wife of the editor, was able to read Tolstoy, Brjussow, Dostoevsky in the original. Communism? There wasn't any. But anarchism, pacifism, anti-authoritarianism, and anti-militarism. How the young poets were attracted by all this! Ernst Blass far example. He came "breezing through the town / With a black hat on his poet's head / And a soft down of happiness for his crown."[3] Then there were the many unknowns, who were never included in any anthology, never became famous. And the ones who died young in the first year of the war, like Ernst Stadler and Robert Jentzsch. There was a genuine humorist among them, a humorist-philosopher— perhaps the greatest since Morgenstern. (Satirists were ten a penny; until Tucholsky became supreme.) The humorist-philosopher's name was Salomo Friedlaender and sometimes he used the name "Mynona", which was Anonym(ous) spelt backwards . . . And there was Wedekind, who naturally did not have to be discovered by the *Aktion*, he telegraphed his quips from Munich, whether against theatre censorship or against the Prussification of Bavaria . . . A paper like that was only possible in Berlin. Its boldness (sometimes called "impudence" by its enemies) appealed to all those who looked for some change in the written and spoken life of the future. In politics this meant: no more rhetoric *à la* Wilhelm II, no "Panther leaps to Agadir" or appeals for the slaughter of the socialists. How Franz Pfemfert managed to escape a charge of *lèse-majesté* is a mystery. He even had the nerve to compare Frederick the Great with the Kaiser.

"A policy of enlightenment" was the slogan; and in art the left wing of the *Aktion* came out against "Yesterday's Naturalism", portraits of wretchedness *à la* Hauptmann—because they had made no attempt to *change* the world, which seems rather unjust criticism to us today. Even worse and more unjustly the Expressionist Movement saw in the great Hofmannsthal not the renovator of language, but merely the "Conservative Viennese". Others besides myself found it impossible to convince our friends of the contrary. What the Berlin Expressionist writers really wanted was so difficult to express that one of their leading prophets, Kasimir Edschmid, would have preferred to abandon the term. Finally, however, he did find the words to differentiate Expressionism from Instant Impressionism, which was reviled as an irresponsible cult of the moment; and also from crude Descriptive Naturalism; and thirdly (and this was fundamental) from the priestly remoteness of Stefan George and his circle. "The Expressionist poet", wrote Kasimir Edschmid, "does not see, he beholds. He does not describe, he experiences. He does not represent, he forms anew. He does not accept, he seeks. Now there is no longer a chain of facts: houses, factories, sickness, whores, screams and hunger. Now there is the VISION of these things. Facts are significant only in so far as the hand of the artist reaches through them to grasp what lies beyond. He sees what is human in a whore, what is divine in a factory. He weaves the individual phenomenon into that great pattern, which goes to make up the world".[4]

If this was right (and it was!) then the look of Berlin itself should really have upset the Expressionistic intentions, should perhaps even have destroyed them. For at first sight the houses were entirely expressionless and boring. Only if one sensed behind them a whole mountain range of secret lives—only then did the city no longer offer any resistance to "Expression". All it needed was for a poet to come along with genuine X-ray eyes and genuine love-hate for Berlin. The poet's name was Georg Heym.

Georg Heym, born in Hirschberg, Silesia, a provincial who came to Berlin for the next stage in his professional training, turned into a visionary, a surrealist super-Berliner, such as had never been seen before. What did these houses really conceal? Were they mines, lunatic asylums, or rebel islands which would explode their roofs into space? Heym loved the explosions of colour in the pictures of Van Gogh and hoped he would one day rival them in words. The poem of poems for him, however, was Rimbaud's *Le bâteau ivre*. He himself spoke abominable French, but was convinced that only chance had stopped him from becoming a contemporary of Napoleon and Stendhal. (His dream diary[5] discusses this.) But since he did not know Paris, Berlin represented all cities for him. For months he strove to master Berlin slang, although being incredibly shy this task did not come easily to him. And naturally there was no dialect in his poems anyway: "Tarry casks rolled from gateway large / Of dark warehouse to soaring barge. / The tugs began to pull. The cloud of smoke over oily water soared. / Two steamers came with bands on board." This poem which was naturalistically accurate down to the very smell was still not really naturalistic. It was visionary: "Behind the idyll we saw the night-flare of giant smoke-stacks".[6]

Everything which resisted the vision Heym found fundamentally hateful. So the façade of optimism, the sterile polka-bliss of the superficial Berlin entertainment industry, the music which filtered out of the Metropole Theatre on to the street—above all the composer Paul Lincke. I shall never forget the disgust with which Georg Heym snarled the words and music of Lincke's big hit: "That's the smell of Berlin,—in, in, / It's like jasmine, in— in, / You can feel it begin,—in,—in, / The smell of Berlin—in,— in."[7]

Heym, who read poetry very badly (his delivery was staccato yet withdrawn), would never have been heard in the Berlin of those days if he had not found friends, who propelled him almost by force into the limelight. Kurt Hiller and his New Club did just this. They forced Berlin to listen to Heym. No greater contrast could be imagined between the highbrow atmosphere of this club and Heym's physical appearance. Square and clumsy, he was at the same time "racially handsome". His brown face and his blue eyes would have stamped him a Germanic Idol under Hitler. Fate spared him from having to say farewell to his Jewish friends when they were later hounded out of the country: Hiller, Erwin Loewenson, John Wolfsohn, David Baumgardt and Jakob van Hoddis . . . For Heym was drowned at the age of twenty-four while skating on the Wannsee on January 16th, 1912.

For many of us the death of Heym was the real beginning of the Great War. At least it appears so in retrospect. If he had not drowned in the Wannsee, perhaps he would have been killed at the Battle of the Marne two-and-a-half years later. None of us had felt the coming war as clearly as he had. Not politically—he had no head for that!—however, he saw it striding towards us as a poetic vision. Like the Cyclops raising its club to shatter mankind: "He that slept long has arisen, / Arisen from deep vaults far below. / He stands in the dusk, huge and unknown, / And crushes the moon to pulp in his black hand."[8]

No, we did not see it coming, the collapse of our world. On the contrary one could say: the closer we came to August 1914 the more hectic and sweet the grip of the intellectual hurly-burly of Berlin became. Books, authors, actors! Berlin attracted them all as if by magic. Sternheim's polished stories and Alfred Döblin's first novels: they could not have existed without Berlin, could they? Werfel and Max Brod were from Prague. But where did they raise their voices? Hamburg, Frankfurt, Leipzig, Brussels, Dresden, Vienna, Cologne or Breslau were over-night all turned into suburbs of Berlin. For Berlin was where the publishers lived! Axel Juncker deserves his place in history for making unknown writers famous, and so too does Erich Reiss and above all Ernst Rowohlt who in the spring of 1911 printed Heym's volume of poems *The Eternal Day* and later the posthumous volume *Umbra Vitae*. Already well established were the producer Max Reinhardt, the Deutsches Theater and the Kammerspiele; now suddenly there was a concentration of new establishments. Everything was throbbing: matters of life and death were scarcely conceivable; everything was life. Werfel composed his *Being Alive*. We were filled with the future, and never did just "being there" seem more attractive than at the *Aktion's* "Revolution Ball".[9] The ambiguous title of the theme was just a colourful theatrical gag. One after another the couples fell on their knees before a laughing guillotine as if it were a bed of love—this was the extraordinary thing—to be beheaded. At my side knelt Dora Hiller, with her brown eyes and blonde hair . . . What a world of balls and concerts! Never had Beethoven sounded so freedom-loving, and never had the Chorus to Joy from the Ninth Symphony seemed so truly ours.

Suddenly that unwelcome day, that fateful August 4th, 1914, approached and with a lowered look announced mournfully: "End of the line, Ladies and Gentlemen, everybody out! The Carnival is over!"

Armin T. Wegner
Awakening. Berlin 1910

The sun is shining on the Kurfürstendamm. Whenever I look back, as only an older man can when his past youth reawakens within him—why is it that then there was always a sun shining in the sky? Nothing can be more unjust than memory for it passes over much in silence, and nothing can be more just. It is the summer of the year 1910. In Charlottenburg, too, all is light and bright. Along the Hardenbergstrasse come two law students deep in lively conversation. They have just left a lecture, given by the Professor of Criminal Law, Franz von Liszt, where they met for the first time.[1] Both swear by a new kind of art, called Expressionism—an ambivalent-sounding foreign label.[2] Despite this they have chosen to read Law and Political Science at the university. As in their poetry they were no longer content merely to record the impression received from the world, but to impress upon it the expression of their heart and mind, so too they wanted to change the world.

From the way they move it is possible to tell how different they are. The one who is a year older, and shorter in stature, is distinguished by a high forehead beneath a prematurely receding hair-line. With his intelligent, penetrating, yet not unkind eyes and the precision of his words he reminds one of a scholar. His step is firm and thoughtful, while the younger with the long, swinging stride which will soon take him across half the world, allows his eyes to roam. One is a sage, the other a wanderer.

Kurt Hiller is the name of the older man, who even then had already gathered around him a circle of disciples of the new Expressionist art. The other is the old man who here recounts his youth. On the way along the Hardenbergstrasse they have both called in at the printer of the journal in which the poetry

23

of the awakening century appears. As stirring as the verses and the drawings of faces which look as if they are shattered by dumdum bullets is the name of this journal: *Aktion*—action, deed, fight. Here Kurt Hiller has handed in the proofs of one of his articles, on which with the precision of an engraver he examines every single comma, every paragraph. Not one of the young writers is as good as he is at mortally wounding his enemy with the thrust of a single sentence. As a thinker, who is an artist at the same time, he knows that a fencer must always ensure that every thrust dazzles by its superiority and technique. Eight years later, when in the midst of the upheavals of the German Revolution we forced our way into the Reichstag to establish an "Intellectual Workers' Council", the art of formulation, at which he was a master, was to put a rope round his neck.

The sun is about to set as the two young men reach the Café des Westens on the Kurfürstendamm, where the General Staff of our artistic conspiracy spend their evenings. During the day we hardly ever went there. We have scarcely sat down on the red plush seats beneath the *trompe l'oeil* mirror, when an acquaintance passes me the latest issue of the *Aktion*. Before me I see columns of verse, the poems of Georg Heym printed on grey paper. When I look up, the eyes of my friends are all staring curiously at me; because many of us rejected these poems at first. I was filled with admiration not only for the language and form of the verses, with their echoes of Baudelaire and Stefan George, the unique quality of the poetic images, but also for the supernatural vision of the future which rose up before me, and I was overcome with awe at this image of war. What did I read?

He that slept long has arisen,
Arisen from deep vaults far below.
He stands in the dusk, huge and unknown,
And crushes the moon to pulp in his black hand.

Into the evening noises of the cities there falls far away
The frost and shadow of an alien darkness.
And the round bustle of the markets stops and turns to ice.
A growing silence. They look round. And no one knows.[8]

24

These lines were written in peace-time. Heym drowned two years later in the Wannsee, without experiencing the fulfilment of his prophecy. Poets have always been visionaries, yet seldom if ever was such a mighty pronouncement of impending doom placed in their mouths as was the case with these young artists. Faithful to the rallying cry of their art, to put the imprint of their soul upon the world, they withdrew deep within themselves. But what did they find dormant in their own blood? Starving people, misery, blackened rivers, factories glowing at white heat, pestilential hospitals, prisons, the blinded, the executed, morgues crammed with cancer-riddled corpses, battlefields, popular rebellions, murder, war and death. Who inspired them to such visions? They themselves did not know. Like sunken leaves in a well turned to silver by the water the visions rested there, moved uncannily before their eyes—testimony to a future as yet unknown. Could the poets do other than stammer in half-choked words, when they drew up to the light, what awaited mankind, what nobody wanted to hear and, if it was heard, what nobody believed? Horror seized them by the throat so that the words came mutilated from their mouths, shattered sentences poured from their shattered souls, one single tormented shriek! Unwittingly by uttering their warning pronouncements they conjured up destruction. Quite a few took part in this destruction; before what they prophesied had come to pass, they started to demolish their most precious possession, their own language.

Three years after I had read Georg Heym's poems of war I saw a man standing on the Kurfürstendamm outside the Café des Westens. He did not look like an ordinary newspaper vendor. Over his left arm he carried a pile of copies of a new journal entitled in blood-red letters: "Revolution!".[4] Among its contributors were Hugo Ball, Johannes R. Becher and Gottfried Benn. The title page showed a rebellious mob amid collapsing buildings carrying in its hands a banner bearing the word "Freedom"—and this five years before the popular uprising in the streets of Berlin. At about the same time the disciples of the new art form organized a masquerade at Carnival time under the slogan "Revolution Ball".[5] The walls of the hall were draped in blood-red light. On the heads of the dancers hung the fiery Jacobin caps from the days of the French Revolution. Whenever an art critic or reviewer of the older generation entered the ballroom he found himself seized immediately and dragged to the "execution". He was placed on a covered chest, the death sentence was proclaimed, and then the board was pulled out from under him and purple with embarrassment he sank into the chest until only his legs were left sticking up.

If we look back today on that astonishing generation which, at home in two centuries—the nineteenth and the twentieth—and impelled in equal measure by faith and anger, had set out fifty years ago never to arrive, its ultimate fate seems dark indeed. While it is true that many writers like Franz Kafka achieved fame, even perhaps immortality, the majority were only too soon to take the path to another eternity. Seldom has a generation bled to death so quickly. The Great War demanded many deaths; young poets were prevented from maturing in peace. And then the great eclipse which came over our people in 1933 drove others into exile or to a brutal death. They died all manner of deaths : before the black muzzles of guns, in prison, by the rope at their own or the hangman's hands or snuffed out like vermin in the gas chambers. Others were spared nothing by way of despair, and died of disease, some even of starvation or else eked out a miserable existence in the soup-kitchens of various lands, forgotten and alone. Their sad end would appear less fateful if they had left heirs behind. Their works burned and banned, the silence was too long and too deep for their voices to be capable of reaching the right people. Abroad, or in Germany with the barbed-wire crown of thorns on their head they were silenced for a long time, perhaps for ever. Now, when scarcely anybody remembers them, grandsons and great-grandsons are beginning to ask about them. They borrow their works from the public libraries, hunt for them on the shelves of second-hand book shops like precious treasures or copy their poems out of the only too few remaining editions. What attracts the young people is not only the uniquely creative expressionism of these poets of the beginning of the century, but also the now legendary fate of the poets associated with it. When the young raise their heads from such books, pamphlets, pictures, or journals they seem in some way transfigured; for several of the departed among this noble generation became martyrs and saints in a godless age by reason of the courage and boldness with which they professed their faith.

Ernst Blass
The old Café des Westens

Where did I sit in those days? Where do I sit today? Time has passed and what a time! Things are in print under my name but what I am starting here is an article about the old Café des Westens at the corner of the Kurfürstendamm and the Joachimsthalerstrasse. The corner is still there, the café was closed down.[1] It hadn't been the same for years. Soon a new one will be opened there which will not be the same either. As I said, it's all over. Over—yes, but not over and done with. If I think back can I reconstruct? Hardly. 1910—what's that? I wrote this and that and became the poet of something-or-other. And really I had no such public intentions. I was studying law. 1910—that was before the war. Yes, at that corner, as I said. That was the time for youth, for making a start: genius forging its path and all that. Or at least: the mule groping its way in the mist.

And was I anything more than a corner—this or that came past? Probably, but I am not always aware of it. The sun-horses of time tore away all too hastily with our fate's light chariot (to quote Goethe)—and maybe they weren't even sun-horses.

How can one know what it was really like at the Café des Westens in those days? It's all gone vague and blurred. The faces bring back neither joy nor sorrow. Eighteen years later. The tail-coat was coming in for gentlemen. Smart ladies were wearing hair-pieces. The cocottes were pompous, with their gigantic hats. In my room, at my parents', the stove was short of fuel as usual.

Fine. I still remember the café in all-powerful Berlin. The drowsy gaslight. Lots of people with determined faces. Newspapers and waiters. Just as it ought to be. Everything tasted of smoke. And even in those days we suffered a great deal from boredom. There were still no so-called "Pro-s". What was there

27

in the way of real experience when one was so young, so bedded in youth? Certainly very little—but what there was of it was good.

The café lay in darkness for me and I myself lay in darkness. As yet nothing was clear. I was interested in literature and modern art. That was certain. I read journals, knew what was going on. A year before, in my second semester at Freiburg university, I had read an essay by Alfred Kerr in the library—it had moved and gripped me; it was a conversation with Lessing's ghost about Brahm's Theatre. I had even written poems and lost them again, certainly no great loss.

One day I got to know some people. Students mainly, their chairman was a Herr Doktor. Heinrich Eduard Jacob (I had known him from school but now he had just published a story in the *Welt-Spiegel*)—had said to me: "Why don't you go to the New Club² in the Nollendorf Kasino?" I went along and found a number of people there. Jacob was not among them. I gave my name and I was offered a chair. Soon the chairman came, Dr. Kurt Hiller. I was treated very politely, felt excited and embarrassed. I listened to discussions, essays, poems. A new member read aloud a poem about Berlin. Hiller praised the poem greatly. The reader was tall and fair. His name was Georg Heym.

The club members frequented the Café des Westens, called Café Megalomania by the philistines. I went there too now, sat with the others, was invited by Dr. Hiller to become a member. I accepted gladly, although I felt very young and insecure and regarded the others as older, more qualified to judge, better versed in philosophy, perhaps because they were, perhaps only because they spoke authoritatively.

How I came into my own I scarcely know. I was encouraged, made to write poems and reviews. Things began to snowball. People asked: Have you written anything new this week? Blass poems appeared, at first playful and imitative, then with more feeling, more self-consciousness. But how it all came about I have as little awareness as the Baron in *The Lower Depths*. It came to pass, I did it timidly, just to see how it would turn out.

Things became clearer both inside and around me and I was more capable of seeing what was going on. That then was the Café of my sufferings and forebodings, of my timidity and my thirst for fame, of my friends and foes, later too of my first passion. And what I was engaged in, there amid all my personal sufferings, was a literary movement, a war on the gigantic philistine of those days, who was almost as bad as the bestial snob of today. Yes, it was a spirited battle against the soullessness, the deadness, laziness, and meanness of the philistine world. In the Café, soul was still worth something. Yes, it was an education in art, this institution to which I think back as to a hard preparatory school, not without some feeling of pride at having been through it.

It was a place of refuge and an unparliamentary parliament. Even the timid and the silent learned how to talk and express themselves, learned to recognize what it was they really felt deeply about. It was an education in emotional sincerity.

What was in the air? Above all Van Gogh, Nietzsche, Freud too, and Wedekind. What was wanted was a post-rational Dionysos. Van Gogh stood for expression and experience as opposed to Impressionism and Naturalism. Flaming concentration, youthful sincerity, immediacy, depth; exhibition and hallucination. The term "Expressionism" was coined by others; but in our circle we had been sailing in Expressionistic waters for a long time. Van Gogh: that meant the courage of one's own means of expression; Nietzsche: the courage to be oneself; Freud: the hidden depths and problems of the self; Wedekind: the problem of human relationships exploding (in brilliant visions). There was much talk of Visions. Visions were the criteria in pictures, foreboding and universal sensibility the criteria for poems.

As some of us were city types and didn't want to lose contact with our milieu, city and intellectual problems were exploited as our material. It was our attempt to give an age of progress its own art—giving the word art absolute value; we supplied the poetic side of rational or technical facts, or rather we experienced these consciously as poetic facts. We used to speak a lot about the politics and the politicizing of mind and art alongside the poetics and the poeticizing of the mechanical and the intellectual. In this respect the proclamations of Kerr and Heinrich Mann were not ineffectual. Both of them could be claimed as modern Expressionist poets and intellectuals. One demand of Kerr's was for the "clear-sighted" bard.

I keep saying "we", but who were "we"? Just a lot of different people who frequented the same café. We didn't all sit around in big ugly clumps carrying on discussions. There was a great deal of distance between one individual and the next, one table and the next, often suggesting a rather formal atmosphere. Opinions or achievements were carefully weighed, sharply criticized. There were, it is true, enthusiastic friendships between particular individuals, but on the whole life in the Café des Westens was made up of different individuals with different opinions even when they appeared to be saying similar things. We were not Bohemians in the usual sense; we had a sharply defined feeling of responsibility, were radical and middle-of-the-road; we were young and doubtless did not have the widest possible horizons, but we were artists who were striving to achieve and who did create something worthy of regard even today. What we did then developed into the wild iconoclasm of Expressionism, but what came after cannot really be held against us. And if today we have become more personal, without a public centre, there is one circumstance of those years which must be considered apart from our present situation, a circumstance which cannot be valued too highly.

We were definitely the opposition. There were two camps. There was the enemy and the opposition. In those days one could afford the luxury of despising the philistine not only with one's fist in one's pocket; but one could snub him. One could be anti-capitalistic and acapitalistic and cut oneself off completely. There was no thought of careers and incomes. One rejoiced at recognition without any desire for success. It was a completely different atmosphere from now. Today much has been accepted, even if wrongly and improperly accepted: Van Gogh is a master, everybody knows Freud or Kerr, Heinrich Mann or Wedekind. They may be ignorant of who they really are but with celebrities this has always been the case. For ages, they have been writing for newspapers and publishing with any publisher they like; the only exceptions that occur to me are Stefan George and Karl Kraus who were also among our mentors. The introvert spirit which ruled us could not hold out in such a casual world. In the end we were delivered up to success or failure. For all I know there may well have been some philosophy of history behind this—there always has to be one—or at least a sociology: in any event it has become almost impossible to be anything but central and collective, a situation which is harmful for art and does nobody any good. There is enough money about to protect and support art, but taste is undermined. Philistinism and the sporting classes have taken over to a horrifying degree. Any aesthetic sport-lover thinks the times of Pindar have returned. Any common-or-garden philistine thinks he too has a Roman's heart. No amount of money or publicity can purchase what is essential to art or mankind!

Please excuse this diversion. I couldn't help thinking about it when I thought of my old friends. There was nothing of the anarchist dive about the Café des Westens. It was simply a meeting-place for non-philistines. In those days there were periodicals with a specific flavour: Herwarth Walden's *Sturm*, Franz Pfemfert's *Aktion*. Wilhelm Herzog's *Pan*. In them, items appeared which concerned and excited us. Café-extracts conceived in carefree, commerce-free nights. In them the courage to be different, to be yourself, came to flower. I'm thinking of Walden's exhibitions and readings. I remember the first Kokoschkas I saw at his place, staggering visions of humanity, colourful expressionistic genius: Kokoschka was the painter genius of the generation. I remember early meetings with Pechstein, the first exhibition of the New Secession, what it looked like and what it meant to us. I remember an evening with the Futurist leaders Boccioni and Marinetti who spoke crazy French; Else Lasker-Schüler listened for a while, then pointed to the bright stone of her ring and said with her Rhineland accent *couleur*. I think of her poem about the Tibetan Carpet, that miracle of language, love and womanhood. Our meetings in the Neo Pathetic Cabaret. The Cabaret Gnu. Of Georg Heym's roaring visions and chords, which the young cyclop strung together one after the other. Of correspondence and long night walks with Hiller. Of Hardekopf's diabolic depressions, and his witty peevishness. Of Carl Einstein's cleverness. Of Leonhard Frank before anybody had heard of Leonhard Frank. Of Dr. Alfred Döblin who apart from his little beard gave no other indication of what he was going to turn out to be. Of Wilhelm Herzog's empathetic temperament. The subtlety and analytical cunning of Rudolf Kurtz. The possessed, fascinating, apodictic poet Jakob van Hoddis who was slowly afflicted by a serious psychosis. And again I think of Kurt Hiller, the best friend anybody could have had in his youth.

It is hard not to become sentimental.

While I write this down it's as if I were sending out greetings to acquaintances and strangers, to friends, foes, detractors. Today they are different and scattered in different places. Where are they, where am I? Somewhere between stability and instability. Many may be still the same but they seemed different then. Did one tend to grapple with more significant things? Did one try harder or was one simply younger? Many made their names, played their parts. What about the forgotten ones who never became famous! Maybe they are the ones who really matter. The present and the past merge and become one.

I can see myself on my way upstairs to a Simmel lecture reading a poem to the student Rudolf Kayser; it was called *Childhood* and to my amazement it appeared shortly afterwards in the *Fackel*.[3] I remember the first scrupulous lyrical pieces Wolfenstein gave me to read. I saw young Leo Mathias but knew nothing about him. What we were doing was more private, more recessive in intention. We had no thought for public acclaim and its agonies. Hiller was acquainted with Max Brod whose *Nornepygge Castle*[4] had moved and enriched many of us. Brod read from his works in Cassirer's Salon on an evening arranged by us. I was in charge of taking tickets at the door. Brod said to me: "Could I please have an especially good seat for my friend Franz Werfel."[5] The name was still unknown, maybe I didn't even catch it correctly, never saw the man in question. Months later Brod read aloud from his friend's poems. Among them was the *Maid-Servant*, the *Beauty* and many others which have since become favourites from the *Friend to the World*. Then I came across poems by Werfel in the *Fackel* or in the *Herder-Blätter* which Willy Haas published in Prague.[6] It could hardly be called our worst time. Soon I got to know them both. In the Café naturally. They were amazed at how formal and "Prussian" we were in our circle, how seriously we regarded trivia, how we "took issue" with everything, drew up resolutions, played polemics almost without knowing it.

I remember the extraordinary stimulus which radiated from Franz Blei and his journals, the *Hyperion*, the *Loser Vogel*. And from Wilhelm Herzog's papers. When Kerr was editing *Pan*[7] he asked me by phone for a contribution (I did not get to know him personally till some time later) with the words: "Write what you really feel deeply about." We could do that in those days, we were expected to, we wanted to. We expressed ourselves directly. Only later were we distracted by the atmosphere of notoriety, one's "work", one's "career". In some cases it was also the desire for stability in the spiritual sense, to escape from the instability of adolescence.

It has not been my intention to deliver a funeral oration. I did not want to become melancholy. But in those early days many of us lived through bitter suffering in the shadow of suicide; experiences in our private lives were far more important than fame. And we had countless detractors, who hurt us—we were sensitive, we didn't know who we were or who we were becoming.

A lot more could be said about all this, enough to fill a book if anybody would be prepared to read it. I break off at this point. Just as I suddenly broke with the Café in those far-off days and went to Heidelberg. In search of more space, more stability. Leaving important work behind.

What I have written here is pretty fragmentary even for a subjective report. Maybe it was not like that. But today it looks at least three-quarters true. No wilful falsification or arranging.

Alexandra Pfemfert
The birth of *Die Aktion*

It was at the beginning of February, 1911 about two o'clock in the morning when my husband woke me with the words: I have it, I have it. I knew at once what he was referring to, the name of his new journal. That evening at our table in the Café des Westens, hours had been spent trying out names for the new paper. With us were our friends: Carl Einstein, Jakob van Hoddis, Anselm Ruest, Ludwig Rubiner, the painter Max Oppenheimer (Mopp for short), and others.

Until that day Franz Pfemfert had been editor of the weekly *Der Demokrat*. The publisher and owner of this paper was Dr. Georg Zepler, then a leading figure in the Freethinker Movement. About the second half of January, 1910 Dr. Zepler had made Franz Pfemfert the following offer: Pfemfert should take over editorial control of the *Demokrat*, while he, Dr. Zepler, would edit the last two pages in the interest of the Free Thinkers. Each was to be independent of the other. Pfemfert immediately accepted this suggestion. On the *Demokrat* Pfemfert already had working for him Georg Heym, Jakob van Hoddis, Carl Einstein, Ludwig Rubiner, Myona, Kurt Hiller and others who later formed the main staff on the new journal *Die Aktion*.[1]

Their arrangement worked quite well until the end of January, 1911 when one morning the printer of the *Demokrat* informed Franz Pfemfert by telephone that Dr. Zepler had killed an article by Kurt Hiller which was already in type. Pfemfert immediately phoned Zepler and protested against this intrusion on his editorial autonomy. When Zepler told him that as publisher he could not accept responsibility for this article Pfemfert explained to him that he carried full responsibility for that part of the paper. And as Zepler did not retract his objection, Franz immediately broke off association with the *Demokrat*. His collaborators all came out *en masse* with him.

The very same day Franz sought out his friend Tom, the printer Tominski, who had just bought a small printing works, reported what had happened and asked him if his works could bring out a new journal about the same size as the *Demokrat* within eight days. Tom promised to do so, even if it meant having the page-proofs printed by another press.

And so a name had to be found for the new journal. Mopp (Max Oppenheimer) who had taken part in the hunt for a name had declared his readiness to sketch a lay-out for the title page in the shortest possible time.

When Franz said: *Die Aktion* at 2 a.m. I liked it immediately.

Eight days later the first number of the *Aktion* appeared.[2]

Claire Jung
Memories of Georg Heym and his friends

In the summer of 1911—I was then nineteen years old—I experienced what was to be the most important encounter of my life: I was introduced to the literary circle of the *Aktion*. This literary and political journal had been founded that year by Franz Pfemfert and in it was to be found the avant-garde literature of the time. For many young writers this journal was the first spring-board to fame. Poems by Gottfried Benn, Johannes R. Becher, Max Herrmann-Neisse, Georg Heym, Else Lasker-Schüler, Jakob van Hoddis, Alfred Wolfenstein, Ernst Stadler, Alfred Lichtenstein, Oskar Kanehl, Richard Oehring and Ernst Blass appeared in it, together with prose works by Franz Jung, Ludwig Rubiner, Franz Blei, Ivan Goll, Walther Rilla, Heinrich Schaefer, Erwin Piscator and many others. Prints by many young graphic artists of the time made their first appearance in the *Aktion*. Political commentaries were regularly written by Franz Pfemfert himself. Among the contributors to the *Aktion* were Karl Liebknecht and Rosa Luxemburg.

My first acquaintance with the Action Circle came about through Georg Heym. My friend Hildegard Krohn had come to know Heym and a deep love sprang up between these two young people, very much against the wishes of her family. So, as Hilde's best friend it was up to me to provide a cover for their friendship. What I did was to pick up Hilde at her home every day and return again with her some hours later, thereby creating the impression that she had been with me all day.

About this time in Berlin the literary meetings organized by the *Aktion* and Herwarth Walden's *Sturm* were taking place in the art galleries of Paul Cassirer or in the Secession on the Kurfürstendamm and in the back-room of the old Café Austria in the Potsdamer Strasse. At these meetings the latest works of young and mostly unknown poets were read aloud for the first time before a fairly large audience. This audience, which included Hilde Krohn and myself among its most faithful supporters sat eagerly attentive in these tiny generally smoke-filled rooms. The audience consisted mostly of young people. Even if much of the poetry was strange and not always entirely comprehensible we felt that in the rhetoric of the lines or the prose passages which were delivered against a setting of pictures by Kokoschka and Kandinsky, Max Pechstein and Franz Marc or Paul Klee, a new life force was being expressed pointing to the future and mobilizing the whole of man's intellectual forces.

I remember the first evening devoted to the work of some new poets who called themselves the Neo-Rhetoricals. We had come on the advice of Georg Heym. The evening was dedicated to Else Lasker-Schüler whom I saw here for the first time. She was a true poet. She knew the magic of words and captured a better and lovelier world in her verse. What Thomas Mann said of poets could be applied to her: "the poet is not somebody who invents things, but somebody who creates something out of things as they are." She herself once expressed the meaning of her own creative work when she met me in the street, sad and confused over some conflict I was going through: "My dear child, write a lovely poem. Out of every suffering a poem must blossom to alleviate another's suffering."

In this poet there was something of the world of the Orient whose radiance is captured in so many of her longer poems and her poetic miniatures. She wanted to beautify the world with the magic of her imagination, make it light and gay. "You have to look for heaven within yourself," she wrote in one of her books bearing the significant title, *My Heart*. "It flowers best in the human breast. And whoever finds it should tend the heaven of its blossom." Else Lasker-Schüler is dead. The Black Swan of Israel, as her friend and countryman Peter Hille once called her, has ceased to sing, and the world is the poorer by one radiant beauty and one brilliant spirit.

From the perspective of our unsettled, disturbing time the years before the First World War seem an age of profound peace and perfect harmony. But to the older members of the pre-war generation who actually lived through that decade this bears no relation to reality. The creative works in which the expression of this age has been captured already show the dissolution of form. In all of them the disintegration of the old social ties, the collapse of an all-embracing and till then generally accepted faith is already visible, but also the quest for a new one, a return to a set of rules. Already the signs of a coming conflict were appearing on the horizon of the age, already discernible in the symphony of a satiated life were the discordant notes of the call to battle made by a strangled and deprived life force.

For, like all things living, man's soul is also the product of an organic development, it too is subject to natural laws and is perhaps the first to detect the coming of a new age. Hence what is clear from all the artistic creations of that time is this hyper-sensitivity, the prophetic awareness common to all creative movements that a revolution was brewing, a re-orientation of culture and a struggle for a totally different way of life and a new kind of relationship between man and man.

After the Impressionist poetry of resignation, whose most beautiful works were verses of a deeply melancholy nature by Hugo von Hofmannsthal or poems of weary renunciation such as can often be found in Rainer Maria Rilke, a new form of art attempted to bring about a revolution in style by activating all man's powers. Not only would a transformation be achieved in artistic form, Expressionism also intended to evoke a revolution in the general attitude to life. To German literature of the pre-war period the poet Georg Heym seemed to be one of the white hopes of early Expressionism.

From an ancient Silesian family active in the Civil Service and the Church, Georg Heym came to Berlin at an early age. The intention was for him to become a lawyer, but a legal career was not really acceptable to his liberal spirit, although he did manage to get his doctorate. In a letter to Hildegard Krohn he once wrote the sentence: "Whenever I enter one of those court buildings I have such a horrible feeling of my own human worthlessness and wretchedness that I always seem to myself to be completely out of place. The people running around there in gowns always look like walking statute books." So Heym turned to literature. His first poems appeared in *Aktion*. His volume of poetry *The Eternal Day* was produced in the period from March, 1910 till January, 1911 and published by Ernst Rowohlt in Leipzig, who also published the second collection of Heym's posthumous poems *Umbra Vitae*. The twenty-four-year-old poet never lived to see the appearance of this work whose title, *Shadows of Life*, he had himself intended for it. Friends saw to its publication in May, 1912. The poet Georg Heym had been drowned on January 16th, 1912 while skating on the Havel near Schwanenwerder with his friend, the poet Ernst Balcke. Eye-witnesses who saw the accident from the bank, but who were unable to get there in time to help, described the incident as if his friend Ernst Balcke had intended to commit suicide by leaping into a hole in the ice and Heym had drowned too while trying to save him.

A tragic feature of the accident was the fact that Hildegard Krohn could not take part in the skating party as Heym had wished. In order to avoid conflict with her parents she had Heym's letters sent to her via a *Poste Restante*. She received the card with the invitation to come skating a day too late, as she had not been able to go out for several days because of illness. I had gone to fetch her as usual and together we went to the Post Office where Hilde found Heym's card. The evening papers that day carried the news of the accident on the Wannsee. Hilde was in complete despair, for she had the feeling that if she had been present the mood and conversation of the two friends might never have veered towards the depths of depression which was the cause of Balcke's suicide. Although Georg Heym could often be youthfully gay and full of boisterous high spirits, nevertheless none of his works are free of the shadows cast by events that were to come. The soul of Heym the poet was filled with a consuming and constant unrest. His heart was with the suffering and the rejected, the poor of this world. In his poems he spoke of the mad, the blind and the deaf, the captive, the sick and the dead. He foresaw all the torments of war as well as the destruction of cities. His poems *War* or *The City of Torment* could have been written in our own time. And that's what still links his poems with us to this day. It's as if they spoke of our suffering, as if their author had experienced in one vast vision all the horrors of our days and their shadows cast a spell of sadness over his art, even where it speaks of love. The tone his powerful, picturesque language prefers is always the sombre, the dark colours, their rhythm filled with passionate drama. His dreams were linked to the time of the French Revolution, which he felt to be a turning-point in the history of mankind. This is how he expressed it in a letter: "I have been depressed for several days—a kind of apathy had settled over me. Now I know my sickness: nothing to stir the soul, no great activity. If only I had been born during the French Revolution. Nowadays there is nothing you can get enthusiastic about, nothing you can make your life's work."

Heym's poetic models were the French poets Verlaine, Rimbaud, Baudelaire and Flammarion.

The last of his poems written the day before his death bears the title *Mass* and is filled with a premonition of death; the voice of the Beyond can already be heard in it. Already, in his earlier poems, Georg Heym had experienced and suffered death by drowning: in the *Death of the Lovers* and in *Ophelia* the vision of the eternal grave in the watery depths is a painful enticement towards that shadowy forest he conceived to lie at the bottom of the sea.

Georg Heym was the first to take Hilde Krohn and myself to the Café des Westens. Much has been written about that famous Café Megalomania of the Kurfürstendamm, on the corner of the Joachimsthalerstrasse where the Berlin Bohemians met. Some of the little marble tables had drawings and sketches protected by a glass plate laid over them. Perhaps the great room of the Café was not particularly attractive, but it did have something of an atmosphere of intellectual tension, which is nowadays completely lacking in all our Artists' Clubs. Forced discussions, clubs for actors and journalists and various others from the artistic *métiers* will never by conscious effort create an atmosphere like this. It must be something that has grown, developed out of the real conflicts of the age. When the Café des Westens was closed the Romanische Café by the Gedächtniskirche took over its rôle and its patrons. But the old Café Megalomania, where at any hour of the day or night one could meet the people one wanted to talk with or start a paper with, open a studio with, form a group with—Café Megalomania—was no more. In the Café des Westens I once met Ernst Rowohlt, the courageous man who published all the young poets. Heym spoke with great respect of this man who published his third book *The Thief*, a collection of short stories. He called him his literary father and sponsor.

After Heym's death Hilde Krohn and I remained faithful to the *Aktion*. First of all some friends of Heym's (David Baumgardt, Golo Gangi, W. S. Ghuttmann, Jakob van Hoddis, Robert Jentzsch) had seen to it that a posthumous volume of his poems was published. Franz Pfemfert also arranged a Heym Memorial Evening at which his poems were read.

My own intellectual development, my own literary work was decisively influenced by this time. Naturally, I too wrote poems, naïve and rather romantic ones; the models I emulated being, of course, Hofmannsthal and Rilke and Richard Dehmel. [. . .]

One has to understand the fascination this first encounter with the world of intellectual enthusiasm had for young people. It was at this time that the Schiller phrase: *"Schnell fertig ist die Jugend mit dem Wort"* was adapted to read: *"Pfemfertig ist die Jugend mit dem Wort."*

Soon after that we got to know Pfemfert better. He was a small, very kindly, lively character, who, unless I'm mistaken, started life as a printer. In any case, the tips of his index and middle fingers were missing on his left hand having been ripped off by a printing press. He was married to Alexandra Ramm, a Russian who was also active on the literary scene and known particularly for her translations from the Russian, as was her sister Maria, who was married to the writer Carl Einstein. I spent many an afternoon and evening at the Pfemferts'. In the little room overflowing with books and newspapers sat Pfemfert rolling cigarette after cigarette. *Papyrossi* were smoked and endless cups of tea were drunk in the Russian manner. The phone rang all the time and visitors were constantly coming and going. In this way I once met Rosa Luxemburg in the dark corridor of the apartment; she was just coming as I was going. Pfemfert introduced me and for a moment she gave me her hand and looked at me. Knowing of her speeches and writings without, I must admit, having the slightest idea of their political significance, I was still surprised by her petiteness and delicacy. Her visit must have concerned something important, because she at once plunged into conversation with Pfemfert and I remember the words: "We'll have to do something immediately."

Johannes R. Becher
On Jakob van Hoddis

When I speak of my past, my literary past that is, I wonder what haven't I done to correct the Expressionist Rebellion *post factum* and to adapt my clumsy poetic monsters to suit my present viewpoint, thereby only robbing them of their grotesque attraction. So I recently flipped through a bound volume of the *Aktion* and I was amazed how dead and antiquated most of the contributions seemed to me. It's true, occasionally an article had the power to make me read it again or some fact or other was capable of impressing me, but—gone. Gone, all the uproar and tumult, gone the *Aktion*, gone our youth with its poetic, often grotesque, errors and mistakes. I tried to imagine myself fifty years younger and tried to explain to my younger self what this time had meant for us. The young man I had turned into shook his head. He couldn't understand, he could find nothing in the past capable of inspiring such intoxication, such literary excesses . . . It's true a novel could express it all, bring the past back more or less as it was, but how poor even this would seem, or so it appeared to me. And yet we have to try to recreate if we are to produce works of art. Everything, even the most up to date, is historical because it always follows events no matter how hard it may try to be abreast or even ahead of them. Yet the past can be recreated, but differently, quite differently from what we, who were in it and passed away with it, are prepared to believe. While it is true that the past cannot be reproduced with its specific aroma, if I may be pardoned the expression, yet we can reproduce it and produce it anew in the sense that it had helped to create the present which we experience. By recognizing in the past how our present has been created out of it and is still being fashioned by it, then to that extent the past cannot ever be lost. But the recognition that the past may be recreated in this particular way implies that we give up all hope—and the decision is frequently painful—of recapturing the specific dream-like quality peculiar to the past which remains irrecoverable.

I do not have the literary talent to recreate the effect of the poem I want to talk about now. It would stretch even the wildest dreams of my readers to breaking-point were I to attempt an account of the magic there was for us in that poem by Jakob van Hoddis, *End of the World*.[1] These two stanzas, these eight lines, seem to have transformed us into different beings, to have carried us up out of a world of apathetic bourgeoisie which we despised and which we did not know how to leave behind. These eight lines helped us escape. We kept discovering new beauties in these eight lines; we sang them, we hummed them, we murmured them, we whistled them to ourselves. We went to church with these eight lines on our lips and we sat whispering them to ourselves at the cycle races. We shouted them to each other across the street like catch-words; we sat together with these eight lines, freezing and starving, and speaking them to each other so that the hunger and cold ceased to exist. What had happened? In those days we did not know the word : metamorphosis. Not till later was there talk of transformation and especially when real transformations had become scarce. But we had been metamorphosed by these eight lines, transformed, and even more, this world of apathy and ugliness suddenly appeared to us as if it too could be stormed and captured. Everything that had caused us fear or anxiety before had lost its power over us. We felt like new beings, like creatures on the first day of creation, a new world was to be ushered in with us, and we swore we would cause such an uproar that the bourgeois would be struck deaf and dumb and consider it a blessing to be sent straight to Hades by us. We stood differently, we breathed differently, we walked differently, we suddenly felt as if our chests had expanded to double their ordinary size—for we had grown physically, we had turned into giants. And the poem we bore before us as a talisman for our campaign, to usher in a massive Rennaissance for mankind, went like this :

> *The bourgeois's hat flies off his pointed head,*
> *the air re-echoes with a cry.*

Roofers plunge and hit the ground,
And at the coast—one reads—seas are rising.

The storm is here, the savage seas hop
On land and crash thick dams.
Most people have a cold.
Trains fall off bridges.

Well, I myself find it impossible to recreate its "contemporary", as we would have said then, epoch-making impact. Dozens of poets have since written imitations of this poem and cheapened it, and in many anthologies devoted to the Expressionist Decade I have found no mention of it.

Would I give some idea of its impact if I were to describe its author Jakob van Hoddis? Ludwig Meidner has sketched him, attractive and animated as he scarcely imagined himself in normal life. He was dwarflike, of bedraggled appearance, grey, unshaven, pimply—unspeakable hands—at all times he was wrapped in a woolly scarf which desperately needed washing, shy, quite whimsical and already a little mad and soon afterwards he did end up in an asylum in Thuringia. But this poem, whose power even today stuns me, possibly because of the extraordinary experiences and events to be read between the lines, expresses in a broken, fragmentary and almost crazed voice the strange mood of the century.

Some poems and some poets have since had a similar impact on me. I cannot say that Dante's *Inferno*, Petrarch's sonnets, the works of Rimbaud, Baudelaire, Swinburne, Flaubert or Stendhal did not grip me as deeply and turn me in other directions. Perhaps it is difficult for many people to imagine today what a world-shattering event the reading of some books was for us. Yes, Shakespeare's sonnets were a world-shattering event and we spoke of nothing else but their stanzas. We would buttonhole all our acquaintances, even complete strangers, about them and attempt to explain to them the beauty of these poetic miracles. We may have been considered mad, but we did not let this distract us from our belief in the beauty of poetry, the mission of poetry, our belief in the poetic principle. Yes, that's how it was. Can that time be recreated? Not until a similar epoch emerges which will evince once more a passion for literature—then perhaps this new age may remember that earlier one and recognize its kinship. This, as I see it, is the only way the past can possibly be recreated.

We seemed to be in the grip of a new universal awareness, namely the sense of the simultaneity of events. Some learned literary types found a label for this quickly enough, namely "Simultanism". Jakob van Hoddis, however, lectured us while we wandered night after night from one end of the city to another (you see, we were peripatetics) to the effect that even in Homer's time this feeling of simultaneity had already been expressed. According to him a comparison in Homer was not there just to show a thing, but to create in us a feeling of simultaneity, of worlds without measure. If Homer describes a battle and compares the clash of arms with the sound of a forester's axe, then the poet only used this comparison in order to show us that while the battle was going on the silence of the forest was also being shattered by the axe-blow of the woodcutter . . .

Roofers plunge and hit the ground,
And at the coast—one reads—seas are rising.

These are the words in Jakob van Hoddis' *End of the World*. At the same time as the slaters are plunging from the rooftops, the flood-tide is mounting, or, nothing exists on its own in this world, every unique entity merely appears to be so, in fact it is part of an infinite whole. "Most people have a cold" and at the same time "trains fall off railway bridges". The catastrophic event is unthinkable without a simultaneous triviality. All things great and small intermingle, nothing can exist sealed off by itself. It was this experience of simultaneity we were eager to express in our poems, but van Hoddis seems to have anticipated all our efforts and none of us managed two stanzas like his *End of the World*. Anything significant in Alfred Lichtenstein and Ernst Blass came from van Hoddis. The experiences of simultaneity became a blueprint, and bureaucratic poetry was churned out, constructed mathematically to the last word, with every statement followed by its opposite until the arbitrariness and lack of order destroyed any kind of connection or sense. Later I discovered that not only in Sinclair Lewis but even as early as in Balzac and in many other writers this awareness of simultaneity had been partially expressed without, however, becoming fossilized or doctrinaire. But already new events were casting their shadow with the growing influence of politics on our poetry. The outbreak of the First World War was imminent.

Alfred Richard Meyer
Alfred Lichtenstein and Gottfried Benn

It is no longer possible to imagine our excitement as we used to spend our evenings sitting in the Café des Westens or outside Gerold's by the Gedächtniskirche sipping our modest drinks and waiting for the *Sturm* or the *Aktion* to appear. Our expectation was less for the intoxication of seeing ourselves in print than for keeping a weather eye open in case we were attacked—words could burn like quicklime and sulphuric acid. The air was heavy with an uncanny hostility with which we had to deal. The code of the duelling student societies was hardly appropriate here. Georg Heym was the only one whose potential physical prowess was spoken of in whispers. Had new fronts formed? Could another turncoat be nailed? Which camp seemed about to break up? Were there cracks in the bulwark of any particular friendship? Who was on the way up? or down? The stock-market reports were a matter of supreme indifference to us. We ourselves were the valuable commodities! And everybody was in the know. What was the new man's name? Alfred Lichtenstein-Wilmersdorf. And his poem was called *Twilight*.[1] Would it displace Jakob van Hoddis's *End of the World*?

> A stout kid plays with a pond,
> The wind has got caught in a tree.
> The sky looks pale and washed out,
> As if its make-up had faded.
>
> On long crutches bent crooked,
> And chattering, two lame men crawl on the field.
> A blond poet is perhaps going crazy.
> A pony stumbles over a lady.

> *A fat man is stuck to a window.*
> *A young man fancies a supple woman.*
> *A grey clown pulls on his boots*
> *A pram screams and dogs swear.*

Alongside van Hoddis, this Lichtenstein had appeared from Wilmersdorf—an area only recently incorporated into greater Berlin—he liked to stress. In 1913, scarcely two years later, the pamphlet *Twilight* appeared under my imprint and did much to encourage the boldness of the Expressionist movement.

A sad eccentric, that's what René Schickele[2] calls him, and speaks at the same time of his comic objectivity. But here it isn't easy to fix the borderline between conscious and unconscious, however naturally one is inclined to allow more play to the latter—and particularly so when Lichtenstein later split himself in two and became a Kuno Kohn as well, adding by this invention a certain masochistic touch to his nature. Following the poet's death in battle his complete works, two volumes in all, were collected by his friend Kurt Lubasch thereby ensuring the preservation of the more tragic notes from which Lichtenstein was never free. The case with van Hoddis was similar: garden-work in mental twilight, not unlike the later Hölderlin: "Vision and exhaustion, twilight and silent knowing." (Wilhelm Michel.) Light growing, fading. Not nearly so simply as Schopenhauer conceived the definition of the comic to be the discrepancy between the concrete and the concept.

Tragedy.   Dullness.   Humour.

Don't we come closer to the roots of the matter if we use the terminology of I. A. Richards, and speak of the "isolated ecstasies"? For even Kurt Hiller's obsession with manifestos or the fulminations of Marinetti, chieftain of the Futurists, against libraries and museums. They, too, remained isolated like their ecstasies, because they were not so much masters of the current as carried along by it.

Something more must be said about the decisive year 1911, and 1912, its equal for feverish intellectual meetings and stormy parties. To reach the desired serenity by way of as much turmoil as possible: *intranquille tranquillitatem, inquiete quietem?* The war was to intervene as the cruellest caesura of all, the war of which Lasker-Schüler, Ernest Stadler, Ludwig Meidner, Theodor

Däubler, Gottfried Benn had had such uncanny premonitions.

Gottfried Benn? Even as late as March 1912 nobody had ever heard of him. Except for a few of his friends. This included Adolf Petrenz, the editor who passed on to me a confused manuscript which I found irritating to read : it made me want to flick through its pages and close it as quickly as possible until I came to a cycle of poems, tacked on as an appendix, which seemed to me to be completely unlike the verses that had gone before. I shouted out loud. Whoever wrote that was not guided by any theory, but by his experience of medical practice. *Morgue*, the cycle was called and the individual poems had the titles *Little Aster, Handsome Youth, Circulation, Negro's Bride, Requiem, Hall of Women in Labour, Appendix, Man and Woman Go through a Cancer Ward, All-night Café*. The pamphlet was set up and printed in eight days; it bears the date March, 1912. It is doubtful if the press in Germany has ever reacted to poetry in such an expressive, explosive manner as it did to Benn's. Immediately Richard M. Meyer classified Benn in his literary history as "Hellhound Breughel" himself. The Augsburg *Evening Post* screamed :

"Disgusting! What an unbridled imagination, devoid of all mental hygiene, is here laid bare; what sordid delight in the abysmally ugly; what debased pleasure in dragging into the light of day things which cannot be changed . . . A licentiousness of taste such as would scarcely be surpassed by the notorious horrors of the Black Mass and the crazy excesses of Montmartre." The good Hans von Weber in Munich who was always well disposed to me and who later (1922) wrote of me as "richer in ideas than any other publisher in Germany" moaned in his *Zwiebelfisch*[3] (resurrected in the twenty-fifth series, 1946, under the editorship of Anna Roith as *Zeitschrift über Bücher, Kunst und Kultur* in Munich-Obermenzing) as follows (this instead of a review) : "If you intend to read these—poems, have a stiff drink to hand. A very, very stiff one!" The Munich paper *Janus* did not take long to decide which face to show but gave us this testimonial : "In the old days when somebody was mad he would merely see white mice dancing. Modern Berlin has definitely made progress in this respect. It sees rats . . . It is not my business to write about the perversity of these poems. I leave this interesting case to the psychiatrists."[4] How did the

Berlin *Post* come out of this affair? "At last a poet has been found to lift us out of triviality and assign us some high goals for the future. Goethe must now abandon his place on Mount Olympus: another will take his place and this man is called Gottfried Benn . . . We may think ourselves lucky to be born into an age in which such a poet lives."

PRAGUE

Max Brod
The young Werfel and the Prague writers

I got to know the nineteen-year-old Werfel through his somewhat younger schoolmate and best friend, Willy Haas.

It was all quite simple. Willy Haas' mother and my mother
knew each other. One day Frau Haas said her son wanted to
discuss something important with me. So I invited him to come
and see me.

Werfel was born in 1890; Haas in 1891; I belonged to the 1884
age group. An age gap of six or seven years in the early stages
of life means an awful lot. It is remarkable how quickly this
becomes less and less significant as one gets older.

Haas told me there was a phenomenon in his class (the eighth
in the Stefansgymnasium), a great poet hardly anyone knew
about except for a few class-mates who looked up to him. The
eighth class in an Austrian Gymnasium, corresponding to the
upper sixth in Germany, was the last class before the final
school examination and the inevitable university. I too was a
"Stefanese", that's to say I had graduated from this High School
in Stefan Street and for many years after the final examination,
as a young lawyer and potential Civil Servant, I kept up a certain
interest in the activities of the school.

Haas showed me some poems, none of which was futile, none
full of the meaningless phrases common to all the poetry
beginners usually brought me. Everything moved in a new light.
Haas had a lot to say about the sad fate of his protegé who,
it seems, was in a bad way and on the point of failing his
examinations but who kept on inexhaustively improvising new
poems of the kind demonstrated, and was well worth some
encouragement.

"He certainly is," I exclaimed, delighted by the samples.
"Bring him along next time you come to see me."

Franz Werfel came: of medium height, blond, high forehead, rather plump, with a ravaged childlike expression, very subdued and shy. However, his manner changed immediately when he began to recite. He knew all his poems by heart. He spoke them from memory, without falter or mistake, with fire, and a throbbing, intense or triumphant voice, whichever was appropriate—now loud, now soft but always in very rich, varied modulations. And he wouldn't stop. I'd never heard anything like it. I was captivated. As always when confronted with great art, I felt an enormous gift had been bestowed upon me, the kind of gift one never finds in any other sphere of life.

There was nothing of Werfel's in print, although by the time I got to know him a book of marvellous poems was ready and after the manner of the old oral tradition, was already circulating. Enchanting phenomenon! If I am not mistaken there were already among the poems I heard at this first meeting some later included in *Friend to the World*. For example, that very personal poem *The Good Pal* that for days I could not get out of my head, it was so original and true.

To clarify my position *vis-à-vis* the much younger Werfel ("much" younger? Yes! See above) I shall have to say something about myself: my position in the world of letters had already been indicated by some books,[1] of which the first, a collection of short stories, *Death to the Dead*, had been astonishingly well reecived (praised, for example, by Max Mell, Felix Braun, Stefan Zweig, Blei); another called *Nornepygge Castle* (a novel which today I reject in all but a few respects, for example the parts dealing with Berlioz's music) had unexpectedly gained me quite a circle of passionately partisan readers in Berlin with Kurt Hiller at their head;[2] in 1907 my first rather daring book of verse, *The Way of the Man in Love* had appeared, of which Rainer Maria Rilke wrote to me at the time that he was sure this *Way of the Man in Love* would soon change into the *Way of the Lover* (how far-sighted and discerning this great poet was!).

In 1910 the essentially far simpler and (as I believe) more personal *Diary in Verse* had followed. It was these poems that Werfel followed with his *Friend to the World*—as was to be pointed out later by, among others, Heinrich Eduard Jacob in his preface to the anthology he edited, called *Poems of Living Poets*.[3] What was happening was the unusual case of the teacher on his knees before his disciple.

Some years later I used this remarkable relationship as the impulse for my novel *Tycho Brahe's Path to God*; and some decades later still, in a King Saul Drama which has appeared in Hebrew in a translation by a friend I had made in Israel, S. Shalom. It is only natural that in those days of tempestuous relationships, my intellectual infatuation with the young Werfel would be taken amiss by all sorts of people—I was warned against him, warned that I was encouraging a rival. I mention this merely in passing. Besides, these "well-intentioned" philistine warnings generally came from distant relations, not from my two real friends, Felix Weltsch and Kafka. The three of us had never been able to understand the rôle of political manœuvres and tactics in the world of art or philosophy.

But I was not content with adoration. I sent some of Werfel's poems to Camill Hoffmann, who had both influence and good-will. There were probably more influential men in Vienna, but none so willing to help. He was about five years older than myself, came from a little Czechoslovakian township (Kolin) and in his younger days had befriended Stefan Zweig. With Zweig Hoffman had edited a volume of good translations of Baudelaire's poems which long adorned my library, then unfortunately disappeared. The translation of the finest of Baudelaire's poems, *Spleen*, has survived and is still in my possession. It is today the only tangible memento I have of the good-natured Camill Hoffmann . . . It was to him I owe the first production of one of my plays, for he recommended my one-acter, The *Height of Feeling*, to the Dresden Theatre producer, Wolf, who put it on with Iltz and Marlé in the leading parts. That was about 1917 and while, it is true, it could not banish my heaviness of heart at a time of world war, nevertheless it was for a brief moment a bright spot in the enveloping darkness.

Once again I imposed on Camill Hoffmann when he had become Press Attaché to the Czecholoslavkian Embassy in Berlin. Despite my violent opposition, part of Kafka's literary remains had been left in Berlin with Frau Dora Dymant and had been confiscated by the Nazi "cultural authorities". I asked Hoffmann to find out what he could and see what he could do. This time his efforts were in vain. Soon he himself disappeared in the maelstrom of that period and I have never found out exactly what happened to him. Auschwitz? The Berlin Kafka papers must presumably be considered irrevocably lost.

This then was that splendid fellow Camill Hoffmann to whom I wrote, presumably about 1910, warmly recommending the newly discovered young Werfel. Both in those days and later when I turned to the publisher Axel Juncker, Werfel's dearest friend, Willy Haas, helped us with the selection of poems in an incomparably expert manner. Even then he was incredibly well read and mature (the first man to introduce me to the name Kierkegaard). "Werfel's Kurwenal" I used to call him to myself. But the sixth-former Haas had no literary "connections"—by the law of seniority they were my domain.

Hoffmann was the literary editor of the Vienna *Zeit*, which a short time before had set up as a new daily in competition with Benedikt's almighty *Neue Freie Presse* and became the mouth-piece of all young talent. We had great hopes for it as an organ for the modern literary movement of free speech and unchau-vinistic Viennese politics. But it could not muster great powers of survival and in a few years it was dead: I think I am right in saying that for a time even Hermann Bahr and the then famous, but nowadays sadly neglected poet, Otto Julius Bier-baum, were its editors, and that one of its first numbers had some social lyrics by Bierbaum set to music by Humperdinck (I can still remember the words and the melody).

This was the newspaper to which I recommended Werfel's poetry. I was able to point out, not without pride, that I was myself a contributor to the *Zeit*, as some of my work had been appearing in it since 1910.

Hoffmann printed the least characteristic poem of the whole bundle. The sensational public image we had expected did not take place. The *Gardens of Prague* was the title of the poem, and Werfel, as far as I know, never included it in any of his subse-quent collections. Apart from its appearance in that Sunday Supplement of the Vienna *Zeit* I have never seen it since.[4]

Haas sent me Werfel's poem when it appeared, with a visiting-card which I have since come across again among my papers. It read:

Dear Herr Doktor,

I have great pleasure in conveying to you the most sincere thanks of my friend Franz for your friendly encouragement which, as you can see, has had for him a most gratifying issue.

Yours sincerely, Willy Haas.

No one will be surprised to hear that I was quite beside myself with excitement over the new star which had appeared on my horizon.

We formed the kind of friendship only possible when one is young, in which mutual trust throbs with boundless excitement; a friendship borne along on a naïve wave of mutual admiration.

The supreme accolade I had to bestow was an introduction to my two friends Franz Kafka and Felix Weltsch. Soon after I started my university studies I had formed a very close mutual association with both of them, one which never suffered any serious rift. The ties with Kafka were broken only by his death, which means they lasted for almost twenty-two years of undiminished intensity. With the philosopher Felix Weltsch I am, to my own great delight, still in closest contact, this being made possible by the proximity of our homes in Jerusalem. I yearned for a friendship of similar depth with Werfel. Any kind of friendship that was not constant and intense was unknown to me. It was beyond the scope of my imagination.

Naturally I introduced Werfel to my two "old" friends and after about a year we were on Christian-name terms. We remained friends in this manner, although our friendship soon suffered a few upsets. In the last years of Werfel's life we were once again close to each other . . .

Kafka and Weltsch were as profoundly impressed as I was by Werfel's poetry and by his frank nature and powers of genius. We met each other either at my place or at Werfel's lovely apartment (we still lived with our parents and had only one room for our own use) or at the wise blind poet's, Oskar Baum, who strangely enough was the first of us to set up house on his own and make a living outside literature. Baum was an organist and music teacher; his first two books, *Existence on the Brink* and *Life in the Dark*, had received a most favourable response. A leading critic of the time wrote: "He is the first blind modern poet and thinker. His novel *Life in the Dark* will take its place among the great *Entwicklungsromane*." The vicissitudes of fate which befell this aesthetic and courageous champion—(blind from birth in one eye, he lost the other at eleven during a fight at school)—led me to ponder the ways of terrestrial and divine justice, and also resulted in a life-long friendship between us until his death under Hitler.

For his part, Werfel introduced me into his own circle. Besides

Haas there was Ernst Popper, bursting with ideas which at the time seemed remarkably vague . . . A polite smile always played on his fat, round, bespectacled face. This gentle smile, however, meant "no", not "yes"—I have never met anyone who was more gentle, more polite, or more stubborn in the way he disagreed with you. I believe Werfel took Ernst Popper as model for the ghostly figure of Franz Adler in his *Graduation Day*. The séance in the middle of *Graduation Day* records the experiences we shared in his apartment and in that of Paul Kornfeld (or rather the apartment of their parents). The tables floated like boats in a storm, they rose beneath our fingers and gave signs to our horrified senses which made intelligible words and meaningful sentences. A woman in Semlin, opposite Belgrade and thus a long way from Prague, was desperately calling for help. She was on the banks of the Danube and in her light clothing was freezing to death. This woman sent a message to our assembly that she was poor and pregnant, that her time had come and that the Danube, in the wind, was flecked with foam. "Help", "Save me" the table said. We became wildly excited. Finally we decided to send a telegram to the Austro-Hungarian Police Station in Semlin asking them to go quickly to the woman's aid. It must have been about three o'clock in the morning when we broke up and made our way through the silent streets of Prague to the German Post Office. The telegram was duly dispatched. The reply was supposed to come to Kornfeld's address. It never came.

This is how I remember that chaotic night. Werfel told the story a little differently with great imagination and poetic licence, as you might expect, in his novel.

But the talented class which included Werfel, Haas and Kornfeld strangely enough also produced Hans Janowitz, who attracted some attention by his work on the film, *The Cabinet of Dr. Caligari*, and finally in the same group (though from a different school) Ernst Deutsch, who in our circle was famous, first and foremost, for his prowess at tennis and for his beautiful sister, and shortly afterwards as a great actor in his own right, the juvenile lead, *par excellence*, whose performance in Hasenclever's *The Son* was to make him a star, which is how we saw him in our dreams and to our delight also in the flesh at poetry readings. That I would many years later admire him as *Nathan the Wise* was something I could not possibly have imagined then.

We used to indulge in another kind of sport apart from wandering off into the kingdom of sultry spirits, or into the realms of Parnassus and Hippocrene. Weltsch, Kafka and I were great hikers. On Sundays, sometimes even on Saturdays, we were to be seen on the outskirts of Prague, the beauty of whose woods we worshipped with an innocent extravagance. The number of kilometres we determinedly covered was a matter of some importance then which I can no longer appreciate today. But there are echoes of that happy time in several of my shorter prose pieces, in poems, in the *Scene in the Village*, a little lyrical drama which appears in my book *The Height of Feeling*, which was highly praised by Hofmannsthal—the book was printed in 1912, and this particular scene was dedicated "to my dear friend Franz Werfel". "Here I want to live behind tiny window panes" —these were the words of my poem. But in the end it is the city-dweller who realizes: "It's to the city my path leads, there I suffered greatly, there were the turmoils of youth." We alternated in those days between rustic Czech influences and those of the city of Prague, our home, whose influences were predominantly German. In Kafka's letters to me there is much talk of these extended excursions haunted for me by the melodies of Smetana and the inspiration of Berlioz' songs (which are even today among the lesser-known parts of the vast *oeuvre* he left behind and which triumphantly stand the test of comparison with the songs of Schubert, Schumann, Hugo Wolf and Brahms).

We went by steamer to the Moldau Rapids, or by train to Senohrab, where the delightful valley opens up to the quick-flowing Sazawa, or to the Beraun River with walks to the famous Karlstein Castle. We bathed in forest streams, for in those days Kafka and I shared the curious belief that possession of a land-scape is incomplete as long as contact has not been physically established by bathing in the living stream of its waters. This is how we later wandered through Switzerland, practising our swimming in every lake within reach.

So now Werfel was introduced into our band of happy nature-worshippers. One lovely summer's day we journeyed out to the silvery waters of the Sazawa, discarded our clothes in the depths of the forest by an open-air pool which we far preferred to civilized swimming pools and, naked as Nyads and Triads, we listened to the resounding new verses of the *Friend to the World* and then swam for hours. In my memory this wonderful Hellenic day in summer will last for ever.

59

Johannes Urzidil
In Expressionist Prague

How did it come about that German literature and poetry could flourish in Prague of all places in the 1910's and 1920's with such unique energy and originality? What accumulation of life-forces played a part in this poetically fulfilled and creative atmosphere? I should know for I was born there, grew up there and was witness to and participant in that German intellectual life of Prague which was so seething with wide-ranging ideas, ever-changing concepts and ethical enthusiasms. But no facile, clear-cut verdict is possible as to the reasons for this phenomenon and as far as I am concerned social, biological or any other hypotheses based upon an interpretation of material sources can only partially explain it. Any strikingly large conglomeration of creative personalities of highest, high or at least considerable standing over a comparatively short space of time within the confines of one city (as, for example, once in Weimar or Concord, Massachusetts) is fundamentally always a sublime and metaphysical phenomenon. Most of the Prague German authors were Jews, but only in individual cases were they permeated with the sense of being so. Their German linguistic consciousness determined their historical consciousness to a far greater extent than ever their racial consciousness could (to use concepts which the Prague philosopher Felix Weltsch has established very convincingly in his study of Kafka). A certain, though only partial, support for my approach may be found in the idea of form and formal quality which incidentally was also developed in Prague by my teacher, Christian Freiherr von Ehrenfels, and later by the Prague German Max Wertheimer. Perhaps this, more than any other theory, helps one gain insight into the secret of a literary scene whose disparate individual features unite in a total beauty which defies analysis.

61

The Prague German writers had simultaneous access to at least four ethnic sources: German, naturally, to which culturally and linguistically they belonged; Czech, which was the milieu in which they lived; Jewish, even if they themselves were not Jewish, as it formed a vital historical factor in the city, making itself felt everywhere; and Austrian, which had nurtured and reared them and which determined their fate whether they accepted or criticized it. Each of these sources drew its vitality from two spheres: from the local populace of Prague and from the Bohemians attracted to the city. These in turn consisted of Sudeten Germans, some already settled there and some attracted by the German University; the basic stock of Czech country people gravitating to the regional (later State) capital; Czech and German country Jews who, as medium land-owners or tenant farmers, were a group all to themselves; and finally the local aristocracy—some Bohemian, some Austrian but with Czech sympathies (not to mention those with German, which is to say, unqualified Austrian loyalties) with their palaces in the city and their splendid country seats in surrounding Bohemia, ancient, in many cases indeed reaching back to the time of the Přemyslide Kings, an aristocracy, in other words, to whom even the Hapsburgs might appear upstarts. All these sources coalesced and a poet found himself confronted with it and, through it, very soon made his way beyond local concerns to more fundamental issues.

Czech poets and writers, still deeply involved in their own struggle for national identity, could not surrender to this kind of universalism, although signs of it appeared in literature in the work of the Čapek brothers, in the visual expressions of artists who strove for a certain breadth and in modern Czech music: in other words, in those art forms which could most directly and immediately express themselves artistically in cosmopolitan terms while retaining their national image. This was why the personal relationships of the Prague German poets and writers were more cordial with Czech painters and musicians than with Czech authors. The literally grotesque language-barrier also played its part. Not all German men of letters were completely familiar with the Czech language (although most of the Jews among them probably were) and few Czech authors spoke German or wanted to speak it.

For the Prague German writers, the sometimes friendly, but

more often politically turbulent and aggressive, symbiosis, the interplay of warring elements (on the Czech side one by no means entirely free from anti-Semitism), the alchemical fusion wrought in the crucible of Prague, was the *causa causarum* of a literary renaissance which very soon created its own literary expression at all levels—a development violently precipitated about this time by the movement called Expressionism. Thanks to the wealth of her national, social and confessional facets, Prague could offer her authors writing in German, the intellectual potential of a city, a capital, and one more glittering than many a European metropolis far richer in population.

Actually Prague had often had a self-contained German language and literature and its history can be closely traced if we pursue Goethe's associations with Bohemia and later the activities of the "Forty-Eighters", or even those of the poets of the "Liberal Age", which with Friedrich Adler and Hugo Salus lasted on into my own youth. Rilke, too, owed a lot to that "Liberal Age", but, at the same time, it was he who led the Prague Germans into the arena of Europe. From Rilke dates the epoch whose achievements have since reached world eminence with Kafka and Werfel under the decisive influence of Max Brod. Nothing like that had come out of Prague before, although so much German had been spoken there throughout the nineteenth century that the Czech Capital, The Golden City of One Hundred Towers, was thought by many shallow-minded and ignorant people to be a "German city", a mistake which was to have bitter consequences.

Rilke's lasting experience of Czech culture had been at the popular level. Bohemian folk songs echoed in his ear and may well have made their way into many a word-form or turn of phrase. This is a fate none can or should escape in any country, because it is an enrichment of what is one's own. But Rilke soon turned his back on Prague. He never became part of its people and the fates of its city and countryside, shared too little of its joys and sorrows. This could not be said of Paul Leppin or Franz Werfel, nor of Paul Kornfeld or Max Brod, nor of Felix Weltsch the philosopher, nor of Hugo Bergmann the student of religions, of Willy Haas our critical mentor, or Egon Erwin Kisch, the "raging reporter". And naturally least of all of Franz Kafka, in whom Prague is mirrored as much as Zurich is in Gottfried Keller or Concord in Thoreau. All the Prague Germans mentioned became part of the city, owed their best to it, were witness to the mounting political stridency of the Czechs, the ever-diminishing will to live of the Hapsburg monarchy—at the same time, however, they also lived in the sphere of German literature, which was equally their spiritual home and were witness to the liberation of literary expression from the residue of the Baumbach Era. In this revolutionary process they could be far more supranational in Prague than anywhere else in the German-speaking states.

Linguistically and atmospherically they could avail themselves of far more direct access to the great Russians. For example, I read Tolstoy and Dostoevsky not only in German but also in Czech and that means comprehending these authors not merely rationally but coming emotionally closer to them. Modern Czech painting, which was radical and boldly progressive, extended vistas in the direction of France. The immense natural musicality of the Czechs was all around us, and the finest products of the long-cherished, though now gradually declining, Prague Wagner cult were already being surpassed by the creative works of a new musical era ushered in by Alexander von Zemlinsky, the teacher and brother-in-law of Schönberg. Naturally we neither would nor could do anything to escape the influence of Hauptmann and Wedekind in drama, nor that of George and Hofmannsthal in lyric poetry, nevertheless Prague remained an autochthonous—no, more—an autonomous—world of its own, which a Karl Kraus, for instance, from his Viennese vantage-point, could no longer understand: indeed, he totally misunderstood it, even if he did originally come from Central Bohemia.

But the sentimental spell of Prague (such as had still colored the verses of Adler and Salus with Gothic and Baroque magic) was no longer what released the poetic sensibilities of the German Expressionists there. It was real life, the constant change which bears the divine within itself, the social, the humane, the humanitarian, the out-and-out European to which this city above all, a city of constantly conflicting antitheses, hourly sent out its challenge. The Prague Germans were far more radically exposed to this challenge than the Czechs who were tied to their nationalistic feelings or the Sudeten Germans out in the country. (For a while I was editor of a literary journal which I had called simply Man[1] and which was intended to be a supra-national platform common to German and Czech writers. It lasted barely a year, for "what is there of man that could last?" (Goethe).

Prague was the city of *raconteurs,* of the Magic Realists, the storytellers with precise imagination. It is true, of course, that Werfel was a lyrical herald who had made his voice heard far and wide and Rudolf Fuchs was a pure and profound poet whose moral position inspired great respect. It is true that Paul Korn- feld was one of the protagonists of Expressionist drama. But the really far-reaching decisions were made in Prague German prose. This was what proved most effective in reaching the outside world. It was free from constricting provincialism and had the widest possible horizons in its repertoire which was soon shared by those authors who were attracted from outside into the Prague magnetic field, for example Ernst Weiss, Hermann Ungar and Ludwig Winder (all three from Moravia), Oskar Baum or Melchior Vischer (both from Central Bohemia). In the Prague of that era they developed into exponents of cosmopolitan intellectual free- dom.

As I remember the Prague of those days it seems to me essen- tially a Kafkaesque city. Perhaps that sounds obvious and almost trivial, but I felt it (and I was not the only one) even when Kafka was still among us. Although Prague is only occasionally perceptible in Kafka's works, and then only at second remove, yet it is everywhere in his writings, like the salt in the water of the Buddhist parable. Although the salt cannot be seen, none- theless every drop tastes salty. Similarly, it would be possible to point to the Prague background for every character, every situation, every description in Kafka. Take one example: *The Metamorphosis.* Just after it appeared Kafka said to my wife's father, Professor Karl Thieberger, whom he met on the street: "What do you think of the terrible goings-on in our house?" Anybody who thinks that was just a joke does not know his Kafka. Like everything about him, it was ironic, of course, but not just irony, it was also serious, real life.

At the time when Kafka was most productive Prague was most typically Prague and most typically Kafkaesque. It is possible to grasp the essence of the Prague of those days far more com- pletely through Kafka than through any other writer, certainly better through him than through any Czech work of that time, although one should expect the latter to be more suitable for the purpose of presenting Prague. This may be one of the reasons why the Czechs are always trying to make Kafka out to be a kind of secret Czech and to claim him from German literature, and this is sometimes helped by the American habit of fixing nationality by the country of birth, whence Kafka is sometimes called a "Czech writer". This is, of course, absolute nonsense because a writer belongs intellectually to the language he represents, the one in which he thinks and writes. (If Kafka once wrote to his Czech girl-friend Milena Jesenska: "German is my mother-tongue and therefore the one that comes naturally to me, but Czech is closer to my heart", then one must remember that this is not to be regarded as a statement of literary ideology but appropriate only to the Czech girl-friend to whom it was written. Czech was doubtless close to the heart of Rilke, as it is bound to be close to everyone who has learned it from the people and like Kafka, Rilke, Brod and the writer of the present observations grew up in the Czech environment and can speak the language himself.)

Our much-maligned Prague-German which was utterly free of dialect, if not of accent, had survived intact since the Middle Ages on the Prague linguistic island simply because it was not subject to the slurring effects of provincial and regional dialect change. This was a singular blessing for literature. We Prague Germans wrote and still write in the language we live with and which we daily speak. This was already true of Karl Egon Ebert, just as it was of Rainer Maria Rilke and of Egon Erwin Kisch. There never existed any gulf for the Prague German between the written and spoken language: no switching over—no matter how unconscious—is necessary. This absolute integration between the languages of life and art is probably the strongest source of the peculiar form and impact of the Prague writers and especially of Kafka. Anyone who ever heard him talk can still hear him down to the finest nuance in every line he ever wrote. That is the secret of an inner identity which we Praguers have preserved as long as possible and which will vanish with us.

LEIPZIG

Kurt Pinthus
Leipzig and Early Expressionism

One July day in 1909 after a lecture by our literature Professor
Albert Köster, a fellow-student at Leipzig University introduced
me to the nineteen-year-old Walter Hasenclever, a lively, slim,
very active youth with burning eyes set in a gaunt dark-skinned
face, in which many people, including Hasenclever himself,
thought there were traces of negroid ancestry because of the
protruding lower lip, flattened nose and black curly hair (as
Oskar Kokoschka often painted and drew him). I was immediately
impressed by the unusual charm of his gestures and his sparkling,
often ebullient manner of speech with its slight trace of Rhineland intonation, but also a frequent, quick shrug of the shoulders
and twitching of the facial muscles—habits which he never lost.
A close friendship soon grew up between us which lasted for
more than thirty years until his tragic suicide on June 21st,
1940 in the French camp at Les Milles.

At our very first meeting Hasenclever handed me a copy of
his first play, *Nirvana: A Critique of Life in Drama Form*, which
had only just been published. The printing costs of the play
he had paid himself out of winnings at poker from rich students
at Oxford where he had spent his first term writing and reading
intensively instead of studying law. *Nirvana* reads like an
anthology of Ibsen's motifs, characters and techniques, and his
next book too, the volume of poetry *Cities, Nights and People*
contains little that is original though it does strike a slightly
adventurous and impudent note. And yet it ends with the vision
of *The Next Race of Men*: "And before us we saw a race of
men on fire / The red morning sun with kindred / Faces, bright
and young." And as a dedicatory poem for me he wrote: "New
paths point the way to a new land / I feel we are already on
the way . . ." It was in these terms that Hasenclever, like hundreds
of other young people, was seized by the awareness and the cer-

tainty of what was coming, namely a new generation, the ecstatic bliss and tortured screams of whose revolt were already evident in their lyric poetry. Their motto might well have been words of Bakunin: "Every destructive pleasure is creative pleasure."

The student who introduced me to Hasenclever soon led us to the regular midday gathering in the back room of Wilhelm's Wine Parlour, in a square on the Reichsstrasse near the old Leipzig Rathaus. There a few students and young musicians met regularly; but the little circle was dominated by a colossal figure with enormously broad shoulders; beneath a tuft of ginger hair beamed the reddish face with the excessively short, pointed nose. This was Ernst Rowohlt, bursting with vitality and *joie de vivre*, who, while an apprentice with the Paris Librairie Klingsiek, had established the firm of Ernst Rowohlt, Publishers, Paris-Leipzig-London in his little room in the Hôtel de Brest in 1908.

At first the publishing house existed entirely in his imagination. But even so Rowohlt had actually published two booklets, which he proudly presented to me the first time he took me to number 10 Königstrasse. There, in the back room of the Drugulin printing works, as a trained type-setter and bookseller, he looked after the production of the *Zeitschrift für Bücherfreunde*. But at the front of this famous old Printing Works he had opened his publishing house—in a single room (with an adjacent store-room) which served as living-room, office, reception as well as bedroom, from time to time.

The owner of Drugulin had given Rowohlt permission to spend as much time as he liked in his Publishing House cum living quarters. But he had no money. It was then that a small miracle —good fortune born of misfortune—occurred. At the suggestion of Privy Councillor Max Martersteig, who had recently come from Cologne to be director of the civic theatre, the city of Leipzig invited the Rhenish poet Herbert Eulenberg to give the public address on November 10, 1909 in the New Theatre in the Augustusplatz on the occasion of the 150th anniversary of Schiller's birth. This oration did not appeal to public or press who considered his reference to the "grim, evil dregs in the soul of the red-headed creator of radical villains" extremely irreverent. Some time after, when Eulenberg, who had a long-standing invitation to dine with the Leipzig Bibliophiles, actually turned up, his reception was chilly and after the dinner Eulenberg was entirely neglected. But some of us young people gathered around him to express our respect for his courage and for the boldness of his plays. Eulenberg said his plays always flopped and he had no publisher. Up spoke Rowohlt: "Mr. Eulenberg, I shall publish all your works". And another young man, as tall as Rowohlt and also ginger-haired, but very slender, slim and elegant, added that he would be glad to finance the project. This young man was Kurt Wolff.

Probably Rowohlt and Kurt Wolff had met before; they shared the same interests, but Ernst Rowohlt & Co. only really got under way now that Kurt Wolff, son of a Bonn Professor of Musicology, put some money into the business and became a sleeping partner. He was married while still a young student to the even younger Elizabeth Merck. She was a descendant of Goethe's friend Johann Heinrich Merck and an heiress of the great chemical works E. Merck in Darmstadt. And so it happened that these two young idealists became friends and partners for a number of years and as a result the older contemporary authors who had failed to gain recognition as well as the emergent "Youngest Writing" found a home.

Rowohlt, grandson of a Bremen sea captain, now set under full sail into the sea of print. The first booklet to appear under his imprint in 1909 was *Hang-over Poetry* by the eccentric Paul Scheerbart with whose drinking capacity and fantastic imagination he felt a certain affinity. In the following year Scheerbart's *Pepetuum Mobile* appeared. Then Rowohlt contracted for almost all the early, new and future works of Herbert Eulenberg, especially *You may Commit Adultery* and *Budding Life*.

In addition, many collections of poetry and plays by the now sadly forgotten rapturous globe-trotter Maximilian Dauthendey as well as novels and plays by the gentle giant, day-dreamer and visionary Carl Hauptmann, were published along with a continuous stream of two-tone, finely printed Bibliophile editions of classical and modern German and French poets at very low prices, under the imprint of Drugulin Press. With these very successful Drugulin Press editions and the works of standard older (though for those days problematic) authors: Scheerbart, Eulenberg, Dauthendey, Carl Hauptmann (whom we looked to as fore-runners of our own, later to be called Expressionist, generation) the young publishing firm had a firm foundation on the basis of which Rowohlt and Wolff could carry out and

69

develop their dearest wish, soon to turn into a passion : to publish as many young, new, unknown authors as possible.

At the beginning of November, 1910 Rowohlt had read a sonnet by an unknown poet, Georg Heym, in the defunct Berlin journal the *Democrat*. This poem seemed to him so powerful and so different that he immediately invited the author to submit a manuscript for publication.[1] The appearance of *Eternal Day*, Georg Heym's powerfully expressive visions hammered into precice poetic form, in April, 1911 evoked astonishment and acclaim. A second book, a collection of stories called *The Thief*, the author himself did not live to see, for he died by drowning on January 16th, 1912. In his correspondence with his publisher, in which he pressed for a journal to be started, Heym used the expression "the New Generation", soon to become a slogan for the age, as was the term "Youngest Writing". In the following year Heym's friends put together a second volume of poetry from his papers, *Umbra Vitae*.

In December, 1911 Franz Werfel's poems, which had been given their first public reading by Max Brod—in generous preference to his own—had come out as *Friend to the World*. Werfel's father had first installed him in a Hamburg export firm to direct his attention to business instead of poetry, but now, having finished off his year in Prague, and, following the success of *Friend to the World*, his father had agreed that he should come to Leipzig as reader, not, as he wrote to Rowohlt, "in order to fulfil his obligations by regular activity in your firm", but rather so that he might be given the opportunity to live and write independently of his family. I was the publisher's chief reader and had been so since the firm was founded.

Werfel turned up in Leipzig about the end of October, 1911, very plump, with a liking for broad flowing cravats and equally long flowing hair, and alternating between youthful bashfulness and exuberant high spirits.

With a powerful, though untrained, voice he sang arias from his beloved Verdi (about whom, ten years later, he wrote his first novel) and thunderously declaimed his hymnic poems. Every other day he would come and see me with a new magnificently declaimed poem (all later collected in *We Are* and *Each Other*); this so intimidated me that as an honest critic I abandoned my own attempts at poetry.

The already mentioned midday gatherings in the back room

of Wilhelm's Wine Parlour were now dominated by Rowohlt, Hasenclever, Werfel and myself. We were joined from time to time by the tall, gaunt figure of Gerdt von Bassewitz whose plays published by Rowohlt are now forgotten, but whose fairy-tale *Little Peter's Voyage to the Moon*, also published by Rowohlt as a Christmas Play for Children, is still very much alive in the theatre repertoire today. In addition there was the medical student Philipp Keller who was polishing up a novel, and E. M. Engert, who never stopped drawing and sketching.

It is today no longer possible to establish which of the dozens of authors on the firm's lists (most of whom had never been published before) were discovered in the next few years by Ernst Rowohlt, by Kurt Wolff, by Werfel, or myself. Many vanished as quickly as they appeared; most developed further in different directions and have taken their place in the histories of literature, some even in world literature.

The surprising thing was that we never needed to look for them—the authors were simply there; they not only sent their manuscripts—they came in person and they brought along others. A great deal has been written about the *Sturm* and *Aktion* groups in these years, and the Munich group, but the midday gathering in Wilhelm's Wine Parlour has scarcely been mentioned, though it really became a breeding ground, then a centre, a place of pilgrimage for the young writers from the German-speaking world. Whenever any writer of the young or older generation came to Leipzig from Berlin, Prague, Munich, Vienna, West Germany he knew that he would meet Rowohlt and Werfel and Hasenclever and me and others like himself in that wine parlour. And he knew that he would then go on to the traditional coffee houses: the refined Café Felsche, called Café Français for that reason—on the Augustusplatz; the stark Café Merkur frequented by intellectuals and journalists; or Café Bauer on whose old-fashioned red plush benches generations of men of letters had sat. This is where we went once with Frank Wedekind whom we all worshipped, after he had acted in one of his own plays in the Old Theatre. He talked on that occasion of one thing only: the responsibility of young people to take up a collection for a monument to the inspired Hermann Conradi who had so loved sitting here and who had died at the age of twenty-eight.

In the years 1911–14 it was almost a ritual for us to meet again in the evenings, generally in the restaurant on the Kleine

Fleischergasse am Markt called Kaffeebaum. It was founded in 1692 and had been a haunt of Goethe's, later of Robert Schumann, Wagner and Liszt. Augustus the Strong had had a relief put up over the Baroque portal with a Turk sitting under a coffee bush holding a huge coffee pot while a cherub is passing him a cup of what the Leipzigers call the "hot stuff". Here Rowohlt reigned at a clean scrubbed wooden table where great quantities of Pilsner were drunk and many ham and egg sandwiches consumed. This was rounded off by a session in the spacious Central Theatre Bar, on the first floor of a café. And there about midnight we would really let ourselves go, especially Ernst Rowohlt, full of enthusiasm, laughter and boisterous good spirits.

This was the finest, possibly the happiest, time of our lives. Our little group and the many who joined us—all of us had the feeling that we were at the start of something new, although we didn't exactly know what; and that we shared a common bond, that too being undefined. Gradually we discovered when our books and pamphlets began to appear all over the place in great numbers, not only in Leipzig but also in Berlin, Munich, Heidelberg, Vienna, and often in complete series right from the start, we had been part of what was later called Early Expressionism.

Alfred Richard Meyer, Rowohlt's old friend and mentor, now his colleague as publisher and connoisseur of drink, often came along. In Berlin Meyer edited what was probably the first of these series (Benn and Goll, Zech, Hermann-Neisse, Lichtenstein and Leonhard appeared for the first time under his imprint). Frequently his merry, plump little wife, the *diseuse* Resi Langer, came along too, as well as some of the above-mentioned authors. But Meyer also brought along the poet Else Lasker-Schüler, black-eyed, black-haired, small and dark, wearing bizarre jewellery and always in the throes of some passionate love-affair. She read her poems with the same intensity with which they had been written, sent everybody poetic postcards decorated with coloured stars and flowers and profiles, fell in love with the pale Baron von Maltzahn, one of the youngest of our circle, whom she christened the Duke of Leipzig and addressed some of her loveliest poems to him. There came, too, the young Johannes R. Becher, Kurt Hiller, the lucid thinker and stylist, propagator of *Advanced Lyrics* and later founder of "Activism", but also his opponent Albert Ehrenstein, the bitterest poet of the century whom I called the "cosmic Schlemihl", while of himself he said he was "harnessed to the coal-cart of his melancholy".

From Prague came Max Brod, the senior member of the remarkable Prague Literary Circle—he told us of his blind friend Oskar Baum and he brought Otto Pick, the mediator between Czech and German writing. Werfel from Prague was already there: and then on June 29, 1912 Brod turned up with a tall, thin, very pale, very shy person who hardly spoke at all: Franz Kafka. Brod assured us Kafka was a great writer, but that he had great difficulty in deciding to publish anything. So we asked him to send us a manuscript and he sent us the slimmest jottings we had ever received from a young writer, quite short pieces of descriptive prose writing called *Consideration*. The manuscript was so scanty that we printed it in a gigantic type-face with the widest possible margins to make a book of ninety-nine pages. Rowohlt only risked a printing of 800 copies. Kafka, who, with the pleasure he took in misfortune, would have preferred to have had the thing back, wrote when he sent it in: "When you get down to it, no matter how much experience and understanding you have, you can't see what is wrong with it at first glance. The commonest trade mark of every writer is the way each conceals weaknesses in his own particular fashion." The taciturn introvert had observed us closely at the midday gathering and depicted each of us with a few well-chosen words in his diary. In addition he wrote: "Strange daily gathering at noon in the Wine Parlour. Large, wide wine goblets with slices of lemon." (This was Schorle-Morle.)

There came the mighty Theodor Däubler with his dishevelled Zeus-like head, to read his mighty poetry with equally mighty voice, sounding the long vowels with a throbbing ring. There came the fatherly Carl Hauptmann with his wart-covered face, long nose jutting out as much as his goatee. Finally there appeared our idol Heinrich Mann, author of the stirring essay *Mind and Deed* which inspired all of us, speaking with quiet voice and aristocratic poise, his little beard *à la Henri Quatre* (about whom he later wrote two of his most mature novels). Many others turned up too, among them the learned and amusing Franz Blei, who had founded more journals than anyone.

But just at the moment when the firm had taken the lead in

c*

the publication of modern literature the split between the two partners came about. The broad-shouldered, robust, rosy giant Rowohlt, who liked noisy drinking in public places and occasionally shattered the bar mirrors with oranges he had picked up off the counter, was not really well matched with the extremely cultivated, diplomatic and reserved Kurt Wolff who was not only a silent partner, but as well had been a silent observer who, in the meantime, had learned from his associate the art of publishing and producing books. Kurt Wolff took over the Rowohlt enterprise in November, 1912 as sole proprietor and continued with it very successfully from February 15th, 1913 for another eighteen years of steady expansion. Emil Preetorius, whose folio of lithographs had already appeared in 1911 with Rowohlt along with other art books, now published a cartoon: Wolff and Rowohlt as separated Siamese twins, Wolff marching off with the books, while for Rowohlt there was nothing to do but watch him go.

In those months, both before and after the split, there appeared the following works by young writers: Albrecht Schaeffer's *The Sea Trip*, Max Brod's *The Height of Feeling, Scenes, Verses, Consolations*, Adolf Andreas Latzko's *The Wild Man*, Fráň Šrámek's *Flames*, Mechthilde Lichnowsky's *Gods, Kings and Animals in Egypt*, Arnold Zweig's *Tales about Claudia* (the first volume of his stories to have a major success) and the tragedy *Abigail and Nabal*; by the members of our group there was *Mixed Feelings*, a psychological novel by Philipp Keller (the only one by the man who later became a Professor of Medicine) and shortly after that volumes of verse: Walter Hasenclever's *The Youth* and Franz Werfel's *We are*. The last two both bear the imprint of Kurt Wolff, the signet drawn by Walter Tiemann of the Capitoline she-wolf suckling her young Romulus and Remus. From now on the firm expanded rapidly, with a great increase in number of authors and their output.[2]

In spring 1913 Wolff, Hasenclever and I were sitting one evening in a bar. The decision was taken to put out a series of slim volumes, each of which, unlike the already flourishing Insel Books, was to be written by a young or still unknown author. But what about the name? On the table lay the proofs of Werfel's latest volume of poetry, *We Are*. A pencil was stuck into them at random and the last line on the page selected, 116, began, "Oh. *Jüngster Tag!*" Thus was born the most representative series of the emerging literature, *The Last Judgement*, which (at 80 pfennig a volume) introduced many names to the reading public for the first time.[3] The earliest issues after February, 1913 included Werfel, Hasenclever, Kafka, Ferdinand Hardekopf, Emmy Hennings, Carl Ehrenstein, Georg Trakl (the publication of his poems in book form), Francis Jammes, Maurice Barrès, Paul Boldt, Otokar Březina, Berthold Viertel, Carl Sternheim, Leo Matthias, Marcel Schwob, Gottfried Kölwel.

It was not only through this series, however, but also through the general publications of the firm that our group and its publisher became of greater service to the new generation. Exactly one year after Kurt Wolff had taken over the firm, his first Almanac, The *Gaily Coloured Book*, appeared with a *List of Publications 1910–1913* which alone took up sixty pages, and a *List of Authors and Artists* containing about 150 names, among them now, apart from those already mentioned, Max Brod, with everything he had written and besides a literary yearbook called *Arkadia*, in which he introduced a number of as yet unknown authors: Martin Buber, Kurt Hiller (*The Wisdom of Boredom*, a *Polemic* in two volumes); Oskar Kokoschka (*Plays and Pictures*); Karl Kraus; Ludwig Rubiner; Paul Claudel; R. J. von Gorsleben; Robert Walser; Else Lasker-Schüler. Soon there followed Johannes R. Becher, Ernst Blass, Kasimir Edschmid, Albert Ehrenstein, Ludwig Meidner and the dramatic and narrative works of Carl Sternheim.

It was one of Kurt Wolff's talents to be good at finding rich young men who considered it a privilege to be active in some form or other in his firm or its associates. In this way the "Verlag der Weissen Bücher" was founded in 1913 with E. E. Schwabach; the works of René Schickele, Else Lasker-Schüler, Paul Zech, Ernst Stadler appearing in it. More important, however, after October, 1913 was the monthly *Die Weissen Blätter*, which, after a brief interregnum with Schwabach and Franz Blei, was directed in an extremely lively and forward-looking manner by René Schickele and (after the pioneers *Sturm* and *Aktion*) developed as it were into the classical journal of literary Expressionism.

So in a short time our little circle in Wilhelm's Wine Parlour had grown as it were into a reservoir of the most divergent trends and personalities of Expressionism, for the whole movement found support here not only from an active publishing house, but also from one which was financially solvent. At the beginning of 1914 Willy Haas joined us in Leipzig as reader; but only for a short time, for in the radiant summer of that year war suddenly ripped apart this great community united in the common cause of far-reaching innovation. But the war which separated us also bound us closer together in the awareness of the coming collapse and of the longed-for reconstruction.

As a symbol of this Walter Hasenclever had written to René Schickele as early as November, 1914: "Shouldn't we, the intellectual warriors, the best and worthiest of them all, hold a council, somewhere in the middle of Germany, in Weimar for example? At the end of the year, New Year's Eve 1914–15?!" This meeting in fact took place in Weimar in the ancient Elephant Hotel on New Year's Eve, unfortunately without Schickele; but Martin Buber, Ernst Rowohlt, Hasenclever, myself, Paul Zech, Rudolf Leonhard, Albert Ehrenstein, Heinrich Eduard Jacob and others all turned up. At the stroke of midnight we stepped out into the deep snow of the market-place and put on a race, which was won by Martin Buber. We raced out of the old year into the new, out of the old self-destructive age into the new, into the future.

MUNICH

Richard Seewald
In the Café Stefanie

As a bohemian city Munich ranked second only to Paris. *Tradition* and *freedom* are both necessary for art to thrive in a city. Paris has always had both, Rome had them at the time when it became the Mecca for the German Romantics. Berlin had never had the former; nor had London or New York, Munich had both. Its *joie de vivre*, which was not without its atmosphere of mystery, attracted the Knights of the Windmill like magic. The Schlawiner, as the citizens of Munich used to call all the long-haired characters from the East, from Russia and the Balkans, streamed into Schwabing, the northern suburb of the city, whose streets are absolutely straight from East to West and North to South so that good light falls into its numberless glass-roofed studios. By day the high glass walls reflected the clear sky, by night they shone with yellow lamplight until daybreak.

But there was as well an influx of blond giants from the North, from Scandinavia—Gulbransson, for one, came with them and stayed. Some wit dubbed them the Nordic Schlawiner, since their conduct was on a par with that of the other bohemians. There must have been "playgrounds" up in the North, cafés, clubs, and such like, but we knew from Strindberg the frigidity of their world and the rapidity with which it thawed into naked despair. But despair is natural for the Bohemian who fails to escape from a Bohemian existence. In my own generation there is probably not a single artist of stature who has not passed through the purgatory of bohemianism which means that he must have been wedded to despair, or at least lived with it as his mistress. And sometimes the old flame comes back to haunt him. But to despair is to encounter the void, and of such encounters the present-day generation has made a parlour-game.

I soon swopped my student's quarters for a studio in Schwabing. The furniture: table, chair, sofa and easel I acquired from the second-hand dealer next door. But I did not make my entry into the *Bohème* until I had pushed back the thick baize curtain behind the glass door of the Café Stefanie, seated myself at one of the little marble-topped tables and ordered an absinthe. The Stefanie was a Viennese café, frequented almost exclusively by artists and writers. It was on the corner of Theresien- and Amalienstrasse and was popularly called Café Megalomania. When bombs destroyed it during World War II it had already been dead for a long time; it was nothing but an empty shell, a pod without a pea, for the *Bohème* had long since disintegrated. It had two rooms, a large one with two billiard tables and a buffet bar on a low ramp, and a smaller one at whose windows the chess players sat. Anybody who came into this place with the intention of becoming a regular had crossed his Rubicon. Here he could lay the foundations of future fame or degenerate. Here, in the course of conversations lasting endless hours, he could enmesh himself in the tangled thickets of opinions and philosophies, each expounded with religious fervour or else give himself up to the sheer seductiveness of argument and end up a life-long Bohemian.

Let me push aside the curtain once more. I step inside like Odysseus entering the Halls of Hades; and out of the mists of time, through the clouds of tobacco smoke, the shades of those who used to sit here approach. I cannot give them the dark blood of sacrificial lambs to drink, but the black ink of my pen may perhaps bring them to life for a moment, even if only by invoking their names. I pour out votive offerings. To name all is impossible and if I try to embrace them they escape like apparitions, whether they are in fact dead or, as some of them, still alive. Some may turn their backs on me ill-temperedly like Ajax with Laërtes. But what they thought and wrote, spoke and created while alive, I shall try to tell elsewhere, for all of it was part of the voice of the age I lived through : the background to the man I see when I look in the mirror. We hear the chorus: *épatons le bourgeois!*

They come in no special order. I'll name them as they emerge out of the mists.

In the smaller room the chess-players sit crouching silently over their boards : Gustav Meyrink, who popularized magic and horror, is playing with Roda Roda, who substitutes for the officer's uniform he used to wear the obligatory red waistcoat and the monocle in his rubicund bulldog face. Beside him sits Erich Mühsam, a *pince-nez*, the only thing distinguishable amid his chaotic black hair and equally chaotic reddish beard, playing with another former Austrian officer. The latter's name is von Westendorf, who wrote a little book called *The Law of the Beast* about the brutal bandit wars in the Balkans. Mühsam was putting out his *Cain, Journal for Mankind*[1] just about this time. They are joined by Heinrich Mann with his romantic French waxed moustaches. In those days he meant far more to us than his famous brother Thomas Mann, who probably never set foot in the Stefanie. Thomas Mann never lived with despair as his mistress—that is absolutely certain. His early suffering was at most a minor disorder. Himself a bourgeois, he wrote books for the bourgeois. Weisgerber, at that time Munich's most promising young painter, is hovering in the glare of the light over the poisonous green expanse of one of the billiard tables and moves the ivory white balls along their prescribed course. Behind him on the long bench under the mirror sit Höxter and Spela. Leo von König, the last of the real portraitists, has painted them, the morbid *décadent* always dressed in black, his pale horse-face topped by a bowler-hat and Spela with her long, dead-white powdered face above their absinthe glasses. What did they live on?—There are various ways for a woman. About himself Höxter once said philosophically that cadgers were always necessary. I saw him for the last time in 1936 looking like a ghost making his way from table to table in the Romanisches Café in Berlin borrowing money as usual. He didn't look any older, for he had always been old.

The tobacco smoke near the door moves and Lotte Pritzel, the Puma, rather awkwardly and boyishly pushes her way in and moves through the tables to where her friends, the Strich brothers, the philosopher and the literary historian, are sitting. Kalser, the actor, is one of their circle. Ah, everybody has lain across Lotte's path at some time or other, said Mühsam with euphemistic blasphemy. She was the most endearing amoralist I've ever known; generous to the point of self-sacrifice for a friend; endowed with a penetrating intellect and a cynical wit which always hit its target. If she called some girl the "anxious night" or the "coal scuttle" you knew immediately whom she meant. The lanky Schiemann she dubbed the "Thing with a Head". (Could almost be the title for a Klee drawing, couldn't it?)

Emmy Hennings, with her blonde page-boy fringe, flits in and out. She's singing somewhere. "Fast, but never vulgar, always smart, in life or on stage, must be the tart." Her varied life took her from the stage to the street. She was a considerable poet and later Hugo Ball's faithful wife and companion until his death. His sad face too peers out of the mists.

I recognize Johannes R. Becher—but we no longer acknowledged each other when we sat at neighbouring tables in the same hotel in Düsseldorf in 1952, where he had come as Leader of the East German Pen Club. I can see van Hoddis, small and dark with thick lips, and Klabund who sits not far from him like a good sixth-former already marked by tuberculosis for an early death. (He and I produced a silly picture book of the war.[2]) And the psychoanalysts: the unhappy Dr. Gross, son of the famous criminal psychologist, his waistcoat sprinkled with cocaine, who was put away by his father; Dr. Gösch, a pale cheesy face with little black eyes, who translated the psychoanalytic doctrine straight into life, lecturing to an attentive following on his idea of circular marriage, Leonhard Frank whose *Cause*[3] made him famous because he introduced psychoanalysis into literature. Many years later when we were sitting in the luxurious armchairs of the Prinz Carl Palais I could not suppress a smile. At both of us.

The forest of rustling newspapers hides many faces, but I can see Franz Blei, an eminent Chinese mandarin casting admiring glances at a young girl's ankles through his horn-rimmed spectacles; and Sörgel, his monocle clamped into a staring eye, limps from table to table, listening to the conversations (we suspected him of owing his book on architecture to this kind of spying . . .).

Bonjour, Henri Bing (he has been a well-established art dealer in Paris for years now)! His bowler pushed back, his stick under his arm, he is signalling to the curly-haired Bruno Altmann. He needs a joke for a cartoon in *Jugend* or *Simplicissimus* and Altmann produced them to order for five marks a piece (often for me, too). Bing came from East Prussia and claimed that his father was the corn Jew from Gumbinnen who used to advance money to an uncle of mine on his crop. The Nazis killed him in Paris.

From the Paris "Dôme" comes the painter Bolz, bowler-hat on head pulled down over his eyes, accompanied by a woman in bowler, hers not so rakishly perched. One of her eyes is still visible. Albert Bloch calls me over. "Don't forget me." He later became a well-known painter in America. (At that time it was my passionate desire to be called Bloch or Bolz or Bing, because it seemed to me impossible ever to become famous with a sentimental name like mine.)

There are many foreigners: the Roumanian artist Forel, silent and gentle; the blond Vinko Milic from Serbia, noisy and rowdy, better boxer than sculptor and at the moment Spela's boyfriend; Luxardo the son of the Maraschino King and the descendant of a Byzantine Emperor Kantakuzen. Anikusa had herself painted as a charming Manet girl by Unold and won a gold medal at the Secession.

Whom else do I see? They are fading away—Carossa has faded almost completely; there he sits, the *ingénu* from the forests of Bavaria, teaching Marietta, who is pretending to be young and innocent; and my last look falls on Rolf von Hoerschelmann, who reminds me not to overlook him for he is as tiny as his brother is big, the friend of everybody, especially all the second-hand dealers in Munich.

But before the mist closes in, yet another figure emerges: Arthur, the waiter. Above his head, on three fingers, he is ingeniously balancing a tray clinking with cups and glasses: a cup of coffee, two eggs in a glass, one absinthe. He acted as banker for all of us; you could always borrow money off him. The nonchalance with which he stuck his hand into his pocket and threw the change already counted on to the table was inimitable. It was always right—or wrong—according to how he felt. He was an incurable gambler. (. . .)

Marietta
Klabund

It was in Munich in spring.

The time was 1914 [or 1912].[1]

Lectures on Theatre, Literature and Art History were given at the university by Professor Dr. Artur Kutscher.

Many original talents emerged under his intellectual tutelage Alfred Henschke was a member of one of his tutorials.

He came from Crossen on the Oder.

Earliest poems were written on telegram forms.

He sent them to the journal *Pan*.

Alfred Kerr encouraged the young poet.

Theodor Etzel was the publisher of *Lese* (Digest).

He was sitting in Simplicissimus with Henschke.

Marietta performed there and was introduced.

The young man said he had some poems to be typed.

Would Marietta be willing to do them because the words were too outspoken for a nice and respectable typist.

She was willing, because Becher had got her a job as Private Secretary with Bachmair the publisher.

She was to pick up the poems next day: Kaulbachstrasse 68, the summer house on the ground floor.[2]

She did so.

"The poems are by Klabund," the young man said and read her some. Did she like them?

"I'm going away for a few weeks. When you've finished, deliver the manuscript to Dr. Groth, Ungererstrasse, No. 5, third floor. Klabund will come and get them there."

The young man left the house with Marietta.

The sun was shining.

They reached the top of Veterinärstrasse and went in the direction of the university.

By the fountain Marietta said: "Faith, Hope and Charity, that's what the Münchners call these three buildings. 'Faith' is the nickname of the Georgianum for young theology students, 'Hope' is the nickname for the university, and the girls' institute on the right-hand corner is called 'Charity'."

A flower girl was standing there.

The young man bought a bunch of carnations.

"I'm pretty sure you are Klabund," Marietta said.

"What makes you think so?"

"You look it."

"No, I'm not Klabund. My name is Alfred Henschke. Klabund lives on the Ammersee. I'm going to visit him." At the Siegestor the young man took his leave and gave the girl the carnations.

The publisher Franziskus Seraphus Bachmair was at the International Publishers' Congress in Budapest.

Johannes R. Becher was his reader.

Marietta came and sat down in the next room with the poems.

Becher came in. "What are you doing here?"

"Typing poems by Klabund."

That didn't suit Becher.

Next day he didn't leave the key with the next-door neighbour.

Marietta went into the yard.

The smallest window in the building was open.

An old broom for sweeping the snow was found.

Using it as support she climbed the wall to the upper floor. From there she could reach the window-frame to hold on to.

She swung herself up and managed to squeeze her slim body. through the narrow little window.

She was in the building.

Marietta sat down at the typewriter.

Becher came in with Dorka.

He used to shut himself away with her for days and nights on end and wrote his first story, *The Affaire*. *New Art* was the name of the eminent journal that published it.

In her haste Marietta not only made many typing mistakes, but she also misread some lines and distorted their sense.

Yet the manuscript was finished. "Sunrise! Klabund! The days are dawning!"[3]

Marietta delivered it.

In a later poem Becher commented on Marietta:
... She whom the T.B. Poet brushed against ...
... And angels filled your lap with red marbles ...[4]

Three weeks had passed. Marietta came into the Café Stefanie.
To the right by the entrance sat Hugo Ball, Hans Harbeck
and Alfred Henschke.

The introductions were spirited: "May I introduce Klabund?"
Hugo Ball asked.

"I've known him for three weeks."

Loud laughter.

Where did the *nom de plume* come from, Harbeck wanted to
know.

"Where I come from, the bogy-man is called the 'Klabauter-
mann'—and poets are always treated as vagabonds. So you take
the Kla- and the bund and you've got my name, Klabund."

There was some discussion of anagrams. Jakob Davidsohn had
changed the letters of his name around into Jakob van Hoddis.

Klabund was certain the name *Decamerone* came from *Cento
novelle de amore*. c=hundred, only the first and last letters of
novelle are used and *de amore* is all there. All that's needed is to
invert the order of two letters.

Hugo Ball, Marietta and Klabund used to meet often. The
three of them collaborated on comic poems, which could be
called fore-runners of Dadaism. The moment they were by themselves in the Café Stefanie or after dinner in the garden of the
Max-Emanuel Brewery, they pulled out their pencils and started
fencing with verses. They invented an author for these poems
which they claimed had been written by "Klarinetta Klaball".
One of these poems read:

> *Embrace the dear Fatherland and all his love!*
> *And hold him tight with all your might,*
> *For the man who finds he can't any more*
> *Just loses him from sight.*
> *The best place to lose him, don't laugh,*
> *Is Pomerania or Pasing.*
> *They caught up with him about Biberaff*
> *And gave him a lovely epitaff.*
> *Published by Velhagen and Klasing.*

Klabund's first volume of poetry had been published by Erich Reiss.

In the Torggelstube am Münchner Platzl there was Max Halbe's historic bowling alley.

Even if everybody present didn't actually play, most of the well-known authors of the time had visited there at one time or other.

Thus it happened that the young poet Klabund was taken there and allowed himself to be introduced as Alfred Henschke, one of Kutscher's pupils.'[5]

After the game there was some talk about new books.

Klabund had already caused some stir because of the outspokenness of his verses. He was the main subject of conversation this evening:

> *Doing his hurried café stint*
> *Randy for absinthe and bint . . .*
> *One evening Klabund spotted something funny:*
> *The rich are the only ones in the money.*

Max Halbe, Alfred Henschke and some others were on the Ludwigstrasse going home.

Although Frank Wedekind was a close friend of Max Halbe, the author of *Youth* would not allow too free language and attacked the young poet Klabund repeatedly.

One or twice the student Henschke dared to raise some objections. This only made Max Halbe more angry and in the end he said furiously: "Be silent, young man, you're still wet behind the ears!"

Henschke shut up.

But when they were saying goodbye at the Siegestor, he said to Max Halbe: "Please excuse me, Herr Doctor, if I annoyed you with my objections. I only dared to voice an opinion. You see *I* am Klabund."

In the Bunter Vogel there was a one-night cabaret. Ernst Moritz Engert had painted the poster: "The Red Line".

Emmy Hennings sang songs by Aristide Bruant in Ferdinand Hardekopf's translation:

It's never seemed worth while
I never got very far
Now I've got the "clap" in jail
In Saint Lazare.

Silently Klabund and Marietta sat in the audience.

Marietta had been in Paris in 1913.

On their walks home together along the Poplar Boulevard of the Leopoldstrasse she had told Klabund of the powerful impressions Paris had made on her. Many bunches of carnations had withered in the meantime.

Today there were white roses on the table.

Klabund scribbled a poem :

MARIETTA

At the cabaret called the 'Red Line"
The 'Bright Coloured Bird'
Fluttered gently over your head
and mine.

You and I—this and that
Beneath the flowers on the moss
One tiny white rose
You plucked from the water glass.

Once I felt your leg
Tiny rose of gentle lust
Great mother you became to me
And I was like your grand-son.

Thirteen-years old and young
As though when I must die,
Mist and memory,
I fell between your breasts.

Later these lines were included in a volume of verse called
Jacob's Ladder.[6]

Summer came—and with it the dog days. The heat of August
brought war.

The serious-minded young people from the Café Stefanie fell
silent or hovered between patriotic romantic heroism and
Dostoevsky-type Christianity.

Klabund wrote a comedy: *Small Beer*,[7] which was produced
in the Munich Chamber Theatre. Of the three acts the first took
place in England, the second in France and the third in Russia.

I still remember verses from a song in the Third Act:

> *Little Czar needs his Cossacks for attacks,*
> *Oh what larks,*
> *Hey diddle diddle*
> *We'll show the foe how cossacks fiddle*
> *Fie-ie-i-ie*
>
> *Little Czar needs his riders alongside*
> *To sleep beside*
> *All his generals' little whores*
> *Who used to travel in coach and fours.*
> *Fie-ie-i-ie*

After its *première* there was a lively discussion of it in the
Bunter Vogel and all the Kutscher disciples tried to say something witty about the play. Marietta didn't say anything. Suddenly Klabund said: "Marietta hasn't said anything yet. What
does Marietta think of the play?" And Marietta answered:
"What do you expect? Klabund!—The name tells you what to
expect. Small Beer!" Everybody laughed in astonishment and
there was general agreement that this was the best comment on
the play.

But war fever was undiminished. Klabund volunteered, but the
Medical Officer sent him home. Klabund already had tuberculosis
of the larynx. (. . .)

Heinrich F. S. Bachmair
A publisher's report 1911-14

When I look back on the seventy years of my life, I can see now that of the various people who influenced me, very few had as lasting an influence as Johannes R. Becher. It was ultimately he who (unwittingly, perhaps) led me into the publishing profession which I had considered in passing, but never seriously. I was to be a publisher for nearly four decades—and would become one again if I had to make the choice.

In 1909 Waldemar Bonsels, who was a publisher as well as a writer, had published my one youthful extravagance—a completely insignificant book about Detlev von Liliencron. The only gain from this venture, which proved as negative commercially as it did from a literary point of view, were the frequent visits to the hospitable home of my publisher, which I continued even after Bonsels had given up his business and had moved from Schwabing to Schleissheim. "Gain," I said, for conversation with famous as well as still unknown writers and painters enriched my knowledge and matured my appreciation of the arts. At the time I was not yet twenty-two years old.

Summer 1911. One Sunday afternoon I went to Schleissheim again. While the other guests were as usual much older than myself this time I also met a young man of about my own age. Some time earlier he had submitted a collection of his poetry to the publishing firm Bonsels & Co. But when he had been informed that it could only be published if the author assumed the costs of printing and distribution, he withdrew it. He too, however, kept up occasional social visits because he like myself was attracted by the atmosphere of the house.

As the youngest of the circle we quickly established contact and plunged into animated conversation. We travelled back to Munich together and arranged to meet in the next few days.

It was holiday time, my new friend had just finished school examinations and I was about to start my third university term. We met every few days, roamed around Munich, went to the amusement park in the evenings behind the Bavaria monument, where all sorts of entertainments were offered and girls in search of male company strolled up or down.

So my first acquaintance with Johannes R. Becher was completely "unliterary". It was to develop into a firm friendship deepening as it lasted over the years. We got on so well together, partly because we both came from "very good" homes, but were struggling to break out from our backgrounds and as a result— each in his own circle—were regarded as black sheep.

But it was more than that. It may have been that Becher felt lonely and was looking for someone of about his own age who could give him understanding and genuine sympathy and who was also ready to treat him with some regard even if opinions and views were different.

I have often thought about the fact that I never met earlier friends of his, nor ever heard talk of any, whereas I introduced Becher to many of my friends from schooldays or from my Schwabing circles. With some of them, Amberger in particular (the Josef in Becher's story *The Affair*), he even became very close.

It naturally followed that I soon introduced Becher to my Pasing home. My generous parents had been used to this for years. My brother and I were always bringing home all sorts of people. In primary schooldays our backyard was always full of school-friends and neighbours' children, and the son of a director of Wagon-Lits International was the same in my mother's eyes as a boy whose father worked in the paper factory. This continued with friends from high school, from the university, the Schwabing *Bohème*. Becher, who soon felt at home with us, was always a welcome guest in my parents' eyes because of his un-affected manner and his conversational gifts. Afternoon visits tended to last until the last tram to Munich made departure compulsory.

My few visits to Becher's parents at Trautenwolfstrasse 6 were completely different.

I immediately felt that the family atmosphere was not as liberal as ours. His mother, whom, like his father, I only met in passing, left a colourless impression. (It was not until many years later in 1945–46 when I visited her again a few times that I saw her deep and sincere feelings, especially for her son Hans.) She was very charming, while the Herr Director of the Assize Court, Dr. Heinrich Becher, showed impeccable politeness, but otherwise remained completely unapproachable.

Once in Becher's room, the first things he showed me were not his poems. I'd known since that first afternoon at the Bonsels that he wrote poetry. We often spoke about that—but literature —especially his own literary efforts—in no way formed the main topic of conversation on our forays through Munich. He opened up a writing desk crowned by a few metal monstrosities and my astonished gaze fell on statuettes of swimmers poised for the start, cups, bowls of various shapes and sizes. These were the numerous trophies he had won in the last few years by his swimming prowess. He made no secret of the fact that he was prouder of these than he was of his poems.

Before my next visit he had probably mentioned that there was always coffee at the Bachmairs. This time Christine brought coffee up to his room. And this is how it was from then on. I was never invited to join the family for a meal.

Christine had been in service in the house for years and was very attached to Hans, which did not stop her from expressing her disapproval occasionally if she thought it necessary. In *Farewell* and in a poem dedicated to her[1] Becher has immortalized his childhood nanny . . .

In the course of our conversations on modern poetry we often mentioned the name of Richard Dehmel, whom we both admired very much. When I mentioned that I possessed two postcards from the poet in which he had replied to my queries when writing my Liliencron brochure, Becher produced a letter, which Dehmel had written in reply to some poems he had sent, inviting the young "harum-scarum" to look him up when he came to Munich shortly. This visit was already some months past.

In winter 1910–11 Dehmel gave a reading from his works at a meeting organized by the "New Club".[2] I had taken advantage of this opportunity to get to know the poet personally. I remembered that on the steps to Dehmel's flat I had met a young man of about the same age who was apparently just leaving the poet. Becher and I agreed that this must have been the first time we met.

The most valuable outcome of our far-ranging conversations I still consider to be a greater understanding of the works of Hölderlin. Of course I knew and loved a few of his poems, but I had read neither *Hyperion* nor the *Death of Empedocles* nor many of his other works. Becher insisted on my reading him thoroughly: he loved him as one of the greatest German poets, no less than he loved Goethe, and read me passages from Hölderlin's works.

If our meetings had already been interrupted for several weeks because of my trip to Vienna, it now looked as if they were to end for some time. It was my intention to move to Berlin for two semesters to attend the lectures of Erich Schmidt, Richard M. Meyer, Gustav Roethe and a few other prominent professors of that time.

So I took my leave of Hans and travelled to Berlin about the middle of September, 1911, where, after a short search, I found a room to suit me in the Memeler Strasse, today called the Marchlewskistrasse.

I hadn't been there for long when Becher wrote to say that he, too, was being allowed to study in Berlin. I never found out how he had managed to persuade his parents. A few days later he turned up. When I described to him the district I lived in he wanted to take a room there too. In the Memeler Strasse there hung on practically every door a little board with the notice printed in large letters: "Well-furnished room to let". The first notice I had come across on my search for lodgings had been at house number 1a for a room on the third floor. I was too lazy to climb so many stairs. Directly opposite there was a room vacant on the second floor with the widow Caroline Sowinski, *née* Riemann. I took up lodgings with her. The bright, pleasant room had its own entrance and was in fact completely private.

Becher, an experienced mountaineer, had no objections to the third floor. He moved into the room I had rejected, the one being let by a furrier's widow called Pauline Zlotorzenski, right next door to the Café Komet.

In those days a furnished room in that district cost 20 to 22 marks a month. In addition one had to pay for breakfast, prepared by the landlady, light—generally gas—heat and occasionally laundry. All together it came to 30 marks.

Becher senior gave his son 150 marks a month, which was exactly the same as I received from my parents, but he was rather careful, for Hans was still a minor. So he sent 30 marks monthly to Frau Zlotorzenski and wrote and told her that she would receive this amount from him every month. If it was too little she was to ask his son for the difference. If it was too much she was to give him the balance. The remaining 120 marks he divided into two instalments, so that Hans could always rely on a Postal Order for 60 marks a time on the 1st and 15th of the month.

Hans first matriculated in arts, as was compulsory for a medical student. Like myself he spent more time in the libraries than at lectures and in addition he really got to know Berlin and studied the life of the big city. In those days that was entirely possible within the framework of "academic freedom" and it made us feel happy and lighthearted.

At midday we ate somewhere in the city—together if our timetables permitted it: in the Linden restaurant which had a lunch for 1 mark 50 or Thick Pea Soup at Aschinger's for 25 pfennigs with as many free rolls as you could eat.

We generally spent the evenings together—when funds ran low, either in Becher's room or mine. Often all we had was a plate of Maggi soup with rolls. I still remember how we both hunted feverishly for a penny I had dropped. We needed it to make up the exact amount for two portions of cheese. When we had enough money we would go out and for convenience we preferred the Café Komet, which was on the first floor of a building on the Helsingforser Platz.

They soon got to know us there and in the not always well-founded expectation of a round of beers the band would play the "Poet and Peasant" overture or the Barcarolle from the *Tales of Hoffman* when we came in.

Our financial existence was a perpetual ebb and flow. Our parents guaranteed the change in tides by strictly observing the dates for the monthly cheques. Hence it came about quite naturally without any special arrangement that we lived on a kind of joint property basis. Whichever of us was in funds paid. From the 20th of the month on, the second instalment of Becher's allowance had to keep both of us for some days; then when my cheque arrived on the 26th/27th, Hans' lean time was over as well. The year 1911 had a beautiful autumn. So we used to leave the city on Saturdays and Sundays. Because Treptow or Grünau were closer than Grunewald, for example

—which we did not visit (including Kleist's grave) until the following year—we generally went there, and we would go rowing without a care in the world, to the annoyance of many a yachtsman whose bows we crossed. (I wonder if Becher suffered the same kind of annoyance years later on his own frequent sailing trips?)

And we liked the countryside, even if we were a little homesick for the dark pine forests of our native Bavaria. But the girls we picked up occasionally were in no way inferior to the home-grown variety and were ample compensation for the supposed deficiencies of Berlin's surroundings.

We had scarcely any "literary" company. It's true I associated with the circle round the publisher and writer Alfred Richard Meyer who had his regular table in the Wilmersdorf Biberbau. But Becher could never be induced to go there. Now and again, but only from 1912 on, we went to the Café des Westens, but there we only met and talked with casual acquaintances. One exception was "Mopp" Max Oppenheimer the painter. We often visited him in his studio. He wanted to draw a portrait of Becher which was to appear under my imprint as a single sheet. There was some advance advertising for it, but it never appeared.

Meanwhile, we did not neglect our studies in German literature and philosophy, even if, as mentioned, we pursued them on our own initiative in the reading rooms of the university and the Prussian State Library. In addition Becher was working on his novel *Earth*.

The founding of the firm of Heinrich F. S. Bachmair, Publisher, was the turning-point. It happened quite spontaneously and at the time I was completely unaware of the consequences this decision would have for the course of my professional life.

It was October 20th, 1911. Becher was at my place. Reading the paper I commented that there were to be celebrations on November 21st to mark the centenary of Kleist's death. Whereupon Becher said: "I have written a Hymn to Kleist." I said: "We'll print it!"

Immediately we drew up a written agreement. When I asked about the manuscript Becher replied that all his poems were in Munich in the hands of Albert Langen, Publishers, to whom he had sent them before coming to Berlin. He did not possess any copies. We sent a telegram to the publishers to send back the manuscript, then entitled the *World of Youth*, with all possible speed.

The manuscript included the Hymn along with a series of shorter poems. We entrusted the work to one of my landlady's sons who worked with the Printers, E. Künstler and Son. I visited the works in person and discussed all details of the lay-out. The work was printed in 500 copies on German machine-made parchment. Naturally a luxury edition in ten off-prints on hand-made Van Gelder parchment had also to be produced. All this splendour didn't cost much—about 40 or 50 marks, which I paid off in instalments from my monthly allowance.

In good time for the anniversary it appeared: *Johannes R. Becher / The Contender / Hymn to Kleist*, with a wrapper: *On the Hundredth Anniversary of Kleist's Death, Price 75 pfennigs*. (Today this twelve-page pamphlet is one of the most precious rarities in the secondhand book market!) Then I peddled it to all the booksellers who already knew me as a customer. I would enter the shop, buy something fairly cheap, and then produce the work I had published myself. The answer was always the same: "Hm—poetry. An unknown author." After some persuasion I got several shops to take the book on a commission basis. I probably bought about 20 marks' worth of books in order to get rid of a few copies of a "book" costing 75 pfennigs in the shop. Setting up a publishing house was extremely easy, selling the books a bit more difficult!

But production had to go on. I had agreed with Becher that I would publish his poems and the novel he was still working on. In the Kleist Hymn there is already an announcement of forthcoming works—*The World of Youth*, poems and a novel *Earth*. But that was not enough. I had a bundle of my own poems lying around. I wrote to my parents, enclosed the Kleist Hymn and the first approving reviews, whereupon my parents sent me some money. In the same way Hans successfully appealed to his father for a contribution towards his first volume of poetry, which, including binding, probably cost about 200 to 250 marks. To this had to be added—and this was what cost most—the cover by Willi Geiger. I had got to know him in Munich at the Bonsels; as he had moved to Berlin in the meantime I visited him occasionally. So I asked him for a cover for my latest book because I thought this would have good publicity value. Geiger demanded a 150-mark fee: I got something of a shock at what seemed to me the immensity of the fee, but as the artist agreed to payment by instalments I thought I could afford this expense.

The volume of verse no longer had the title Becher originally wanted, namely *World of Youth*. We had a pretty violent fight about this. But in the end we came to an agreement and the volume eventually appeared under the title we had both agreed on from Becher's various suggestions—*The Grace of a Spring*.

At the same time my own poems came out. They were to be followed by Becher's novel *Earth*. But these seemed to us too little which which to launch a new firm. Above all we needed an established name. At the Bonsels I had met the authoress Frances Külpe whose books were published by Georg Müller in Munich, at that time one of the most respected publishers of *Belles Lettres*. Hers was a name of some standing even if only in the sphere of light reading. Despite her English maiden name James, Frau Külpe was a charming and intelligent middle-aged lady. It was only natural with her majestic figure and short masculine hair-cut that she should smoke cigars. Both Becher and I enjoyed visiting her and often went to see her in Zeuthen, where she lived with one of her two daughters by her first marriage and another lady. She let me have a little collection of stories called *On the Volga*. Her daughter Else von zur Mühlen drew a bloodthirsty dust cover, which we thought very effective. As I advertised both volumes of prose together the well-known name of Frances Külpe made quite a few book-sellers order the other book with which the reading public was not quite so familiar. Besides, *Earth* was a novel and at worst it could always be put into the shop's lending library.

While I stayed on in Berlin, Becher went home for Easter, 1912. Because his father wanted him to continue his university studies from next winter in Munich, Becher got my parents to agree to support my publishing to some extent if I too came back from Berlin. They saw my collaboration with Becher as some guarantee that my youthful undertaking would not just be a flash in the pan, but would develop well.

As the summer term drew to a close we began to prepare for the removal of the firm to Munich, to Schwabing, which we felt the only possible location for it. Becher's parents lived there;

most of the great publishers of *Belles Lettres* like Georg Müller, R. Piper & Co., C. H. Beck, Delphin and others had their domicile in the artists' and writers' quarter of Schwabing.

At 39 Kurfürstenstrasse I found a fourth-floor part-flat of two rooms, and when, after a few months, the lessee of the other half moved out, we took over the whole flat. There the firm was set up. Becher was matriculated at the university, but devoted most of his time to the firm. He read and reported on all the manuscripts that came to us, most of which unfortunately were no use to us, and helped me with the correspondence which we typed ourselves. I looked after the technical side, production and advertising and relations with the book trade. A messenger called Franz, our factotum, completed the staff of the publishing firm Heinrich F. S. Bachmair, Munich and Berlin.

The success of our labours was not overwhelming. All the same, there was steadily growing recognition. Some newspapers and journals commented on them with benevolent condescension, others published exhaustive reviews of our latest books. So *The Contender* was already reviewed in Michael Georg Conrad's *German Literary Journal*[3] and in the Munich literary journal *Janus*.[4] It went something like this: "A young talent of extraordinary range and tremendous explosive power here throws off his shackles for the first time under the guise of the struggling Kleist. The language is of great originality and a strong stream of new and lively images floods through this tiny work. It is not going too far to claim that something of the feverish genius of Kleist rages in the swollen veins of this work. This is blood of his blood, and spirit of his spirit." At the same time, it must be admitted another journal said: "This is the same kind of fanaticism the Schlegels denounced in Schiller, but in modern dress." The *Berliner Lokalanzeiger*: "Well, I have tried devilishly hard to make Becher's poems an affair of the heart, but failed." (The expression "affair of the heart" came from my blurb for *The Grace of a Spring*.) "I shall not deny"—the man continued—"that there are good verses in the book, but that's a matter of taste." So with the Scherls literature was a matter of taste. Franz Pfemfert's *Aktion* reviewed Becher's early publications and was completely positive.[5] In March, 1912 it had a first contribution from him and from then on Becher published poems and little stories regularly in Pfemfert's weekly for some years.

In Munich a lively association with younger writers and painters soon developed, some of whom I engaged either as authors or as contributors to our journals.

With one of them Becher soon became friends: Albert Michel, a young business-man, came to us with a manuscript of poems called *Spring* and a list of acquaintances who had ordered the book in advance.[6] As the verses showed promise, I accepted them, especially since the advance orders reduced the commercial risk. On Becher's advice Michel sent some poems to *Aktion*, which printed one now and then. When Albert Michel was killed in The First World War Becher dedicated a volume of verse to his memory.[7]

Munich's typical bohemian café, the Café Stefanie, saw very little of us. We spent our evenings in the one opposite called Café Bauer (later Glasl) and as we were never safe from publisher-hunting authors, free copy cadgers and other similar types, no matter how late the hour, we changed over to a completely respectable middle-class place, the Café Fahrig at the Karlstor.

At night, on the way home, we often used to improvise "neopathetic" poems. A young poet, Jakob van Hoddis, whom I had met in Berlin, possibly through Else Lasker-Schüler, was just publishing his first poems. A kind of school grew up round him, whose followers called themselves Neopathetics. At first they seemed to us utterly harmless and, despite their new get-up, rather belated Impressionists. Anything at all that caught our attention in the street—a poster, a lurching drunk, a solitary lit window high up under the eaves—became the cue for the first stanza, which Becher or I declaimed aloud. The other had to add the second verse, and so a poem yards long grew and grew until we parted for the night. We had a lot of childish fun with this nonsense. But it would have seemed even greater nonsense to go beyond this and perpetuate these nightly elaborations in print.

We often went to the Kathi Kobus' artists' dive, Simplicissimus, in the Türkenstrasse, where regulars were given a bowl of soup with liver dumplings after midnight. Here Becher discovered one of the few genuine Schwabing characters, an extremely young artist's model, Marie Kirndörfer, nicknamed Marietta. She was a good-natured girl with quick repartee, and the close friend of a number of us. Marietta often paid us a visit at the office, as Klabund described with some embroidery in one of his short stories.[8]

It was in the Simplicissimus too that Becher's great love for the poet Emmy Hennings began.[9]

Before that there had been the gloomy "Dorka" affair which caused his friends considerable concern. Once it was all over he recorded with ruthless self-criticism,[10] the experience in his short story *The Affair*.

At the beginning of our time in Munich I lived with my parents as before. Becher usually came to us on Sundays and we discussed the current issues of the firm, often during walks in the near-by wood, which usually ended up in the Lochham country inn. At the office we could never find the time. Either that or he read me his latest works, among them once his *De Profundis Domine*.[11] I immediately declared myself willing to publish this work and had it beautifully printed in a limited edition on Dutch paper with a half leather binding. Some time after the appearance of the book, when the title no longer appealed to him, Becher reproached me: I with my Catholic upbringing ought to have known better than he who came from a Protestant family that the beginning of the 130th Psalm went: *De profundis clamavi ad te, Domine*.

This work, which was written partly in prose, partly in verse, has never been reprinted in its original form. In *Decay and Triumph* the verse and prose was published separately. The poems are grouped together under the one title *De Profundis* on pages 64 to 97 of the first volume and show occasional variants. Nor has the order of the first printing been retained throughout. In addition two poems from *The Grace of a Spring* (X and XI) have been inserted. The prose text is at the front of the second volume. Under the title, *De Profundis*, it has been textually amended and abbreviated as well.

In the course of these Sunday-afternoon talks the plan also matured for a series of publications, in which younger writers could present their attitude to the preceding generation of writers. We called the series: *Die neue Zeit. Beiträge zur Geschichte der modernen Dichtung*. The first "book" contained five contributions, among them a *Speech on Richard Dehmel* by Johannes R. Becher.[12] As we anticipated some success for these works I had 3,000 copies printed. But scarcely 300 were sold. Before we had this flop remaindered—which seemed to us absolutely vital in view of its failure—we gave some thought to how it should go on, for we already had several essays for the coming numbers on order which would have to be paid for.

We decided to transform the series into a journal, while retaining the title. However, there was already a *Neue Zeit*, a Social Democrat monthly published by J. H. W. Dietz of Stuttgart. The advice given by Becher's father, to whom we turned for a legal opinion, was not such as to encourage us to risk a legal tussle with the Stuttgart firm. So we abandoned our old title and called the journal *Die Neue Kunst*.[13] A number with about 100 pages was to appear every two months. Becher and I provided the material for the first number ourselves. Soon we were joined by two friends of earlier days: Josef Amberger, whose volume of verse *The Endless Way* I published, and Karl Otten, whose *Journey through Albania*[14] was no great success although that country was very much in the news at that time. The four of us edited the journal in great harmony. Becher was represented with poems in every issue. In addition the first contained his short story *The Affair* which, when reprinted in the second volume of *Decay and Triumph*, was renamed *The Little Life*.

Die Neue Kunst was the first journal of any size to come out decisively on the side of Expressionist Writing, but there was not enough money to keep it going and expand it. So it never got beyond one half-year's volume of three numbers, although we did everything in our power to make the journal known and enlarge its circle of subscribers. To this end we put on some performances before invited audiences. We hired the Munich *Kammerspiele* for one evening, engaged actors (as star attraction the subsequently much beloved Leontine Sagan) and under Hugo Ball's direction the play *The Wave* by Franz Blei with the author acting in it went on for the first and probably the only time.[15] (My seat in the front row of the stalls was the most expensive theatre seat of my whole life.)

The second function, a literary cabaret, was on a more modest scale. It took place in a room in a public house in the Schillerstrasse near the Central Station. Among those taking part was Becher reading some of his own poems. The name of the cabaret was invented by Emmy Hennings who also took part. Two or three of us were sitting in the Café Glasl, discussing the programme for the evening and possible names for the cabaret (which we intended to be a permanent institution). None of the suggestions put forward found general approval. In the end

Emmy Hennings: "I've got it! The Den of Murderers!" ("*Mördergrube!*") She shouted this so loud that all the other patrons in the café looked round in surprise.

The evening was a great success. The pub whose platform was adorned with a giant bat was packed. The newspaper reports were sarcastic, but very extensive.

The *Den of Murderers Evening* was not, however, Becher's first public appearance. Under the guidance of Dr. Artur Kutscher, a lecturer at the university (extraordinarily popular with his students, friend and biographer of Frank Wedekind), the *Neue Verein*, a progressive bourgeois literary club, put on so-called "intimate evenings", at which young or still little-known writers read from their works. As member of the club, above all as a former student and the current publisher of Dr. Kutscher, I suggested an evening with Johannes R. Becher to him, and this in fact then took place in the Mirror Hall of the Hotel Bayerischer Hof. (The lines: "In the mirror hall of the Four Seasons Hotel / I stood in Dinner Jacket, reciting poems . . ." in the dedicatory poem "To Munich" must be a lapse of memory on the part of the poet.)

Besides the *Neue Kunst* I later published the bi-monthly journal *Revolution*, done on newsprint, which lasted for five numbers.[16] Some of Becher's writings were published in this journal too.

With time our rooms in the Kurfürstenstrasse had lost their charm for us. The four flights of stairs kept many people away. We also had to consolidate the hard-won confidence of our suppliers. For this more impressive rooms in a better location were essential. We found a suitable ground-floor flat at No. 4 Horscheltstrasse. It was a bit off the beaten track, but the house and accommodation satisfied our increased requirements.

In the meantime Becher had been very busy writing. An imposing series of new poems was already in existence. He had also composed a few short stories, which, apart from *The Affair*, had mainly been printed in the *Aktion*. So the plan arose to publish one or two books of greater volume than *The Grace of a Spring* (70 pages) and *De Profundis Domine* (52 pages). The Publishers' List sent out at the end of October, 1913, *The Second Year*, announced as "in preparation": *Hans*, short stories, and *Decay and Triumph*, new poems.

I didn't like the title *Hans*. Even at the preliminary stage I had objected that it was too "autobiographical" and would arouse false expectations in the reader. After lengthy mutual deliberations I accepted Becher's proposal to publish Verse and Prose together under the one title *Decay and Triumph*. The first volume received the sub-title *Poems*, the second *Experiments in Prose*.

In spring 1914 while it was still printing with the firm Poeschel & Trepte of Leipzig, I realized that the shaky financial basis of my firm was not sufficient to keep it running as a going concern. Personal factors came into it too, so that I had to consider selling my undertaking. An interested party was soon found, but he could offer no guarantee that he would carry on my policy.

Besides, it was time for Becher to be published by a firm of better standing. Most of the well-known authors of our generation, like Leonhard Frank, Hasenclever, Werfel, Wolfenstein and many others had been giving their books to publishers like S. Fischer, Insel-Verlag, Georg Müller, Kurt Wolff. So we decided on Ernst Rowohlt, who shortly before had become director of the rejuvenated Hyperion-Verlag. Becher travelled to Berlin and entered into negotiations with him about his taking over the work which was in the process of being printed. But at first Rowohlt was a bit doubtful about introducing a new author with a two-volume work. After lengthy discussions all that Becher achieved was an agreement that the Hyperion-Verlag would take over the books from me on a commission basis. The name Hyperion-Verlag was prominent on the title page, but all business with the printer and the binder was still dealt with by me. The publisher's blurb I put out before the book appeared shows clearly by numerous quotes that Becher was already acclaimed by leading critics at home and abroad, by reason of his earlier publications. The Belgian Literary historian R. Hallemans wrote in 1913, for example, in an Antwerp paper: *"En lisant ce représentant de la jeune-Allemagne littéraire, on a l'impression qu'il conquerra sa place sous le soleil non seulement dans le pays germanique mais aussi dans la littérature européenne."*

BERLIN 1913-14

Fritz Max Cahén
The Alfred Richard Meyer Circle

I dropped in on the Alfred Richard Meyer circle in the summer of 1913, having left Paris behind me with much Cauchy, Henri Poincaré, Boutroux, mysticism, Celtic excavations, the Mona Lisa viewed from all sides on visit after visit, the Musée Cluny, the Guimet, Montparnasse with Delaunay, Braque, Severini, Picabia, Carl Einstein, Ludwig Rubiner—Immersion in Neo-Pythagoreism—and much more. The reason why—with the railways' dust still on me—I rang A. R. M.'s doorbell in Wilmersdorf one forenoon was absolutely prosaic, however poetic its origins. He had bought a poem of mine and I needed the honorarium. You might say I needed it desperately.

He was not at home. He was at the office of a feature syndicate where he was editor. As a publisher he always had to have another job. What he required for his personal needs he earned as a writer and editor—in later years he was even employed for a time by the Telegraph Union. What he had of his own he put into his publishing. I got my honorarium and an advance on a newspaper feature as well. I had never written that kind of stuff before and it turned out a ghastly flop. Not many years later leading journals fell over themselves for features by me, but then usually to no avail.

This was my introduction into the Alfred Richard Meyer circle, which amounted at that time to two apartments and three regular cafés. The Café des Westens was a long way off in the background. Regular café gatherings were as much a part of A.R.M. as the creases in his trousers and the duelling scar on his prematurely wrinkled face. Munkepunke's entry into the literature of the century had come about as follows: having failed his law exams for the second time, he was taken on as a trainee for the literary page of the *Norddeutsche Allgemeine* which at the time groaned under the rod of Rudolf Herzog. A.R.M. published two booklets *Rattled* and *Barnim*, which got the law out of his system and built up a publishing firm instead.

One of the apartments was his own—with Frau Resi Langer, formerly Paul Rohrbach's secretary, now a *diseuse* (when she read Morgenstern's *Gallows Humour* the room of Reuss & Pollack's bookshop was decorated by Grieneisen, the undertakers)—the second belonged to Victor Hadwiger's widow. His was nearer the Bayrischer Platz, the other near the Südwestkorso. and Meidner's studio a little further down the corso. Dr. Anselm Ruest—an anagram, like van Hoddis was for Davidsohn, for Ernst Samuel—played host. He used to be the closest friend of Victor Hadwiger, the social democrat. Roaming round the sessions at Frau Hadwiger's place was my fellow countryman Kristian Krauss who had a novel published by Grethlein, strove in vain for a stage success, had another historical work published by Borngraeber, later became a travelled Orientalist, and ended up as a newspaper tycoon, at all times unhappily in love with modern literature—and on the sly a gentle Satanist with a taste for Black Mass.

The most important of the gatherings was given the name "Paris" by Munkepunke. It assembled several times a week in the coachman's pub near the Bayrischer Platz. Meyer, gourmet of the first order, with complex desires for mixed drinks (cf. Munkepunke's *Drinks Book*, his articles on cooking in many papers and much else besides) along with crisp meat balls and good strong pickled pork—with Kümmel and barley wine to perfume the products of the Berlin Breweries—sings the praises of the "Hay Burners" parked along the kerb outside. The lyrical pamphlet *Paris* caught the atmosphere of this circle.[1]

Rudolf Leonhard—monocle screwed in—takes the chair. He has just brought out his *Angelic Stanzas* and his *Beate and the Great God Pan*.[2] Gottfried Benn drops in, still a young doctor, pale, undernourished. His *Morgue* has been published by Meyer, his *Sons* beginning to take shape.[3] Rudolf Kurtz with his square skull set over his beer. He is working on a Dostoevsky edition. Once at his house—far from the city centre—there was a wild debate on the meaning of categories. Died-in-the-wool Hegelian. At intervals: Paul Erkens, crazy about fun-fairs, later stage designer in Munich, always thirsty; like Felix Lorenz of the

Berliner Tageblatt who drops in now and again. Occasionally Kanehl turns up too, originally from Wickersdorf, about to move somewhere else, where he is to be resident playwright at one of the better theatres.

The second meeting-place—name and place have been preserved in the lyrical pamphlet called *Dance-Hall*[4]—takes us to the Boulevard Quarter. Here René Schickele usually joins us, in panama hat and concertina trousers, at once powerful and unsure of himself. *In the Hornet's Nest* was the title of his book and he lived up to it all his life. Max Herrmann-Neisse still lives far from Berlin, but the correspondence with him is brisk. A few other *Dance-Hall* poets too: out-and-out provincials, at least judging by their addresses. As usual Arno Holz still reigns at the Potsdamer Platz.

The third meeting place—a matter of some complexity. It is situated, or rather it is in session, in a *bodega* near the Kurfürstendamm, while the other corner is generally occupied by Ernst Rowohlt and entourage. Anselm Ruest's beat. Usually with us is Dr. Otto Buek, from Marburg like myself, a first-class Greek scholar and co-editor of the Cassirer Kant edition then in progress. Ruest: probably the best Stirner expert of the time, pupil of Dessoir, acquaintance of Lasson of Hegel fame. Rudolf Leonhard, the lawyer, has also sat at Dessoir's feet . . . After a preliminary tussle with Friedrich, the exponent of popular philosophy—seated at Rowohlt's table he looks like the living embodiment of Nietzsche—the mild air beckons Kantians and Hegelians alike to take an evening stroll in the Tiergarten.

Anybody who goes for a walk with A.R.M. alone—I used to do so often, since my Apollinaire translations were on the way, the double volume of *Maiandros*[5] due, and besides I was looking after various things connected with the edition of Pückler-Muskau's posthumous works which Munkepunke planned—ends up drinking Berlin pale ale, in clouds of tobacco smoke, surrounded by watch-chained bellies not far from Unter den Linden or in a fantastic Italian wine shop near the Potsdamer Bridge, where the tramp Peter Hille, flanked by an admiring band of Alcibiades, once lifted his Socratic beard in drunken rapture. On the other side of the canal in the Patzenhofer pub you meet Richard Dehmel who has come into the city from his small-holding out in the marchlands. Lautensack: only seen by those he cares to invite; off the beaten track for most Berliners; too

D*

highly strung, his little pointed beard always quivering with excitement and frequent impulsive gestures. But he and his wife are both charming hosts—bubbling over in Munich dialect, Wedekind in every corner of the room and a ghostly Delvar occasionally haunting the pauses in conversation. That then was the close circle.

Café des Westens. Else Lasker-Schüler's colourful hair-band. Albert Ehrenstein: coat too long, narrow-brimmed hat, pushed too far back on his head, infinitely unworldly. Ernst Wilhelm Lotz, Slav cheek bones, a dreamer's mouth, a dreamer's eyes. What a room! Right out in the back yard, washing, drying scarlet runner beans, climbing; picture of a smiling girl on his desk. She smiles somewhere in the German East he left to come to Berlin. Juniper blooms in his room. In the Café: the philosopher Itelson, pear-shaped skull, an aura of mathematics; a shrivelled-up old woman by his side. Blümner discussing with Franz Blei, tense histrionics beside narrow face of visionary.

Suddenly Henri Guilbeaux is in Berlin. To give a lecture. I write it up for *Maiandros*. Long night with him and Meyer: from Maeterlinck to Verhaeren, from Claudel to Louys. His fate is well-known: veered further towards the left, mutineer in the Black Sea Fleet, appalling difficulties when he returned to France. A.R.M. at his peak on such occasions. A crafty fighter yet hypersensitive, well versed in all the highways and byways of modern literature; hypererotic flows from his lips as easily as ecstatically sublimated academic humour. Apollinaire comes to life, the Parnassians are a bit shaken at the gentle spleen vented upon them, Rimbaud rampages past, with many a quote from pulpit oratory. He gives ample proof of what made him "tick" and why he is a publisher.

This makes one realize how little the narrower circle is the whole circle, which can be seen more clearly—although there, too, incompletely, in the *Mistral*[6] of the *Maiandros* series. Hundreds of men of letters loosely held together by one thing, the fact that they are consciously striving for a new age. At the same time—difference between the Meyer Circle and many of the other young publishing houses—the "new" is not meant politically. If the art for art's sake principle was upheld anywhere, it was by Munkepunke and his inner circle.

Nineteen-hundred-and-fourteen rips the publishing concern apart. Everybody is called up or volunteers. Lotz, so young, so very young, and Stadler are killed, like Lichtenstein and others. Even John Höxter—the living caricature of a soldier—marches off to Verdun. It's true he doesn't get very far. He is discharged. As for myself—back from the front—I'm in Copenhagen writing for German newspapers. Dr. Ruest is working in the War Office Press Bureau. Rudolf Leonhard asks me one day if I can't use him. I put in an application for him. The C.-in-C. for Brandenburg/Prussia denies him permission to leave the country as an incorrigible pacifist—since when? He had never had any political opinions of any kind in the past. When in 1918–19 I am Graf Brockdorf-Rantzau's Press Attaché in the Foreign Office, he becomes my liaison officer with the U.S.P.D. I also get him to write broadcasts for Nauen. Slowly but surely he drifts into the Red camp: our friendship does not change, but our conversations are no longer so uninhibited as they were. After 1919 I remained a political commentator.

A.R.M.'s publishing house had been in difficulties since the beginning of 1914. With the *Maiandros* series he had bitten off more than he could chew. After the sixth book only very few of the green supplements appeared—no more books. Gone were the days when he had produced his gay *Fleas' Circus*—drawings by E. Th. A. Hoffmann—and got Peter Scher to strum his *Horse-Fly in Summer*. His post-war activity also remained vague. Finally Meyer wrote only for other publishers.

How had Expressionism started anyway? Weren't the artists the pacemakers? It's true we all loved Impressionism. But we were sick of art exhausting itself in the fragmentation of form and the use of the visible world as its sole point of departure. Lucretius' flock of sheep, visible blobs of colour, had been done to death, when Seurat painted his *Cancan*. What the Expressionist movement had done was to raise in an epoch-making way the noblest and oldest problem in aesthetics: how can the amphiboly of inward and outward reflexion lead to art—from without to within or vice versa. People had been aware of this problem since Plato differentiated between τὴς εισωχοπουκὴς εἴςη ςύο and εἰχαστιχήν και φανταστιχήν In Dürer—see the Albertina —purely cubistic tendencies in the drawing of the draperies! Beginnings of Expressionistic excitement in the Colmar Altar! New epochs are generally not so new as they seem or would like to seem, at least when it is a question of those spheres of human activity which include the relationships between the creative individual in interaction with the object-world. They merely throw a new light on them.

If one were to single out the Meyer Circle from the overall stream of the *Sturm und Drang* of the time one can say that it identified the trend of the time before anybody else, that it fostered more than others the connections with French modernism, especially as regards lyric poetry. Apart from A.R.M., those of the Circle who are still remembered as outstanding are Gottfried Benn, Rudolf Leonhard, both of them *despite* their political evolution and essentially regardless of it also, Carossa and the Lautensack of the pre-Expressionist period. Of the others, only this or that poem, this or that essay or whatever it may be. A quantitatively small, but in no way and no respect insignificant, contribution to the development of contemporary literature. There just aren't any modern classics.

Walter Mehring
Berlin *avant-garde*

Every morning before my father took me to school on his way to the office, I would find him at the breakfast table with a huge blue pencil circling communiqués and articles in a pile of daily papers, material for his satirical poems, polemics and caricatures in his comic political weekly called *Ulk*—anything which incited him, the progressive, freethinker and "Dreyfusard" to social protest, militant pacificism and *lèse-majesté*.

And naturally I read *Ulk* although that didn't please my father very much ("without a solid grounding in the classics you'll just spoil your taste!"). But I also read the newspaper cuttings he had marked before their processing and so precociously sharpened my instinct for irony. And while rummaging around in the illegal and otherwise offensive printed matter which my father collected in cardboard boxes I came across a particularly vicious attack on him—angrily crossed out in blue—which gave me something of a shock. For my father, who had been repeatedly reprimanded, imprisoned, even condemned to six months' hard labour, who had stood up for Jean Jaurès, Hauptmann and Wedekind, was my idea of the aggressive, completely "modern" minded journalist. But here he was being ridiculed as the Editor-in-Chief of an "antediluvian" and unspeakably dull comic paper. This excited my curiosity so much that I immediately acquired this irreverent journal—with the pocket-money my father sometimes gave me to take a little girlfriend to the ice-cream parlour. He never guessed what I would use it for.

The author of this sneering comment, who as I now discovered made fun of my father and the whole Berlin Press all the time, was a certain Herwarth Walden, editor of *Sturm*, Germany's first Expressionist journal, founded in 1910, inspired and instigated by Walden's first wife, Else Lasker-Schüler, the sacred muse of the German *avant-garde*.

Apart from *Sturm*—to which I later became a contributor at the beginning of the First World War and shortly before the death of my father, who had been arrested again for anti-militarism—there existed since 1911, another "scandal sheet of Berlin Asphalt literature", Franz Pfemfert's *Aktion*, to which I also subscribed for that reason.

I was a sixteen-year-old adolescent when I drifted into the *Sturm* and *Aktion* milieu drawn by the same irresistible attraction as to any other den of vice; and so I joined the Bohemians who conspired together round the tables of Berlin's old Café des Westens—Café Megalomania—and in every other European capital complete with their sacred cows (the Marquis de Sade, Walt Whitman, Rimbaud, Laforgue, Dostoevsky and Strindberg), secret talents known only to the initiated (Apollinaire, Franz Kafka, Franz Werfel) and martyrs: the vagrant Peter Hille, who starved himself to death, the Russian Social Revolutionary Senna Hoy, whose *Letters from Siberian Captivity* were answered by a demonstration of sympathy by the intelligentsia, then still capable of complete solidarity.

The decade from the turn of the century until World War I became the decisive epoch of that last great revolution which displayed no national flag of any land, a revolution which took place not on barricades, but on easels and palettes, and simultaneously in a shack in Montmartre, Paris, the "Bâteau Lavoir", where Cubism was born (created by Braque and Picasso, baptized by Matisse), and in a Bavarian hostelry in Sindelsdorf, which gave birth to the "Blue Rider": Kandinsky's and Franz Marc's *Almanach 1911*,[1] the first year of grace in our artistic calendar. "What is at stake is a real revolution, a total reversal in questions of taste, whose consequences are still unforeseeable!", Franz Marc, the painter of legends like the *"Animal Fates"*, had prophesied.

It spread from Munich to Zurich and in 1912 to Berlin in Herwarth Walden's *Sturm* Gallery with the first Berlin Exhibition of the Futurists.[2]

On the way to school at the Wilhelmsgymnasium in the Bellevuestrasse I had been in the thick of it when the bald-headed Caesar of the Futurists, F. T. Marinetti, had flung his manifestoes on to the pavement from his taxi window:

"We stand on the platform of the centuries . . . Destroy the Art Galleries! Burn down the libraries; . . . We attack moralism, feminism and all other expedient, profitable cowardices."

I chased the taxi blindly round the corner to the *Sturm* offices (34a Tiergartenstrasse) and the most turbulent show of pictures I had ever set eyes on.

I had never dreamed that an exhibition could be such a tempestuous affair; never thought it possible that disputes over problems of style could develop into pitched battles between invited public and foreign guests of honour; into shouts of: "*Evviva l'amore!—Evviva Garibaldi! Evviva Futurista!*" and: "Chuck them out!" and "Where's the Police?", who promptly appeared, moustachioed and helmeted . . .

Today, looking back, it seems to me scarcely conceivable how Guido Severini's *Pan-Dance in Monico*, a gay colourful ragtime of faces and thighs, Balla's, *Boneshaking Coach*, Boccioni's *Laughter* shattering into azure blues—how such historical experiments in art, long since become museum-pieces—could cause such hysterical manifestations in the public.

In effect what was happening was an explosion which fundamentally recast perspective, symmetry, all the traditional concepts of beauty—at the time only very few decadent artistic types were aware of it . . .

In Berlin Herwarth Walden (*Sturm*) and Franz Pfemfert (*Aktion*) came on the scene as the ringleaders of the "real revolution" at one with each other against the prevailing taste of *blasé* snobs, cultural philistines, the old masters of Academy *Kitsch*—and irreconcilably opposed to each other . . . Walden sardonic, subtle; Pfemfert crude, a typical cheeky Berliner. Contrasts even in external appearence: Walden—a straw-maned Rumpelstiltskin; affected, bristling; but also capable of throwing off his bristles when he went into ecstasies over some work of art that enchanted him; Pfemfert—something of the socialist boy-scout, a cunning, crude plebeian, but basically just as much the ardent enthusiast when it came to "Art, Culture and Politics".

Walden and Pfemfert, fanatics and ideologues both, represented the international Bohemians who considered any popular success suspect and despised any journalistic concession as a crime against principles.

In his *Sturm* Art Gallery, which usually stood empty apart from

the *vernissages* when the crowds stood and gaped as if in a wax-
works, at the *Sturm* evenings at which Dr. Rudolf Blümner's
and my recitations of August Stramm works ended in boos
and hoots of laughter, at his private receptions, looking very
fragile alongside his commanding Swedish wife, Walden assumed
an arrogant air of ceremonial, which impressed even such a
superior philisophical intellect as the painter Kandinsky, or such
a soberly pedantic craftsman as Piet Mondrian—even that strictly
Prussian Police Councillor H., his protector...

Walden always spontaneously won over the young neglected
talents at whose attempts he sniffed short-sightedly, but with
sure instinct, through his gleaming glasses; with infallible self-
confidence he converted the sceptics by the rich imagery of his
paradoxes, which he produced with all the rhetoric of a
reformer:

"Much that was rootless but dared raise its head above the
ground has been driven out by *Sturm*. Much that had borrowed
life from the world of being instead of that of appearance has
been destroyed by it. For the being of the sun and of art is
appearance . . ." by his cutting sarcasm—he seldom laughed—
he horrified the critical experts who, in order to tease him, asked
what they were supposed to admire more—the impudence with
which these fellows from *Sturm* propagated these barbaric paintings as revelations of a new art of the future, or the despicable
sensationalism of the art-dealer who gave over his rooms to
this insanity in forms and colours...?

But it was certainly not thirst for sensation that motivated
the eminently unbusinesslike Walden. It was rather his naïve
speculation on "his" Expressionism, his prophetic superstitious
belief in the "Art of the Present which is already the Future"!

"Art is inhuman," he preached. "So we must be prepared to
sacrifice all humans to it!"

This stood in crass opposition to the radically materialistic
dialectics of Franz Pfemfert, who warned stubbornly and mono-
manically that "the Czarists and big-wigs of all countries and
of all parties were to a man helping to lay the foundations for
the coming catastrophe."

"Art without social content is empty humbug!" he declared,
loudly enough for all to hear, including the people from *Sturm*
at the next table.

"If, however, it should come to pass," he added, "that Socialism should behave in such an authoritarian manner as the worst of reactionary philistines, then before anybody else does, we shall attack it."

Pfemfert placed naked tendentiousness above "pure form"; above the "work of art in words" in the manner of August Stramm, the Post Office official and most consistent of the Abstract poets, above the apocalyptic poems of the unfortunate Jakob van Hoddis, the Berlin *poète maudit*; and above all literary fantasies he placed the noble anarchistic Utopias of the Russian prince Peter Krapotkin.

And if Pfemfert included in his *Aktion* a Ludwig Meidner poster: "Revolt of the Mothers against War", a Matisse nude, an early Georg Grosz caricature, or if he printed in his *Aktion* book club *Der Rote Hahn*, the *Aeternist* and *Neopathetic* poets like Ivan Goll, Carl (Bebuquin) Einstein and Ferdinand Hardekopf and the "Northern Lights Dante": Theodor Däubler, and the poet of *Morgue* Gottfried Benn, M.D., then he always did so on purpose to annoy the narrow-minded philistines of the "right" or the "left". This was certainly his intention when in the autumn of the first year of the war in the midst of the Pan German Victory fever, he published an *Aktion* special number[3] on the arch-enemy, the French: Poems by Baudelaire, Mallarmé, essays by Henri Bergson, Paul Claudel, André Gide, by Braque, Picasso; it was dedicated with black edging:

TO THE POET CHARLES PÉGUY VICTIM OF THE WAR

This was certainly "political propaganda" too, but just as noble and courageous as Walden's advertisement in *Sturm* at the same time publicizing the art of the Italian Futurists, the French Cubists, and the Russians Archipenko, Chagall, Kandinsky . . .

Walden and Pfemfert,

the two rebellious, typical Berlin characters—in their life-time neither had deigned to acknowledge the other with either word or nod,

and yet they were to suffer the same fate; impoverished, outlawed, forgotten:

death in exile,

Herwarth Walden in Soviet Siberia—

Franz Pfemfert in Mexico. . .

"This is the kind of madness hatred of art can rise to! Such things can neither mislead nor hinder my friends and myself in their endeavors!"

Herwarth Walden had declaimed in his opening address at the First German Autumn Salon in 1913.

as watchword for the artistic *avant-garde*,

"qui meurt, mais ne se rend pas..."

Rudolf Leonhard
Marinetti in Berlin 1913

I met Marinetti for the first time before the First World War,[1] in Berlin, when there, as everywhere else, a form of art was being born which we took to be something absolutely and entirely new (something every generation of artists does). We thought there had never been anything like it, and above all we thought it had no connection whatsoever with the comings and goings of what had been accepted immediately before us. None of us—or at least very few—had any idea how much of the present was already contained in our heads and our hands; we saw dimly in our poems but not in our conscious thoughts how closely the past with its weapons of war and its conservatism, at best culturally disguised, already hung over us; hence it was little wonder that those of us who placed the creative artist higher than the created work, and would have preferred to renew Rembrandt and the Romantics rather than cherish them faithfully, found the hated word Passéism incomprehensible and the term Futurism so enticing! This was about the time when the Frenchman, Alexandre Mercereau, was in Berlin and Döblin refused to put his signature to a letter to Hauptmann, perhaps—perhaps?—because he already sensed the latter's weakness and coming betrayal, but neither would he write to Richard Dehmel—that great poet who had unjustly been pushed into the background, simply because he didn't correspond with "such people"—whom he considered a wretch. This was the pre-war Berlin of extreme tensions and extreme self-confidence.

In the same side room in the Café Josty where this happened, we shortly afterwards met Marinetti, General of the Futurists, delegate of the Anti-classicist youth of Italy, who, we understood and believed, were trying to replace the land of Art Galleries with one which was alive and vital, the land of tourists and hotel-keepers with one of writers and creative artists. The session was presided over by Herwarth Walden, yellow-maned, ivory-faced, sharp-nosed, alert and lively, jealously and cleverly classifying and guarding every new "trend". Marinetti jerked about on his chair with a Mediterranean elasticity which was always calculated; already bald, with extravagant elegance and extravagant but precise gestures, with a great deal of exactly drained—and well trained—vivacity: not so much frothing as bubbling over, but the bubbling over was evenly distributed to all sides. He looked around in all directions quickly, with sharp, sparkling, perhaps mistrustful, excited eyes set in a soft, pale face which he kept tautening and tightening. He was always engaged in conversation, he talked a great deal, he liked Berlin enormously. It was as if this were a special Berlin, his Berlin, his domain, as if Berlin had been made ready for him, as if it were suddenly full of him. Now I know that he was no poet, no artist. He was an ambassador; one who concealed the fact that he was only an unofficial ambassador by the din he created, one who had no other credentials than the signature on other people's pictures, no other *agrément* than our indiscriminate interest in the Café Josty; and it is now obvious that he was no organiser, but an *entrepreneur*. And by heaven it is no mere pun if I say that his wily, jerky gestures were those of a Marionette.

We didn't read his poems until after he had gone. Alfred Richard Meyer published them in his poetry series. Rudolf Kurtz wrote a short compressed preface which was a masterpiece of judicious ambivalence.[2] Am I wrong—it is all so remote like a chapter of prehistory—or did I write about it myself in some long-forgotten journal?[3] What was positive about the loud, uninhibited flow of the hollow inflated verses was at best the Schillerian rhetoric. Drugged exuberance of puberty, caught in the style of advertising slogans; rhapsodic style with no object and a subject as good as shapeless; feeble rhythmical fluency without direction or light; din for din's sake; verbal diarrhoea.

I last saw Marinetti at a congress of all the Writers' Unions in Paris. Now he was every inch the Ambassador, was officially, His Excellency, the exponent of Fascist literature. The bald patch on his head no larger, the gestures no less unconstrained, the glance no freer, the self-assurance, however, more impressive. I could not deny myself the pleasure of reminding him of our encounter in the dim and distant past of his unofficial pre-Excellency days in Berlin; he was enough of the official and His Excellency to be all quick and enthusiastic as if he remembered precisely, quite precisely. (Between myself and the Fascist delegation there existed from the very first minute till the concluding formalities of the session an instinctive hostility, certainly not consciously willed by either party.) At the concluding banquet, too, Marinetti also spoke; he was the only one who did so in an official capacity; he spoke of the extraordinary artistic sensitivity of his extraordinary leader; only one pair of hands at one table clapped once; it was extremely embarrassing.

So he went on being His Excellency—for Germany he was an Axis artist and yet decadent, or rather: decadent and yet an Axis artist, and the *agrément* had to be wrung from our critical *Führer* in a moment of distraction.

But what was this art of the future?—*was*, because it no longer is, it is past. Always a man of many parts, Marinetti invented "Bruitism" for music, with remarkable awareness of the fact that music is connected with noise; he did not make any serious attempt to harmonize and synchronize the noises of real life for film and radio, which is what others did, but rather tried to dissociate by putting things round the easier way, disorganized music into noise. In order to make the theatre interesting he did not, for example, advocate better plays better played, instead he suggested selling the same seat to different people and making them fight for it or smearing a few seats with glue before the performance. He wanted to reform the theatre with the cheapest schoolboy pranks. He put out proclamation after proclamation, even more vulgar and flat than the tendentious, ridiculously pompous declarations of D'Annunzio, whom he had hated for being a Museum artist and poet of the past, and whom he had joined in the Academy. Yes, he was sufficiently *passé* to become His Excellency with a seat in the Academy—when the Academy went Fascist. He merely moved his revolution to the right where all it did was make a noise but did not affect the *status quo*, or the Establishment. He loved and worshipped war, because it made a noise and because he had no desire to know what else it did. With his noise for noise's sake he genuinely but unintentionally caricatured art for art's sake. He was successful with it because there are plenty who, in order to be *au fait*, accept what is now for the sake of the noise it makes, without asking whether the new is also good, or even if it is really new. Him, an innovator? Not even the opposite, and not even a clown; a man of affairs, if you like a machine just ticking over beautifully; a nonentity that kept erupting. And when in the Louvre, or anywhere else, he proclaimed his *aeropeinture*, flight-painting, then for all the violence of his scribbling he never mentioned what his friends sticking to their aeroplane seats were painting with: brains and blood—other people's. (. . .)

Franz Jung
Franz Pfemfert and *Die Aktion*

We left Munich without regrets. But the general exodus of Art and Literature from Munich was already well under way by 1913. Only a few months later in the Café des Westens on the Kurfürstendamm Margot was able to meet again most of the people she used to sit with in the Café Stefanie.

In the meantime I had published another book called *Comrades* with Weissbach in Heidelberg without worrying about the reception it would have from the reviewers. All the same it brought me into contact with the *Aktion* circle and I soon became a regular contributor of essays, generally of social criticism. I remember an appeal in the form of a short story, "Morenga",[1] to save the Hereros in German South West Africa, whose cattle the German Colonial authorities had taken away to secure enough pasture land for a dozen white settlers. It had developed into an uprising which had been extended into a colonial war by the German Government, with an Expeditionary Corps and daily victory bulletins in the press. The Hereros, armed for the most part with sticks and one or two English fowling-pieces, had no chance against the German automatic rifles and machine-guns. The military operations were confined to separating the various tribes and pushing them back one by one into the desert where they died of hunger or thirst, forty thousand men, women and children.

Around Franz Pfemfert, the editor of *Aktion*, there had gathered a circle of young poets, of what could justifiably be described as the *avant-garde* literary generation. Whoever had any point of view in whatever form, in smooth or clumsy verse, was welcomed to the journal; what mattered was the will to expression, the inner compulsion, the dynamic force of the statement.

There seemed to be nothing tangible holding this principally youthful circle together. Nor was there any label which you could apply to this literary movement in so far as there was such a thing. All this came later, retrospectively.

Franz Pfemfert published these young poets of *Neopatheticism* —Alfred Lichtenstein, Ernst Blass, van Hoddis and others like Gottfried Benn and Oskar Kanehl, Richard Oehring, within a framework of essays on politics and social criticism, leading articles on the social problems of the day, and interpretations of Bakunin, Krapotkin and Proudhon. Whether he wanted it or not, the poet was educated in social criticism, regardless of the fact that these poets later in wartime went their different ways again.

This educational process, if one can call it that, was helped along by the co-operation of those who had already "arrived" on the literary scene. I'm sure that in those years there was scarcely a single writer of stature and significance who was not proud to appear in *Aktion*; he owed it to his own prestige to do so. This degree of cohesion within a framework of pronounced social criticism was the particular hallmark of the *Aktion*.

If nowadays literary histories call these years and this circle of contributors German Literary Expressionism, then I must immediately add that this Expressionism was a form of protest against the narrowness of observation in Naturalism, a kind of barrier against the danger of a Neo-Romantic revival, against Neo-Classical imitations of the past. What was original and peculiar about this conglomeration of such mutually conflicting factors was the impulse to place the individual ego at the centre of things against all influences from without, as defence mechanism and counter-attack against the *status quo* in society. It was a long time before literary histories discovered the common line in language, form of expression and diction. For the language also had become too restricting, too fossilized and frozen, too inflexible. The poets themselves did not realize this at the time. Strange how fresh the language of Expressionism has remained. It has been buried by two wars and their aftermath, but it has remained so much alive, in both the written and the spoken forms, that one could begin to build on it anew any time. It is wrong to see this development from the worm's eye view some of its followers adopt nowadays. The perspective is broader:

Expressionism was already part of a revolutionary movement with very strong social and political overtones.

In the inner circle round Franz Pfemfert and the Ramm sisters, Ludwig Rubiner was the outstanding personality. His essay *The Poet Intervenes in Politics* made exactly the point we all felt. To this circle belonged Karl Otten, Kurt Hiller for a time, Carl Einstein, Sternheim and Landauer and as good friends, so to speak, the great publishers Fischer, Kurt Wolff and Rowohlt, strange as this may seem today, and in addition Alfred Kerr and Maximilian Harden.

This is the phenomenal thing about Pfemfert: how was he able to manage this enormous task?—and right throughout the war . . . Where did he find the money to keep the journal alive—to which had to be added the costs of his book-publishing concern? It's true the *Aktion* paid its authors' no money, but that is not the decisive factor; perhaps not the money at all but the work, the correspondence with authors and the hundreds of people from all parts of the world, the technical labour of editing, printing and distributing . . . a phenomenal achievement, as any professional will admit.

Pfemfert never had any help apart from Alexandra Ramm, his wife. He lived in the Nassauische Strasse in the Wilmersdorf Quarter of Berlin in a rear flat on the fourth floor. This had a kind of office, and Pfemfert sat at a table facing a mountain of letters and manuscripts, in front of him a cigar box full of tobacco from which he constantly made cigarettes. He was always accessible to everybody from early morning till late at night. The door was open for any visitor.

I shall not conceal the fact that I did not feel quite at home in the *Aktion* circle. I was treated with a kind of friendly reserve. Although later in the war Pfemfert published my works in quick succession and they are the ones with some claim to lasting value, even if only as characteristic of a narrowly restricted period; yet there was hardly any close connection between us. Unfortunately I had little or no contact with Ludwig Rubiner, and with Carl Einstein I probably spoke no more than a few words. My guess today is that these works of mine, which for the greatest part were written while I was a prisoner in Spandau or shortly after, including the novels *Sophie, Sacrifice* and *The Leap from the World*,[2] may have been considered appropriate material to counteract the superficiality of wartime literature—

the fate of the individual especially in his relationships with woman and the world he lives in leaves the war entirely out of account, the war is not much more than an annoying and persistent rumour—but Pfemfert never talked to me about it. These works were soon forgotten in the general upheaval of war. They have a certain rarity in the book trade today for the few dozen literary fanatics who attempt to uncover the roots of Expressionism.

If Pfemfert counted on a greater impact when he published them, then the disappointment which one only became conscious of some years later must have been extremely bitter. My ambiguous position as Stock Exchange correspondent, my own indecision whether to break with the Stock Market or with literature, and my display of grievance made it very difficult for me to be properly accepted into the *Aktion* circle. (. . .)

Nell Walden
Kokoschka and the *Sturm* Circle

My first encounter with Oskar Kokoschka took place at the beginning of 1913 in Vienna. I already knew his wonderful visionary drawings from the first set of *Sturm* in 1910,[1] as I had already read the first numbers of *Sturm* as a young girl in Sweden. After leaving school I had spent a few months in Lübeck and so I was able to read them in German and understand their contents.

Full of enthusiasm and excited by all the new ideas which were very attractive to a high-spirited and lively girl such as I was then, I had met Herwarth Walden by pure chance in Sweden in 1911. We were married in 1912.

Before I got to know Kokoschka in person I had seen the first *Sturm* exhibitions. *The Blue Rider, Oskar Kokoschka, The Futurists, Picasso, The French Cubists.*[2] It was like a revelation. I now knew what modern painting and artistic form meant.

Kokoschka's splendid dark portraits I saw for the first time in Berlin in colour: *Peter Baum, Herwarth Walden, Rudolf Blümner, William Wauer* and others. The transcendental manner of treatment which seemed almost magical, the revelation of aspects of character in the subjects, were for me quite shattering. I attempted to imagine what the artist would be like. Kokoschka turned out quite different from how I had imagined him.

What Kokoschka created at this early stage, at such a young age, will certainly last and in my opinion has never been matched since.

In January, 1913 Herwarth Walden and I had to take a trip to Budapest. A *Sturm* Exhibition in the Nemzety Salon, the hanging of the pictures and an opening address by Walden made the trip necessary.

At that time I knew many *Sturm* artists. The "Blue Riders"

had all been at the *Sturm*, which had its publishing house, editorial office and exhibition gallery at 134a Potsdamer Strasse. Although it is true that the first exhibitions—until spring 1913—took place at 34a Tiergartenstrasse. Franz Marc, August Macke, Heinrich Campendonk, Paul Klee, Kandinsky, Gabriele Münter, Marianne von Werefkin, Jawlensky and the Frenchman Delaunay with his wife Sonia, Léger, the Futurist Umberto Boccioni and Marinetti the leader of the Futurists had all visited us. But the artist I wanted to meet the most was Kokoschka.

Herwarth Walden decided to stay a few days in Vienna first, to see his friends there and to introduce them to me. We arrived in Vienna and visited Kokoschka the very next morning. We climbed up the many steps to his studio and rang the bell. He opened the door himself and he and Herwarth Walden embraced joyfully. Meanwhile I had both time and opportunity to observe Kokoschka: a young, handsome, cheerful character, charming and pleasant; about my own age, but looking a bit older. His most striking features were his blue eyes with their powerful gaze and his stubborn chin.

We liked each other from the start and Herwarth was pleased we got on so well together. "Koko" laughed and joked and discussed thousands of plans for exhibitions and for the future with Walden. I had the impression he was just as optimistic and enterprising as Walden. While he was talking with Herwarth Walden, he studied me intently and immediately took out charcoal and paper to sketch me. From the windows of his studio we had a view of the gay, brightly coloured roof-tops of Vienna, dominated by the spire of St. Stephen's.

The few days we spent in Vienna were full of meetings with friends and *confrères* of Walden. The evenings found us in the Café Central, the Viennese artists' café. There I saw Karl Kraus for the first time, sitting alone at a table almost buried beneath a pile of newspapers and weeklies. Here we met the "group": Kokoschka, Albert Ehrenstein the poet, Arthur Holitscher and above all Adolf Loos, a good friend of Herwarth Walden. Loos was one of the finest men I have ever known. This man, the great (perhaps even the greatest) architect of his day, is unfortunately almost forgotten and yet he was the founder and revolutionary innovator of the architecture of our age. The clean uncluttered lines of his beautifully designed house near the "Burg" filled me with admiration. You could hardly imagine a greater contrast.

No man in Vienna was more hated than he, nor was there any so uncompromising. I shall never forget his fine features, his slender hands—one hand always cupping his ear as he was slightly deaf. Kokoschka has made a drawing of him in which Loos' sensitivity, his intellect and deafness are wonderfully expressed. This young artist, Kokoschka, had something very few possess—a great visionary gift of empathy. The portrait of Karl Kraus, as well, is unbelievably revealing and expresses all that is characteristic of that man.

The evenings in Vienna among the large circle of artists and friends in the Café Central were rich and full of unforgettable impressions. The discussions about art, the jokes, the sarcasm, so characteristic of Herwarth Walden, the feeling of really being part of the vital stream of art, all this was enchanting and wonderful for a young Scandinavian wife like myself. It always went on far into the night, for the few hours we were to be together had to be exploited to the full. Often we ended up in the early hours of the morning in a little *Delikatessen* shop where Prague ham and crisp rolls put fresh life into us. Vienna with its tradition, its gaiety and charm absolutely delighted me . . .

But time was pressing. We had to go on to Budapest. The great Pussta brought an entirely different landscape. It's remarkable: the endlessness of the steppes, resembling undoubtedly the Siberian tundra, the desert and the sea, certainly spectacular, but equally oppressive . . . We travelled past stations where there was not a soul to be seen—only occasionally a Hungarian landowner in big riding boots, carrying a riding crop. I had my first glimpse of what the fabled East must be like.

Budapest meant more work and many parties given for us by the artists. The Hungarian is quite different from the Viennese. His Budapest is beautiful, it is true, but somehow brutal and hard. The old decadence of Vienna, characteristic also of our Northern capitals, was completely missing here. But the city, splendidly built up on both banks of the Danube, delighted me. The artists and the exhibition committee did absolutely everything in their power to welcome us. Nights were turned into day with gipsy music, visits to night clubs, champagne, flowers.

The second time I saw Kokoschka was in Berlin, 1916, after he had been wounded in the war. He stayed a longer time on this visit. Kokoschka came to the office of the *Sturm* every day and painted the pink portrait of Princess Lichnowsky and one of me in blue with a yellow flower in my hand. He also did the grey-blue portrait of the poet and his friend Albert Ehrenstein (Tubutsch). He did a lot of portrait painting at this time. A second one of Rudolf Blümner, this time different, harder, more taut. Also Gertrud Eysoldt, Claire Waldoff, Hermann Essig, Adolf Knoblauch and one of myself in blue charcoal because he saw that the black was too hard for me.

His paintings from this period show brighter colours. The scuro-style of his work before the war was over. At that time the *Sturm* publishing house brought out a beautiful edition of his play *Murderer, Hope of Womankind* with four drawings which appeared in the first year of the journal, whereupon half of the subscribers cancelled their order for the paper— a fact which did not deter Walden from publishing Kokoschka drawings throughout the year. As title page Kokoschka drew a self-portrait which he dedicated to me. (This sheet from 1916 was stolen from me along with eleven of what were probably the best drawings from Kokoschka's early period [1908] in the course of the travelling Kokoschka Exhibition in Germany, 1950–51.) The dedication in my copy of *Murderer, Hope of Womankind* read: "Dear *Sturm*-Carnation, please accept this book with the proviso that the best is still to come. It is a promise. Your devoted Oskar Kokoschka, Berlin, 6.10.1916." For the luxury editions of this set he aquarelled the drawings by hand. He came to the *Sturm* every morning and in my little office he painted in the pages. At that time I wasn't painting much, being too busy with my journalism. So he used my paints and brushes. When the water and the brushes got too dirty I took the liberty of providing fresh water and cleaning them. When he arrived and saw everything neat and tidy he became sad and said: "Carnation"—this was his nickname for me—"I actually need filthy water and dirty brushes." So I relented and only rarely tidied up his table. We were really very, very good friends.

He could be as solemn as he was happy and gay. His relationship with Herwarth Walden was very good. Walden had discovered him, after all, and had a very high opinion of his talent. Their conversation generally revolved on serious artistic questions, but they could be very bright and witty too, especially when Rudolf Blümner was present. Then there was no end of amusing cracks and sarcastic comments on their contemporaries, especially the art critics, who at that time damned us to a man.

Kokoschka was at that time on very good terms with the charming actress Katja Richter. Every Wednesday the *Sturm* evenings took place in the gallery rooms. Rudolf Blümner, the great *recitateur*, delivered poems by the *Sturm* poets, especially those by Stramm. After the performance we regularly repaired to the little Huth Wine Parlour, a few doors along towards the Potsdamer Platz. Here a little room was reserved for us every Wednesday. We regulars assembled there and visitors to the *Sturm* evenings knew where to find us. Everybody could order what they wanted, depending on what there was. This was 1916, the famine year . . . But material pleasures were unimportant to us. Wonderful times and good talk. Koko and Katja were always there.

Before my *Sturm* time Kokoschka and Walden had been regulars at the Café des Westens, as had all the artist circle in Berlin. This was the daily meeting-place. Talents, great and small, set the world to rights, wrote their articles, their poems at the Café tables, borrowed from each other or from the red-haired hunch-backed waiter Richard who was everybody's confidant. In Berlin this Café was called Café Megalomania. When it was later closed the whole scene shifted to the Romanisches Café opposite the Gedächtniskirche. Richard went too and Duff the newsboy. I was seldom in the Café des Westens. When Walden opened his gallery in the Potsdamer Strasse 134a, he had made the Café Josty on the Potsdamer Platz his regular haunt. This was where the *Sturm* poets and its foreign contributors met, in the evenings so that we should not suffer too many interruptions at work during the day. The new Café Megalomania (Romanisches Café) I later often visited with my second husband, the Berlin Doctor, Hans Heimann. We lived directly opposite. The new Café was split into the Big Bath Tub and the Little Bath Tub, and many doctors were regulars in the little tub.

Later it was Aenne Maenz's turn in the Augsburger Strasse. Here there were more actors than anything else. Fritzi Massary, Pallenberg, Jannings, Gussy Holl, Conrad Veidt and other stars went along to Maenz after the theatre. Ringelnatz was often here, and Munkepunke (Alfred Richard Meyer), who wrote a pretty little volume *Maenz—Maenzliches—Allzu-Maenzliches* (a pun on Nietzsche's *Menschliches, Allzumenschliches*). This is where Duff the newsboy went in his old age. I still remember how the door was barred at midnight (the official closing time) and thick curtains were drawn over the front windows. But I suspect that Aenne Maenz, a very businesslike Berlin woman, knew how to handle the police and they turned a blind eye, if not two. We were never raided, we just ate our sausage and drank a syrupy drink called "Sea Dog". I never did find out how it got its name.

Writing down these memories now is like re-living those times. It was a wonderful, bright world. To come back to Kokoschka! His Berlin period was at an end. He went first to Stockholm, later he accepted an invitation to become professor at the Dresden Academy of Art where he was active for a number of years. This meant another interruption in our friendship, for, in consequence, Kokoschka signed a contract with the Paul Cassirer Gallery which guaranteed him a regular income, lived in Dresden, and rarely appeared in the *Sturm*. (. . .)

Hans Flesch von Brunningen
Die Aktion in Vienna

In Vienna Neo-Romanticism was all the rage. My friends wrote poems full of lush rhymes. Their models were Hofmannsthal, Vollmoeller, Stucken. I come from Vienna. But all that silk and gold brocade and Bolognese poodles sickened me. Just to be different I went into a bare room and wrote my first prose sketch on toilet paper.

My mother said: "What are you doing? That's disgusting. Nobody will ever print that." In the sketch there was something about rape in a drawing-room with golden mirrors. Inspired by a scene from *Don Giovanni*.

True enough this sketch was never printed. But others very soon were. And poems. And longer sketches. Of course, they were not printed in Vienna. But in Berlin. A hand picked me up from afar. It set me down. And I've been on the same spot ever since.

I was seventeen. You don't grow more clever with age. The year was 1913.

I must give some idea of what Berlin meant to us in Vienna in those days. Everything really. Berlin was infamous, corrupt, cosmopolitan, anonymous, gigantic, the place of the future, literary, political, artistic (as the city for painters). In short— the bottomless pit and paradise all in one. I went up the Gloriette Hill behind Vienna with one of my friends. It was night. To the North the sky was aglow. "That's where Berlin lies," I said. "Berlin's where one should go," I said. "Why?" my friend asked, being of a practical turn and thinking of the expense. "That's where they recite poems in cabarets. That's where they print anything that's *avant-garde* and modern. Not your kind of rubbish about purple passion and splendour." And shortly afterwards somebody must have sent some of my writings to Franz Pfemfert. First there was a story—I still remember—it was

E   129 called *The Metaphysical Canary*.[1] I can't remember what was in it, though. An uncle who had the reputation in our family of being very clever said this was all very well, and he could understand why I should be proud to be in print at such an early age; but in his young days this kind of thing was called a "flash in the pan". What my father said was indescribable; moreover he asked me if I got paid for it.

Now it was a point of honour in those days not to accept any kind of payment from the two leading journals *Sturm* and *Aktion*. At least that's what I was told. It's also what Franz Pfemfert wrote to me on lots of cards illustrated with lovely pencil drawings by "Mopp", Harta, Egon Schiele. I never set eyes on him. But in effect his was the hand that reached out from the oppressive distance of Berlin to seize the rebellious innocent lamb I was then.

Soon things got even better and even more exciting. A card arrived from Pfemfert telling me to go to Schiele at once. Schiele was to do a pencil drawing of me which would appear on the title page of the *Hans Flesch von Brunningen* special number of the *Aktion*. By then it was the ominous year 1914.[2]

One hot summer day my friend Heinrich Nowak took me up to Ober St. Veit. There I saw Schiele. And Schiele drew me. In five minutes a sheet was ready. A splendid sketch. There are copies of it with all my various wives, divorced and otherwise. The original is somewhere in the United States and unfortunately cannot be traced.

And the whole number was ME. It was a great time for manifestos and summonses to Battle, War, Life, Revolution. My contribution to this was called *To Death (A pamphlet for the Metropolis)*. I began with the frivolous simple statement: "There are too many of us on this earth, that's obvious." And I closed with the macabre, paranoid threat: "The generation marching up over the hill of childhood bears my name on its banners." How wrong one can be! But we really believed it. What did we believe in? In ourselves, our own power and glory. A thoroughly pagan breed. And we have had to pay for it. Let us never forget who held the stirrups for us—no matter into what unknown wastelands the ride might take us. Without *Aktion*, without Franz Pfemfert, I should never have become what I am today. This is no value judgment. No expression of regret. Neither hurrah, nor alas. Just a statement of fact.

HEIDELBERG BONN STRASBOURG

Jacob Picard
Ernst Blass, his associates in Heidelberg and *Die Argonauten*

Biographical Fragment

To say something about an amorphous phenomenon like literary Expressionism is not easy. Even if one is not required to give any theoretical definition but only chase memories of various people who are reckoned as belonging to such a movement. Basically they did not really belong together, rather were they original forces going their own way and as such obeying the incalculable impulse of the spirit of the times and its *melos*. There was perhaps only one group which followed a programme produced by communal brooding—these were the youngsters around Kurt Hiller about 1910 and the group called "The New Club" in Berlin, a whole body of friends to which Ernst Blass belonged and which was joined for a while by the most important of them all, Georg Heym, before he went his own inspired way. From the creative point of view they had nothing in common. They just set the tone for something vaguely new, for something in the air which later had farther-reaching effects with Werfel and then with Edschmid.

To talk purely about lyric poetry—because formally this was where it all started—what was produced was certainly entirely different from all the faded Romanticism and cheap Impressionism which had been the order of the day since the turn of the century in purely literary as well as bourgeois magazines (not forgetting, of course, what George, Hofmannsthal, Mombert and Rilke were already offering, for their influence was the predominating one especially in South and West Germany long after the First World War).

For someone like myself who consciously stood apart from the new ideals, but who was otherwise involved in it all, it is perhaps easier to detect the differences. I can risk plunging therefore deep into the shaft of memory to tell of my personal experiences with people who were reckoned as part of what was then, if often only apparently, modern.

I was personally closest to the Heidelberg group which centred around the *Argonauten* journal[1] and especially its editor Ernst Blass. At this point it must be interjected that this journal was one of those which, by reason of this man, who gave it its style and it character, consciously avoided anything that might be called an Expressionist programme, unless *anything* with new goals in those days is to be called Expressionist. Above all my own view is that Blass's own art does not possess those elements which are normally called Expressionistic—however modern it was, it lacked pathos. That he felt this himself, though perhaps not completely, became obvious by the speed with which he, the twenty-two-year-old student from Berlin and already famous on account of his first volume of poetry, came under the formal influence of George, without becoming a member of the George Circle. He was the pure uncommitted lyrical poet responding to his identification with what he recognized in George as the most fundamental source of artistic creation; and in general the influence of the "Master", who lived in Heidelberg, was very powerful on many others besides, on Friedrich Sieburg for example, the youngest of us. The Berlin Group which Blass had deserted was offended by this confession of faith and even more so by the essay he published in 1920, *On the Style of Stefan George*. Blass was a pure poet, who, like Verlaine, or even more, Baudelaire, found inspiration in the *melos* of the big city. This was something completely new for Germany which until then had never seen big city poems such as had been written for decades in Paris. The kind of thing that was to be found in Blass's *I Come Breezing Through the Town*[2] which had appeared a short time before with Richard Weissbach the Berlin publisher, had been unheard of in German until then.

The thing that really made Blass a representative and speaker for modernism apart from the novelty of his poems was probably the aggressive, provocative preface to this collection, which in the language of a Kerr made programmatic statements about intellectual aims which had clearly been discussed over and over again among the circle of Berlin comrades; the rejection of bucolic elements of Swiss and South German origin was at the top of the list. As for the impact of these poems themselves, they are the forerunners and heralds of a series of lyrical phenomena of the next few decades now generally well known, for without Blass neither Erich Kästner nor Mascha Kaléko nor Walter Mehring would have been conceivable, however individual they are. This must be emphasized.

The journal *Die Argonauten* began to appear in 1914, with Richard Weissbach, the same publisher as brought out his poems. The bright blue format with magnificent layout had an introduction by Ernst Blass which contained the words: "May Lynceus and Orpheus be the guardian spirits of our ship in which the singer is joined with the voice of reason, the look-out with him who senses beauty in virtuous voyage." What a difference from the manifesto of two years before!

Die Argonauten cannot be mentioned without giving some attention to the publisher Richard Weissbach, who deserves all credit and without whose obsessed idealism the whole thing would not have been possible. He was a constant enthusiast, a book-bewitched, over-friendly character who never lost his composure and who not only looked after the business side of things, but also, despite the fact that Blass had the last word, exercised some editorial influence among his friends and advisors. I have never managed to find out where he got the money to support this expensive undertaking, although he did have a list of committed subscribers (above all in academic circles in Heidelberg) who did not all come from the humanities but shared the same high cultural level of the time above and beyond their special disciplines. The atmosphere permeated by Max Weber, Gundolf, Gothein, Neumann and others of this type in the city . . . That the *Argonauten* should ever be identified with Expressionism can only result from ignorance and probably from the fact that, apart from the aforementioned poems, the first anthology which might be called Expressionistic, namely Kurt Hiller's *Der Kondor*, was also published by Weissbach in 1912 and contains poems by Blass. There was really no such thing as an "Argonaut Circle"—only a number of young, more or less well-known authors, many of whom did not live in Heidelberg, but were encouraged by Blass and themes as varied as the personalities of the authors, although the general quality was always of the highest. Every issue included poems by Blass himself which in content became less and less like what one had earlier been accustomed to by him, even showing traces of the once despised bucolic in pure lyrical form, his genuine creativity responding not merely to his new literary surroundings, to classical works and the discipline of George's style, but also to the experience of the South German landscape so entirely different from that of his youth. Fellow contributors were Ernst Bloch and Radbruch, Leonhard Nelson the Neo-Kantian, Max Scheler, Robert Musil, Walter Benjamin, Friedrich Burschell, Arthur Kronfeld, the doctor and philosopher, to mention only a few—and Rudolf Borchardt.

What an event it was when Borchardt gave the lecture organized by Weissbach at the beginning of December, 1914 in the Heidelberg City Hall on the theme: *The War and German Contemplation*, in which he spoke, albeit with some nationalistic concessions to the spirit of the times, about "the collapse of aesthetic culture in Germany". I was present myself, it being the first time out of hospital where I had landed after my first experience of war as a volunteer in Flanders. I had received the Iron Cross, which was rare in those early days. The Cross itself was worn and not just the ribbon; and there Borchardt stood at the lectern, also in the uniform of a reserve battalion (it was the 142 Infantry Regiment of my own division), and spoke in his spellbinding sonorous voice. I couldn't actually follow everything he was saying, not only because I couldn't help thinking of comrades left behind a few weeks before in the cold, rain, fog and danger, but because Borchardt, in front of whom I was directly seated, kept staring at me as if he were speaking to me alone, probably because of the decoration, the only one in the room. Bravery? Certainly not! The reason why I received the Cross so early was that at this stage of the war I was simply not conscious of how dangerous it was to be shot at; I realized soon afterwards. There had not been a war for so long. I have to put this in to keep the record straight, in order to explain why I was inhibited and distracted by the lecturer's gaze. I only realized fully what he had been saying when I read the lecture which Weissbach printed as a special number of the *Argonaut* series[3] nor was I in complete agreement with everything he said. In all events, this had absolutely nothing to do with Expressionism . . . As a general movement Expressionism was spoken of in only very vague terms, for there was no real name for anything then.

My part of the country was quite different from that of Blass. I came from the bucolic reaches of Lake Constance and had been several years in Munich where I had been a member of the Academic Dramatic Club, which, if I remember correctly, had been founded by Michael Georg Conrad. In any event, there I used occasionally to see the old man still resplendent with his red hair. Various people of literary stature came out of this Club, but also leading men of the theatre before and after the war. Otto Falckenberg, for example. The literary aims and ideals of the Club were more in line with what I had grown up with. My models had originally been the great Swiss poets of the last century, until George's relentless discipline and also Hermann Hesse's first collection of verse showed me the way beyond my first juvenile mentor, Emanuel von Bodman. Von Bodman's poems regularly appeared in *Simplicissimus* and several of his collections of verse had appeared under the imprint of Albert Langen. It was he who first encouraged my own poetic efforts. However, my close friendship with Hans Heinrich Ehrler, who lived at the lake in Constance, endured for more than thirty years until in 1938 I had to give him his marching orders and that for the bitterest of reasons. He read my new poems and I read his, but in the end we went entirely different ways . . . This then was my background when I came to Heidelberg, and although I was never asked for a contribution by Blass, we were as close to each other as possible for one as reserved as he was. He appeared rather unfriendly and not very talkative when one met him. His large broad face beneath its thick dark brows had almost a gloomy appearance occasionally illuminated by a gentle smile. Kokoschka's picture of him in Bremen captures it with almost staggering precision.[4]

As we both lived in Neuenheim by the edge of the meadows and orchards we met almost every day and shared the same "South German night skies" above them. What he thought of me and my lyric poetry of that period can best be seen from the fact that he occasionally called me "Bodenseele" [earth-soul]. He never said much to me about my verse as far as I can recall, but in my volume of poetry, *The Shore*, published in 1913 by Hermann Meister of Saturn Publishers, I dedicated a poem to him, "The Poor People's Park", which he must at some time have praised. That poem, written in Freiburg, 1911, before I had experienced much of what was going on in the big cities, even in literary circles, was the first to derive from a social motif and it had an unfamiliar hymnic sonority with strange premonitions until then quite foreign to me. In view of all this I was very surprised, indeed deeply moved, when in 1959 I received as a present from Blass' sister in Israel, on the twentieth anniversary of his death, a postcard he had sent her in November 1913 on which he wrote: "Picard's book *The Shore* is out and I like it very much. He has dedicated one poem in it to me. The lines are so similar to the kind I used to write a long time ago, before my book, so Verlaine-like." I myself never thought of comparing myself with Verlaine, though he meant a great deal to me . . . It was a strange coincidence that shortly before I received this card, I had published in the *Tagesspiegel* an article in memory of the twentieth anniversary of his death in which I had compared him with the French poet Verlaine. I was one of the few who had been present at his funeral in January 1939 at the Weissensee Cemetery in Berlin.

Blass stayed in Heidelberg for another two years after the *Argonauten* had begun to appear. By the time the last numbers came out the war was in progress and we were all scattered . . .

The journal in Heidelberg at that time which had something resembling Expressionistic aims was *Saturn*,[5] which Hermann Meister edited and published and to which he even contributed. In addition, as an enthusiastic rugby player, he edited a Sports Paper which was typical of him. Among others who contributed to *Saturn* were Rudolf Fuchs from the Prague Kafka circle, Paul Mayer later for years reader with Ernst Rowohlt, Rudolf Leonhard, Kurt Erich Meurer, in other words the people whose poetry he had published in book form including myself, but above all Albert Ehrenstein whose *Tubutsch* with Kokoschka's drawings had already appeared and made him famous. As a poet he was in the first rank of those who can really be described as Expressionists unless one is inclined to call him a Surrealist because of his peculiar style. He occasionally came over from Vienna on a visit, as did Werfel, to give a reading from his *Friend to the World*. Reading?—more like roaring.[6]

But it is not right to talk about the literary life of Heidelberg in those pre-war days without mentioning something else. Long

before the *Argonauten* and *Saturn* had appeared, Weissbach
edited a monthly literary supplement for the *Heidelberger
Zeitung*,[7] to which we all contributed. These were our first
attempts at criticism and we were very conscientious, not passing judgment in the insolent, gloating way half-baked critics
do it nowadays. We had some sense of responsibility which was
supported by the knowledge and the standards of the great
German and French essayists of the preceding decades and earlier. Our immediate models were perhaps Moritz Heimann and
Josef Hofmiller, not Alfred Kerr, whom we nevertheless read
with pleasure, and of course, Dilthey's *Literature and Experience*,
which had appeared only a few years before.

Sometimes there were vistors. One day Blass reported that
George Heym, whom he knew very well from Berlin, was coming, and all of us who had been enthralled by his first volume
of poems *The Eternal Day*, which had come out just a short time
before, were filled with expectation. But one evening when we
were sitting round the little table in the café Blass came in,
very pale, and said with quivering lips: "George Heym has
drowned!" I myself was so moved that first thing next morning
I felt compelled to write a long obituary. It appeared in the
Frankfurter Zeitung[8] and was probably the first appreciation of
that unique outsider and of the poetry that was then so modern,
in any of the big respectable dailies.

Once Weissbach gave me a slender volume of poems to review
which I held suspiciously in my hand till I saw that it had come
out in *Insel*. The name of the unknown author was Hans Carossa.
Anyway, I took it with me and after I had read a few things
I was captivated. This was something new, traditional but pure,
modern poetry. What I wrote about it I no longer have in my
possession, but I know that it was an enthusiastic welcome.
When, many years later in the twenties, I entered into a short
correspondence with Hans Carossa, for some reason or other,
he informed me that for a long time he had carried my review
about with him in his wallet, as it had been the first affirmative
one. For me his lyric poetry has lost none of its freshness to
this day.

Contributors to the literary supplement of the *Heidelberger
Zeitung* were academics as well as men of letters: the philologist
Weinreich, at that time I believe assistant in the Archaeological
Institute, the doctors Weizsäcker and Otto Meyerhof who later

received the Nobel prize, both with philosophical pieces on the Neo-Kantian school of Leonhard Nelson, Erich Lichtenstein the literary historian and sometime publisher of exquisite books in Weimar, who is still conscientiously at work to this day on the *Tagesspiegel*; also Friedrich Burschell and Georg von Lukács, and the biologist Graf Uexküll as well as the psychiatrist Arthur Kronfeld, and above all Ernst Bloch and Hermann Sinsheimer, old school friends and like Burschell from Ludwigshafen; also Bloch wreathed in a black wig. Sinsheimer was already writing the Mannheim theatre reviews for Jacobsohn's *Schaubühne* in Berlin, which sometimes also published poems by me. The philosopher Lask, a quiet, very friendly man, also worked occasionally for the paper; he was killed early in the war on the Austrian front. Naturally not all the contributors knew each other.

By the outbreak of war which scattered us all I was no longer in Heidelberg. Many never returned: the murderous September–October of 1914 already tore great holes in the lists of those of our generation we knew; Ernst Stadler fell in Flanders, Ernst Wilhelm Lotz on the Aisne like Alfred Lichtenstein and Ehrenbaum-Degele, the Berlin friends of Blass, who also had to make the break with Heidelberg. And when we came back, those of us who had survived, it was all different and the *Argonauten* were past history.

Karl Otten
1914-Summer without autumn. Memorial to August Macke and the Rhineland Expressionists

When I look back over the forty years of war and revolutions to the year 1914 the last months before the outbreak of war seem, for unsentimental reasons, like islands of paradise. I do not mourn for these times or for my youth. It is something else entirely that moves me—the realization that we young people were then the first champions and heralds of the European Idea, that we helped to found in Europe an intellectual, not a materialistic, industrial or military, power. And it is for reasons of continuity and of obligation to dead friends that I remember them.

Today the poets, musicians, painters and sculptors of that time are no longer in dispute. They have international reputations. And yet between then and now there yawns a chasm, the battlefield of two world wars which has buried all they really strove for and helps to perpetuate the sickness of discontinuity from which Europe suffers.

At the beginning of our century the European style wrought the miracle of an amalgam of all the normally disparate arts. Poets defended painters, composers set modern poetry to music, painters like Marc, Kokoschka, Kandinsky and Klee took up the pen. Scattered all over Europe these champions of Expressionism gathered together into groups who knew and helped each other.

One of these groups had grown up in Bonn around the painter August Macke, and it is about him and his friends that I should like to write, because I knew him well and myself belonged to this group.[1] His little house was situated in Graurheindorf. About the beginning of spring 1914 there gathered here painters, poets, sculptors mainly of Rhenish origins. In those days the

Rhine had a significance for us which it has only acquired politically in recent times. In our eyes it was a cultural no-man's land leading to Belgium, Holland and especially France.

The first time I visited August Macke he was standing in the middle of his airy studio in a loose sweater and corduroy trousers tied at the ankles, the incarnation of a Barlach sculpture. In his hand he was holding a book, Däubler's *Northern Light*, and he was reciting from it in Däubler's own fashion, at the top of his voice:

> *My grave is no pyramid,*
> *My grave is a volcano*

Still full of a long trip through Greece—my first book *Journey through Albania*[2] was lying on Macke's desk—I told him about my experiences in the temples and mountain monasteries of Hellas.

Macke, just returned from spending the spring in Tunis painting with Moilliet and Klee, discussed his idea of the purity of colours with us non-stop, his technique of applying unmixed colours on to the canvas with his palette knife, his notions of the possibilities of abstract forms, such as were peculiar to Kandinsky and Klee. For every aspect of modern life he looked for an explanation appropriate to his time, while never negating the transcendent poetic and imaginative power of the artist. "The new elements: cars, express trains, aeroplanes, films and machines simply must give birth to a new artist, impart impressions to him that Böcklin and Lenbach never knew. Machine conquers man. The artist must adapt to this invasion while at the same time never sacrificing Maria in the Capitol or the Madonna with the Flower. This synthesis must be our aim."

Macke was a universal man, whom nothing in the world of art escaped. Kairovan and the Cologne Museum for East Asian Art brought him the Orient, especially China and Java. The Rhenish Primitives, Negro Sculpture, the Russian Ballet—they all agitated his artistic sensibility. One morning he surprised me with a new idea which was strongly inspired by his Javanese dream castle, Burubudur: "The painter must work out the forms in three dimensions. As it were, get to know their weight, find out what these symbols represent in nature. Everything we produce is nature. Just as we are natural by nature, so mind, idea, soul, art, creation are natural too." And he showed me in his garden a series of bas-reliefs which he had made with an electric drill out of massive chunks of wood: among great masses of blossoms and runners were hidden people, animals, houses. To crown it he painted them all and it looked like a Macke painting come to life.

Despite his Westphalian background, Macke was a fanatical Rhinelander, a worshipper of the great river which he would study for hours—no, days on end—in order to be able to crystallize the ultimate nuance from its foam-yellow body. When we went strolling along the woodland paths and village streets around Bonn and Graurheindorf with Macke snorting and laughing like Pan, big and strong in body and soul, bursting with *joie de vivre* and as full of real gentleness of heart as a child, the images and forms came to him like the true inspiration of home. The simplicity of form which at that time he was struggling to attain was something like this: "As a generally accepted form of male presence I give the men a bowler-hat. The women are well turned about the neck and the hips, with parasols through which shines the light. And the girls, the girls are dressed in frivolous blue and white aprons and tilting Florentine straw hats. With these formal elements I mix the chestnut-tree, whose leaf makes the clearest symbol of tree possible, avenue, shade and use of space. And then there's the Rhine, space itself in flux, a sky in flux, river-banks and villages in flux. Movement simply cannot be presented more clearly and significantly."

Out of these artistic elements of his native ground, Macke crystallized in often desperate efforts the prismatic fire and at the same time the rich shade of the Lower Rhineland-Dutch paintings which were created in those few fruitful months.

Around Macke a host of young painters had gathered, meeting at his hospitable house and hammering out plans. Plans which under the driving energy of Macke very soon came to fruition. We would sit in the shade in his garden by the Rhine blinking into the sunlit summer. Macke, Max Ernst, the gentle hunch-back Paul Seehaus, the slim infinitely talented Franz Henseler who had been washed up from Munich. Often Heinrich Nauen

141

would appear and Franz Marc mount his blue horse to paint the monkey frieze round the studio. Occasionally the drainpipe figure of Haru Engert would wriggle in like a ghost, squat on his haunches and cut silhouettes.

Arising out of our European conversations—we looked upon Cologne and Bonn as suburbs of Paris, Vienna and Rome—Macke develped the idea of a representative Exhibition, the first exhibition of Rhineland Expressionists which sprang into existence without any preparation or outside help. One July morning in 1913 the six-foot lengths of a red and a blue banner swung from the upper storey of Cohen's Bookshop in Bonn. Above the door was the sign in straight solemn lettering: EXHIBITION OF RHINELAND EXPRESSIONISTS.[3]

I can remember some of those pictures to this day: Heinrich Nauen's two peasant children in blue smocks, one of whom is clutching a huge loaf of fresh bread to her bosom. Macke's avenue with *flâneurs*, flooded with the red light of our summer, girls playing and the sailing boats on the Rhine. Then the Rhineland Madonna by Franz Henseler, the constructivistic ghosts of machine-men by the splendidly fanatical Max Ernst. Gentle English landscapes by Paul Seehaus, landscapes by Campendonk, and a series of pictures from Soest by Christian Rohlfs, the German Cézanne as we called him, the man August Macke looked up to as to a miracle-worker and oracle. Wilhelm Lehmbruck exhibited a number of ecstatically exaggerated sculptures.

Among those visiting the exhibition another poet had caught my attention, my friend Johannes Theodor Kuhlemann, dark-skinned, black-haired, looking more like a Frenchman or a Spaniard than a dyed-in-the-wool citizen of Cologne. He was secretary to Collofino-Feinhals, the rich cigar-dealer who wrote a book about tobacco and collected pictures. So too did old Soennecken, the founder of the fountain-pen concern, and the lawyer Joseph Haubrich. And above all Edwin Suermondt from Aachen, discoverer of le Douanier Rousseau, friend of Delaunay, Derain and Picasso, who incidentally used to come to Cologne every year to study our primitives. In Aachen, too, lived Jules Talbot Keller, a very gifted writer who bought up all Franz Henseller's pictures and also possessed one of the finest Rousseau's, *Le Repas du Lion*. Suermondt, as Heinrich Nauen's patron, commissioned him to paint the frescoes in his family castle Drove; and of these I still remember the "Harvest", and the March of the Reapers over the Rhenish Fields.

To complete this panorama, from the background of all our activities and plans arose the great Werkbund-Exhibition of 1914. Cologne became the centre of the new art. Two great exhibitions of Cézanne and Van Gogh, which the Düsseldorf art-dealer Alfred Flechtheim had helped to bring about, surrounded us rebels with an aura of tradition.

In the summer of 1914 the censers swung higher and higher and overturned. Macke and his friends sat in a sailing-boat and sped down the raging stream, right under the bows of clattering steamers towering above us. That's the last thing I remember. The radiant shores of our lives, villages bedecked with flags, Rifle Clubs firing off their guns, roundabouts and big dippers, open-air dancing. Into this riot of living came the sound of the shots in Sarajevo. The forbidding pictures of the Balkan war I had witnessed on my Greek trip rose up again before my mind's eye. My fears were met with disbelief. "It is simply impossible, quite impossible that there might be a war," Macke repeated over and over.

The only one to share my dreadful premonitions was Max Ernst: "The machine-men are going for each other only to discover that while it is true they have no mind, they can still die . . ." His handsome, slender face with its strikingly blue iridescent eyes lay smooth and masklike behind an evil grin, that played over his machines and wire figures.

About the middle of July we parted, never to meet again, each fleeing to the fate that Europe's destroyers had in store for him. September 14th, two weeks after we parted, August Macke was killed. Marc and Henseler followed him. Then little Seehaus died, then Lehmbruck—there was no end to the dying.

Otto Flake
Life half lived

A doctor gives his medical opinion when somebody is dead, that's his profession. But a man of letters is not supposed to be a coroner and an obituary is not compulsory, it's an act of remembrance. Here it is, then, more a page from a diary than an "appreciation". It is dedicated to Ernst Stadler.

The end of July was a time of which one could write in biblical language: and it came to pass that each and every one wherever he dwelt made haste to hie him home, for the peoples of the world threatened to overrun each other with war.

I had just arrived in Innsbruck with a Trieste-Constantinople ticket in my pocket and my baggage all ready in the Adriatic port. But instead of going over the Brenner I went through the Vorarlberg, Switzerland, and Alsace up to Strasbourg, the ancient harbour-city.

Once I had put my affairs in order I began to move about the seething city, this buzzing ant-hill inside its ring of fortresses, and as is customary when one returns home, began to look up my friends.

One lived on Cathedral Square, his window looked out on the rose-window above the portal and I came across him there packing his Cubist paintings away in crates and putting them down in the cellar along with enough canned food for six months. This fellow had an *idée fixe* and was firmly convinced there was going to be a siege. A second lived by the city wall and could see with his own eyes mountains of trousers and jackets being tried out on the barracks' square; the third lived in Kehl and already there were Saxon or Pomeranian soldiers on guard-duty on the Rhine bridge carefully searching men and women for bombs. But where did Ernst Stadler live? That same spring I had wanted to come over from Holland to visit him in

Brussels where he was lecturing at the Free University, in autumn he was to become Professor of German in Toronto, which sounds Italian but is in fact in Canada—in the meantime he was giving some lectures in Strasbourg to keep his name on the staff list.[1]

At last I found pinned on the door of some flat or other his visiting card with the three academic and awe-inspiring titles which always made his friends laugh when they thought of the man who had had them printed. He was just saying goodbye to a student, not much younger than himself, who was thanking him for signing his report card, then we said hello. The thirty-year-old professor had the good fortune to be short-sighted so that in public he always wore horn-rimmed spectacles *à la* Franz Blei, which gave him a certain dignity. When among friends he wore a monocle which made his clean-shaven face look remarkably like Chamberlain, the British Imperialist, not Houston Stewart Chamberlain.

As one would have expected of a university professor, there were books and journals all over the place. To glance at them was however quite a revelation. There was the *Cahiers de la Quinzaine* series of his beloved Péguy—another one to die a victim of the war on the other side; the fine white *Nouvelle Revue française*. Works by Jammes (whom he translated), Rolland, Ch. L. Phillipe; there were Schickele and Sternheim, the German authors, of whom he thought highly, *Aktion* and *Neues Pathos* and all the latest, anything up to date and not in the least academic; better to be literary than academic was this Professor's maxim, and he followed it without any of the snobbishness of certain German philologists who are hyper-modern, only to take the wind out of other colleagues' sails. Then too there were English books and the draft of an English essay which he wrote when he had been a Cecil-Rhodes Scholar at Oxford and had lived the college life prescribed for upper-class young gentlemen.

Taking it all in all, what was he? An Alsatian, a genuine German, who needed the culture of another country besides his own, in this case even another two. He was beginning to develop great universality and all-embracing vision. The way he brought different cultures together was most fruitful and gave promise of intellectual and cultural cross-fertilization that would not have remained hidden in far-off Canada, but would have made its way to Berlin. Not without mishaps perhaps, for despite the high opinion Erich Schmidt, his teacher, had of him and certain of his historical textual studies, it was dangerous to be so modern—yet this young lecturer wrote in a style which was too lucid not to make its mark. He would have become what we did not have then and still do not have now, namely, a historian of modern literature, a critic. And let it be clearly understood, not one prepared to leave the actual production to others or who considers criticism to be as important as creative work (and this is quite justified, although we cannot boast of such a person either), but a man who works critically to clear away the rubble, to find a point of view, to produce clarity for himself and for the nation—a critic by reason of his own creative vitality, who no longer accepts the German academic tradition and for that reason spends his time on *avant-garde* material.

Despite the monocle he was by no means a lounge-lizard, more of a heavy-footed than a light-footed person, but for that very reason endowed with the German love of the perspicuous period, the clear intellect and the bold, steeply rising life-line; once again: an Alsatian who would have nothing to do with the phoney concept of Alsace as a Buffer State between France and Germany and half inclined to the belief that the real mission for Alsace was to demonstrate how one could be selective in what one imported and appreciated. His was a European approach based on mutual comparisons and understanding.

Far from seeing everything with German eyes his Alsatian standpoint on the periphery made it easier for him to be objective and critical, easier for him to build bridges to themes which were not German. Son of a high civil servant who could have had his professional path smoothed for him and who, being well brought up, was prepared to make such concessions, as were absolutely necessary, he was at the same time fundamentally independent, no revolutionary, for that was not his nature, but possessing the toughness of a man who has imposed upon himself the obligation to speak the truth as he saw it. The future would often have forced him to face difficult decisions, he would always have done so with dignity and consistency.

If he was going to be shot, it was his own fault, he said. For in Brussels he had completed the written part of the Interpreters' Examination, leaving the oral part to be taken later in Strasbourg. But whether from absentmindedness or because he was feeling

creative and was busy writing poems, he missed the deadline
and when he got round to it he was a week late. He was no
coward and took the war seriously, but some of us would have
been happier if he could have been found a less dangerous position, one where men like him can do their duty to the full. He
was not practical, not selfish enough, and people like him have
to pay the tragic penalty.

The last days of July arrived: Friday, July 31st came when the
State of Emergency was declared. That historic evening Strasbourg was seething, the suburbs had emptied into the city centre,
where the old streets were crammed; such paths the patrols
made as they forced their way through simply closed behind
them; the asphalt still boiled from the heat of the day, the first
searchlight beams moved across the starry sky like the arms of
windmills, in the cafés the "Wacht am Rhein" was being sung
while regiments were in fact marching to take up their positions
on the Rhine; according to an announcement the guns on Fort
Mutzig were going to fire a practice burst—no cause for alarm—
and there were many who could remember the fateful weeks of
August 1870. We sat packed in the café, Stadler, his brother
who administered a region in a quarter that was half French,
and a few others. They were all Reserve Officers, all studying
their marching-orders. Most of them relieved the nervous tension
of waiting for the last decisive news by seizing on anything and
making a joke of it, turning ideas upside-down and juggling with
them. Stadler thought this was wrong, he said this was the wrong
note; his own seriousness was just another form of nervousness.
Everyone in the café was singing again, the band had to play one
patriotic song after the other. This enthusiasm from those who
were to stay behind became unbearable, we moved off.

On the Kleberplatz there was a human wall in front of the
guard, waiting for nine o'clock to strike from the cathedral, then
the fateful notes of the Last Post were sounded. We went past the
Iron Man, that quaint symbol of medieval defiance which hangs
a tiny sign above a chemist shop, and turned into the Wine
Market. Before us was Valentin's, a white, little, restaurant, well
known to connoisseurs far beyond Strasbourg, a bright pearl of
French *cuisine*, a little bit of Paris at its best.

Why shouldn't we go in? It was bright with not many people
inside, a few gleaming uniforms, a few dinner jackets and here
too an historic mood, a melancholy question: when will such

pleasures as these be possible again and who will be still alive to enjoy them? In one corner a few members of the *jeunesse dorée* sat dining, real cocks of the provincial roost. There was nothing offensive about this, it had the additional blessing of good form. For the last time the waiter was performing his advisory and intimately respectful function—next day he would be called up. Dark Burgundy against a white cloth, choice dishes on silver plate.

A gentleman from the Ministry came in the door quietly imparting the news: it's as good as certain. What a blessing! And at once the feelings only to be expected of decent people in this position began to stir, restraint and deep down a last gentle gaiety while still remaining fully aware of the gravity of the situation. There was talk, aims and ideals were reviewed. A happy victory, *auf Wiedersehn, auf Wiedersehn*!

Next morning I went round the shops with him; in his hand he had a long list of all the things an officer needs. But things like a revolver or a torch were not be had for love or money. At lunchtime he received a telegram; he immediately left for Colmar to join his division and I believe he marched into battle the same evening. Then some news from him occasionally, parcels of cigarettes he never received, a newspaper-cutting that he had won the Iron Cross, then another that he had been killed and the same day a card from his commanding officer.

There's nothing left but a volume of poetry. And that's something that will endure. Read the *Aufbruch* which appeared in the Weisse Bücher series[2] and you will realize that in one respect at least he was fortunate—he was able to leave behind this monument.

DURING AND AFTER THE WAR
1915-20

SWITZERLAND

Emil Szittya
The Artists in Zurich during the war

I

Münzer's naïve novel[1] in which everything is nicely romanticized really ought to be forgotten. During the war Zurich was not only a hot-bed of espionage, it was also a city in which all this cruel age's longings for something clean burst into explosive and chaotic proximity. Because of the war Zurich certainly gained one of the most interesting pages in its artistic history. There does not seem to be any certainty about whether man is fundamentally good, or not, if he is, where does all the Evil come from we keep stumbling over all the time? There must therefore be some ultimate goal (or law even) behind everything that happens. But if, forgetting Nietzsche and questions of Good and Evil for the moment, we consider the Great War, it really is astonishing how all the intellectuals in the countries at war, even the finest and most individualistic, became as one with the mass mentality. There was something in the air that clouded the mind, robbed one of the will to breathe. People in the countries at war became absolutely horrible. Who can really blame Arno Holz for writing jingoistic poems? What right had the younger generation to move away from Richard Dehmel because he wrote war poems? Was it really only charlatanism that made Kokoschka and Moissi rush to volunteer? Was it all hatred of one nation for another? Is there really such a thing as a war-crime? I must confess that when I travelled through the countries at war, Belgium, Italy, Germany, Austria and Hungary and my route took me near the theatre of operations. I reproached myself bitterly for not being in it. However much one might condemn war, it nevertheless shows a lack of solidarity with the sufferings of the many to hide behind well-guarded cities. And yet, already in 1915, Hugo Kersten, who died so young, and I were among the first to rise *au dessus de la mêlée*. But that was in Zurich. This *petit bourgeois* city pervaded by a smell of cheese and its women wearing size nine shoes, nevertheless had an atmosphere during the war which made it possible to breathe and in which one could think lucidly about the bloody things happening across the border.

To arrive at a clear picture of Zurich during the war, we must review the three phases of the Café Megalomania.

II

In the Café Astoria there was a remarkable gathering of regulars at the beginning of the war. Karl Bleibtreu (who wrote dozens of war stories and novels and one anti-Semitic book) used to sit there welcoming everybody with the greeting "Gott strafe England" (although he himself—perhaps rightly —was dodging the war); he would make bold speeches about why the Germans couldn't help winning. His opposite number Professor Bovet, editor of *Wissen und Leben*,[2] would often pop into the Café to speak about German war-guilt and why one absolutely must support the *Entente's* war of liberation. (Among his associates were people like Dr. Altmann, a well-known Munich Bohemian who was such a good patriot that he volunteered in 1915 and was killed in the first battle he took part in.) From among these coffee-house artists Paul Altherr founded the Cabaret Pantagruel which was the first ever to ridicule the whole war. A fairly mediocre poet called Vincent V. Venner became its director; in Switzerland he was famous not only for this or because he changed wives every two or three years, always leaving the previous one with two or three children (in this way he became the proud father of fifteen children), but also for being the most successful of all the Swiss poets at tapping financial sources. The most notorious was Steinmann, a Zurich millionaire homosexual, whom he got to finance a journal called *Ähre*.[3] It was quite an amusing literary rag. Venner invited all his friends to dump their rubbish in it. It cost Steinmann vast sums. This money was then drunk away in a Spanish joint in the Niederdorfer Strasse. In the end the paper devoured so much money that the wretched millionaire was legally restrained by his relations. Venner was very concerned about the integrity of his friends; he once had Leonor Goldschmitt beaten up by his friends because he thought he was a German spy. (Incidentally, Leonor Goldschmitt is another of those amusing characters in German literature. Twenty years ago he was said to have written some books with supposedly socialistic leanings about which even Gerhart Hauptmann expressed himself favourably, but then along came Erich Mühsam, who suffered slightly from persecution mania and claimed Goldschmitt was a stool-pigeon. There followed endless, long-drawn-out court-cases. After that Goldschmitt's literary career was finished. The whole affair had a detrimental effect on his life and wherever he went it cast a shadow across his path). However, the innocent Venner himself was apparently not all that innocent. In 1916 he was arrested on suspicion of espionage and convicted as a French spy. (That's what the papers wrote, whether it was true or not is hard to say because his wife claimed he was innocent.) (This kind of thing happened even in Switzerland during the war.) One day Venner brought to our regular gathering, Leo von Meyenburg, a young, very talented poet (who cooked up a strange concoction of Mallarmé and Verhaeren and who maintained that the re-establishment of the French monarchy was the only possible salvation to emerge from this ghastly war.) The most endearing member of our company was the young Rhineland poet F. W. Wagner, an enormously tall gaunt figure who could be seen tottering about the Café in a morphium stupor. He used to write twenty or thirty little poems every day which he would sell by the dozens to an old rag. But he was really very talented and later helped to start the Steegemann publishing concern. It was said, alas, that he had been in an asylum a few times already.

That's what Café Megalomania looked like at the beginning of the war.

III

Café de la Banque is the other place we must take a walk through, because it reveals Zurich's second and fundamentally more important period during the war : that is the period of the birth of the Cabaret Bonbonnière. The Café de la Banque opened a cabaret under the above title. In this cabaret extremely radical, anti-war material was put on, but the audience consisted mostly of profiteers and spies. By the end of 1917 all the countries engaged in the war realized that it was not to be won on the battlefield, and that they would have to find other means to victory. The Café de la Banque and more especially the Café Terrasse and the Café Odeon were certainly the most suspect of means. For a spell Zurich had become a metropolis. The Cabaret Bonbonnière had started a trend. Cabarets sprung up everywhere eager for the money of all the spies, profiteers, confidence tricksters and patriots of various hues. Zurich was full of money. I'm convinced Zurich has never seen so many remarkable characters and so much money as it did during the war. While thousands were dying most horribly on the battle-fields, it was possible to have a wonderful time in Zurich and so it is not surprising that people like Albert Ehrenstein and Werfel intermittently came to live in Zurich. It was particularly amusing to read ex-Socialist Otto Ernst's silly manifestos which, however, were never published by the Swiss newspapers he sent them to.

IV

In 1915 when Hugo Kersten and I founded the first European journal *Mistral*,[4] we not only reaped a harvest of abuse from the entire Swiss press, but it also took a long time before our paper, which was supposed to bring together people from all parts of the world, was taken seriously. At the time Kurt Hiller wrote an ultra-patriotic essay for us. Carl Sternheim was alone in supporting us by taking out a subscription for a year. Later the *Mistral* was to become the focal point of one of the most remarkable artistic movements during the war. Immediately upon the appearance of our journal Hugo Ball and Richard Huelsenbeck had sent us a broadsheet from Berlin in which they came out not only against the war, but also against intellectualism in art. Artificial intellectualism they considered to be yet another reason why no one was outspokenly against the war despite all the international outcry. At the time Kersten and I did not have enough steam to carry on the movement on our own, but we were soon joined in Zurich by the above-mentioned pair and Emmy Hennings, and they were able to take the movement for Internationalism much more firmly in hand than we could. This marks the start of the most important time for Zurich during the war. Hugo Ball had experience in the revolutionary movement of German literature. Before the war in Munich he had founded a journal called *Revolution*[5] whose very first number was confiscated. He was among the first to be revolted by war and flee abroad. In Zurich he first wrote poems for *Young Guard*[6] whose editor at the time was the man who was later to become famous as a leading Communist, Willy Münzenberg. Ball and his wife, Emmy Hennings, were starving most of the time. It was he who first drew the attention of the world to Henri Barbusse's *Le Feu*.[7] In Zurich he founded the "Voltaire Cabaret" where absolutely nothing but revolutionary works were performed. It was Ball who created Dadaism as a reaction against intellectual confusion, though it was later successfully exploited by others like Tzara. In this circle the international body of artists met again. From all corners of the world artists streamed into Zurich. Ball arranged international art exhibitions. In the Cabaret we met Else Lasker-Schüler, Christian Schad, Hans Arp, Slodky, Hans Richter, Viking Eggeling (later, the last two tried to create something new they called— Art of Movement). By the way, Hans Richter is supposed to have been as successful with women as d'Albert. Dozens of women kept threatening to commit suicide if he refused to love them. Many celebrities frequented the Cabaret as for example the Swiss novelist J. C. Heer, who found it great fun. Despite the success of his own workmanlike sentimental trash he was quite willing to devote his declining years to Dadaism.

Of course Dadaism was under fire from all sides, but nevertheless it was undeniably the only international art movement during the war. It was the first movement to break completely and for all time with any kind of Romanticism in art. Possibly this movement was of little avail against the vast confusions of intellectualism, but at least Dadaism tried to make people realize they should not let themselves be blinded by geniuses, and that was what helped the movement to become international. When Hugo Ball got bored with Dadaism and turned to politics Walter Serner suddenly became very interested in Dadaism. He travelled to Paris to find a backer for the movement and this turned out to be Francis Picabia. Picabia was very rich and could well afford the self-indulgence of being a Cubist painter. Naturally he also indulged in

157

Dadaism. Paris now became the centre of Dadaism. The Dadaists were swimming in money and drowned the whole world in Dadaism. The founder of German Dadaism was Raoul Hausmann. He was really a remarkable man and for a long time his followers called him Dadasoph. He was quite a mediocre painter, but long before George Grosz he had recognized the deficiencies of all -isms in painting. He loved scandal, because, as he saw it, this was the only way to ridicule respectable citizens. He loved to laugh at absolutely everything. That's what made him a Dadaist. He was the most systematic of them all in his use of irony at the expense of this over-civilized age. It is a pity that while others made a great deal of money out of Dadaism he should remain so poor. (Just as this book is being printed [1923] I get the news that Hausmann has acquired a bank account by marriage.)

Blood made Baader a Dadaist. (He is said to have been a master-builder. However there are those who maintain he was only a labourer on a building-site, and once when Hausmann was furious with him he wrote that he had been a tailor.) His mania began with wanting to be like Schmidt, the founder of the Mormon sect. He believed he too was singled out to create a new bible. Hausmann, who knew this Dada master best, writes, "As a tramp Baader traversed many countries. He was a grave-digger, master-builder, property-owner, spent several periods in a lunatic asylum, was a clairvoyant. At the beginning of the war he wrote to the German Emperor's youngest son : 'My dear boy, I, Baader, the ruler of the universe, have a very poor opinion of your father and I instruct him to put an end to the war at once.'" Naturally, the ruler of the universe was immediately carted off again to the asylum. On his release he attended a church service and made a pacifistic-dadaistic speech whereupon he was carted off once more. The revolution set him free again. Then he devoted himself entirely to Dadaism. When the National Assembly met in Weimar he made a speech from the balcony to the horror of all those present. Then he wrote a Dadaist Bible which he hoped to sell to an American millionaire for 100,000 dollars. When this came to nothing he got in touch with Count Keyserling who was delighted and wrote him a very nice letter. Baader exploited this new connection for publicity purposes, whereupon Keyserling announced in all the papers that he didn't even know Baader. But he could not shake off our hero as easily as that because the Dadaist simply published Keyserling's letter in the same papers. So far this has been the ruler of the universe's last act, but he has assured me that a great deal can be expected of him in the immediate future. He is looking for a backer who is ready to exploit his potential commercially. (I get no commission from him for this last item of information!)

Among the enthusiastic followers of Baader is Dr. Döhmann who calls himself Daimonides. He is a gynaecologist on the Kurfürstendamm in Berlin. Wears horn-rimmed spectacles à la Franz Blei and a fur coat, of course. He writes chocolate-box poems for ardent ladies on the Kurfürstendamm. He can do the foxtrot and the shimmy better than anybody in Berlin, yet he has very little luck with the ladies. He also intends to write a foxtrot opera. At every Dada evening he is there functioning as Dada pianist.

Christian Schad
Zurich / Geneva: Dada

In the summer of 1915 I left the Munich train which had brought me from the German maelstrom to Zurich, the island of peace. As a young painter and designer with publications and a driver's licence to my name I was of age and liable for military service and should have been in field grey lying with the millions of others in the fiery mud or even under a plain wooden cross. Instead, thanks to my assumed weak heart and the connivance of a clever doctor, I had been released to attend a Swiss sanatorium and so had escaped the cogs of the war machine and was now in the Bahnhofstrasse, Zurich, in a totally different country ...

The impression of this first moment was overwhelming. Back there on the other side of the border I had just crossed, a gigantic and hybrid mechanism which sucked in everybody willy-nilly to slave, starve and die, went relentlessly on its way —where I was now, people lived for the sake of living. All the poetry and philosophy the Germans are so proud of had been transformed by Prussian discipline into the one watchword: "God, Emperor and Fatherland", the Officer was the ideal man and the War the supreme test; all that Man could look for in life was now restricted to subservience, his best qualities were crippled.

It must be admitted that existence for a German was a tragic problem reaching far beyond such simple mechanics. Presumably ordinary citizens, especially the young ones, have always seen the soldier's uniform as the fancy dress of some adventurous game without realizing that in its seams like poisonous lice lurk murder, suicide and total destruction. A fancy dress to facilitate the escape from a dull normality overcast with dread forebodings. And now—just as a uniform brings release from the destructions of civilian life—war was to bring release from society itself with its calamities and crises like a thunderstorm clearing the stifling atmosphere.

At the outbreak of this First World War a mad wave of fatalism, which substituted force for reason, came and overwhelmed not only the normal citizens—it swept along many of the Expressionists and Socialists as well—one need only remember the long list of names of those who fell as volunteers, Franz Marc, Ernst Stadler and others. The number of those who right from the start renounced the use of force as a possible means of solving national and social difficulties was very small —and some of those had managed to escape, often under extremely difficult circumstances; so the people in Zurich in those years represented basically a delegation of the critical Expressionists in opposition, whose intellectual position inevitably developed into aggressive Dadaism and later into the ironic detachment of "New Objectivity" and Surrealism.

Now I too was in Zurich. The day after my arrival I enquired at an art shop for the Russian painter Slodky, who, like myself, was a contributor to Franz Pfemfert's *Aktion*—the shop-assistant pointed to a young man : "Slodky—he is standing right there." Great was the general rejoicing; he took me straight to Angela Hubermann and Walter Serner. The Swiss by and large respected those who had run away from "Wilhelm" and everybody hoped he would lose the war so that the Prussian spiked helmet would not rule the world. Besides, there were hardly any illusions about this because with Zurich being one of the most important Stock Markets for all war materials from iron ore to secret information and anything else in short supply, everyone was very well informed.

Serner and I met fairly regularly and in the course of our evening and nightly walks and talks—daytime was for work and sleep—we always came back to the dream of a journal, the first of whose eight numbers did in fact appear in October 1915 under the title *Sirius*.[1] Soon we were being secretly pointed out in the writers' Café de la Terrasse and the letter-box of the small flat we had taken in order to economize became too small. Max Herrmann-Neisse, Else Lasker-Schüler, Ludwig Bäumer, Alfred Wolfenstein, Theodor Däubler, Leo Sternberg, Alfred Kubin, even Peter Altenberg, that inexhaustible writer of witty letters full of crossings-out and exclamation marks—

162

all said they were ready and willing to help. We even printed some early Picasso.

We spent a great deal of time with Hans Arp, Hugo Ball, Emmy Hennings, Leonhard Frank, Ludwig Rubiner and the famous Marietta who was appearing as *diseuse* in the Café de la Banque Cabaret in the Bahnhofstrasse. I often took a stroll there with Arp deep in extremely Dadaistic conversation and it was through him that I met Laban and Mary Wigman who afterwards visited my studio in order to dabble in graphic-rhythmic experiments; I must admit I did not like them drumming and dancing to Nietzsche. However, what mattered more to us than the primitive writhing of their beautiful souls was some form of dynamic action against the boring repetitiveness in art and disgust at deeprooted, senile tradition. What Hugo Ball experienced every day, or rather every night, was nearer the heart of the matter: he accompanied Emmy Hennings while she had to sing the hackneyed old songs of the Belle Epoque in the "Stag", a dive situated in the brothel area of the city.

This was the quarter that produced something new in the Cabaret Voltaire, the cradle of Dadaism, which was in a way an offshoot of Expressionism. Of course fifty years earlier Dostoevsky with his *Sketches from the Underground* and then Isidore Ducasse, not to mention Lautréamont with his *Maldoror* and his *Poésies*, had been far ahead of their time with similar ideas. In any event, Dadaism arose out of the reaction against an intellectualism which was banal because it used memory instead of reason. As a result it had to be alogical (like Zen nowadays, for instance) so as not to be assimilated by the philistines. The shock experiment was successful, but only as regards form, not morals: no one felt inwardly shattered and forced to reflect; the roofs of indifference had not been reached.

Tearing out these roots was precisely Serner's goal. Our journal had expired with its eighth number for financial reasons, if you like; our friends had demanded no fees and Heuberger the printer had shown himself a true lover of the *avant-garde*, but sales didn't cover the expenses—a balance that told its own story. In the last number, in one of the stories, Serner's last sentence was: ". . . he hurriedly left the café." In a sense this cafe represented the religious-metaphysical standpoint, which *Sirius* had tried to express. It had now been done away with by a complete *volte-face* though this did not mean that

163

Serner had lost any of his humanitarian impetus. Where before
he had quietly employed flanking attacks, these now became
frontal and radical in order to undermine the soothing comfort of life's illusions and the commercial elements in intellectual
life. His *Con-Man's Breviary* was written in Lugano in 1918
and was published in 1920 by Paul Steegemann as *Ultimate
Dissolution*. It was followed by the book *The Blue Chimp Inn*.

He reaped his reward in the wrath of the good citizens who
marked Serner down as a total destroyer of all order, paradoxi-
cally what they particularly held against him were exactly those
activities which satisfy the most intimate needs of traditional
society: the possession of one or even more brothels and the
trading in virgins and state secrets. That he should personally
be believed capable of such things and that this caused him
serious unpleasantness was only to be expected. That his
Breviary represents an obvious turning-point in Dadaism, by
giving it an ideological content which goes far beyond the
merely formal revolt, justifies him in our eyes; the seven-
volume collected works published by Steegemann must be considered one of the foundations of Modernism today. His motto
was: the ultimate disappointment is when the illusion that
you have no illusions turns out to be one . . .

For me he was the most important man in Zurich. I know
there were men like Leonhard Frank who once starved so long
that he almost forgot how to eat and who said to me the vital
thing was not to have a Fatherland but a home: the feeling you
get at night looking through a warmly-lit window. And there
were also Europeans like René Schickele or Otto Flake, writers
who are now widely recognized though often attacked. But
they mostly lived by the lakes and were not accessible to us
young people. Then, too, there was the secondhand book-dealer
Hack who paid as good prices as he could for our home-made
drawings or books we did not need so that we could get a plate
of soup at the stall. He died a horrible death: he was always
ready to share his morphia and one day he gave a girl friend too
much and she died—in despair he tried to hang himself, but the
rope broke, so with the end dangling round his neck he jumped
into the Limmat and was drowned.[2]

In 1916 I went to Geneva and found it to be the French equi-
valent: the sanctuary of French-speaking pacifists Frans

Masereel, Henri Guilbeaux, Romain Rolland and many others who lived and worked there, and like us refused to play the crazy flag-waving, man-murdering game. They tended to gather in the Café Landolt where I met Archipenko, Masereel, Buchet, the woman painter Epstein and occasionally Lenin, or they tended to mix among themselves as in Zurich. Francis Picabia and Tristan Tzara kept in touch with us from Paris; Philippe Soupault once came over on a visit. As one might expect, Serner also spent some time there.

We formed no group—we never did. Serner was not one for groups, but he was a marvellous friend; groups were stable and anything that was stable bored us; we were Dadaists and not even treating the necessary chores of organization as a joke or a technique could attract us. We remained birds of passage—I met Serner later after the war in Rome, or Genoa, Naples, Frankfurt, Vienna, once even on the Tegernsee; his life was just like his stories in which somebody is always arriving and going away again and doing the strangest things in between. He was always open to the infinite possibilities of existence. Sometimes we would roam from dusk till dawn through the harbour area and squat in crude music-halls—neither of us would have done it so readily on our own, but it was the right background for his brilliantly spontaneous *aperçus*. I last heard of him in 1927 —he asked me to represent him in Berlin at the première of his *Posada*, of which all further performances had been banned in advance. That he should disappear without trace is characteristic of him . . .

In Geneva I managed to produce a Dada programme of a kind in as much as I was experimenting with camera-less photography—a paradox full of extreme possibilities which Tzara immediately christened 'Schadography' and which was discussed in various French and American publications; some of these papers are to be found in the MoMa, the Museum of Modern Art, in New York. The year 1920 found me in Rome in the company of Jules Evola, who later became a mystic, and Prampolini. I was also in the Salon Bragaglia; in the course of time I got to know top-ranking military men as well as the equally strange aristocrats who live a magically *mondain* life in their palazzi. Then I was drawn to quietude again—I went to Naples which offered me the nearest hermitage, an immediate and subterranean existence; there my first surrealistic pictures came to me including the one of the low life melodrama I had gone to with Serner. Dada was dead and gone—we had to find new ways of discovering the New Man. Perhaps it was more than mere chance that made me paint a portrait of Kisch (the famous "raging reporter") on my return to Berlin . . .

Richard Huelsenbeck
Zurich 1916, as it really was

I first met Hugo Ball in Munich in 1912. He was then dramaturg with the Kammerspiele. He immediately impressed me by his superior intelligence and his profound knowledge of things. We became friends. With the help of Hans Leybold and Klabund we founded the *Revolution*,[1] which was our form of resistance to Imperial Germany. Ball wrote a poem against the Virgin Mary which brought about the journal's downfall. Several law-suits were launched against us and we were scheduled for the same fate as Panizza. But they failed to realize that we were much younger, more resilient and aggressive. Invective, threats, bureaucratic unpleasantness poured off our backs. The measures taken against us could never be as bad as our worst imaginings. We knew the 'blimps' and bureaucratic antiques behind their desks and ink-wells before they even let fly at us with their decrees. No verdict against us could match the level of hatred we felt for them. It's still interesting that it was Ball who wrote against the Virgin Mary.[2] Later, in Ticino, he would have considered it a deadly sin, but in Munich he would have nothing to do with religion.

Shortly before the outbreak of war we met in Berlin. If I'm not mistaken, Ball was editor of Reclam's *Universum*[3] at the time. Or maybe it was some other illustrated journal. The life he led was miserable, but he was unremitting in his efforts to grasp the intellectual values and underlying spirit of the age. When war broke out our hatred for official Germany changed and everything associated with it changed into a kind of paroxysm of rage. We couldn't see a uniform without clenching our fists. We considered our most practical course. Revolutionary resistance to the well-oiled war machines would have been madness, Pfemfert's *Aktion* could offer some intellectual consolations, it

167

is true, but no way to freedom. My reaction against the "spirit" which I identified with Imperial German post-classical culture began. Side by side with the sabre-swinging officers strode the German University Professor, a volume of Goethe clutched to his heart like a charm. The Manifesto of the German Men of Letters seemed to me the height of hypocrisy. It is completely grotesque to reproach us and say we should have worked for the proletariat then, for there was no proletarian organization, legal or illegal. For the pure-minded pacifist there was only one solution: to leave a country whose actions and politics one could not accept. Was Germany guilty of starting the war? No? Then stay in your country and fight. Is she guilty? Yes? Then leave for Switzerland and try to deepen your knowledge of the situation from a neutral standpoint and take action when the time comes. To a certain extent we were misinformed because we thought Germany and its leaders at the time far more cunning than they really were. We thought it was all cold calculation, we saw the Emperor, the Victory Allee, the gleaming uniforms, the Krupp factories, we heard the demand to shoot at fathers and brothers and we sensed a deep-seated plot aimed at all the fundamental values of humanity. We saw the Generals as a kind of intellectul advance party of the Devil. We dragged men who were probably mindless idiots up to our own level and made them morally responsible.

On the other hand, we considered it morally right, valuable, and absolutely essential to turn our back on Germany because for one reason it was dangerous to do so. Anybody could let himself be called up and keep up a stream of critical comment. But they did nothing to stop the war machine. Our aim was to record our insight into the real causes of the war. Often we were unsure. Was it really Germany's fault? Is it possible for a country, such a great country and one that was our spiritual fatherland after all, to set the world alight? In Zurich a pamphlet appeared which claimed to have proved this beyond the shadow of a doubt. Not *Entente* propaganda. A German had sat down and written a confession of the things he knew. It shatters me to this day when I think how anguished we were over the truth. Bowed down and heavy with such ideas we arrived in a city in which the scum of international profiteering had begun to settle. I saw very little of the Swiss themselves during the war. We had the feeling they didn't like us, that they felt we might disturb their peace, and the really important things we had to say ran completely counter to what they thought. Among the whores, speculators and *petit bourgeois* (who gaped with red-rimmed eyes at the relaxed moral standards) moved the uniforms of captured French and German officers. When they became aware of each other they went as stiff as ramrods, but they still saluted each other. That made a deep impression on us.

And would it have been better for us to join a workers' organization instead of founding a cabaret? Anybody who argues in this way knows nothing of the conditions as they were then in Zurich and reveals a surprising lack of insight into the human psyche. Personally, I have stopped making demands on people and what they should do till I know the facts. A fundamental precept in World History seems to me to be "Shoemaker stick to your last". I have never been a politician and even today I don't see myself as one. I am simply not cut out to be one. My *métier* is writing; there will always be people like that. I'm in favour of everybody realizing what he is capable of and pursuing what he is best at. This seems to me a fundamental principle which cannot be qualified by any political or economic theory, it's more of a precept of human tolerance without which relationships between men are wicked, unbearable and morally perverted. I have no reason for holding back with my confession of faith. I shall never deny that I am a Socialist, but my socialism has a humane basis. I am what orthodox party members contemptuously call an "emotional Communist". I have an inherent watchful instinct that protects against anything brutal, mean and socially unjust. I am ready to fight tooth and nail with heart and soul to see justice done, but it is impossible for me to believe that the world can be summed up in one party programme. I am perhaps not the revolutionary one has to be. I understand that there have to be politicians who look different, are differently constructed psychologically from me. I just am what I am. I know where my goal lies and where I can accomplish something. In those days I associated with the Cabaret Voltaire and Dadaism because I realized that some form of cultural protest (and Dadaism was never anything more) was necessary and that this was where I could accomplish something. I devoted myself to Dadaism first in Zurich and later in Germany with such intensity that it undermined my health and my so-called literary career. That was no joke. In the term Dada we concentrated all the rage, contempt, superiority and human revolutionary protest we were capable of. Had I joined a political party, no matter which, I should have accomplished far less at the time. After all, several million people must have heard the word Dada resounding in their ears and a few tens of thousands must have realized that Dada was the ironic and contemptuous response to a culture which had shown itself worthy of flame-throwers and machine-guns.

Ball's case is much more difficult. While I grew more and more convinced that the world should and could be changed, Ball believed that no compromise could be found between the feeling for what was right and just and the force necessary to bring about social order. To be truthful, one must admit that there is an intellectual stand which simply does not fit in with the world as it is. One must also admit that sources of intellectual energy do exist whose effects lie on a plane completely different from the calculations and considerations which physical and political events arrange themselves into. Ball is one of the most sensitive and spiritual men I have ever met in my life. His path from the painful protest of Dadaism to belief in a spiritual power which works according to its own laws is one I can understand though not necessarily approve. That Ball should call his Cabaret "Voltaire" indicated that he was obsessed by cultural criticism. He fought Germany and Protestantism because he considered these powers unethical, socially inferior and culturally corrupt. He detected a connection between Protestantism and Hegelianism and became suspicious of all exploiters of dialectics as a result. He dreamed his way into a spiritual sphere which, knowing neither "yes" nor "no", had room for the absolute. The enormous, almost exasperated sincerity with which Ball fought for his truths places him far above many of my literary acquaintances who simply clung to some comfortable traditional conviction and steered a steady course towards comfort and security. Ball was so poor he often starved for days on end, but this didn't bother him. He saw only the path before him, the decisions to be taken. The Cabaret Voltaire and Dadaism were as serious and important to him then as his devotion to the Church was to become to him later. I have always rejected this piety, I do not understand it, religious dogmatists are even more alien to me than political ones, but I am prepared to accept that Ball fought his way through to his conviction with uncommon sincerity and that no one is entitled to tell him what he ought to have done. If in those Zurich days Ball had wanted to play politics or if he had joined a party he would not have been Ball. All his political ideas, all his economic and ethical thinking was concentrated into the founding of the Cabaret and into his cultural criticism. Any other attitude would have placed him in an impossibly ambiguous position, reduced his achievement to nil, and would have exterminated him as leader and human being. The Cabaret Voltaire in which Dadaism was born was nothing like the usual run of crude comedy (this is the picture our latter-day critics seem to have of it); no, it was a cultural platform on which everybody could give free expression to his opinion. Germany has never seen anything like it. Even if only for the reason that no deals were made there. This was where people were prepared to express opinions which could not be expressed elsewhere. That these opinions were mainly on cultural matters was simply because we are intellectuals. They can do what they like to us, but that's what we are. Shoemaker stick to your last. Ball did in fact once become active in politics when he took over the *Freie Zeitung*[4] in Berne, but then the reaction against an activity which by his very nature left him cold must have set in, and he fled to Ticino and that was the beginning of his Catholic fiasco. Ball was far less of a politician than even I was; he was incapable of making compromises. He simply could not adapt to changing trends and differing opinions. He was inflexible. He would have died rather than go along merrily with the stream. He did die—of starvation, debility, poverty, bitterness, isolation. I reject Ball's Catholicism; I demand that the world be changed, I find popery abhorrent; I consider it a disaster that Ball became entangled in religious mysticism. But I respect the man of the spirit; I respect his fate; I know what it means to die for one's convictions. It is infinitely more difficult to die for one's convictions than for an armed power.

Zurich 1916 as it really was?[5] It was exactly like our ideas. There weren't any Swiss around in Zurich in those days. There were crooks, whores, international rabble and our spiritual hunger for truth. Were there any workers' organizations? Yes! A totally fossilized, scared Social Democrat Party, no Communists. A group of discontented Social Democrats who gathered round the "rebel", Brupbacher, who in those days called himself

an anarchist and who is now a Communist member of parliament. We had contacts with all of them, exchanged opinions.
There was also one great man who was later to revolutionize one
part of the world: Lenin. He lived in the street where we had
our Cabaret, directly opposite.

Seeing the racketeers on the terraces of the Baur au Lac one
had the feeling that decadent European culture stank to high
heaven. People moved like puppets, like projections on a screen.
Whoever said anything worth listening to? What was there to
stir anyone's feelings? Where could one see any escape from the
spiritual and physical pressures of war? Neither Brupbacher
nor the "rebels" nor the orthodox SPD members were capable of
making any decisive impression on us. Lenin, who shared the
same street with us, was silent. The emigré Marxist Russians who
lived in Zurich fought out their battles behind closed doors.
Nobody broke these down for long, least of all the Zurich
Socialists who were rightly regarded by the Russians as insignificant. Zurich could never be the starting point of a world clean-
up, this was only an intermediate stage for hunted men, a cover,
a temporary lodging to get one's breath back. Lenin was biding
his time. The Zurich Socialists' time has still not come.

Social differences are not very extreme in Switzerland. Only
in the large cities is there a class barrier and even there the
connections with the favourable conditions of the countryside are
so prevalent that party programmes tend to peter out into compromise. No, Swiss social conditions were no concern of ours. The
cultural protest we put on was a beacon for all in Europe with
eyes to see. Portrayal and reminder of the collapse of post-
classical middle-class culture. Revelation of a new emotional,
primitive path. In this work we have given of our best, expended
all our energies. It would be ridiculous if after the event we
were to claim to be something different from what we were.
The collapse was something we experienced collectively as a
group of intellectuals who stayed at their posts and knew what
they were doing. Afterwards Ball left for Ticino, I myself went
back to Germany towards the end of 1916. Here conditions made
action imperative. The people were starving, the soldiers were
beginning to revolt. The Naval Mutiny had just been put down
with draconic severity. This was it. There's nothing I said or did
then I want to take back. The German Revolution did not fail
because I appeared in a Cabaret. It did not fail because certain

people who felt competent on cultural issues took part. It did not fail of a surfeit of romanticism, but of a lack of romanticism, a missing impetus, a pathological lack of revolutionary temperament. In my opinion it failed because of the small-minded, timid and therefore malicious spirit of the mediocre type of German who, incapable of any heroic gesture, is frequently found among party officials. If the German Revolution, German Social Democracy had known how to attract more men like us, it would not have failed. Every movement which despises the spiritual is bound to get bogged down. This has all been said before, but the Germans cannot be told often enough.

Hans Arp
Dadaland

Disgusted by the slaughter of the World War in 1914 we devoted ourselves in Zurich to the arts. While the thunder of guns roared in the distance we sang, painted, pasted, wrote poems for all we were worth. We sought an elemental art to cure men from the madness of the age and a new order which would establish the balance between heaven and hell. We sensed that gangsters would appear who in their obsession with power would simply use art to brutalize mankind.

In 1915 Sophie Taeuber and I painted, sewed and pasted pictures which are probably the first examples of "concrete art". These works are self-sufficient, independent "realities". They have no rational sense; they do not arise out of everyday reality. We rejected everything which could be mere imitation or description in order to liberate within ourselves the elemental and spontaneous. Because the distribution of planes in these works, their colours and interrelationships did not look deliberately worked out, I explained that these works were arranged "according to the laws of chance", chance which is for me a part of the inexplicable reason, the fathomless order governing the universe. At the same time Russian and Dutch artists were also producing works which seemed related to ours but were born of entirely different intentions. They are glorifications of modern living, confessions of faith in the machine and in technology.

In his place on the Upper Zäune in Zurich Janco slaved away for a time at naturalistic painting. I forgive him this secret vice, for to it we owe the faithful picture of the Cabaret Voltaire. In a packed dive some absolutely crazy characters are to be seen on the stage representing Tzara, Janco, Ball, Huelsenbeck, Emmy Hennings and your humble servant. We are creating an unholy din. The audience are shouting, laughing and clapping their hands above their heads. To which we reply with sighs of love, belches, poems, with the "moo, moo" and "miaow, miaow" of mediaeval Bruitists. Tzara is waggling his bottom like an Eastern dancer's belly, Janco is playing on an invisible violin and bowing to the ground. Frau Hennings with the face of a Madonna is doing the splits. Huelsenbeck is banging the drum non-stop while Ball, as white as a ghost, accompanies him at the piano. We were given the honourable title of Nihilists. The Ministers of Misinformation call everybody that who does not follow their path. The great matadors of the Dada movement were Ball and Tzara. In my opinion Ball is one of the greatest of German writers. He was tall, somewhat haggard and had the face of a Pater Dolorosus. At that time Tzara was writing his *vingt-cinq poèmes*, which belong among the best of French poetry. Later we were found by Dr. Serner, a romantic character, author of detective novels, master of ballroom dancing, skin specialist and gentleman-burglar all in one.

My dear Janco, are you still singing the devilish song of the mill at Hirza-Pirza with your wild laugh and a toss of your gypsy-locks? I still remember the masks you produced for our Dada mainfestations. They were terrifying and generally dripping with blood-red paint. Out of paper, horse-hair, wire and rags you fabricated your love-lorn foetuses, Lesbian sardines and ecstatic mice.

In 1917 Janco was working on abstracts, especially plaster reliefs. Their significance has still not been fully realized to this day. Janco battled passionately for our art.

Tzara, Serner and I wrote a cycle of poems in the Café de la Terrasse in Zurich: *The Hyperbole of the Crocodile's Hairdresser and the Walking Stick*. This kind of poetry was later christened "automatic writing" by the Surrealists. Automatic poetry springs directly from the poet's guts or any other organs which have stored up usable reserves. Neither the postilion of Lonjumeau nor the hexameter, neither grammar nor aesthetics, neither Buddha nor the sixth commandment should stop it. The poet croaks, swears, sighs, stammers, yodels, just as he feels like it. His poems are like nature: they laugh, rhyme, stink like nature.

Trivialities, or what are commonly called trivial things, are as valuable to him as elevated histrionics; for in nature an atom is as lovely and important as a star, and only men have the temerity to decide what is beautiful and what ugly.

Eggeling I had met in 1915 in a Paris studio. At that time he was busy looking for the rules of a kind of concrete counterpoint; he composed and drew its first rudiments. He was plaguing himself to death with it. In 1917 I met him again in Zurich. Now he had written down on long rolls of paper some kind of hieratic ideograms, figures of extraordinarily balanced beauty. These signs, these figures, grow large and small, split, multiply, move to different places, become entwined, sink away, come to the surface again partly and form in their sequence a magnificent construction, a kind of vegetable architecture. He called these picture rolls "Symphonies". Eggeling died in the year 1922, but not before he had realized his creations in film with his friend Hans Richter.

Augusto Giacometti from Graubünden was already an established artist by 1916; despite this he was friendly with the Dadaists and often took part in their demonstrations. He looked like a prosperous bear and perhaps out of sympathy for the bears of his home canton he wore a bear-skin hat. One of his friends confided to me that he had a well-filled bank book hidden in the lining. On the occasion of one Dada soirée he presented us with a thirty-yard-long garland of honour in all the colours of the rainbow and covered with eulogies. One evening Giacometti and I decided in all humility to make some unofficial publicity for Dada. We marched along the bank of the Limmat from one hostelry to another. Giacometti would open the door carefully and then articulate with loud clear voice: *Vive Dada*. Then he would close the door again just as carefully. The startled citizens almost dropped their sausages. What on earth could this mysterious cry mean, uttered by a respectable man in his prime who did not in the least look like a wastrel or one of those foreigners only there on sufferance?

Giacometti was painting star flowers, cosmic conflagrations, sheets of flame, seething caverns about this time. These paintings are related to ours in that they are immediate representations of forms and colours. Giacometti was also the first to attempt a mechanical statue. For this "Mobile" he remodelled a wall clock and made its pendulum swing coloured shapes backwards and forwards.

Despite the war those days were full of unusual charm and in retrospect they seem almost idyllic to me. At the time Zurich was occupied by an army of international revolutionaries, reformers, poets, painters, politicians and apostles of peace. They tended to meet in the Café Odeon. There every table was the extra-territorial possession of some group or other. The Dadaists took up two corners by the window. Opposite them sat the writers Wedekind, Leonhard Frank, Werfel, Ehrenstein and their friends. In the neighbourhood of those tables the dancer couple Sacharoff held court in precious attitudes and with them the two painters Baroness Werefkin and Jawlensky. A jumble of other people jostle about in my memory: the poetess Else Lasker-Schüler, Hardekopf, Jollos, Flake, Perrottet; Leo Leuppi the painter, the founder of the *Allianz*, the dancers Moor and Mary Wigman; Laban the Granddaddy of all dancers, male or female and Cassirer the art dealer. Quite oblivious to all these swaying figures General Wille sat all alone with his little glass of Velt-liner. In some cases it was the body that was swaying somewhat by midnight, in others the mind. In a few cases the mind became so shaky that they decided to put an end to their own lives, which is what happened to the strange bookseller called Hack who ran a little bookshop in the Oetenbachgasse not far from the main street. He was a drug addict who had fled to Switzer-land to escape the war. I shall never forget his horrible death: he only succeeded in killing himself with the help of the River Limmat after the biggest possible dose of morphia had had no effect and the rope he had tried to hang himself with had broken under the weight of his own body. Joyce, the Irish writer, Busoni and my countryman from Alsace René Schickele, preferred to direct the fates of the world over a bottle of cham-pagne in the Kronenhalle.

Not far from the Cabaret Voltaire in which Dada first saw the light of day Comrade Lenin lived a few houses farther down the Spiegelgasse. Some of my friends claimed to have seen him in the Cabaret Voltaire. However, the writer of these lines was never aware of anything suspicious. The short-sighted citizens of Zurich had no complaints against Lenin, because he was inconspicuously dressed. Dada, on the other hand, really got under their skin. The friendly way we produced our warnings that the good old days were over made them absolutely blind with rage. They wanted their world, that charming little garden sanctuary, to go on just as it was. The good citizen regarded the Dadaists as dissolute monsters, revolutionary wretches, uncouth Asiatics with an eye on his clock, cash-registers and medals. The Dadaists thought up practical jokes to rob the citizens of their sleep. They sent false communiqués to the newspapers about hair-raising Dada duels in which their favourite writer, the King of Bernina, was supposed to have been involved. The Dadaists made the citizens aware of chaos and distant but powerful earth tremors so that their clocks began to whirr, their cash registers wrinkled their brows and their medals went all spotty. "The Egg Board", a sport or party-game for top people in which the participants leave the field covered from top to toe in egg yolk; "The Navel Bottle", an enormous object in which bicycle, whale, brassière and absinthe-spoon engage in intercourse; "The Glove", which can be worn in place of the old-fashioned head— all were to make the good citizens aware of the unreality of their world, the futility of their activities, even of their so lucrative patriotism. Naturally this was a very naïve undertaking on our part because the ordinary citizen has as little imagination as a worm and in place of a heart has an over-life-sized bunion in which he feels twinges only when the barometer falls, that's to say the Stock Market prices go down.

BERLIN

Erwin Piscator
The political significance of *Die Aktion*

Even as late as 1944 a prominent Frenchman wanted to leave
a memorial service being held for Romain Rolland in New York
when he heard that a famous German writer was coming. And
perhaps Thomas Mann came just to demonstrate publicly how
great his own mistake had been. The mistake, which he shared
with many other German authors in 1914, of not having
listened to Rolland's warning and not having answered his
appeal. For his part, Rolland left his homeland, France,
at the outbreak of war and went to live in Switzerland.
But Thomas Mann was not the only German writer and poet
who in 1914 welcomed with surprising patriotic enthusiasm the
forces of bourgeois imperialism which till then they had viewed
with suspicion. And not only the artists and intellectuals to
whom one could always concede that pure politics was not their
business, no, the whole German Social Democratic Party had
toppled over to a man when the Emperor announced that now
there were no party differences. But for a minute number of
M.P.s who voted against, the party voted for the war credits.

The pen dipping into the past sticks, for in striving to draw
a bright picture of one man, the picture of the others comes out
very black and full of pain. The picture which stands out bright
against this dark, divided background is that of Franz Pfemfert.
But the only way to do him justice is if one knows that his
mission was by no means easy. He stood out against everybody
(against almost all his friends and acquaintances—and almost
against his own people). The more confused the others were, the
more clear-sighted he was. Uncompromisingly! They were all
guilty, not only of a political lapse, but of a crime against the
spirit as he saw it and he nailed them down for it—artists and
critics who had failed in the decisive moment of their lives. And

this was a feeling shared by a small number of the young people then. Many volunteers stumbled into the trenches of Lange-marck, Ypres, Verdun and the Eastern Front, with the blessings of their favourite authors and the false claim of the politicians that the international brotherhood of men was no longer valid and that there was every good reason why they should be hurled into the fateful and inevitable inferno of heavy bombardment and every good reason why gas warfare should be their inevit-able fate.

"I set up this journal against the face of this age." When I read these words in the very front-line, when I saw the title *Aktion* before me, when one poem after the other gave precise poetic expression to my suffering, my fears, my life and my imminent death and when I found myself among those real comrades for whom the only higher command was that of humanity, then I realized that no divinely ordained fate pre-vailed, no inevitable fate was leading us into this filth. It was all quite simply a crime against mankind. I owe this awareness to Pfemfert and his *Aktion*! Was Pfemfert political? Was the *Aktion*? Did they all become "Communists"? Anybody who has been through a heavy bombardment from about 2,000 guns aimed at a little section of the front, just smiles: the 2,000 guns speak far louder than the Communist Manifesto. You don't need to have read Marx or Lenin then! Man screamed. Stammered. You could hardly expect him to write in well constructed Rilke-type verses—the word exploded in his mouth. That's where the real, the genuine Expressionism was born. No extremism, or radicalism—not the kind of politics commonly confused with diplomacy—no, what was born was the kind of unswerving and unconditional truth which will stop at nothing or nobody—one might almost say not really politics against the politics of war and the subjugation and oppression associated with it, but just the Truth regardless of what one means by it.

In any event, for us young people Franz Pfemfert exemplified this Truth with singular purity.

He was the cleansing agent, the purge, the settler of accounts, the principle of black and white like the wood-cuts or lithographs on the cover of the *Aktion*, on the white rather rough paper, without embellishments or adornments, or over the poems—those revealing records of this dreadful time. Fundamental state-ments. All in all I have always regarded the war as my teacher, but if this question is put to me again as now on the occasion of this series in commemoration of our revered Franz Pfemfert, then I must put on record the extraordinary influence the journal *Aktion* had on me. It was instrumental in setting the pattern for my views on war at that time and for my later thinking. In our state of total abandonment our confusion was great. Faith in our experience, our studies, our culture, had faded. The working-class was divided—indeed in the trenches we never heard anything from that quarter.

But we did hear from Pfemfert! How many times have I had *Aktion* in my hands at night—and felt like taking it across to the English and Canadian trenches. Look, will you. There's this too! Another Germany! Pfemfert was the embodiment of that other Germany. And more. Pfemfert could not have been all this without his faith in mankind. The faith undermined by the powers of war was kindled anew by him. This commitment to his faith made him pitiless to friend and foe alike, this was why the greater defection of an enemy shocked him less than the small defection of a friend. Defecting in this case meant defecting from the absolute. He saw politics as something metaphysical in the totality of its demands (e.g. being not only anti-nuclear, but anti-war and everything associated with it). No tactics, no compromises. He reproached me later for putting on Toller and because the bourgeoisie came to my theatre on the Nollendorfplatz—concessions which were not permissible. Well, I made them and, as it seemed to me, with every justification. At the same time it was good to have him as a critic. His uncompromising attitude, his anger served to preserve purity in the choice of means. He was one of those who would never again shake hands with anybody who had gone wrong (e.g. by being pro-war). (There wouldn't be many people for him to shake hands with today!) But prophets are usually without honour in their own country, as the saying goes (perhaps least of all in Germany). Woe betide the man who turns out to have been right all the time. He always was and always will be punished more severely than the man who was guilty like the rest. You don't have to lower your eyes before him. This is what made Pfemfert inflexible, lonely. A lonely man disappointed and embittered by everything happening around him, he foresaw the events of 1933 with the same clarity as those of 1914.

He was no "apolitical character", he did not ride the wave

of "neutral art", he was not infatuated with art for art's sake nor with politics for politics' sake, he made no deals in either sphere, neither with his person nor with his publishing concern. He remained what he was right from the start, a man working for mankind—naturally a political man in a highly political world—but one whom even politics could not divert from his path.

Recently somebody sent me one of my poems which I had forgotten. It was in the *Aktion*. Pfemfert had collected it.[1]

How many poems from the trenches would have been lost (probably all of Kurd Adler's) if it had not been for *him*, the collector.[2]

Expressionism? Politics?

"I set up this journal in opposition to this age," he wrote. Which age? The age ceased in 1918. Was the time limit a party, which was then not yet in existence? Liebknecht's Spartakus was not founded till later.

Pfemfert's aim lay beyond party politics. I have never received a political request from him—but he printed my poems—I don't even know whether he liked them, but they were from a front-line soldier and that was enough for him. This was presumably his approach to his other authors, too.

What bound us all together was the age we all lived in and it was the age we lived in that also formulated our thoughts. In time we became a kind of collective, but we were no party and Pfemfert was no party-leader. Still out of the exigencies of war the hope of peace was born in the end. Only we were cheated out of it then as now.

His disciples could be divided into various types : "O-Mankind" dramatists and poets making their passionate appeals to "Brothers" who were in fact already threatening to smash their skulls with gun-butts; Expressionists creating a "style" out of historical necessity; Dadaists ridiculing art because they felt let down by it; right, centre and left-wing Communists often as Tucholsky put it, further left than their own shadows; and those who gave up and bowed to the inevitable. Pfemfert remained upright. He never bowed to anything. He never gave up, though he became very embittered. For the group he had gathered about him—and which had survived the war—could have been the hope of a new Germany. But there was simply no leader among them whom the German people would have acknowledged as they did Hitler. So he can only serve as a never-to-be-forgotten example (though he is forgotten already). It is very sad to have to write about such a man—for how great was the struggle, strength, talent that went to the grave with him and his age. And yet again—how encouraging it is that over and over again an age like this produces a man prepared to stand out against it, a calm dispassionate person prepared to engage his talents and everything in his power to change it. And that is his message for us now: there is no fate governing our destiny, it is up to us as human beings to change the conditions, which produce anti-social injustices and cause wars. That was his aim and the aim of his journal *Aktion*, which he naturally wanted to turn into a vehicle for real "action"—was that politics? Was it love of mankind?

Sylvia von Harden
Memories of days gone by

During all the worries of my years in exile I used to comfort myself with the thought: "What a wonderful, exciting, rich intellectual life has been my lot! What extraordinary personalities I have been associated with!" Today—at sixty-eight—I often think back on those countless fascinating literary, artistic and human experiences.

Was it my boundless ugliness that helped me ensnare the *avant-gardists*, great and small? My romantic nature that enthralled them?

In this context I remember my old friend, the painter Ernst Fritsch saying to his wife after the First World War: "That crazy, ugly, restless girl has the kind of charm the loveliest and richest women cannot compete with."

How could I ever forget the day in December, 1915 on which I first met Ferdinand Hardekopf, parliamentary stenographer, poet and translator, that genius of a man to whom I gave my first love? It's been forty years—since he left me in 1921—it's like a dream. I know he was to be my great love, a love which for me was to last a life-time.

His sharply defined profile, his greying hair, the large dark brown eyes under the bushy eyebrows, his powerful nose, the strangely challenging mouth, his lovely hands, the magic of his mind were mine to worship for the seven years I spent with him as his mistress in Berlin, Munich, Zurich, Mannenbach and back again in Berlin. Anyone who has had the great good fortune to live with "Hardy"—as we used to call him—will remember it for a life-time.

He introduced me into the artistic life of Berlin—through him I got to know the glamour and the misery of the artist élite. Since then his poems in *Aktion*, in *Sturm*, in the *Weisse Blätter*, his

187

unsurpassable versions of Baudelaire and Voltaire, his translation of the *Faux Monnayeurs* by André Gide, *Le Rêveur* and *Le Grand Troupeau* by Jean Giono have taken their place in literary history.

Through Hardy I met the philosopher and writer Mynona, alias Dr. S. Friedlaender. Once Mynona invited me to coffee. As far as I can remember today, he used to live in a summer house in Wilmersdorf. So there I sat beside the man whom I fanatically adored, completely enthralled by his thick, silvery hair, his aristocratic features out of which gazed the eyes of a dreamer, his classical nose and the always sarcastic mouth. He made me a present of *Rosa the Lovely Policeman's Wife*. I already had his grotesque pieces *For Dogs and other Humans*, *Red White and Black* and later acquired every book he published. Any man who could call himself the friend of Karl Kraus, Anselm Ruest, Georg Simmel, Alfred Kubin was an unusual personality. I used to send him enthusiastic cards and letters from Switzerland and when I came back to Berlin in 1921 I used to sit beside him every afternoon as he played chess because he confessed to me that he had taken a particular liking to me.

I had expressed the burning desire to be introduced to Johannes R. Becher because everybody always seemed to be talking about him. One evening Hardy brought along the tall, slender youth who in 1916 looked like an Apollo and he aroused a certain curiosity in me. He somehow managed to meet me alone occasionally. Then I would stroke the locks from his brow, gaze into his light blue eyes and study his pale features. This wild and talented morphia-addict was writing like one possessed. He gave me a copy of his first volume of verse, *De Profundis Domine*; I had his books, *Decay and Triumph*, *To Europe*, *Poems for Lotte*, the fabulous Lotte Pritzel in Munich who started a minor revolution among children with her fantastic wax dolls. If he wrote verse like one possessed, he also engaged in politics the same way. That's why I left him again.

One afternoon Hardy introduced me to Ludwig Hardt, the unforgettable récitateur with the uncontrollable temperament, the clear face, the squat figure, a voice that fascinated the whole of Berlin when he presented his unsurpassable imitations of famous actors: Alexander Moissi, Albert Bassermann, Friedrich

Kayssler, Eduard von Winterstein, Max Pallenberg, Rudolf Schildkraut, Ernst Deutsch, Fritz Kortner, etc. How could I ever forget the years he made me his favourite.

Every evening spent with Hardy brought some new surprise, like the time when John Höxter came over to our usual table. He was a man with long black hair, glittering mouse-like eyes, yellow complexion, shaking hands and nervous voice—painter, drug addict, who kept repeating over and over his sarcastic ditty:

> If many a Mann knew
> The real Thomas Mann,
> Then many a Mann
> Would give Heinrich Mann
> His due.

Every day in the Café Megalomania and later in the Romanisches Café he collected as much money as he needed for his expensive vice. He rewarded his little Café Maecenas by entertaining them with his wit, sarcasm and poetry.

Theodor Däubler remains one of my most unforgettable encounters. A Colossus pushed through the revolving door of the Romanisches Café and steered his way straight for our table. Opposite us he dropped into a couple of chairs. I stared at his silvery grey, straggly beard and only recovered my wits when he pulled a copy of his *Star Child* poems from his pocket and pressed it into my hands. He inscribed it with six words: "For the girl who loves Hardy!"

It was from him that I first heard about George and Eva Grosz, to whom I was taken a few years later by my dear friend. John Förste, whose sarcastic poems in *Simplicissimus* caused something of a stir.

As my thoughts range further into the past, I remember the immense impression Franz Pfemfert made on me. It was through Hardy that I also met the *Aktion* editor. Pfemfert, the tough man with the brilliant beady eyes, the pointed nose in the stubborn face, with his sing-song voice, but above all with his political personality, meant an inexpressible amount to me. What heroic courage it needed in those days to smooth the path for the young Expressionist writers. I only fully realize this when I study the *Aktion* volumes which Cotta have just re-issued.

I was already enthusiastic about the pictures of my old friend, Heinrich Maria Davringhausen, the painter, at a time when nobody appreciated this new style. The loveliest women in Berlin were crazy about him. His elegant appearance, his polished manner, his enchanting nature all helped. To this day we still share very close artistic and intellectual interests.

I ran into Ewald Mataré at one of those marvellous Art Balls. His hair already silvery even then, his rather tormented expression, his gentle nature—all this fascinated me year in, year out, as much as his pictures did before he turned from painting to sculpture. He had the gift of telling crazy stories brilliantly. We used to walk up and down outside my house in Friedenau all night long. He would absentmindedly miss the last tram and have a two hours' walk home for my sake. I still call on him whenever I'm in the Rhineland and we have a good laugh over our memories of days gone by . . .

Then came my years of itinerant apprenticeship. Munich first stop. Hardy had written Erich Mühsam asking him to meet me at the station. There he stood on the platform as the train pulled in. I'd have recognized him immediately in any crowd. In 1916 he still had dark brown hair and a dark brown beard. He ran to meet me full of enthusiasm because Hardy was his friend. Zenzl and he really looked after me devotedly.

Mühsam played chess every afternoon in the Café Stefanie. Through the publisher F. S. Bachmair I made the acquaintance of his friend, the immensely tall, gangling bookseller, Leo Scherpenbach, who later edited the journal called *Bücherkiste*[1] and published my first prose piece, a parable called *The Mask*.

Also haunting the place was tall, pale E. M. Engert, whose marvellous silhouettes used to appear in most of the literary journals. He was one of the darlings of the Schwabing *Bohème* (and with good reason) because he was most entertaining. I was one of his ardent female admirers.

I didn't see Hardy again till Lugano—at his old friend Olly Jacques' place, the divorced wife of Norbert Jacques. Her literary salon was the meeting point for the most important artists from all corners of the earth.

I left for Zurich with Hardy following me, till he stopped off in Mannenbach, at that time a little village not far from Kreuzlingen.

In Zurich I had the great good fortune to meet Stefan Zweig, whom I adored. He procured a job for me with Max Rascher, the publisher on the Limmatquai.

Here in this sleepy city I met many artists who were to play an important part in my later life : the painter Ellen Bing and her husband Henri, famous for his drawings in *Simplicissimus*— the very gifted Russian artist M. Slodky—Klabund, with whom many years later in Berlin I was to give a recital through the good offices of Lutz Weltmann, Hans Arp and Sophie Taeuber. I was one of their admirers at a time when this extraordinary artistic couple were still completely unknown and I have remained faithful to them to this day.

Richard Huelsenbeck, the witty, imaginative, charming Dada-specialist pleaded with me to babble one of his poems in the Cabaret Voltaire. Unfortunately I was not able to comply, despite my great admiration for Huelsenbeck, because I had to consider my position with Rascher the Publisher.

I spent my weekends with Hardy in Mannenbach. There we would sit with his friends round a solid peasant table drinking wine—with the lively del Vajo, Spanish correspondent in Zurich, in 1917, later prime minister before he had to go into exile— with the dazzlingly charming Jerwen, who was crazy about old films and had built up a most significant film archive—and with Dr. Buek, the politician now over eighty who lives in an Old Peoples' Home in Paris.

It is impossible to do justice here to all those whom I loved, revered and esteemed. There will be more about this in my memoirs, *My Life with Ferdinand Hardekopf*, and *My Platonic Affairs*.

In the meantime the great romantic feeling is gone. But the so-called "Golden Years" between 1915 and 1930 can in a sense be compared with the present : its Teenagers, Beatniks and all the rest. Then as now there was a generation of lost European youth!

Lothar Schreyer
What is *Der Sturm?*

When August Stramm was asked: "What is *Der Sturm?*" he replied: "The *Sturm* is Herwarth Walden."

Herwarth Walden was the founder of the *Sturm* and the director of the *Sturm* from first to last. What was the *Sturm?* A journal, an exhibition, a publishing house, an art school, a stage—but that doesn't cover it. It was not a society of artists, not an organization. It was a kind of turning-point in European art. This was a magnet which irresistibly attracted the artists who were to change the direction of art in the first decades of the twentieth century. This magnet was one man, Herwarth Walden. Artists from all countries, Expressionists, Futurists, Cubists entrusted their works to him, knowing that this man truly appreciated them, sensing that this man was endowed with the driving power to push them and their works not merely to success but to total victory! Herwarth Walden committed his whole life's energy unconditionally till this goal was reached.

Herwarth Walden fought for this goal with word and deed. Herwarth Walden was no painter or sculptor, he was an artist with words and music. Along with other close friends I shared this fight with him for more than twelve years. We were held closely and fatefully together by bonds of work and friendship, sharing the joys and sorrows of all those years. If the joys were great, the sorrows were even greater. The joys were seeing all the new art and creative work. The joys were many hours filled with scarcely conceivable mutual understanding. The sorrows were that so few people supported the new art, the misunderstandings of the blind, the scorn and contempt poured over our friends and us, the disappointments inflicted upon us by many friends who suddenly turned their backs on the *Sturm*, the human weaknesses and failings, not least our own which impeded the good work.

The name the *Sturm* had been coined by Else Lasker-Schüler, Herwarth Walden's first wife. This was the sign over everything that now inevitably happened. The storm purifies, uproots, destroys. But it also roars through the world like the Holy Ghost. It is the never-ending transformation, the renewal from the ground up, the cypher under which the spiritual truth of the Absolute meets the frailty and hope of temporal existence. Hope —even if often despairing—brings us the joys, our frailty the sorrows.

My first meeting with Herwarth Walden took place between two trains. Lotte Möbius, a girl I had known since childhood, one day sent me a journal of very shabby external appearance called the *Sturm*; in it there were pictures of the kind I painted and poems like the ones I wrote. I knew then I was not "crazy" as many claimed, but that there were people who were striving for the same goals and aware of the same things as I was. The journal came out in Berlin where the *Sturm* Exhibition also was. The journal reached me during the war just when I had decided to volunteer as a "medical orderly dog-handler" in Leipzig. I was so impressed by the paper that I immediately sent a copy of my play *Night*[1] to the editor, Herwarth Walden. I travelled to Leipzig to enlist by way of Berlin. Between Lehrter Station and Anhalter Station I had a bare two hours between connections. Not far from the Potsdamer Platz in Potsdamer Strasse 134a I found the *Sturm*. The art gallery on the ground floor at the back of the house consisted of three narrow rooms. A serious young Jewess opened the door and led me into the gallery. Here I saw, for the first time the pictures which were the fulfilment of all my artistic hopes. Franz Marc, Jacoba van Heemskerck and Heinrich Campendonk immediately appealed to me most. I mentioned my name and asked to see Herwarth Walden. The young girl hesitated a little and looked me up and down with a certain fanatical seriousness—I was being weighed up. As I learned within the next hour, this was Sophie van Leer whose gentle fleeting verses I had read in the *Sturm* with so much pleasure. She led me along a narrow dark corridor into a tiny little office in which sat Herwarth Walden behind a desk. He peered at me through heavy *pince-nez* glasses. So, I thought,

very short-sighted, looking at the characteristic musician's skull
with its long blond hair.

"Lothar Schreyer from Hamburg?" he asked.

"Yes," I said.

He had a cigarette in the corner of his mouth and he offered
me one.

When it was lit he said with gentle irony:

"You sent me a manuscript for the *Sturm*, didn't you."

"Yes," I said. "But that's not why I've come."

He said:

"I congratulate you. Not for not coming because of the manuscript. I congratulate you on the manuscript. I shall publish
it in the *Sturm*."

A great joy came over me. But I didn't say a word of thanks.
I felt this would be out of place with the strange man before me.

Suddenly he said while lighting another cigarette:

"You're a bit young, aren't you?"

"No, I just look it," I answered, involuntarily taking up his
ironic tone. At the same time Herwarth Walden did seem
ancient to me. To me he looked like an old Jew. And he said
with his flippant Berlin twang:

"Thought you were going to tell me why you've come to my
office."

"Yes," I said. "I've just seen a *Sturm* exhibition for the first
time. I'm on my way to the barracks. I'm sort of joining up. I'm
volunteering as a medical orderly dog-handler, if that can be
called soldiering."

Herwarth Walden roared with laughter: "Volunteer-medical-
orderly-dog-handler! Imagine that! Poor unfortunate German
language!"

But at once he added: "But you'll be back. The *Sturm* needs
you."

He said this with open sincerity. He had cast a net of friendship over me which was indestructible.

"I hope I'll be back," I said. "But I'd like to take something
with me. Can I have a wood-cut by Franz Marc?"

"Have you any money?" he asked, straight out.

"What does Franz Marc's *Riding School* cost?" I retorted.

"Can you afford 30 Marks?"

"For the *Riding School*—yes," I said.

He hesitated. "I don't know for sure whether I can sell you

195

the print. Franz Marc is at the front. My wife and I are very worried about him. Frau Maria Marc has written to stop the sale of all his pictures. But as she lists all the pictures individually and does not expressly mention the prints, maybe I can take the responsibility of letting you have it. The copy you have seen in the gallery has to stay there."

He brought out a folder. In it lay a few wood-cuts by Franz Marc.

"Here is the *Riding School*," he said. "This one was also run off by Franz Marc and signed and numbered by him. It's number three. Franz Marc printed only ten copies of his wood-cuts, signed and numbered."

He handed the print to me across the desk. I took it and thanked him delightedly.

"Excuse me," I said, "if I now complete the ridiculous trans-*action*," and laid thirty marks on the desk.

"*Ridiculous* trans-*action* that's good!" roared Herwarth Walden. "Let's settle the trans-*action* then."

At the time I had no idea that the *Sturm's* rival was called *Die Aktion*. And he put the money into his wallet. I stood up.

"Now I have to get to the Anhalter Station as quickly as I can."

He came with me as far as the front door.

"*Auf Wiedersehen!* As soon as possible!"

"As soon as possible," I confirmed.[2]

After a few weeks I was released from service as a medical orderly and went to tea with Herwarth Walden and Nell. Nell Walden was a beautiful young Swedish woman, incredibly blond, incredibly intelligent, yet so charming and feminine that the timidity which usually comes over me in the presence of blue-stockings immediately disappeared. It developed into a life-long friendship.

For many years I was able to observe at close quarters the *camaraderie* of Nell and Herwarth Walden who together dis-covered the artists and poets of the new art movement—and the action group they formed for a brief number of years which even broke down the barriers created by the World War. As an artist I had found my niche in the *Sturm*. Herwarth Walden soon put me in charge of the editorial side of his paper. I shared his sorrows at the early death of Franz Marc and at the early death of August Stramm.[3] Both of whom I only knew through their works. Many other *Sturm* artists and writers from abroad I met personally as soon as the war was over. It was still the burning age of artistic change.

I shared Herwarth Walden's unrelenting battle against the opponents of the new art. I saw how Herwarth Walden, i.e. the *Sturm*, made itself unscrupulous enemies by the wounds which his critical comments inflicted on conceited and often malicious critics. Step by step Herwarth Walden would go over from defence to attack. He was not just right "behind" the new art and its artists as it is often put, he was always right out there in the front line. In battle he was afraid of no art-historian or critic, no matter how distinguished, if that person was lacking in knowledge or insight. Herwarth Walden's blows were such that his victims rarely got over the pain they inflicted. He was lethal, whenever any doubt had been cast on the good faith of his artists and poets. Out of the wounds he inflicted a harvest of hate for Herwarth Walden sprang up which was a constantly renewed threat to the *Sturm* and its contributors; and the effects can still be felt to this day obscuring and falsifying the memory of the *Sturm* and Herwarth Walden.

I know that our battle for modern art has largely been to no avail. Many of us have become "famous", it's true. The works of the famous hang in the art galleries and collections of the whole world, contemporary dealers in twentieth century works live almost exclusively off them and also—because they don't know any better—off commercially-minded fellow-travellers and weak imitators. But on the whole people can still be divided into enthusiastic followers of genuine Modern Art on the one hand and its opponents on the other and the opponents are still in the majority.

Herwarth's sorrow was also our sorrow whenever one of the *Sturm* artists left the *Sturm* to associate with an art-dealer who employed the usual capitalistic practices which the *Sturm* did not use. Herwarth Walden then felt "abandoned". But he always summed up his natural disappointment in the words: "He has to be forgiven a great deal, for he is a great artist."

The most profound sorrow I experienced on the *Sturm* was when Herwarth Walden and Nell Walden, whose combined work the *Sturm* was, had grown so far apart that a separation of these two people became necessary. With the separation of Herwarth

197

and Nell Walden, Rudolf Blümner and I saw the end of the *Sturm* as imminent.

And so it was.

The labour for the creative arts had been accomplished in about a decade and a half. This achievement is part of the history of the art of the twentieth century. What Herwarth Walden was—apart from discoverer, defender and untiring helper of the new art—is known only to very few survivors. Of the musician Herwarth Walden there are only a few songs and piano pieces in existence. Of Walden the man of letters there is a great deal in existence but it is buried in the almost forgotten numbers of the *Sturm* and in the few books Herwarth Walden published of his own. All the same, these works—criticism, polemics, plays, novels, poetry, letters—are among the chief documents of Expressionist literary art. Herwarth Walden's few remarks on the theory of literature are—scarcely regarded—but fundamental insights into the very nature of literature.

Herwarth Walden's literary products are now as good as forgotten, like all the literary products of *Sturm*. As surely and indisputably as Herwarth Walden reached his goal for the visual arts, so just as completely ineffectual was Herwarth Walden —that is *Der Sturm*—in literature. Completely ineffectual as far as external results are concerned. Even though I know the value of an insight does not depend on its being generally accepted, nevertheless the sorrow remains that so many insights are not accepted by the world. New insight into literature gladdens the heart. That our insights were not accepted by the general public, indeed scarcely even noticed, is sad.[4]

Der Sturm, Herwarth Walden's creation, slipped through the fingers of Herwarth Walden, its creator. The work accomplished was scattered abroad as widely as the bounds of human endeavour permit on the one hand and the limitations of human failure on the other. All that was left behind was a lonely man who had lost everything, who had given his all, from whom everything had been taken, everything but for the faithfulness of a few friends. I went back to Berlin once more to make my farewells. Herwarth Walden had only a little art gallery left on the Kurfürstendamm—magnificent as to the actual works, but as a place utterly miserable. Miserable because it was laden with misery. Not only with hopeless physical poverty. The art revolution had no radiant centre any more. The *Sturm* time was over.

Every happening has its day and its day was over. Even the Bauhaus finished long since—i.e. by the end of the Twenties. It too was in the same state of decay as the *Sturm* and no radiant centre any more. Herwarth Walden knew that his work for the art revolution was finished. He still had hopes of aligning Expressionist Art, which had started off as an intellectual revolution, with the political revolution, in effect with the Communist Revolution.

When I came to Berlin to say good-bye, I knew that Herwarth Walden already had the necessary papers and the passport for Russia. He had accepted an important literary commission from the Soviet Government.

We walked silently through the last exhibition.

Then we drank a cup of coffee in a little café and smoked a few cigarettes.

There was nothing more to be said. We just looked at each other. In friendship. That was the only thing that was left. He knew that I respected his path to Communism even if I did not understand. I knew that he respected my path to the Christian Church even if he did not understand. The lack of comprehension was mutual.

When we shook hands and said good-bye there was no trace of irony on Herwarth Walden's face. And I felt only awe now that the end had come.

In 1941 Herwarth Walden was banished to Siberia for reasons still unknown.

Paul Westheim
How *Das Kunstblatt* was born

"Even a publisher can have ideals," I once wrote in the pages of the private Hall of Fame somebody had acquired under the nice euphemism "Guest Book". He didn't happen to be a publisher. Actually, when I come to think of it, in my literary life I have had dealings mainly with publishers who *were* true idealists, obsessed with projecting ideas, presenting intellect and intellectual values to the public: Hermann Reckendorf, Dr. Ernst Rathenau of the Euphorion Publishing house and Gustav Kiepenheuer who had the courage to bring out the *Kunstblatt*,[1] *Die Schaffenden*,[2] and those magnificent monographs on living artists, which began with Kokoschka and Lehmbruck and carried on with Chagall, Klee, Ensor and others. This certainly called for courage and vision; these artists were not world famous then, on the contrary they were extremely controversial figures, to say the least. This was also the case with literature as far as Kiepenheuer was concerned. I remind you merely of Kaiser, Toller, Kasack, Hans Henny Jahnn. And I cannot believe it was chance that these same idealists succeeded in building up publishing concerns which were also genuine commercial successes.

Remarkably enough I was to find this confirmed yet again in the new world. Like the Insel-Verlag which Alfred Walter Heymel had founded to afford the modern literature of the turn of the century some avenue of publication, The Fondo de Cultura Económica, the firm which put out my book on the ancient art of Mexico, was originally an association of idealistic men who had recognized the need to offer Mexican academics and students the specialist literature, particularly on economics, which, being written in foreign languages, was not accessible to them. And it was this same idealistic and non-profit-making undertaking which in the course of fifteen years brought out over 700 books and developed into the most significant and flourishing publishing concern, not only in Mexico, but in the whole of Latin America.

The first number of the *Kunstblatt* appeared in 1917 while the war was still on. Our programme was: "Everything of lasting value in the art of the present." Reproduced in the first number were works by Munch, Kokoschka, Lehmbruck, Barlach, Kirchner, Heckel, Nolde and some gothic statuary. I think one may say all these artists have proved to have lasting value. And many others too who followed in later issues: Klee, Grosz, Dix, Marc, Macke, Hofer, Chagall, Rohlfs, Max Ernst, Schlemmer, Baumeister, Nay, Werner Gilles, Scholz, Marcks, etc.

The idea of founding the *Kunstblatt* was not conceived in the midst of the hustle and bustle of the art game itself—far from it. As a soldier in the First World War I had exceptional opportunities to think about what is called the "art game". In a World War of this kind it's a question of killing time as well as men—this was the "Heroic Time". So in the hours and days which could have been used for playing pontoon or for going over barrack-room rumours, various things became clear in my mind: that a new artistic generation was in existence, creative spirits full of *élan*, spurred on by a new artistic will aimed at intensification and spiritualization. The works of young masters, real masters, were still being virtually ignored, if not totally rejected. For example, a Berlin critic wrote of my friend Lehmbruck's *Dying Warrior*: "This microcephalic statue with the unbelievably long legs and neck will probably find its well-earned resting place in some fair-ground Chamber of Horrors." It was clear to me that these artists who, I was convinced, represented the art of the age, the art of tomorrow, lacked one thing: a platform from which they could show what they were, what they could achieve. To produce this platform in opposition to the apparently so marvellous art-trade seemed to me an enticing, not to say essential task. So the idea for a journal with the modest name *Das Kunstblatt* was born.

Chance—and what a decisive rôle it plays in so many great affairs—chance would have it that one day in the Brigade H.Q. where I was to complete my military career a devil-may-care fire-brand who didn't care for office work at all took over. He soon disappeared again. However, on his first morning he rushed into the orderly room and promoted everybody in sight. He made the lance-corporal a corporal, the corporals he made sergeants and he tried to put two stripes on my sleeve. In view of this I took the bull by the horns and asked him if he wouldn't rather give me a pass for Berlin. "Marvellous," he said, "then I won't have you hanging around the office. Make out a rail warrant for yourself!" As it happens, there was an exhibition of the Secession on in Berlin. By chance I met the owner of the *Graphisches Kabinett* on the Kurfürstendamm, I. B. Neumann, full of enthusiasm as always for anybody with talent and promise. As the exhibition was not particularly exciting and shafts of spring sunshine were beginning to appear, we sat on a bench in the garden of the Secession and there I developed my *Art-Sheet* idea to Neumann just to hear the opinion of a man who had some idea of the situation in general. Some months later when my military services were no longer considered necessary, I suddenly saw from my balcony a man hurrying across the yard waving a paper in his hand. It was I. B. Neumann. He shouted up to me: "I've bought paper. Now we'll start that journal!" Paper in those war-time days was an important item. So I put the first number together. We printed it. When the copies were all ready to appear Neumann, who was an Austrian, got his call-up papers. "Doesn't matter," he said. "My wife and you can bring it out together." I wasn't in favour of that. To start a journal you need money and the idea that we should be squandering Neumann's money while he waged war in the trenches or maybe even in an orderly room, didn't appeal to me. I suggested postponing production till after his safe return.

Two months later in Frankfurt I was invited to dine with a man who had a marvellous art collection. There was a young lady sitting beside me at dinner. And when in the course of the evening there was some mention of the printed but still un-published *Kunstblatt*, she said: "Perhaps Kiepenheuer would be interested. My brother or brother-in-law (I can't remember exactly) has just started with Kiepenheuer. Couldn't you let me have a sample copy?" I gave her one. Just out of politeness really. Kiepenheuer was the famous literary publishing house, which had brought out those lovely little volumes in the *Book-lover's Library* series and also all sorts of exquisite literature. How could they be interested in an art journal? I could already foresee the usual letter coming: ". . . other commitments . . . in view of the troubled times . . . regret cannot take it upon ourselves . . ."

But. Scarcely was I back in Berlin when a telegram arrived

from Weimar. "Our Mr. Kiepenheuer is in Berlin tomorrow and would like you to call on him at the Hotel Fürstenhof." We discussed the plan of the journal in great detail. Kiepenheuer was vitally interested, bubbling over with enthusiasm was my impression. In a word we were "agreed in principle". In the next few days I was to come to Weimar for discussions on the technical details. I relate this episode because it revealed to me one of the qualities of the publisher in Kiepenheuer which I later often had occasion to observe and admire. Instead of becoming immersed in pros and cons, in house traditions and all the other possible inhibiting factors, he was open-minded, interested in new ideas, new possibilities, immediately grasped the importance of new initiative and had the courage to say "yes" when the time came. That behind this talent for taking decisions—one so rare in publishing—there was also sound judgment, is proved by the list of the firm's publications. Scarcely a dud among them.

He had asked that brilliant architect, "lay preacher" in the modernization of architecture and crafts, and untiring advocate of high quality workmanship, Henry van de Velde, to join our deliberations in Weimar. During those discussions van de Velde said something which I have never forgotten and which has become one of the guiding principles of my work: "You must bring out these youngsters as if they were Rembrandts. If you don't believe in them yourself, how can you expect the public to?!" Kiepenheuer himself took this point at once, being already committed to real quality in the appearance of his own books. He procured magnificent paper on which the reproductions came out like masterpieces, had the *Kunstblatt* produced by A. Wohlfeld in Magdeburg, one of the best printers not only in Germany but in the whole world.

On New Year's Eve I took the train back to Berlin. About the middle of January, 1917, the first issue appeared.

Naturally we were savagely attacked. Not only by the eternal conservatives who had a right to resist new developments. "Anti" us was the whole clan of specialists, the "serious" art historians, the gallery-directors, the critics, even the ones on the "progressive" papers. They reached the stage of the most despicable personal insults. We were all too fresh, too full of life and *Sturm und Drang* awareness of being a turning point in art history, too lacking in routine, too lacking in the proper art-school atmosphere.

In view of this resistance on the part of "public opinion" I seriously considered whether it wouldn't be better simply to pack the whole thing in. I still remember I was just engaged in putting together a special number on the nature of sculptural form. But then, when I had the galley-proofs of Barlach and Lehmbruck before me, I thought: "We'll show them!" And what encouraged me more than anything was Kiepenheuer's attitude. He did not let himself be led astray for a moment; he was and remained convinced.

And then quite different voices began to make themselves heard, especially from the young artists out there at the front. After I had published one of Picasso's brilliant pictures, one of his great heads, Helmuth Macke wrote for example: "*Kunstblatt* just arrived. Just after a shell had exploded beside us. Twenty dead. The head by Picasso seemed to me like an illustration of what had just happened." In October, 1917, we brought out a special Kokoschka number, for the first time a pictorial survey of the whole creative work of this great artist. The issue was sold out in a few weeks, we had to print a second run—something quite extraordinary for a journal. The spell was broken, the *Kunstblatt* was "made", the young artists had their platform, were accepted for what they were, namely young creative artists, their works found their way into the art galleries, run by the same directors who had been so "anti" at first, until the Nazi philistine mentality came on the scene and removed this art and pilloried it as "debased". If the *Kunstblatt* was able to do something towards helping the young generation of the time to gain the recognition it deserved and which it will keep in the history of art, then the credit is due to one man, Gustav Kiepenheuer, who for years put his great publishing concern, his means, his personal efforts, his organizational and technical experience and his faith in the significance and the cultural achievements of these young artists into this journal and the numerous artist monographs and art books which grew up around them.

Hermann Kasack
Wolf Przygode and *Die Dichtung*

The two journals in which the first wave of Expressionism found visible expression bore the names *Sturm* and *Aktion*, names so characteristic of the fighting spirit of those years. Both journals had been appearing in Berlin since 1910 and 1911 and in their own way (and often with the same contributors) they formed the reservoir and starting-point of *avant-garde* painting and literature. A more temperate title was the monthly called *Die Weissen Blätter*, 1913–20. It was superior in quality and size. It sought to document and make the substance of literary Expressionism amenable to the public as it developed through different stages.

In 1918 the first issue of a journal with the pretentious sounding title *Die Dichtung*[1] began to appear at irregular intervals. This was an undertaking which in its design followed fundamentally different aims and intentions from any other journal before or after it. This becomes obvious from the story of its birth, which must now be told.

During my time in Berlin in 1915 I had got to know another law student barely a year older than myself who was surprisingly well-read in modern literature and unusually receptive to new impulses. His name was Wolf Przygode (pronounced with a "sh"). His father, a leading educationist and at that time director of the Mommsen-Gymnasium, had written a Greek primer which I had used at school myself. After only a few meetings Wolf Przygode and I were close friends and in complete agreement on all the literary problems which concerned us.

On his initiative and after some thorough ground-work we began to organize private readings in May, 1916, in order to present our conception of what we understood by poetry to more public scrutiny. We typed the programmes and invitations ourselves, thus giving them the personal touch, and sent them to a small circle of acquaintances mostly older than ourselves. Possibly about forty persons would turn up regularly and then depart after the poetry reading without comment or further conversation.

In general we read the passages we had selected after long deliberations alternately. From the end of May till the middle of July five readings took place. Today, forty-five years later, it is very revealing to see what was read. This is why I want to quote in detail from a few programmes I have among my papers. It must be remembered we were only twenty years old and the war was on.

On the first evening, May 29th, 1916, we read: *Poems* by Ernst Stadler; *Going for a Walk* by Heinrich Mann; *Man Screams* by Albert Ehrenstein; *Fairy Tales* by Fjodor Sologub; *On Ibsen* by Frank Wedekind. On the second evening: the poems *To the Reader* and *Sarastro* by Franz Werfel; *The Leprous Forest* by *Kasimir Edschmid*; a short story by René Schickele (in place of the originally planned chapter from his novel, *Benkal, Comforter of Women*); the poems *Ode to Youth, The Ultimate, Smiling* by Hermann Kasack; Leonhard Frank's short story *Gothic*; Rudolf Kurtz's essay, *The Young Poet*; one chapter from Franz Blei's *Modern Man*. On the third evening, poems by Stefan George and Ernst Blass were read, prose by Lothar Treuge and Ludwig Klages' *Stefan George's artistic faith*. The fourth evening was dedicated to French literature, the contributions were read partly in the original, partly in translation. The vast programme, which in all essentials was put together by Przygode, deserves to be listed in full because it shows as far as literature was concerned there were no trenches: Henri de Régnier's poem, *Twilight Picture*; Ernst Stadler's essay *Jean Christophe*; a chapter from Romain Rolland's *Jean Christophe, L'Aube*; Paul Claudel's poem, *Charles Louis Philippe*; Jean Viollis' *Étude sur Charles Louis Philippe*; the second chapter of Charles Louis Philippe's, *La mère et l'enfant*; a Jules Romains poem from *La Vie unanime*; the end of André Gide's *An Experiment in Love*; Paul Fort's *Night Ballad*. Then after the interval: extracts from André Suarès' *Light at the Heart of the Gem-Stone* and *Psalm of Excess*; Jacques Rivière, *On Claudel*; acts two and four in part of Paul Claudel's, *L'annonce faite à Marie*; Pagoda, Ballad; Edmond Pillon's *Francis Jammes*; Paul Claudel's poem, *Saint François-Xavier*; Francis Jammes'

Baptismal Psalm; J.-J. Rousseau and Mme. de Warens' *Prayer for one last Wish.* That seems to me to be a company no one needs to feel ashamed of. On the last of these evenings we read, among other things, poems and prose by Else Lasker-Schüler, Georg Heym, Rilke (from *Malte Laurids Brigge*), René Schickele (*Whitsun*), Theodor Däubler, Georg Trakl, Gottfried Benn (*Express Train*), Paris von Gütersloh and we closed with Nietzsche's *The Sun Sets.*

This last evening, too, included contributions by poets who were then practically unknown to the general public and who are now counted among the most significant of their time. Before the start of the second cycle of readings in winter 1916–17 we wrote a letter to the participants to the effect that the readings would only be continued if "there is the assurance that everybody accepts the organisers' choice of material. Once again it is unequivocally stressed that the organisers are concerned with one fundamental issue only: to gather together people who are united in their view of art; to form a circle in total agreement about the material presented."

On the first evening of the second series Przygode expounded these aims and intentions yet again. What he said seems to me by its passionate seriousness to rise above the occasion and be characteristic of the spiritual attitude to art of young people in those days: "Much more clearly than on the first occasions when we invited you to join us we see our goal before us and the path that is to lead us to it. Please understand—and please judge our intentions with extreme severity, but also with absolute respect for our cause. What we have in mind with these evenings is one important thing only: to gather together people who believe as we do that art is not merely a form of entertainment, not merely a convenient means of relaxation, but that art is the absolute in human expression of whatever is of supreme importance in life, namely the Eternal, the Cosmic, the Divine. We believe that the nameless flower of great literature cannot burst out of barren rocks joined together by chance. For our part we wish to help smooth the way for what is to come; this we have recognized as our duty and it is one we have no right to evade. You have understood that for us there can be no such thing as modernism or trends. Complete relevance is our only yardstick . . . If we select our programme with such uncompromising one-sidedness, this is because only where we are pointing does the eternal we mentioned earlier, appear to be present. In our work which—I stress this again—is only a first stage, we are utterly dependent on all those with whom we share acceptance of the goal and the path to it. Let us help each other upwards out of barren isolation to a spiritual community. Let us be uncompromisingly honest and pure: the infinite which is to come will be born only in the cold translucent light of a great height."

What was read that evening was: Ernst Blass's preface to the *Argonauten*; Rudolf Borchardt's, *The Book of Joram*. After the interval: Poems by Klabund, *To us is given*; Max Herrmann-Neisse's *Hymn to the Moon*; Manfred Georg's *Third Song for Maria Carmi*; Arnold Zweig's story, *Movement from a Schönberg Quartet*; Carl Einstein's transformations: *The Third Legend*.

From all this it will be clear that these evening readings were part of the "first stage" operation, which then assumed more lasting form with the appearance of the *Dichtung*. Przygode's ideas quoted above, being aimed at some form of communication between work and reader, also determined the character of the journal edited entirely by him. Its impressively large format (25 × 33cm.), its immaculate type-face and lay-out were enough to distinguish it from all similar publications; besides, it was an undertaking serving literary works exclusively. The four books of the first series, intentionally not called "numbers" because the rather unusual term "book" came nearer to the format and intention of the publication, appeared in 1918–19 in the Roland-Verlag, Munich.

Several authors were invited to contribute and one of these, Hugo von Hofmannsthal, wrote on May 24th, 1917, in a letter from Rodaun: "Rudolf Borchardt has told me that your intentions are good and sincere. For that reason I shall be glad to make available such works of mine in future as will fit in with the general scheme of your undertaking—which incidentally your letter does not quite make clear—my only request is that you should tell me which of my works (or sections of them) you have in mind. Baron Andrian, with whom I talked yesterday, will be glad to allow certain of his poems to be included . . ." And on June 9th, 1917: "Now I grasp your aims completely. It is rather difficult to satisfy the request expressed with regard to the first numbers . . . But there are a few poems friends sometimes reproach me for not including in my collected works which, as I recall . . ." Hofmannsthal, who had no copies, then explained where they were to be found.

Georg Kaiser wrote to Przygode from Weimar on April 14th, 1917: "I have read your letter with considerable interest. I welcome the plan for your journal and am glad to accept the place your favourable assessment of my art assigns me . . . By way of greeting I should like to let you have a very short essay *Das Drama Platons*—the embryo for a more extensive dramatic work centring on Socrates and Alcibiades. It is a small token of my earnest wish to be associated with your most promising enterprise." (In the First Book Przygode printed Georg Kaiser's *Friedrich and Anna/Third of the One-Acters*.)

In the introductory preface Przygode, who tended to formulate his ideas almost too pedantically, called art the "last means of expression of creative spirituality" and while avoiding doubtful definitions for the art of his day came down on the side of "the validly formed expression of observed essential content". And picking up once more the idea of communication from the reading evenings, he continues: "Where the personal element of necessity falls away, objectively founded communion can be transformed into deeply felt community, pure in spirit: to prepare the ground for this is the ultimate aim of the *Dichtung*." The First Series contained considerable contributions from Leopold Andrian, Lothar Treuge, Rudolf Borchardt, Hofmannsthal, Rilke, Gütersloh, Heinrich Mann, Ernst Blass, Kurt Heynicke, Georg Kaiser, Paul Kornfeld, Oskar Loerke, Gottfried Benn, Martin Gumpert, Adolf von Hatzfeld, Georg Kulka and myself. In over-estimation of my youthful attempts the Third Book consisted entirely of my play *The Lovely Girl*, written in 1916.

Before the Second Series a Prospectus, prepared by Edlef Köppen, appeared with the same publisher in 1920. In it once again the continuity of German literature that Przygode had pointed to was stressed: "To grasp in their typical characteristics the connections between one age and another—foundation and superstructure—as immediate feeling, being of today, senses them, to link what is already established with what has just taken shape, to establish inner relationships . . . , is the fundamental task of the *Dichtung*." As a special supplement of the *Dichtung*, the *Book of the Dead* had already appeared in 1919, with contributions by writers who had died in the First World War, Peter Baum, Gustav Sack, Alfred Lichtenstein, Ernst Wilhelm Lotz, Ernst Stadler, Georg Trakl. The special edition contained a wood-cut by Franz Marc and an etching by Walter Gramatté. In the postscript were the words: "The aim was to give these few—who include outstanding talents—a chance to be seen in their proper place in the history of German literature and to make sure they never lose it—these few whose lives whether by aspiration or achievement were of decisive value— with whose passing the art resources of today suffered incisive loss." Przygode then gives reasons why he does not include works by August Stramm, Wilhelm Runge and Reinhard Johannes Sorge. The plan for a second special supplement *Book of Women* with works by the most important women poets never came to fruition, nor did the volume *French Literature*, although extensive preliminary work had been completed.

The Second Series began to appear with Gustav Kiepenheuer in Potsdam, 1920, under the journal's own imprint. Lyonel Feininger designed a colophon specially. Two books twice the previous size were published, the second not appearing till 1923. The contributors to the Second Series were: Paul Baudisch, Gottfried Benn, Rudolf Borchardt, Karl Brand, Paris Gütersloh, Martin Gumpert, Max Herrmann-Neisse, Hermann Kasack, Edlef Köppen, Simon Kronberg, Georg Kulka, Oskar Loerke, E. A. Rheinhardt, Friedrich Schnack, Johannes Urzidil. In the arrangement of the contributions Przygode consciously placed things according to their literary genres, and this meant more than an external formal principle: "The arrangement has been strictly in accordance with the three traditional genres (lyrical poetry, prose narrative, drama) plus the newly established one (sketch), because the completely differing demands of each for critical purposes were seen to be as important today as they had ever been." By "sketch" is meant not the "borderline form of the artistic essay", but as a posthumous remark indicates, a poetic process, which presents both "event and immediate reflection on it". Again and again he pointed out that he was not concerned with the individual contribution: "What is important is not the individual work of art, but arranging individual works into an anonymous work of art of a higher order, in order to establish the unity and inner associations of all literature." Hence the words on the dust jacket of the first book of the Second Series: "Joined together here are stories, novellas, plays, poems and sketches, not as sermon and programmatic statement—this was never the true essence of art—but as formulations of something of poetic and hence human value."

This Book contained a supplement: *The Karl Kraus Affair*. In sharply polemic form Georg Kulka and Wolf Przygode tackled the editor of the *Fackel*, who had accused Kulka of plagiarizing Jean Paul. At the time this was a much discussed literary "scandal" which moved even Albert Ehrenstein to write a pamphlet against Karl Kraus; today it lies buried in the dust of time.[2]

To confirm the "unity of all the truly living artistic sensibility in his time" Przygode also included the fine arts in his publications. In 1921 he published his First Folder with original prints and reproductions from sketches by Lyonel Feininger, Heckel, Kirchner, Kokoschka, Lehmbruck, Macke, Marc, Meidner, and Nolde. This publication which selected out of all the flood of possible material exactly what appeals to us and moves us today reveals an astonishing sureness of judgment. The reaction to Przygode's request for contributions was interesting. Lyonel Feininger writes on March 30th, 1919, from Berlin-Zehlendorf on a page from a writing-pad adorned with a wood-cut: "Many thanks for your kind invitation to contribute to the folder of graphic art you plan. I accept with particular pleasure. In the next few days I shall send you a selection of prints to choose from. In the main I have done wood-cuts; I'll include a few etchings as well; but these date from earlier years. Since 1914 I have hardly done any etchings." Feininger then writes exhaustively about the various reproduction processes and mentions incidentally: "My blocks are made from pine wood and extremely fragile, being very finely and smoothly cut."

The first reaction from Emil Nolde on November 2nd, 1918 was quite different. He writes from Utenwarf near Mögeltondern: "I'm always very unwilling to let my graphic works go to series printings, though I should have been glad to make an exception for your sake. All the same, I'm sorry you have made this request and I beg you not to include any of my prints, nobody will miss me and your venture will manage quite well without me. During the last few years I have been doing very little work of this kind." But Nolde did take part after all, though there seem to have been difficulties over the selection, as the following passage from a letter of September 30th, 1919 reveals: "I don't think I have any better drawings than the ones I sent you. Why haven't you used one of them?" Ludwig Meidner writes an acceptance from Cottbus on October 29th, 1918: "On my return from holiday I find your charming request to contribute to an art-folder. I thank you for the invitation and shall be glad to participate. I just have to obtain permission from my sponsor and from the Paul Cassirer Verlag; for I am under contract to Herr Cassirer." In a letter of March 20th, 1919 he writes: "I am now prepared to etch you a plate for the folder you have planned. I shall probably decide to do an old woman's head which I have studied and worked over many times. I should be very grateful, incidentally, if you could let me have a nickel zinc plate fairly soon (for dry-point, because this is the only technique I can consider, etching blurs and washes out the delicate charm of the hand-drawn line) . . ."

The Second Folder then included *Sixteen Coloured Sketches from the Sketchbooks of Franz Marc*, reproduced magnificently in collotype by the Imperial Printing Works in Berlin.

Also appearing under the *Dichtung* imprint in 1921–22 were separate publications in smaller format by some of the contributors; Paul Baudisch's Tragic Operetta in one act, *Adultery*; Martin Gumpert's Poems, *Homecoming of the Heart*; Hermann Kasack's sequence of poems, *Stadium*. A special printing of Hermann Kasack's poem, *The Year's Song*. Simon Kronberg's prose piece, *Chamlam*, Georg Kulka's *Requiem*; Oskar Loerke's sequence of poems, *Pompeii*.

At the end of the few books of the First Series Przygode gives in each case a survey of those works which he considers to be decisive contributions to the literary climate of the time. This list is an extremely remarkable literary-political attempt to "survey and evaluate", as he puts it, "the whole literary production in Germany for the last thirty years". How great his feeling of responsibility was can be seen from the fact that apart from new books which he treated as a whole, in the case of collections of stories he might single out only one particular story or another as being any good. Criticism was understood as an organizing act of will, not as "leaving it to the judgement of history". It was an obligation "to clear the ground of what was dead and useless for what was recognized as alive and significant for the future". It would be extremely rewarding if some young literary historian were to examine these ideas on the basis of the concrete examples available in his work.

Perhaps something from one of his letters will give some idea of what he saw as *the* criterion for literature, with his own journal in mind: "Not communication by means of words, but transformation into words." In the postscript to the Second Series with which Przygode closed his venture in 1923 he once again differentiates between the ideals of the *Dichtung* and the increasing literary commercialism and journalism, not without a note of sadness underlying the main accusation. Doubt and disappointment can be heard in the concluding words: "Indeed it may well be the case that every musical and artistic effect of a word is the consequence of a confusion, not intrinsic to the intention but a product of some accidental crossing of thought with imagination, not—as we like to believe—its ultimate sense. But yet: if this is a mistake, could there be a more laudible one?"

The essence of an age, the picture of its literary life, "the poor public figure of the poet", as Loerke once put it, can be better seen and determined from journals than from books. What Schiller's *Horen*, Schlegel's *Athenäum*, Kleist's *Phöbus*, Arnim's *Trösteinsamkeit* were for the 1800's, the *Dichtung* was for the years of flux in which the great art revolution of Expressionism took place. As can be seen in retrospect today, in every individual publication it lays down in clear terms the foundations of the New Art. Always with an eye to tradition Przygode attempted to seek out from the writings of the time what convinced him as "Dichtung" (literary work of art), as realization or promise of something new, as "the start of a rising graph". His aims find expression in the words with which he closed the First Series in 1919: "With reverence (for us this goes without saying) let us do what we can for the best possible art of today in the best possible form of today. Where we fail or may fail in the future as our work goes on . . . let our personal shortcomings be severely criticized, but let there be due recognition for the meaning and value of what we are doing." All the pride and faith of his youth can be heard in these words.

Wolf Przygode died young at the age of thirty-one in 1926. My record of the memorial service is contained in the volume of essays *Mosaics*, which includes my commemorative address to him. I knew most of the contributors to *Dichtung*, some very well, others less so. But we were never really a literary circle with *Dichtung* as its literary organ. Przygode always stressed

that. Only very few are still alive : apart from myself only Paul
Baudisch, Kurt Heynicke, Paris Gütersloh, Friedrich Schnack,
Johannes Urzidil. I wonder if they still remember the *Dichtung*
days?

Wieland Herzfelde
How a publishing house was born

Only the fact that even two years after the outbreak of hostilities the imperial régime still considered itself as unshakable as the Rock of Gibraltar, can explain how it was possible for a group of artists to print and distribute their opposition to the war—for some months even legally—despite wartime censorship and the supreme powers of the Governor General in Prussia. Perhaps they were exonerated because, though members of the opposition, they had nothing to do with the Socialists or the Labour Movement. No Prussian Criminal Superintendent would have dreamt of looking for revolutionaries among painters and poets in those days. One can see why. Had not ninety-three respected German artists and professors at the outbreak of war voluntarily attested to "*their* Kaiser" that Germany's war was a just one, and that all non-Germans were some kind of vermin on the face of the earth. Even those who had not given their approval to this sad document of 1914-type *Gleichschaltung* were at best cosmopolitans, pacifists, or individual anarchists—harmless cranks who didn't like the state much, but for whom revolution was no more than an inflammatory phantasy.

Who in Germany was aware then of Lenin and the Bolsheviks? Certainly no intellectuals. Most artists had hardly even heard of Marx and Engels. Not one of those who looked to Rilke and van Gogh, Hofmannsthal and Chagall, Rimbaud and Picasso, Stefan George and F. T. Marinetti as their mentors had ever read the Socialist classics. Certainly before the war they had contributed to journals with names like *März* and *Pan, Sturm, Aktion, Der Anfang, Neue Kunst* and *Revolution*.[1] But these journals folded up at the beginning of the war or they became completely unpolitical. (In 1917 the *Aktion* did again start publishing something besides "pure art".) The politicians who had been on the staff of these journals or edited them either fell silent or they folded up. Only very few artistic contributors to these journals refused to be silent—perhaps because they knew nothing about politics and so were scarcely aware of the danger of what they were getting at. They couldn't grasp why Gogol's or Verhaeren's art should lose its value as a consequence of differences between some potentates. They wanted to go on writing and painting like before the war and thought back wistfully to their discussions with French, Russian and Italian Bohemians. Shoot at them? No, that would have been treachery. So it was a point of honour not to help the war effort. They couldn't kill their own brothers. This professional solidarity and faith in internationalism would not have sufficed to turn distaste into opposition. The mourning for fallen friends, the emotional rather than intellectual indignation at mass-murder and at government lies, the hatred for those who had the audacity to send call-up papers to free men, the contempt for those who could write as Gerhart Hauptmann did:

The campaign cannot really live
Till I've been riddled like a sieve

the sorrow at the illusions about "Humanity" destroyed by the war—these were all conditioning factors; and another was a front-line soldier (called a Field Grey in those days).

This particular Field Gray, a poet by profession, was me. Eighteen years old at the outbreak of war, I had volunteered immediately. Not from any enthusiasm for the war. The schoolmasters and bureaucrats (at the time this was the worst term of abuse I could think of: bureaucrat) were the ones who had instigated the war. That was obvious. But it was equally clear that my young friends would be the ones to pay for it. A feeling of solidarity told me: one must do what one can. I volunteered as a medical orderly. A medical orderly cannot be a murderer, or so I thought. So I played my part in the mass-murders of Flanders 1914–15.

The lads of Dixmuiden and Langemarck whose legend Hitler is again using to entice the young Germans of today to their doom were the lads I helped to drag out of the line on stretchers to the overcrowded field hospitals. I saw them lying on beds of stinking straw, breathing their last in blood and filth. And my eyes began to open. I began to get more and more difficult, contradicted my superiors, felt I was an "accessory to murder" and said so openly to escape my own feelings of self-contempt. The result was peculiar: by the end of January, 1915 I was sent home, a physically healthy returned soldier "not worthy to wear the Emperor's uniform" any more. How humane the treatment of awkward agitators was in the first years of the war! It wasn't till autumn, 1916 that I was compulsorily "deemed worthy" again and sent back to the Western Front in the infantry.[2]

In Berlin I found my friends poisoned with hate, but inactive. Many were still wearing uniform. Franz Jung was at the Eastern Front, Alfred Lichtenstein was already dead. On the way to the front in 1914 the whole country went wild with enthusiasm. And we swallowed our opposition. Now the whole country had gone quiet. It seemed to me now was the time to get ourselves a hearing. I applied for permission to publish a paper, an art journal. And in June 1916 the paper actually appeared. It caused something of a stir, not least because in it drawings by George Grosz were published for the first time. The title *Neue Jugend* didn't mean a thing: a school magazine with this name had existed before the war in Charlottenburg; founding new papers during the war without special permission was forbidden; so we bought the name and to fool the censors we began with Number Seven at page 127.[3] On this first page a poem *To Peace* by J. R. Becher, which was revolutionary rather than pacifistic was printed.

The periodical carried contributions by Theodor Däubler, Else Lasker-Schüler, Albert Ehrenstein, Richard Huelsenbeck, E. J. Gumbel, Gustav Landauer, Leonhard Frank, Franz Jung, George Grosz, Davringhausen, Carlo Mense, apart from the "foreign foes", the French Jouve and Seurat, Ensor the Belgian, Chagall the Russian. The glosses were far more political than the rest of the text. Here are a few samples:

"Archaeologists please note: A not yet extinct Stone Age race.

In the German University Newspaper, Nos. 21/22, Vienna, 20th June, 1916 the following could be read in an article by Major D. Kressmann:

'The word supra-nationalism was invented by Hermann Hesse, the writer now living in Bern. He himself says that he values peace more highly than war and finds peace-work nobler and more valuable than war-work. So he will probably count

himself a pacifist and find a like-minded friend in Herr
Förster.

'How is it possible in the face of this war which sets all the
nobility of our German spirit aflame, brings all our virtues to
fruition, broadens our vision of the future, a war which has
clarified and spurred on our united national consciousness to
take up a cultural and civilising mission for the advancement
of all mankind in freedom, morality and refinement not merely
as a serious and onerous task, but to pursue it with everything
in our power—how is it possible, I say, for a German to claim
quite coolly in the midst of this infinitely great and, for our
people, uplifting and sublime conflict that peace-work is nobler
and more valuable than war-work?'

"Which prehistorical museum wishes to acquire the option on
Major Kressmann's body while he is still alive? (E. J. Gumbel.)

"*demain*, pages et documents. Genève. 1916. Nr. 1–7. Directeur
Henri Guilbeaux, éditeur J. H. Jeheber.

"The journal *demain* fights for peace! It informs you in French
that there are other documents than ultimatums and scare stories
about Belgium. *demain* unmasks the "big Press", serves those who
do not serve governments. For the cause of the Fight for Human
Freedom we should like to put up a neon-sign for *demain* on the
Unter den Linden. (W.H.)"

Besides our journal there also appeared in 1916 the *Almanac
of the new generation for the year* 1917.[4] Later the *First George
Grosz Folder* and shortly after that the *Little Grosz Folder*.[5]

In the postscript to the first number (No. Seven) of the *Neue
Jugend* were the words: "We are merely taking over the title
of the *Neue Jugend* . . . we do not intend to be a purely literary
avant-garde journal: *the time has come for all intellectuals to
unite against their sworn enemy!* At first, however, artistic
matters *will* form the main body of our paper: we live in an
age of manifestos . . .

"All freedom-minded people (Expressionists, Followers of the
Youth Movement, etc. . . . .) will find a platform in the *Neue
Jugend*. The limits of our publications will be set only by the
basic conception, the efficiency of the censor, the number of
pages and our temporary incapacity to pay fees for contributions
. . . All European artists and intellectuals who are not senile,
sober and submissive are invited to contribute and help."[6]

The "efficient censor" let three numbers through. Then I was in the Emperor's uniform again and back to the Western Front. Thanks to my brother's help, another number did appear in October and in February/March 1917 yet another double number of the monthly. Then, however, it was not a case of an issue being banned now and again, the whole journal and the whole firm was banned. What was to be done? Franz Jung had an idea: my brother (who was not a minor) presented a petition to General von Kessel, Governor of the Prussian Marches. The petition ran:

The *Neue Jugend* has been banned. In it a novel called *The Malik* by Else Lasker-Schüler was appearing in instalments. We are under contract to publish the whole novel which is the story of a Turkish prince, in other words an *Ally*. We beg permission to open a publishing firm with the sole aim of publishing this novel. The firm would bear the name of the novel to be published —the Malik-Verlag.

This permission was granted. Else Lasker-Schüler's novel—symbolic-romantic prose, which in reality had as little to do with Turkey as with any other country, appeared years later in the Paul Cassirer-Verlag.[7] What appeared only a few weeks later in the Malik-Verlag was the *Neue Jugend* again. In the meantime its character and format had completely changed. Copies of the monthly had the usual magazine format and were twenty to forty pages thick. Now the *Neue Jugend* appeared as a newspaper in gigantic, American format, with colour printing rather like a poster. The first number was described as the Weekly Edition. The next Prospectus for the Little Grosz Folder. Nearly all the contributions were anonymous. Some characteristic titles: *The Sect 1917; The Need for Resistance; Can you ride a Bike?; Pray with your Skull against the Wall; The New Man; Religion of Extravagance.*[8]

In these two numbers (the printer went on strike over the third number, which was to appear printed white on black crêpe paper—to symbolize death as the Ruler of the Age) the German political version of Dadaism made its first appearance. The address given for the publisher was that of a disused building-site in Steglitz, in reality my brother was living in a Berlin barracks, while I read the proofs during a heavy bombardment of the Witchaete sector in Flanders. Not surprisingly, we could do nothing personally about distribution. This was handled for us superbly by the firm of Georg Stilke, Berlin. It had the monopoly for all railway bookshops and agencies serving the army. We delivered a complete sample edition to it for nothing. Folded so that none of the contents could be seen. Sure enough, the paper reached Jerusalem, Warsaw, Northern Italy, and Ostende. German organization . . . ! The Malik-Verlag circle of authors was not content with that. So-called *Neue Jugend* Authors' Evenings were held in Berlin, Leipzig, Dresden, Munich, Hamburg, Mannheim. They served more as anti-war agitation than as propaganda for the paper. Once in Berlin during the winter of 1916, Gertrud Eysoldt, the well-known actress, gave a reading from the *Almanac of the New Generation*. She recited a poem called *Human Sacrifice* by my father, Franz Held, who had died before the war. It ended with the words:

> *I was born the Kaiser's, went and soldiered.*
> *And a mother lost her son.*
> *One?! Millions of sons died and mouldered—*
> *And the Kaiser's cruel sun shone on.*

Tremendous excitement seized hold of the people filling the Meistersaal in the Köthenerstrasse. There were shouts of: "Down with the War! Down with the Kaiser!", women screamed and wept. People were carried out fainting. Only with great difficulty did the police officer on duty manage to get a hearing and declare the assembly closed. That was the first time during the war a meeting had to be wound up.[9]

Only very gradually did our firm develop after the war into what might be called a real publishing house. But it never became this in the looser sense of the word, publishing the word of the poet for mere material gain. Even long after it had become the representative left-wing publishing concern, it was still governed by the law it had started with, the law of the struggle for freedom, culture, and the dignity of man. The persecutions during the Spartakus battles, the prosecuting counsels of the republic, Dr. Goebbels himself, who had approximately 400,000 Malik volumes confiscated—nothing could make the firm deviate from its chosen path. But the firm learnt something in the course of its twenty years' history. In 1916 we were few in numbers.

222

And—though our isolation hurt us deeply—we were proud of our scarcity value, proud of what we considered our exemplary attitude. We appealed to all, but really only to the "ones who mattered". The October Revolution taught us that these are not few, not some special élite. Born out of the struggle against war which every artist must wage simply out of love for life and his fellow-men, the firm would have been without an aim after the war if it had not grasped very early that its function was to lay bare the causes of war and to fight them in peace-time, more than ever.

Raoul Hausmann
Club Dada. Berlin 1918-20

There is no doubt that the word Dada—hobby-horse—was used by a group of young artists for the first time in Zurich in February, 1916, without any clear definition of what characteristics made it different from any other movement. The Dadaism of Zurich was different from the Cubist and the Futurist movements in the first instance because it did not have any programme, in the minds of its founders it was a protest against antiquated aesthetics and against "reasonable" rules for literature. In Berlin Dadaism was able to gain a hold in 1918, because the journal *Die Freie Strasse* offered a psychological base to work from. The *Freie Strasse*[1] was founded in February, 1916 by Franz Jung and Richard Oehring, its contributors were: Otto Gross the psychologist, Georg Schrimpf the painter, later joined by Raoul Hausmann and Johannes Baader; Richard Huelsenbeck was in the eighth issue, the Dada number.

Die Freie Strasse stood for a new kind of anti-Freudian psychoanalysis. It was Otto Gross who had found the basic formula: that of the conflict in the development of personality between what is one's "own" and what is "alien". This meant a departure from the Freudian formulation that the ID and moral inhibitions result from awareness of the Oedipus complex. The writers and painters associated with *Die Freie Strasse*, who included George Grosz and John Heartfield in their number, developed a new approach to society and to art by accepting that all intellectual creativity represents a kind of self-educational process for man, in which routine and conventions have to be ruthlessly wiped out.

This was the intellectual ferment into which Richard Huelsenbeck[2] threw the word "Dada" on his return from Switzerland in the spring of 1917. After Huelsenbeck's first tentative mention of it on the occasion of a poetry reading in March, 1918 in the I. B. Neumann gallery when he quite unexpectedly spoke about Dada,[3] and after various consultations with Franz Jung,[4] George Grosz, Raoul Hausmann and John Heartfield, the "Club Dada" was launched for propaganda purposes at the beginning of April, 1918 and the first Dada evening fixed for April 12th.[5]

Huelsenbeck wrote the first *Dadaist Manifesto*, which was signed by Tristan Tzara, Franz Jung, George Grosz, Marcel Janco, Richard Huelsenbeck, Gerhard Preiss, Raoul Hausmann. This was the first move away from the anti-aestheticism of Zurich.[6] If there were still a few "existentialist" ideas haunting this first manifesto, then this was certainly no longer the case in the "manifesto against the Weimar way of life"[7] published by Hausmann about the end of April, 1918. In it for the first time the reaction against all traditional morals and aesthetics is quite pronounced thus drawing a line of demarcation between the Berlin movement and the Zurich one. One elementary difference between the two movements lies in the fact that Dada in Switzerland could take the form of an "artistic game", while Berlin had to face the conflicts created from the war and then by Bolshevism.

When Huelsenbeck introduced us to his *Fantastic Prayers* and the Cabaret Voltaire in 1917, the group saw the direction the battle for the New Art could take. Two basic attitudes crystallized: one tendency was a kind of satirical super-realism, the other abstract art. In the fine arts this tendency was adumbrated by the invention of Photomontage (Baader, Hausmann, Heartfield, Höch, Grosz) which introduced different points of view and perspective levels simultaneously into pictorial representation, rather like superimposed film; in literature it was characterized by the significance attached to the "Unconscious" and to automatism, as Hausmann's *Manifesto on the Laws of Sounds* and his *Sound Poems* showed (1918).

The deliberately new intellectual attitude of the Berlin Dada group was underlined by the fact that the readings pursued certain revolutionary but not, as is constantly and falsely repeated, Bolshevik aims. In various public manifestoes they waged war on bourgeois rubbish, wrong-headed Expressionism and empty rhetorical Idealism.

The Club Dada put on twelve evenings and matinées: April 12th, 1918 in the Neue Sezession in Berlin; June, 1918 in the Café

Austria; April 30th, 1919 in the I. B. Neumann Graphisches Kabinett; May 24th, 1919 in the Meistersaal in Berlin; two matinées on December 7th and 13th in the Tribune Theatre; Dresden and Leipzig in January, 1920; March, 1920 in Teplitz-Schönau and two evenings in Prague.

The journal *Der Dada* was founded by Raoul Hausmann in June, 1919; the third number was edited collectively for the Malik-Verlag by Hausmann, Heartfield and Grosz.[8]

Individual functions which caused public uproar were: the public address by Baader in Berlin Cathedral on November 16th, 1918 (We don't give a damn for Jesus Christ) and the distribution in the National Assembly in Weimar of a pamphlet called *The Green Corpse*, in which Baader demanded the seizure of Government by the Dada Central Office.

The first exhibition (May, 1919) of Dada painting and sculpture was put on in I. B. Neumann's Graphisches Kabinett.[9]

The climax and the end of the "dada club" was the great "International Dada Exhibition" in the Burchard Galerie in Berlin in the year 1920.

Richard Huelsenbeck had the *Dada Almanach* published in the Erich Reiss Verlag in Berlin 1920 and he also published a little book *En avant dada* in the Steegemann Verlag in Hanover.[10]

Political events and disagreements among the members brought about the natural dissolution of the Dada movement.

This movement has made valuable contributions to individual and mass psychology as well as that of the artist and the writer.

Karl Jakob Hirsch
Revolution in Berlin

Letter

The Revolution came as no surprise to anybody in Germany; it had been in the air since the time when even the newspapers could no longer deny that Germany was defeated. It was no longer a question of what for years had been called Ultimate Victory, just of how to change over from war to peace.

I remember President Wilson in one of his declarations demanding the abdication of the Kaiser. Nobody was surprised and discussion of what a short time before would have been sacrilege was wide-spread.

I had quit military service in October because the Berlin Volksbühne had asked for me as their professional adviser. So I was already a civilian when the famous November 9th dawned. That morning I happened to be in the business manager's office at the theatre—he was on the phone. This man, Herr Neft, was an old Socialist and Union-leader who had very good connections with the new, rising power of the Social Democrats.

The telephone conversation was unforgettable, it went like this: "My theatre-manager has told me the revolution is on for twelve noon, have you anything definite?" I was standing by the window and could see a group of demonstrating workers with red flags coming along the Linienstrasse. At that moment Herr Neft said: "Oh, I see . . . you're having a meeting this afternoon at four . . . so nothing can happen till then. Well, many thanks, that puts my mind at rest."

I pointed out the workers' demonstration to Herr Neft and said: "They don't seem to know about the meeting."

That was how the German revolution broke out, not exactly

according to schedule, a little ahead of time, but it was a revolution.

I left the theatre with Wilhelm Dieterle the actor and took the subway to Charlottenburg. While we were down below the revolution had been victorious up above, because by the Reichskanzlerplatz everybody was wearing red rosettes in their lapels. My wife was waiting for me at home. She was very excited and I can assure you we were both very pleased with what had happened. Nothing could have kept us at home that day.

You must understand, my dear boy, when I tell you that for us the much abused Revolution of 1918 was really *the* great time.

Don't let them tell you it was a revolt of the armchair soldiers who were sick of going hungry and doing without. It was more than that. It was really the dawn of a new age; the war was over, absolutely over, and it had to be the last war ever. That was the will of most of the enlightened people.

In those days we all believed in a new and better future. Today only the most fanatical optimists can manage to believe in the reconstruction of a totally demolished world. At eight o'clock on November 9th the Council of Intellectuals was formed. I was a member. The first session took place in the Reichstag, demands were formulated, which did not strike us as in any way world-shattering, like: abolition of the learned academies, socialization of all theatres, nationalization of all professions, elimination of all titles and the immediate establishment of a world parliament.

The words were very big, but the will was not small, on the contrary, we all knew that the old way had to be radically done away with. The word "radical" played a very big part in all these manifestoes, it was almost *de rigueur*. It was, as it were, the precondition for the existence of the New Man as we envisaged him.

But despite all the violence one slogan took pride of place—Love of Humanity. It was our business to put it into practice.

This age, in which young people did make a serious effort to build up a new world, is not to be laughed at.

The magnitude of our aims was in no way out of proportion to our powers, it just turned out later that the revolution had not triumphed as extensively as we had wished. The tragic aspect of the German Revolution was its half-heartedness; the

Germans knew in their heart what was needed, but tearing all the barriers down to build something new went somewhat against the grain.

It was more characteristically German that at one of the protest marches through the Tiergarten park-keepers ran along the column reminding the revolutionary mob to keep off the grass!

The war was over, I had survived it unharmed, while my poor brother had sacrificed his left arm. He lived with our mother in Munich; we met once every year. The war had made life in Germany very tight and miserable. After the hunger years of 1917–18 there was decent food again. With the help of American Quakers we received some ham, which satisfied our hunger, even if it did taste of carbolic. The thick chocolate in the shops was called "Kwatta" and it tasted wonderful. But what we young people were really involved in was much more important than these material things.

We were in a state of exaltation. Spartakus could keep shooting or the reaction keep marching, it didn't worry us, because the New Age had arrived, and Leonhard Frank the writer had proclaimed that "man is good".

It's true peace was no reality, but it did blossom in our hearts. We sang and painted and wrote that there could never be another war.

I became a founder-member of the November Group, an association of painters, sculptors and writers dedicated to the Expressionist view of the world. Exalted feelings for humanity in general had reached their peak. Ludwig Rubiner the poet sang of this in his hymns, Alfred Wolfenstein sang his song of praise to the "comradeship of men". And new journals appeared and we were in everything. The sunshine of human happiness shone high in our youthful heaven, while we were little concerned with the real world in which blood was still being shed.

On January 15th, 1919 Karl Liebknecht and Rosa Luxemburg, the left-wing leaders were assassinated by White Guards. We wrote manifestoes in protest, we claimed public allegiance to any movement whose aim was the liberation of mankind.

I met Eugene Leviné. He was the purest example of a completely selfless human being I have ever seen in my whole life. He died before the firing squad of the summary court of justice in Munich when the Republic of Soviets in Bavaria was smashed.

My dear son, I can give you only hints of the greatness and beauty of this age.

It was a great age, not because there were great men in it, but because the most enlightened of us strove for great things.

Today I can understand the great age of 1918 better than ever. It was not the fault of the men of 1918 that our own age has ended in bloodiest barbarity. (. . .)

Hans Rothe
Theatre: From Sorge to Unruh

In 1920 I met a man in the streets of Leipzig, who had been in the artillery with me and had previously played juvenile leads in the Hoftheater in Gera. His name was Wilhelm Berthold and he was now administrative director of the Leipzig Schauspielhaus. Scarcely had we shaken hands when he roared out in glorious Saxon dialect: "Our dramaturg has scarpered, do you want the job?" The academic career I had been pursuing halfheartedly and really only for appearances' sake came to a sudden end. I became the dramaturg at the Leipzig Schauspielhaus, which was a private theatre under the direction of Fritz Viehweg. Research done since then has proved that Expressionism was all washed up by this time. At the theatre then we were not aware of this, just as we had only a vague idea of when it had all started. In wartime, Expressionistic plays had been banned to protect morale. Hence Expressionism was known mainly from the *Sturm* Exhibitions in the Potsdamer Strasse. Not till 1919 did Kurt Pinthus make us realize that a "Twilight of Mankind" had taken place. Occasionally manifestoes would appear. Nowadays they are treated as important, at the time, however, they were not studied so closely. In 1920 people were filled with the promise of "No More War" and all the things that happened in the decade before the First World War—for the Wilhelminian Age was finished long before 1914—were enough to convince us that we had entered a new epoch of great demands but even greater promise.

Sternheim and Kaiser were the great names in the theatre. In Kaiser's *Alkibiades Saved* (approximately 1919) we read: "Tokens and tokens are a cord of great length that strings praise after praise which summoned you to the final step of the exalting steps." This was a new note. So it must have been Expressionism.

Sternheim, who had written nearly all his great plays before the war, sounded like this: "Wafting by on a wave of white linen. Marking the gulf between us. Let me have a sniff at you, my little dove (he walks in Thekla's wake sniffing). Fragrant!" *Bürger Schippel*, 1913.) Because Sternheim's picture of the middle-class hero had reduced the pre-war public to apoplectic fits of sheer uncontrollable rage, it was up to us to see that he succeeded in doing so after the war. This was not so easy as it seems today. There were even some people who thought him *passé*, although he had scarcely ever had a proper hearing.

My contact with the modern theatre had begun in the February of 1918. Käthe Kollwitz had obtained permission for me to be present at some of Reinhardt's rehearsals of Goering's *Naval Encounter* in the Deutsches Theater. Max Reinhardt, whom at that time I did not know, was the producer. The seven sailors were played by Conrad Veidt (young, gaunt, fiery, with frayed trousers), Hermann Thimig, Emil Jannings, Werner Krauss, Paul Wegener, Bernhard Götzke. The seventh was played by a Herr Schönfeldt, whose Christian name I no longer remember. That was the magnificent casting for a matinée performance which, as far as I can remember, was only allowed to be put on once.[1] A representative of the Admiralty tactfully dressed in civilian clothes sat throughout the rehearsals silently making notes on all the defeatist utterances. At a time when clearly the Admiralty was alone in not knowing about Germany's defeat. *Naval Encounter* is Goering's best play, one might almost say his only one. It is one of those plays one should like to think of as having been written by the Unknown Soldier. It opened our eyes to the long way we still had to go. Reinhardt produced very few modern plays and still fewer "controversial" ones. He approved of Unruh's *Officers*, perhaps this author's best and not fully Expressionistic play, and put it on nineteen times (*première* on December 15th, 1912), at the same time he left his assistant Felix Hollaender to do Sternheim's *Money Box* in the autumn of that year and it was performed only once, though it did run for a couple of weeks later. On March 5th, 1913 Reinhardt's production of Sternheim's *Burger Schippel Esq.* was put on and over that year and the next ran to twenty-seven performances. His greatest success with a "controversial" living author was with Sternheim's *Snob*, which he presented for the first time on February 2nd, 1914. It ran for fifty-six separate performances, a fact which must strike us nowadays as a fateful note to start the First World War on. Not till December 23rd, 1917 did the time seem ripe for him to take up the cudgels again on behalf of a "modern": he produced the *première* of Reinhard Sorge's *Beggar* after its author had been killed. The play had been published in 1912. When it became known through its stage version it was read as one of the first works to embody the Expressionist message—I could not see any message—all through the war people were always looking for a message—any more than I could in Goering's *Naval Encounter*. When they are both read together today this first impression is confirmed.[2] Hasenclever's *Son*, which was played in November, 1918 in Reinhardt's theatre, was not produced by him. But it remains to his credit that he greeted the war with the *Snob* and said goodbye to it with the *Son*. Other plays he did not produce himself were Unruh's *One Family*, Else Lasker-Schüler's *Wupper*, Werfel's *Visit from Elysium*, Kornfeld's *Heaven and Hell*, Arnold Zweig's *The Mission of Semael*—though all these plays were performed in his theatre. But he did produce Stramm's *Forces*, a production whose impact was even more overwhelming than his *Naval Encounter*, for while Goering was exciting by reason of his material, Stramm relied entirely on form. This production of *Forces* seems to me to be the purest, strongest and most selfless contribution Reinhardt made to modern theatre. The eye could see the heavens opening . . . and yet this production has remained one of Reinhardt's least well-known. It was put on only four times. As I remember it, the critics felt this was no suitable vehicle for Reinhardt, they found fault with the play as well as with the production, they failed to realize what the effort he had put into this production meant in the artistic life of this man who was always slow to find his way towards anything modern. About then disgust drove Reinhardt out of Berlin. From then on he turned his back on the moderns, never produced a single Georg Kaiser, and, when I tried to persuade him to do Bruckner's *Criminals* in 1928 he refused.[3]

When I came to the Leipzig Schauspielhaus it was already engaged in lively competition with the Altes Theater, the civic theatre whose director, Dr. Alwin Kronacher, was making the conservative section of the theatre public more and more uneasy with one work of experimental theatre after another. He put on Werfel's *Mirror Man* for the very first time and Unruh's

Square (a new version), he presented Brecht's *Threepenny Opera* as his Christmas offering—eighty performances—and he was always getting indignant letters. The Schauspielhaus operated a little more unobtrusively. The two directors, Viehweg and Kronacher, complemented each other brilliantly, and were personally on very good terms with each other—"we do the under-cover work" was how Viehweg put it.

I really became involved with Expressionism when Hans Henny Jahnn handed me a copy of his *Coronation of Richard III*. Moritz Heimann had already drawn my attention to Jahnn in 1919 when he was awarded the Kleist Prize. I sought him out and with enormous enthusiasm, which I have the greatest difficulty in recapturing today, I read the 289 pages of his play. I read it and announced to Viehweg in typical Expressionist manner: "If this play is not performed it's time all the theatres closed down." Viehweg grunted, squinted at the massive text suspiciously, and took it home. At that time I did not know him well enough to realize that he would never read all the way through such a long play, especially as he was quite capable of coming to the first rehearsal of any play he was putting on without the slightest inkling of what it was about. But from some special Berlin experiences, particularly the productions of Toller's *Transformation* and *Mass Man* (in Fehling's production) I was convinced that it was one's duty to attempt what was most difficult and unusual. Somehow or other I managed to get Viehweg to agree.

Jahnn's play is nowadays normally included in the Expressionist repertoire. We were completely unaware of this then. It was different, it was shapeless—all in all: it was wild. It is almost entirely composed in iambic lines of from four to seven feet. I have no idea with what intention the author did this. Even for a production running something over four hours—a good two-thirds of the play had to be cut. It was perhaps not so much the play as Jahnn's potential that we found so convincing. Casting caused some problems. For Queen Elizabeth we had in our ensemble Lina Carstens, still a splendidly powerful actress to this day. Otto Werther had been chosen to play Richard—he was later to succeed Viehweg. When he had read the play he refused. As it happened, Dr. Kronacher was just starting on *William Tell* at the Alte Theater. The lead was to be played by Fritz Reiff. Reiff, later to be at the Munich Kammerspiele for many years, was a modern actor. I managed to come to an agreement with Dr. Kronacher, the boldness of which only theatrical people will appreciate: the Schauspielhaus lent him Werther to do Tell and he lent us Reiff to play Richard. For many weeks all the rehearsals and performances of two large organizations had to be arranged round these two actors, both of whom liked the exchange. When the rehearsals started to get more and more tumultuous with massed soldiers, sessions of parliament (using hired students), Viehweg left Leipzig for his winter holidays in the Harz. Political conditions in February, 1922 were confused, there were strikes, Putsches—so the play opened before the author could get there. After an adventurous journey he turned up before the final scene dressed in a crumpled, soiled suit. Uproar greeted his appearance, but a great deal of clapping too. None of my productions has been subjected to so many searching conmentaries as this one has over the years. Lina Carstens was highly praised, Reiff too, and a young beginner who played one of the Princes in the tower: Luise Glau.

The visit of Jahnn, the Expressionist, had unexpected repercussions in Leipzig. In the audience for the *première*—where he was always to be found on important occasions—was the Thomaskantor Karl Straube and the then twenty-four year old Günther Ramin. Ramin had been my private pupil at the Thomasschule for some time, because he had to be crammed for the school Certificate in Latin and Greek, and through him I had met the Thomaskantor. We all met Jahnn and then it came out that Jahnn was a great organ-builder who knew the Bach organ better than the two musicians who played it. In short, the outcome of this meeting was that from that time on the "swell", the pedal that made the organ tone swell majestically or fade away, disappeared from Bach interpretations. Straube was so convinced by Jahnn's facts that he re-called a volume of Bach's organ works which he had already sent to Peters-Edition for publication, so that he could revise it. Some details about this little known episode can be found in *Günther Ramin* by Charlotte Ramin, Atlantis Verlag 1958, p.45ff.—a book which must, however, be read with reservations. In 1951 I was in the train from Nuremberg to Frankfurt and got into conversation with an American organist. He asked me why Straube had suddenly stopped using the "swell" about the beginning of the twenties (that's how well informed he was). I was able to tell him. As a result of Expressionism, which at the time just could

237

not help making the intellectual atmosphere in every sphere so highly charged that there were new explosions all the time! That was the only good thing really about our *Richard III* venture. Public reaction can be judged from the newspaper which on January 7th, 1922 contained this and other delightful cultural comments: "Well now, My Lords—if this goes on, gadzooks, there's nothing for it but for public and critics to go on strike, forsooth!"

Naturally it did go on. The Leipzig Schauspielhaus presented Brecht's *Drums in the Night*. In Berlin the last great fight recorded in the theatrical history of our increasingly impoverished century took place when on May 14th of that seminal year, 1922, the audience at the *première* of Bronnen's *Patricide* fought a pitched battle in the downstairs foyer of the Deutsche Theater. The production had been by Berthold Viertel, the actors were Agnes Straub, Elisabeth Bergner, Alexander Granach and Hans Heinrich von Twardowski. A play by the same author called *Excesses* which we liked better was published by Rowohlt, but as far as I know never performed by anybody. Bronnen was an author only for as long as he was carried along by Expressionism. Later he was to reveal not a trace of his earlier capabilities or even his potential. But today the important thing is not the quality of the plays which were performed then, but the amount of oxygen they pumped into that short space of time which might be called the Period of Expressionist Theatre, lasting from 1918 till the currency reform. When waistcoats had to be let out again genuine Expressionism didn't have a chance any more.

IN OTHER CITIES

Alfred Günther
Dresden during Expressionism

In 1905 when I was twenty my father died and I returned to the city of my birth from idyllic Löbau, where I had spent my childhood. The Dresden I discovered then had just added a new glory to its Baroque splendour with the first Richard Strauss *premières* under the baton of Ernst von Schuch. Simultaneously, from the studio work-shops of Heckel, Kirchner and Schmidt-Rottluff came the first signal for the dawn of a new art with the founding of the Brücke.

I had brought back with me scenarios and some poems. Encouraged by Dehmel and Liliencron, I sent them off, but only in 1908 did I find a publisher: E. Bonsels & Co. in Munich. He brought out *Phoenix* my first volume of poems which started my friendship with Waldermar Bonsels. Johannes Schlaf wrote in the red *Tag* that he perceived in it an "Oscar Wilde-like instinct for ornamentation, lavishness and colour". In the same year I wrote my first article for a newspaper, a review of Nietzsche's *Ecce Homo*, the first edition of which had just come out in the Insel-Verlag.

In the following years I was writing for the *Dresdner Volkszeitung* on modern literature, art and theatre. So I also made my way to Hellerau where I got to know the people there. Karl Schmidt and Wolf Dohrn had founded this garden-city as a settlement for *Deutsche Werkstätten* but in no time at all it had become the centre of a rich artistic life. Wolf Dohrn, the inspired organizer, had brought in the Dalcroze School of Eurhythmics, he got Heinrich Tessenow to build its living-quarters and the stylish neo-classical Festival Hall, and inaugurated the Festivals to which the whole world came in droves. This was where Gluck's *Orpheus* was performed in 1912 and 1913 with the Dalcroze dancers and Claudel's *L'Annonce* on the bare, raked stage with lighting effects by Adolphe Appia, isolated, never to be repeated achievements to which the war put a speedy end.[1]

In Hellerau Jakob Hegner began his magnificent career with a tiny printing press and a tiny publishing concern. He had translated Claudel and Francis Jammes, had published the first volumes of poetry by Friedrich Schnack, and in his *Neue Blätter*[2] appeared the first contributions by Theodor Däubler who was soon to become the mainstay of literary life in Dresden. Paul Adler the lawyer-poet had arrived from Prague bringing his extraordinary prose-poems *Elohim, You see,* and *The Magic Flute.* Later, at the time of the revolution, he became politically active and founded a "Socialist Group of Intellectual Workers" which did a lot of practical good. The blond Heinar Schilling, publisher and founder of journals, wrote an Open Letter of Conciliation to Henri Barbusse. From 1914 on I was in the literary office of the *Dresdner Neueste Nachrichten* with Camill Hoffman, the poet and essayist from Prague. Many Prague writers came to see us.

Dresden's forum for modern art and literature was the Bienert household. Frau Ida provided exemplary hospitality for all writers and artists and became a generous patron to many of them. This is where the men from the Bauhaus met, Gropius and Klee; the painters of the latest Secession, Otto Dix, Felixmüller, Constantin von Mitschke-Collande, also Lasar Segall the Russian, who later achieved great fame in Paris and Brazil with his visionary pictures. Mary Wigman the creator of the new expressive dance form was there, and Gret Palucca was one of the family. Treated as friends were Otto Hettner the painter, Hans Pölzig the architect and Oskar Walzel the literary historian. We had Meier-Graefe in Dresden, and Oskar Kokoschka, who had come as a wounded Austrian officer to convalesce in the Lahmann sanatorium on the Weissen. Hirsch in 1917, was recruited for the Art Academy. Will Grohmann gave up his teaching post and became the spokesman of the new art. Licho acted in Kokoschka's three plays in the Alberttheater, *Murderer Hope of Womankind, Job* (with Heinrich George) and *The Burning Briar Bush.* Fritz Busch conducted Hindemith's opera based on Kokoschka's *Murderer.* Walter Hasenclever, the eternal youth, was one of us, Licho had put on a performance of his *Son* with Ernst Deutsch. In the Royal Playhouse, as it still was then, the director Count Seebach had Reinhard Goering's *Naval Encounter* performed. In the following epoch Berthold Viertel and Josef Gielen tackled Expressionist drama and had rousing successes with Friedrich Wolf, August Stramm, Carl Sternheim and Georg Kaiser.

Unforgettable for me is my friendship with the brothers Franz and Friedrich Kurt Benndorf, at whose intimate gatherings all sorts of literary themes were debated. Among those present were Ivar von Lücken, who apart from Dietrich the "Goth", was one of the few genuine Bohemians Dresden could boast of. He, too, was painted by Kokoschka.

At the time of the Revolution the astute, cosmopolitan Hugo Zehder, Heinar Schilling who later went over to the Nazi camp and Felix Stiemer founded three journals: *Neue Blätter für Kunst und Dichtung*, *Die Neue Schaubühne* and *Menschen* to which we all contributed.[3] The three art dealers Richter, Gutbier and Rudolf Probst (New Art Fides) all put on exhibitions which played an important part in propagating Expressionist Art.

In Dresden we had a club presided over by Ludwig von Hofmann, at which all open-minded people were welcome and a Monday Circle of a similar kind started by Fritz Bienert. Life at that time was often exciting. I remember the time Johannes R. Becher turned up at my house secretly one day; he needed a hiding-place at the time of the persecution of the Communists; in these weeks I got to know him better than many others did; Franz Pfemfert also came along sometimes. In 1920 my third and last volume of poems *Exorcism and Dream* appeared in the Rudolf Kaemmerer Verlag.

Friedrich Wolf
Felixmüller (On the Theatre in Dresden)

Nearly thirty years ago in the spring of 1919 I was in a hotel in Dresden with Berthold Viertel the young producer of Saxony's State Theatre when I met Felixmüller for the first time. Viertel was producing my Expressionist play *That's You*. Felixmüller was to design the sets. He was about twenty-two at the time, but already enjoyed a considerable reputation as one of our most talented painters. He was a blacksmith's son and even at school his drawing ability had been apparent by the age of thirteen. In spite of the opposition of his father, who had no high opinion of "breadless art", he was accepted for the Dresden Art Academy at the age of fifteen, thanks to the help of Consul Mühlberg. Besides the usual studies he began to do portraits. The exact representation of human likeness and type was the starting-point for his art. It is significant for Felixmüller that after an impassioned journey through the inferno and purgatory of Expressionism he returned to the realistic treatment of man in relationship to work and society and to the human face as the ultimate expression of existence.

In overcoming the problems of portraiture Felixmüller learnt his craft. In portraiture every line had to be just right. No trickery was possible. While he was working on the stage design for *That's You* he made some character sketches of the producer, the lighting-director and the author of the play for the journal called *Der Zwinger*. And although at the time he stood in the full "May glory of his sins" as a wild Expressionist and my portrait was described by the good citizens of Dresden as a "Tulip in a Flower-Pot", all three portraits were highly characteristic and, for all their extravagances, strikingly good likenesses. The individual was discernible. Here again, despite all the Expressionism, sound grounding in technique formed the basis for his work.

Why did I come to choose Felixmüller of all people? In my play the basic spiritual and dramatic principle was the idea that all existence is a constant flux, that man too—especially man—is in a state of constant transformation from the lower forms to the higher. At that time I had read neither Hegel nor Marx. I was up to my ears in Schopenhauer and in the teaching of the ancient Indian philosophy of the Vedas. Human existence had to pass through many different stages. But everything all around you, everything you pass through: "tat twam asi!" "That is you!" With one foot still in the purgatory of the First World War this was how I saw the problem of the responsibility of the individual: each man is responsible not merely for himself but also for everybody else! Your failure also contributes to the failure of others. The awareness of this compels action—transforming oneself, others, the world! So the whole of existence is not a stone, however much "hard" facts and stony hearts and conditions may make it appear to be so. Everything is in a state of flux, in transformation, a fluid process!

This was the basic idea of my play *That's You*. Felixmüller's job was to translate it into visual effects for the stage. Before we had ever met, Felixmüller had worked with Erich Ziegel, the director of the Hamburg Kammerspiele, doing stage designs for Kornfeld's *Seduction*, in which he demonstrated his principle of breaking down the rigid walls of the proscenium arch, using movable props in place of fixed sets and changing them with the curtain up.

My play *That's You* suited this idea of Felixmüller's down to the ground, the basic conception of the play lent itself to this kind of treatment. The prologue and the epilogue had, as it were, pre-natal and post-mortal "beings"; in the play itself these beings appear in action as good, solid citizens. But in the prologue and the epilogue they flit from star to star, as it were. Felixmüller solved this difficult problem by putting the actors into rigid starched canvas costumes, against a cubistic space made of lateral lines in front of an arching horizon. He had numerous arc lights shining upwards on them from below. At the same time with the lights from below and from the wings he could constantly change the spaces into a tiny little pointed star, a flattened box, a plane stretching into infinity, etc. Dramatically and scenically the most important part, however, was the central part of the play which was a down-to-earth, very realistic story about three men and a woman. An apprentice gardener is incited by a blacksmith to seduce the wife of the head gardener to get his own back on him. The young man resists for a long time until one night the two young people fall asleep under the spell of the moon. And now in their dream the "objects" in the room begin to act out a life of their own. The crucifix as a Cross of Christ, the hatchet as a murder weapon, the couch on which they both lie as an evil woman bringing them together. Felixmüller had to express this scenically.

He solved the problem magnificently, and in a simple and fascinating way. The walls of the room, the coverings of the couch and of a second (much larger) axe were transparent. And suddenly, while the light in the young couple's dream fades, the moon starts to come in through the wall, the "faces" of the crucifix, the couch, the axe start their debate as to where these two lovers and dreamers belong. As the room dissolved into nothing, the two people sleep on in an infinite landscape beneath a gigantic moon surrounded by the conflicting spirits of the "objects".

This whole experience of the twilight world stood or fell with the stage design. It could very easily collapse into confusion. It was Felixmüller's achievement to have created optically and dynamically a stage magic which never for a second released the audience from the spell of the word and the image.

For author, director (Berthold Viertel) and stage-designer Felixmüller this work was an experience, a source of creative happiness such as is rarely found in such harmony in theatre work. After that I got to know Felixmüller as a person. He never tried to conceal his working-class background. Snobbishness of any kind is completely foreign to him. He is too much of a craftsman for that. In those tempestuous years following the First World War he was entitled to try to capture the exuberance of heart and hope on canvas in an ecstasy of Expressionism. No empty formalism! No, his accusing pictures after the assassination of Karl Liebknecht came from the same indignation of the heart as his prints against war and mass-slaughter. They arose out of the same intellectual and emotional view of the world. This has to be stressed: the Expressionism of those years 1918–19 was passionate, honest and active condemnation of all wars, past, present or future. It is no accident that many of the Expressionists of that time—including Felixmüller—were denounced by the Nazis as "decadent". These days we often see in the exhibitions and stage-work of our young artists a dull, completely misplaced, plagiarized form of Expressionism which attempts to trick itself out with "surrealistic" and other quickly adopted guises. Empty dilettante formalism without the artistic passion of a genuine intellectual standpoint, often too without even the technical ability. In those days ours was real intensified expression of an extreme intellectual and artistic passion, exploding out of sheer exuberance....

Friedrich Burschell
Revolution and *Neue Erde*

Munich 1918–19 From my Memories

The German Revolution, which I took part in about the beginning of November, 1918, has since been described as a mere collapse or even as a kind of soldiers' strike.

For us, my friends and myself, and for millions of front-line soldiers, the abdication of the German royal family and of the existing power structure meant not merely the end of the senseless, murderous war, not merely salvation and liberation, but far, far more: it meant hope, the assurance even that out of the chaos a new and a better world would arise.

I still remember meeting Rainer Maria Rilke in the Ludwigstrasse in Munich. I was wearing the field grey uniform of a lieutenant in the Bavarian cavalry, from which, as was only right and proper for a revolutionary, the insignia of rank had been removed. I had just been to see the newly-installed Minister President Kurt Eisner in his office in the Promenadenplatz where he had made me a kind of military adjutant. Rilke came up to me, on this forenoon he was as excited as any of us. The deep melancholy mounting sometimes to desperation which I had observed in him over the last few weeks of the war during my visits to his studio flat in the Ainmillerstrasse now seemed to have left him. I remember how he suddenly held out his hand in the middle of our conversation, opened and closed it a few times as if he were grasping something. "The time is so ripe," he said to me, "it can be moulded into shape." I have never forgotten these words, for they summed up completely the mood we lived in then.

I was living at Akademiestrasse 7, hard by the Siegestor, in a spacious ground-floor room in the once well-known Pension

Romana which has since disappeared. My room had a private entrance and could be entered straight from the street. I was living well at the time. Being sociable I didn't mind the many visitors, the eager messengers with the latest news and all the helpful girls from the neighbouring Schwabing boarding-houses. I especially remember the nights we used to sit, shrouded in clouds of tobacco smoke, talking over endless cups of tea. It must have been during one of these nights that we hit on the plan to capture in print the mood we lived in. We had no thought of a journal in the usual sense, even if only because it would have been impossible to find a publisher quickly. For we had to be quick if we were to get across.

Sure enough, to everybody's amazement, the first number of our venture came out two weeks later, amazement because even then I was far from being a particularly efficient character. It could certainly never have been done at all without the help of friends. Two in particular stood by me: Alfred Wolfenstein the poet, unhappy by nature, but extremely ambitious and enthusiastic, and to provide the necessary balance clear-headed Martin Sommerfeld the literary historian who later died in America in exile.

REVOLUTION. TO ONE AND ALL read the title-page of our 30 pfennig weekly in heavy print.[1] It had no cover, was only eight pages long and with its cheap print it looked like an expanded pamphlet. They tell me it has great scarcity value nowadays. I have lost all my own copies in the course of my turbulent life. I have only been able to rustle up one copy, the one which was on view in the Expressionism Exhibition in Marbach and later in other cities.

From the editorial data I now realize—something I had completely forgotten—that I had put my name to it not merely as editor "with the assistance of friends" but also as publisher. This reminds me of a curious episode. Shortly after the appearance of the first number a man walked into my room, introduced himself as a police officer and asked me if I could produce an official permit for my publishing concern. I had some difficulty in making the man realize that times had changed and that he couldn't behave like a royal bailiff in the middle of a revolution.

What I had in mind with this journal can be seen from the beginning of my preface to the second number:

"The only justification for what is now called revolution, is

248

the realization of the only goal worthy of human endeavour, namely community of love and awareness of God.

Politics are necessary, but their ultimate aim must be to make it possible for man to think about why he is here. Politics are not only necessary, they must be taken seriously, their ultimate aim must be to make man free and natural, to give him back to the earth, to his soil, to let him breathe, to make his time his own and to take from him all the stupid, accidental hardships of poverty and suppression.

For there is still enough hardship left even in the best ordered state and in the best of all possible worlds and it is not politics that can make mankind happy.

Man must know what he is living for; what distinguishes man from an animal is his reason; he must have a goal worth the effort, one that brightens the dark dwelling places of this earth with the comforting light of ultimate certitude . . ."

This is pure Expressionism, if not in language then certainly in attitude. I had started to write like that in Heidelberg before the war, for the *Argonauten*, a journal which was edited by the now unjustly forgotten poet Ernst Blass with the help of friends.

A community of friends was a fundamental part of this movement, which, as is now realized, was by no means restricted to literature alone. Yet it was not a collective awareness that bound us together. The concept of the collective did not crop up till later. We were and we remained individualists and this is exactly what struck us as the essence of the newly-won freedom—that everybody could express himself according to his own nature.

In my case everything, or practically everything I wrote then had some religious intent. I derived from Hamann, the dark "wizard of the north", from Kierkegaard and from Tolstoy. I believed in a God, the *deus absconditus*, who calls upon Man and needs his help to fulfil himself. But I believed in none of the existing churches and in my pious radicalism I took the logical step and left the Protestant Church.

The first number of the journal had been written by my Munich friends as no contributions could be expected so quickly from elsewhere. For the second number a contribution arrived from Berlin which particularly pleased me. It came from Oskar Loerke with whom I had been friends since my student days in Berlin. The article was called "The Voice of the Poet". It was of moving humility, quite apolitical and a long way removed from the ecstatic stammering of the "Oh-Mankind" variety which was just becoming fashionable about then.

My old friend and countryman Ernst Bloch expressed himself in similar terms only more bitingly in the same issue. His contribution came from Switzerland to which he had emigrated during the war, like Hugo Ball, Leonhard Frank and others, in order to be able to protest openly against Imperial Germany. Much as he joined with us in welcoming the Revolution, he could not suppress his mistrust at the way things were developing, and he was to prove right.

But this is not the reason why only two numbers of *Revolution* in all ever appeared. Much more to the point was the fact that it was almost impossible to carry on the business of editing in a boarding-house room not designed for the purpose. Besides a real publisher had been found for it: Walter Schmidkunz, the idealistically inclined owner of the Dreiländerverlag which today no longer exists. He had his rooms right behind the Siegestor in one of the palatial like houses on the Leopoldstrasse. Like other publishers Schmidkunz was in process of adjusting to the new times. So there was plenty to do in his firm. I was able to help him to bring out two series in small format: first of all *The Gateway*, a literary kind of collection.[2] A story of Oskar Loerke's appeared in it and among other things one of my own pieces, the dialogue *On Character and Soul*, which I had written in Heidelberg before the war and first published in the *Weisse Blätter*. This series was followed by a second which, in keeping with the character of the times, was called *Documents of Humanity*.[3] According to the blurb this series was to include "as contributors to the current reconstruction of the world, leaders and teachers of human revolt" from Thomas More by way of Fichte, Kant, Wilhelm von Humboldt and Jean Paul with his "Prayer for Peace" up to the early Socialist Louis Blanc. It was a worthwhile selection of short tracts, at popular prices, selected on purely paedagogical and humanistic grounds.

This was the firm which was keen to take over our *Revolution* in altered and extended form. At the request of the publishers I was to assume sole responsibility for the editorial side and after only a few short weeks a real journal appeared carefully laid out and well printed. To make it even more attractive, one or two original prints were included with every number. It was in the course of hunting for these that I became friends with Max Unold and Richard Seewald.

The title too was changed. *Revolution* did sound a bit too loud and categorical to me, with too great a bias towards pure politics. *New Earth*[4] seemed to me to express better the widespread chiliastic expectations of the time. With this in mind I wrote the introduction to the first number:

"It is the aim of this journal to continue the policies already expressed in the two numbers of the pamphlets *Revolution, To One And All*. It will attempt to gather together all the human, generous and passionately vital voices behind all the uproar and purely political comings and goings and to call for the only thing that matters, the revolutionizing of the individual and the awareness that decisively new things are not possible on this earth if they do not derive from genuine heart-searching.

"It is concerned only with integrity and humanity and hence recognizes no individual considerations of any kind.

"It will not be a further contribution to the hatred which has darkened this earth for long enough; and if it does struggle against falsehood, hypocrisy and all forms of brute force, open and concealed, then it does so with the power of persuasion and an unquenchable faith that while the truths of love may not be easy they have to be recognized in all human relationships.

"For understanding counts for a great deal and men ought to be mature enough to take the fate of the inhabited earth into their own hands and bring it to pass that the kingdom of goodness and light is no longer confined to books and promises."

Such extravagantly expectant language would be unthinkable today. Now that everybody has grown soberer, harder or harder-boiled, it is possible to smile at young people like us who had escaped the First World War. But it seems to me this should not be done out of pity, but in the sad realization of how much the poorer we have become.

My earlier contributors had remained faithful to me. New ones joined us: Martin Buber, Regina Ullmann, Hermann Kasack, Adolf von Hatzfeld, Gustav Sack with a posthumous war-story which Rilke valued especially, and Gustav Radbruch, the famous professor of law whom I had known in Heidelberg, with a lucid piece of work called *League of Nations Minded*, written long before the founding of the real League of Nations.

My own contributions were signed F.B. which later gave rise to the curious assertion that Franz Blei was their author. Among them is one which still seems to me to be valid today. I had tackled Lenin's *State and Revolution*, a work which has since become famous. The Russian variety of Communism was just being born and was still hardly identifiable as such. My review is too long to quote in full. The conclusion is all I wish to resurrect:

"Here is the great adversary; there is still nothing to match it, but our lonely faith. Here the gigantic madness of rationalism has become reality. Here can be seen the last ghostly remnants of Hegelian philosophy, the world-scheme without ethics, the autonomous mobility of the Idea.

"It is true that Lenin will have nothing to do with ideas which do not have their roots in economics; they might make him hesitate to do what must be done immediately and without deliberation.

"All he can see is the injustice of conditions to date; you only have to change them and by the simple principle of formal logic whereby a double negative must produce an affirmative, justice is restored.

"Formal logic, the coldest, deadest, most abstract concept is on the march to conquer the world.

"The object of all this, namely man, does not need to be examined any more closely. He is the product of his circumstances, and formal logic will see to it that he is all right.

"The means for reaching the goal need no justification as long as they are efficient and guarantee control. Afterwards things will turn out right of their own accord; for the present meet torture with torture, murder with murder; later it will all sort itself out.

"There is only one answer to this cold madness; no civilization will hold it back by mere military might alone, only faith in the power of the heart born anew, only faith in something not accessible to any kind of reason, namely the truth that one must first strive for the Kingdom of God and of Love, and that then truly everything else will follow."

My fellow contributors and myself would certainly have continued to speak in this tone, expressing this point of view. But the times did not permit it. Strikes, the cessation of postal services and other hazards of daily life stopped the further appearance of the journal. Besides, Kurt Eisner had been assassinated at the end of February, 1919. I was still in a position to write a brief obituary in which I claimed that he had been assassinated because he was the only political leader in Germany whose guiding principle was his moral conscience. The murder victim was the same man who, as I knew from personal experience, was prepared to sacrifice all his plans and even his personal reputation rather than allow people to be murdered.

The republic of Soviets, in which I had no desire to play any part, soon followed and immediately after that came the merciless "White Terror" everybody will know about from German history, or rather ought to know about.

So the *Neue Erde* was buried after three numbers, and I now left a Munich I could no longer stand.

Kasimir Edschmid
In memoriam Carlo Mierendorff

Dear Mierendorff, as I look through the literary remains by which you set no great store, but which your friends felt ought to be published for political as well as literary reasons, as I flick through the slim volume of your writings, many memories come flooding back. Apart from your publisher Joseph Würth I am probably the only one who knew your journey through the catastrophic decades of our generation from its earliest beginnings. So perhaps having been the companion of your youth I am perhaps the person best qualified to mourn you now that you have gone.

Looking back on our lives something must first be said about Darmstadt, which was a little world of its own in those days with a very fair idea of how to shape its young people. We have to behave as friends do who have not seen each other for a long time and then meet among the ruins of their shattered homeland, wander about in the deserted areas, listen to the song of the birds in the still flowering gardens, look out into all this desolation and say: "This was my house—that was your flat, and this is where we used to sit talking at night. That was where we printed this manifesto, that was where a certain meeting was held, and that's all gone, but we are still alive." Are we still alive? Yes, you are, my dear Mierendorff. Your erect, broad, ever youthful figure, the angry brow, the merriment of your eyes, the irony of your smile, your blond hair, your virile, enthusiastic, aggressive dignity—all this is as alive and unforgettable as the power of your intellect to triumph over ruins.

First there was Theo Haubach, who lived a few houses away from ours in the Kiesstrasse. My brother, who was never afraid of Santa Claus, and indeed felt equal to acting the part himself (except that he preferred taking to giving) visited Theo with a beard on his chin and a sack on his shoulder just when Theo was having a bath. He returned home laden with nuts, apples, and aniseed cakes. This was the only scare our family inflicted on the Haubachs. We grew up. My brother went to America. I completed my studies, Haubach moved up to School Certificate stage. He came up to me on the square of the 115th Infantry Barracks when the volunteers were reporting in 1914 and introduced you, Carlo Mierendorff who had also just left school, and you suggested we should all try to get into the same barrack room. One year later you joined me for a while in the hospital on the Olbrichweg, which had been erected originally as galleries for the great art exhibition of the preceding year and then transformed into sick-bays. In these rooms, pleasantly decorated in the style of the Viennese craftsmen, you helped me cart buckets of hot water, though you were sick yourself, and wash the wounded who had been on the move in transports from the Balkans for weeks. It was difficult to tell where their shirts ended and their skin started. You were a true friend.

Meanwhile Joseph Würth, who was two years younger than you and Haubach, was about to take his School Certificate in the Ludwig-Georg-Gymnasium and at the same time was promoting the project later called *Dachstube*. Under this name—and under the names of those who gathered round the enterprize—it will go down in the chronicles of the city, the region of Hesse and indeed of the fate that befell the whole German nation.

Würth, who had organized a series of readings with a few schoolfriends, published a hand-written journal called *Kunstschau*, while at the same time in Offenbach Ernst Müller, who shot himself soon afterwards, published *Das neue Deutschland* in one single number. The two papers were amalgamated in August 1915 and *Dachstube* was born.[1] In the following year letter-press and a copying machine were acquired, and the year after a little hand-press of the Boston type. You, Mierendorff, sent articles from the front. At first each printing ran to between sixty and one hundred copies. By 1918 sixty-five issues had appeared, as well as some brochures, among them Haubach's *Jacques Prince*, Fritz Usinger's *Eternal Conflict* and your *Gnome*.[2] Now the publisher of the *Attic* put out a series called *The Small Republic*,[3] in which the first contribution was your *Autumn in Lorraine*, the *Karlsreis* and Schiebelhuth's *Little*

Calendar, drawings by Eberz, Schülein, Gunschmann, Keil, the
In Memoriam for Lisl Steinrück, the *Bachanale* by Ernst Müller
who died aged sixteen, illustrated by Kahn the painter who died
soon after the war, and Schiebelhuth's *Swasticrusade.* And more
besides.

With number fifty-six of *Dachstube,* however, the stormy period
of your youthful literary group came to an end. In this the last
number (November, 1918) you published a proclamation. With an
extraordinarily sure sense you turned to politics, but in doing
so you raised on high the torch of morality: "Time," you said,
"has become the yard-stick of all values and woe betide the art
form which attempts to ignore it. We await you, friends. Seek
out direction, aims and means. Let our irresistible determination
for the future carry us aloft, let this be the watchword of our
faith."[4]

You founded the journal called the *Tribunal.*[5] This *Tribunal*
extended far beyond its immediate circle and became one of the
bravest and best of those racing towards what was thought to
be a new world. Joseph Würth and you published the first number together. In January 1919. You asked me to write the introduction and then, together we composed the Proclamation to
the Youth of France, which appeared in the *Tribunal,* signed
by the best brains there were in Germany in those days:
Unruh and Schickele, Pechstein and Krell, Däubler and Zech,
Georg Kaiser and Albert Steinrück, Toller and Sternheim, Rudolf
Leonhard and Theo Haubach and many others . . . this was the
proclamation which appealed for a Supra-national European
Community. The answer arrived in flesh and blood in the shape
of Paul Colin, the editor of *L'art libre* and later editor of *Europe*
in Paris, who came to Darmstadt and spoke as a disciple of
Jaurès for the community of European peoples, for the liberation
of German prisoners of war and for a new Germany in a new
world. He was the first to sound such noble fanfares and he
spoke in the Fürstensaal in Darmstadt while the nationalist
organizations sang songs outside in the Grafenstrasse by way of
protest and tried to lynch the French speaker—opposite the
house Georg Büchner once lived in and from which he fled
from Germany to French soil in search of liberty.[6]

Ah, Mierendorff, if we could talk about the last few decades
today two years after the capitulation of the Hitler régime, we
should be forced to confess how miserably fruitless all our efforts

of those days were, for we were deserted not only by the goodwill your enthusiasm rallied, we were deserted by people too, yes even by Colin himself, the man who brought us the gospel of freedom and was later received with full honours in Berlin by Moissi and Einstein; Colin went over to Degrelle and his German protector and became the boss of a Fascist newspaper. He was shot outside his office in Brussels by a man from the Belgian resistance movement. Not only people, ideas too lay bleeding in the streets at this time and the confusion in men's minds has never been nearer the Tower of Babel than in the age in which you grew from youth to manhood. If one thing did remain constant, however, it was the memory of the just wrath and the spiritual power which emanated from you and your followers. This memory is still alive today despite the ruins— indestructibly alive.

You then studied in Heidelberg, Freiburg and Munich and edited the *Tribunal* in Darmstadt. And with the help of of friends you published the delightful *Hessenborn* in which you yourself under many different pseudonyms composed the furious bourgeois protests against the *Tribunal* . . . the *Hessenborn* which, despite its destructive irony, was taken seriously and acclaimed by the bourgeois.[7] It was a ray of sunshine in the midst of so much calamity. In their publications the National Socialists later documented the events of this period stage by stage. Their head- lines show how irritated their little world was by the big world you embodied and how you rose above all these parochial events. Your name comes up again and again in accusations and denunciations: over the appointment of Gustav Hartung as director of the theatre, over the founding of the Secession, the opening of the first International Art Show after the war on the Mathildenhöhe, over the speeches by the General Secretary of *Clarté*, the battles against anti-Semitism, the premières of *Kean*[8] and of *Stürme*. Your name along with Haubach's, Schiebelhuth's, Würth's, Michel's and Hoetger's . . . your circle was contemptuously compared with earlier Darmstadt figures like Büchner and Sturz, Lichtenberg and Merck, whom the Beckmessers of the reactionary circles of those days detested as much as the later exponents of brute force did. Such compari- sons only redounded all the more to your credit. One only has to read in Nazi records to see how many of all the Darmstadt happenings were associated with your name: the decline in milk supplies and the emergency currency issued by the city, the first hand-out of American bacon, the Kapp-Putsch, Rabindranāth Tagore's visit to Keyserling's School for Wisdom, the onion growers' strike in Griesheim, Erzberger's assassination in the Black Forest, the consecration of the Nazi banner in the City Church, the assassination of Rathenau and the price of a pound of butter during the inflation—800,000 mark. "800,000 mark for butter," Hitler's chroniclers wrote indignantly, "and yet the Weimar Coalition still holds celebrations for the constitution." Alas, this accusation was not entirely without foundation: the Weimar Coalition should have been busy with other things than celebrations, for a few months later the leader of the Nazi Party carried out his putsch at the Feldherrnhalle in Munich. The Dollar stood at Two Billion Mark at that time. And that was when you, Mierendorff, entered politics, filled with anguish over the fate of your country.

There was nothing half-hearted about your politics. After some tumultuous goings on you had gained your doctorate, in Heidelberg, you joined the S.P.D., you were elected to the Reichstag, and when your former fellow-student from Heidelberg, Goebbels, marched out of parliament in protest at one of your speeches with all his followers at his heels, you shouted after him: "Stay where you are, Herr Goebbels, if you have the courage to look a front-line soldier in the face." Goebbels never forgot that. It was you who brought to light the Boxheim documents, in which the Darmstadt man Best, who later became Nazi Governor of Denmark, had sketched the draft plan for overthrowing the government, in sentences which always concluded with the heartening refrain: "So and so is to be shot". You came back to Darmstadt to join the administration of Wilhelm Leuschner, the union leader to whose members we had helped to share out theatre tickets, when the right wing had decided to wreck the première of Kean. You supported the Three Arrows Movement, which was supposed to bring down National Socialism. Everybody thought it was finished at the end of 1932. When the Nazis won after all you were dragged through the streets like an escaped animal only a few months later. I can still see the face of my hunch-backed cleaning woman telling me what happened—she later burned to death in her cellar during the bombing of Darmstadt. Your opponent Best had you shipped off to Osthofen and for years you saw the inside of

259

one concentration camp after another. And Goebbels gave you proof that though he had not dared to look you straight in the face he had correctly evaluated the weight of your personality. Yes, even after your release shortly before the war you remained banished from Hesse for ever by the Reichsstatthalter Jakob Sprenger. He was simple-minded enough to force you to go all the way round by way of Würzburg if you wanted to travel from Frankfurt to Heidelberg. That's what they were like, the over-bearing followers of brute force and that's what they'll always be like: petty-minded middle-class citizens and criminals and idealists, it's impossible to tell them apart, and that's what made them so dangerous.

You did not leave Germany, any more than Haubach and Leuschner did, any more than any of those belonging to your circle which extended far beyond Darmstadt. You were of the opnion that the bitter misfortune that had befallen Germany had to be lived through by you and had to be openly attacked the very moment there was the slightest chance of success. If you were still alive today you would realize with astonishment that you would be held in suspicion for this courageous attitude, that you would be slandered and accused—by those villains who, having themselves stayed in the country, now play the part of the raging wolves of that eternally phoney German radicalism. But you knew what your fellow-countrymen were like, you knew them and just how ineradicably provincial they were no matter how fiercely they tried to conceal it, and I'm sure you foresaw this too. It was all the same to you. You always went your way, as you thought fit, and as you judged right and proper. Your personality, your almost arrogant self-confidence, your easily roused enthusiasm concealed, only from those who did not know you, the fact that you always thought only of your duty, not your personal ambition, your vanity or your career.

You were not an easy person, not even for your friends, and often your friends were displeased with you or you with your friends—almost to breaking point. But you were generous and your friends remained faithful to you, this much is true. You yourself had a healthy grip on reality and were capable of correcting any false attitudes you had once held by reason of inexperience, youth or abstract theory. One day, shortly after the end of World War I when Heinrich Simon, the grandson of Sonnemann, had invited the top staff of the *Frankfurter*

Zeitung to his home by the river Main, for talks about whether one should abide by parliamentary procedures and elect a National Assembly or whether Germany would be better governed by *räte*, you spoke out against a National Assembly. Later when you were no longer the "voice of youth" you thought and acted differently. But you never lost the fire of youth. It still glowed about you even when you came out grey-haired from the dungeons of the new dictators.

One evening, in 1919—you were in your early twenties and had just come back from the wars highly decorated with military honours like Haubach and Schiebelhuth—one evening, we were sitting in the historic Café Oper discussing the *Tribüne der Kunst und Zeit*, a series I was editing for Erich Reiss at his request— volumes of Schickele, Goll, Hiller, Däubler, Krell, Benn and others had already appeared, among them Franz Masereel's anti-war *Political Sketches*, which Masereel had published during the war in the Genevan journal *Feuille*—,[9] on this evening I said to you: "Listen, Mierendorff, isn't it strange that everybody is ready and willing to write about art, literature, politics, socialism, young people, force, good and evil spirits, Fatherland and Europe, but not a soul is prepared to discuss the cinema, not a soul has given a thought to the possibilities it may have?" (Radio was known only from hearsay in those days.) "I've given a thought to it," you replied, "let me write about it."

So you joined the company of the most significant authors of your age. What you wrote turned out an excellent book. And the book deserves to be wrenched from oblivion not only for its insight, but also for the form in which you presented your ideas.[10] Some of it may seem exaggerated and intentionally baroque, but a great deal of it reminds one of the young Büchner and his *Hesse Courier* by the confident imagery of its expression.

"Ever since cinema grew up into an enormous cow sprawling over Europe," this was how the book started, "it has been a parasite living out of everybody's pocket. As it lives for all it lives off all. The public of the cinema is the classless public." Even in those days when the cinema rarely got beyond adventure films, you realized how socially rewarding it could be, but also how great the danger was if the cinema were expanded and improved purely for commercial gain instead of for some socially useful purpose. "The cinema will be completely and totally ruined," you said. On the other hand you were already

261

dreaming of surrealistic films when there weren't even talkies yet: ". . . films in which heads are swapped, somebody eats a live ox, bodiless legs go for a walk, a fart sweeps the National Assembly to ruins. I want a Rabelais for the cinema." Ah yes, you were an urbane character. In your wisdom there was always a grain of fun and in your aggressiveness the kind of melancholy that makes men attractive. You were not one of these gloomy philistines of the kind the Nazis came up with, who stay philistines even when committing murder. You always spiced your soup with Attic salt and you put on a merry face when you were hacking your enemies to pieces. "Let's not get backache from sheer solemnity and gloominess," was your cry, as if you had popped straight out of Büchner's *Leonce and Lena*, and at the same time you were his Danton: "Not even the last one-eyed man on the northern or southern hemisphere will escape me. The man who cranks the camera controls the world."

But you didn't get the cinema you raved about in your youth. The man who wouldn't look you in the eye when you attacked him in the Reichstag, Goebbels, was the man who took over the cinema, picked your brains, sent you packing and used the cinema to propagate the ideas of racial extermination instead of extolling the idea of human happiness.

It was always the same tragedy: others took what you were prepared to give and in the end gave stones in place of bread. Schiebelhuth was right when he wrote in 1920: "There is a swastika in the world / Watch out for everybody called Meier / Colour your mind black-white-red / Move closer to the world pogrom! . . ."[11] At the time these ironic prophecies were laughed at. Later it was no laughing matter. Alas, Schiebelhuth too perished. He died of a broken heart in America after translating Thomas Wolfe, writing some excellent nonsense rhymes and some delightfully meaningful verses.

Ah, Mierendorff, the days when we were young and the Rosenhöhe was fragrant with blossom and the plum trees shimmered white on the Marienhöhe and the nightingales sang round the Grosser Woog—alas, this carefree time so full of hopes and dreams seemed to belong to the dim and distant past, when we met for the last time—the day before your last birthday in Berlin.

I had spent the morning with Haubach and V.B., we were to meet again for your birthday, I got out of the S-Bahn at Unter den Linden. You came riding along the lane which had suffered hardly any damage, a fly had got into your eye, you stopped your bicycle by the pavement quite by chance—and we met earlier than we were supposed to. I remember all the little details, even the handkerchief you pulled from your pocket, how you rubbed your face and above all your kind and gentle laugh. So we went up and down in front of the American Embassy where at the time the Swiss were looking after things. In your mind you had already completed the proclamation to be read over the radio after Hitler had been removed. Your main worry was how the centres of resistance in the south round Berchtesgaden could be broken. In the midst of these and other worries you were struck down in Leipzig on the morning of December 4th. It came when you least expected it during an English bombing raid and the bomb which struck the house you were in killed you outright. "The Lord who is ruler over life and death called our friend and colleague Dr. Carlo Mierendorff to Him on the fourth of December" was how your friends Henk and Haubach put it in the newspaper announcement which caused such dismay to all those who were looking to the future and thereby to you.

Würth arranged the funeral in Darmstadt in the woodland cemetery. "A life of unusual grace and of unusual burdens" Haubach said in his memorial address. It was not granted to you to deliver the liberation speech you had planned. Five months after Haubach's speech came July 20th. Haubach, Leuschner and many others of your circle were arrested. Shortly afterwards Darmstadt was destroyed. The house of *Dachstube* and many houses which might have borne witness to your works, your plans, your books and your journal were destroyed. Leuschner was hanged, and shortly afterwards Haubach was dragged to the scaffold where he too was murdered. Not merely a century, a whole millenium seemed to have passed since the time when my brother scared the neighbouring Haubachs as Santa Claus with the sack of apples and nuts on his back. Haubach was not scared beneath the gallows. But the world was scared; perhaps as it had never been scared before.

More has been said about you and Darmstadt than about you and the world, my dear Mierendorff, and more, it seems to me, about politics than about the slim volume of literature you left behind and which I ought to have dealt with in greater detail, even if only for the imagination and boldness with which you approached literature—but in times like these, who could separate the one from the other? From the place which was your starting-point, accept these greetings with which your friends wish to honour you, not for the sake of what you have written, but for the greatness of your heart.

Paul Steegemann
Five years as publisher in Hanover

It's five years ago already . . .

Just imagine : one fine spring morning some tiresome customer demanded picture postcards, stamps and a few volumes of Rudolf Stratz and a young trainee book-seller decided there and then to escape from this kind of serfdom and establish himself as a publisher.

In Hanover.

With the remnants of his salary, a smooth, clean-shaven face, tail-coat, monocle and yellow boots he took a taxi to Edler and Krische, the printers and announced that he was Paul Steege-mann, the Publisher.

And therefore he wanted a considerable credit.

With some hesitation he was given what he wanted.

Whereupon he wrote to some friends that he was the up and coming man.

And he printed books of sixteen pages.[1]

And with the profits books of thirty-two pages.

And with the profits books of sixty-four pages. And so on.

One of the books of thirty-two pages was *Anna Blume*.

In a jiffy 10,000 copies were sold, author and publisher famous.

There were scandals. Because of the book. Because of the advertizing.

In the meanwhile the publisher grew into a businessman.

Very economical.

At first he saved by not having a large office.

He owned a single room with the publishing business under the bed.

And on the phone he was extremely polite. He always answered every call with the same question—which department please? then he put the call through to book-keeping, despatch, main office, the readers, etc.

In the evenings he packed his books himself, dragged them to the post office in a wheel-barrow. So he expanded.

In 1921 he went to the Book Fair in Leipzig for the first time, his entire range of publications for the exhibition in a cardboard box under his arm.

On the tram he asked for "straight ahead please." He was told he would have to get off. "We go round the corner."

That afternoon he met Hans Reimann at the Book Exhibition.

In Germany nothing is held against a publisher more than a lack of policy, national endeavour, cultural mission.

Within the herd clear-cut, obvious decisions are expected. Struggle for the good of the people. That kind of rubbish.

The German simply has not got the sensitive nerves for the nuances of individualism which for him, notwithstanding its achievements in certain spheres, means only one thing—chaos.

Coming on the scene so late in 1919 what was the position of this publishing firm vis-à-vis its rivals? Distinctly disadvantageous.

A publisher needs authors. The famous ones are under contract to other publishers. There is no sale for the new ones. Which is why Paul Steegemann started off by publishing new authors. And said goodbye to his working capital.

But not for long. Soon realization dawned in the publisher's eye-ball. If there are no saleable authors around, then one has to produce saleable books.

He immersed himself in the issues of the day, let his nerve-endings swing free on the end of an imaginary antenna and as a result of these acrobatics commissioned Reimann to write books against popular writers like Dinter, Ewers, Courths-Mahler; a book from Dr. Kurt Hiller against paragraph 175; *En avant dada* from Huelsenbeck; an anti-Rudolf Steiner one from Wilhelm Michel; one from Ossip Kalenter about the private life of Balzac; an anti-war book from Frau Stinnes; the Raffke novel from Artur Landsberger.[2]

And so on. And so on.

Take a look at the new catalogue.

Wagenschiefer, the Public Prosecutor, is a good friend of the publisher. Because he is always confiscating books. And then demanding the death sentence (or the next best thing) at the judicial proceedings. Pity. Because so Paul Verlaine's wonderful volumes of verse *Femmes* and *Hombres* and Aubrey Beardsley's sweet novel *Venus and Tannhäuser* get pulped.[3]

If we ever get the republic we deserve—the republic of Hölderlin, Goethe, Heine—these books will be re-issued. However, it'll take time as Ludendorff put it so succinctly.

But the publisher who every second could see from a stray roofing-slate, a broken Conti-Cord, a misguided stroke of lightening or the brilliance of a shooting-star just how relative everything is, himself and his esteemed contemporaries included, went in for a bit of writing himself on the side in 1924 and just for a joke invented the author Gustav Bock.

Under which precious name he will take his place in the annals of world literature.

Let us drink his health.

And what about money?

There isn't any.

What is there instead?

Debts.

With the printer. The paper-supplier. The distributor.

Every day at noon Steegemann arises from his silken couch and faces the economic cosmos.

Which is why he has chosen this rather unusual method of looking for a silent partner.

Let us drink his health with brimming glass!

Skål!

Hans Harbeck
Expressionism in Hamburg

> *O rule of claw and hunt for marvels!*
> *O heart flung high!*
> *O monument of space!*
> *Hans Leip*

The Hanseatic way of life is utterly incompatible with the violent ethos and the destructive syntax of Expressionism. A poet who—to use Kasimir Edschmid's words—behaves so ecstatically that he seems to be wearing his heart painted on his chest will not thrive very well in the atmosphere of the Elbe and the Alster. Lessing's clear and logical mind forms a bulwark against the onslaught of excessive emotions. At most the Hamburger would be inclined to look with favour on that particular type of Expressionism which Kasimir Edschmid assures us knows nothing of fat bellies and pendulous breasts. "The torso of the work of art grows out of firm thighs and generous hips and rises from these into a well-trained, well-balanced body." That's more like it. That is a view of art that sounds pleasingly sporting. Despite all this—here is the paradox of fate!—Hamburg produced one of the most significant publications of the whole Expressionist Epoch. Despite this there *were* poets living in Hamburg who surrendered with boundless enthusiasm to the enticing possibilities of the new manner of expression. I am thinking of Karl Lorenz and his journal *Die rote Erde*.[1]

You almost need a magic wand to get hold of a copy of these precious documents these days. Before me I have the first (200 pages) and second (289 pages) books of the second series. A glorious sight to behold. The size of an atlas, magnificently strong paper, spacious print and between the texts not just one timid wood-cut, but whole plantations of them. Artists like Josef

Achmann, Kurt Löwengard, Heinrich Stegemann and Willi Tegtmeier present an impressive range of samples of their work. Particularly well represented is the sculptor Karl Opfermann. Who, I wonder, was the Hamburg Rockefeller or Vanderbilt financing this daring undertaking?

While the language of forms exploited by these artists is one which we find completely convincing to this day, the lyrical poetry of Karl Lorenz and his associates leads straight to the heart of the new movement's problematic nature. Even Johannes R. Becher and Georg Heym, the real creators and founder-members of the movement, could not stop their effusions from occasionally becoming simply too long-winded. In Karl Lorenz there are real dam-bursts. He does not shape or form, he paints at great length and wallows in it. Blue is his favourite colour. The stanzas that pour out (though very graphic) all sound the same. An example chosen at random:

My longing for you echoes smiling in the blue flame of your
  cheeks!
The wind's gentle game enters our silent togetherness!
Light strikes us gently from blue lanterns of insects chirping!
Warmly the scent circles over blue boats from the bars
And ever and again dreams rain from the trees?!

While this is still to some extent comprehensible, somebody like Paulfried Martens plunges head over heels into a linguistic jungle and gets completely lost. The reader gives up the ghost and says to hell with all this Expressionist hocus-pocus!

But it is neither the graphic arts nor the verse contributions that determine the real intellectual strength of the *rote Erde*. It is the theatrical and dramatic efforts preserved in it which really succeed in captivating professional researcher and amateur alike. Invaluable contributions by Georg Britting, Kurt Heynicke, Alfred Wolfenstein and Paul Zech go some way towards justifying this elaborately produced journal and lead us directly into the artistic nerve centre of the age.

Of those actually born in Hamburg Hans Leip the poet, who was as sensitive as he was tough, was the only one who was for a time deeply influenced by the movement. Faithfully following Franz Werfel (*Oh Earth, Evening, Happiness, Oh just being alive!!*) he exclaims in 1919: "Oh dancing trees. Oh rims of the hills!" And again, the end of his novel *Servant of Godeke* (1925) goes like this: "Oh waking sleep! Oh unquenched desire!"

His first work *The Pit* has all the hallmarks of the out-and-out Expressionist offspring[2]. If this boldly conceived book were to be subjected today to the blinkered philological approach of pure stylistic analysis it would quickly be seen to contain numerous linguistic aberrations of the kind which strike the modern reader as absurd. The then fashionable predilection for violently exaggerated imagery is frequently exploited to the brink of—unintentional—parody. (I shall never forget the sentence: "The senator smiled like a parson's dog-collar.")

On August 31st, 1918 Erich Ziegel opened the Kammerspiele on the Besenbinderhof. This enterprising little theatre aimed to serve the spirit of the times and take an active part in the formation of a new outlook on life. In the *Freihafen*,[3] the theatre's news sheet, Erich Engel speaks prophetically of catastrophe and ruin although the war was not yet over. But he does believe in the possibility of a change of heart and a rebirth especially in morals. His heart is with the a*vant-garde* theatre striving upwards to the Ideal. Spread the word, reflect, strive upwards—this is his impassioned cry.

And now in the next few years nearly all the really vital Expressionist dramatists went through their baptism of fire at the Besenbinderhof. Barlach, Hasenclever, Kaiser, Kornfeld, Sternheim and Toller—along with Wedekind and Strindberg—dominate the repertoire. The stage becomes a platform, and the productions assume the character of manifestoes. The so-called "Challengers and Agitators" set the tone.

The fame of the young producer Erich Engel spreads very quickly. His exploitation of the new means of dramatic expression is so masterful that they seem to have been designed specifically for him. He does not make things easy for himself nor for the actors. He must have his own way. He hammers at it. He is sometimes guilty of a touch of pedantry. His approach is academic, but inspired. His stage-designs those of a white-hot mathematician.

But—he is always successful. His numerous *premières* nearly always turn into triumphs for his beloved dramatists who proclaim with Expressionist exuberance the idea of humanity.

271

Now just a few words, *pro domo*.

About 1911 in Hamburg a largish number of water-colours and paintings by Emil Nolde were exhibited at Commeter's for the first time. A bold risk. The Hamburg newspaper the *Fremdenblatt* suggested that obviously the bacchanalian painter of these pictures was mad. The conservative *Hamburger Nachrichten*, which employed me as its art critic despite my youth, permitted me to write a panegyric.

In the autumn of 1914 I organized a "Patriotic Evening" in the Munich Kammerspiele, which at that time was under the direction of Erich Ziegel. On this occasion four poets appeared on the stage in person. Frank Wedekind, Klabund and my humble self pleased and delighted the public. The fourth poet engaged by me was Johannes R. Becher, clearly the most expressive of all the Expressionists. This was youthful daring or bravado, if you like, on my part. The inevitable happened. With a few ferocious words Becher painted a picture of the horrors of war which was noisily howled down and he was forced to take to his heels. The person responsible for this disaster was me, without a doubt.[4]

In the spring of 1917 I was in a German orderly-room in Roubaix (France) secretly fashioning one line of verse after another. I was sick of the war naturally and had been for ages and more than anything else I wanted to pierce its dragon's belly with a lance. Besides, I seemed to sense the approaching collapse and had all sorts of visions of radical revolution.

I wallowed in dreams of violence and upheaval. A selection of my verse later appeared in March, 1919 under the concise and succinct title *Revolution*, published by the Dresdner Verlag. The flame-coloured volume was on display in show-case number fifty-two of the great Marbach Expressionist Exhibition.

Occasionally I meet one of my friends who will greet me with a quotation from my revolutionary poems:

> *An overturned burial cart weeps.*
> *A young man waves a canon about.*
> *A tiny bird throws its chest out*
> *And sings: Oh sun that never sleeps!*

When this happens I can't help smiling, but I'd find it very difficult to say what the smile means.

GENERAL REFLECTIONS
IN RETROSPECT

Kurt Wolff
Publishing in general and the question: How do publishers and authors meet?

For fifty-five years people have been asking me: where did you learn your profession. My answer is invariably the same: nowhere.

It strikes me as one of the more attractive features of our profession that it can't be learnt. The usual counter to that is: wouldn't it be useful to have worked for a printer or a book binder? Why? I don't want to set up type or do the actual printing or binding. Or people claim it would at least be desirable to do a little work in a book-shop. Why? Since I was twelve I have spent hours in book-shops nearly every day, both at home and elsewhere. Surely it doesn't make much difference whether I am customer or shop-assistant, on this side of the counter or on the other. Anybody in love with books and publishing feels at home in book-shops. I don't believe in the value of a Ph.D either. Naturally it is an advantage to be well-versed in world literature and to have a knowledge of three or four modern languages to be able to read foreign books in the original and not have to rely on somebody else's advice. But all that comes under the heading of "general education". And that doesn't get you very far in our profession.

One day I moved from the German Department of the University of Leipzig to 10 Königstrasse, Leipzig, the home of the printer Drugulin. I moved into the two-roomed office of Ernst Rowohlt, who was the same age and as mad on books as I was. He had invited me. And I brought nothing with me but the one essential thing study can't give you, and a lot of it at that:

273

namely, *enthusiasm*. Naturally enthusiasm has to be accompanied by taste. Everything else is secondary and can be picked up in practice.

The first essential is to be clear in your own mind what line you want to be active in as a publisher. But that is basically determined by the taste and enthusiasm of the individual concerned. By taste I mean not only judgment and feeling for literary values. Taste should also include a reliable feeling for how a specific book has to be presented—the format, type, binding, dust-cover etc. Literary taste, on the other hand, has to be combined with an instinct for whether a particular book will be taken up by a small section of the reading public or whether its form and content will appeal to a larger circle. The size of the edition and the nature of the publicity are decisively affected by this and one has to be careful not to let one's personal enthusiasm mislead one into mistaken and over-optimistic expectations.

When I moved into Rowohlt's two-roomed office—the third room was the Rowohlt living-quarters—enthusiasm knew no bounds; typographical taste, however, was limited to judging whether type-face, title-page, binding etc. looked good or not. It was quite a while before I was capable of saying to the type-setter: leave two more points, titles in italics, etc. Ernst Rowohlt was well ahead of me on that score. He had served an apprenticeship with Drugulin and learned a lot. On questions of literary taste we were in total agreement; in those days his heroes were Scheerbart and Dauthendey, and it wasn't difficult to infect me with like enthusiasm for both of them. Without false modesty I can also say that we were of one mind in our admiration for the dramatist Herbert Eulenberg. And the Schiller Prize he was awarded for his play *Belinde* seemed to endorse our judgment.[1]

But how does a publisher come by manuscripts, where do they come from? How do publishers and authors meet? Above all, what considerations decide his choice of what is to be published?

You either publish books you think the public *ought* to read or books you think the public will *want* to read. Publishers in the second category, that is to say publishers who follow the public, pandering to its tastes, don't really count as far as we are concerned—do they? They belong to another "ordo", to use the lovely Catholic concept. For that kind of publishing you need neither enthusiasm nor taste. It's just a question of supply and demand. You merely have to know what will have the appropriate effect on the tear ducts, the sex glands, what will appeal to the sport-lover, what will give people the creeps, etc.

Publishers like us, on the other hand, are trying to do something creative even if only on a small scale, we are trying to rouse some interest in what strikes us as original, of literary value, significant for the future, no matter whether it is something difficult or easily accessible. This applies to *non-fiction* as well as *fiction*. Of course we can make mistakes, and we often do. Sometimes we think we have spotted some future promise in the personality or the manuscript of an author and this is not realized. But the effort is worth-while, success is not what matters—that's often a question of luck. Yes, it's often more luck than good management that brings in a good author, but let us not theorize.

Because I had accepted a manuscript by Max Brod and he saw Kurt Wolff as the firm for his whole *oeuvre*, he sent me a young fellow-countryman and friend: Franz Werfel. One day he personally brought along another friend and fellow-countryman: Franz Kafka. Nobody with ears to hear could have resisted the music of the early Werfel poetry, nobody could have remained unmoved by the magic of Kafka's prose.

About this time when I was still a student as well as a publisher, I used to attend Albert Köster's lectures in Leipzig; beside me sat a young man I liked the look of; I got talking with him and over the years he was to become a close friend. This was Walter Hasenclever. And when one day he finished a play he had been working on, he brought it to me to be published. This was *Der Son*. We are not talking here about its literary merits but at the very lowest estimate it was not mere entertainment.[2] As a play dealing with the theme of the Father-Son conflict it was dynamite for the generation born about 1890. It was performed by countless theatres all over Germany; but it is hard for us to appreciate nowadays the tremendous excitement it generated at the time.

Kafka, Brod, Werfel, Hasenclever—they were the firm's first authors, and, as we have seen, it was more luck than good management that brought them to Kurt Wolff's. Naturally one had to have the right nose for how each in his own way and in his own measure was worth the publisher's time.

In the Innsbruck journal *Der Brenner* I read some poems by somebody, I had never heard of, called Georg Trakl. They breathed so powerfully of great poetry that I at once—this was April 1st, 1913—wrote to the author offering to publish his verse in book form. That same year in the *Jüngste Tag* series a volume of poems appeared and less than one year later in March, 1914 Trakl sent the manuscript for a new book called *Sebastian in Dream*, which can, with some justification, be described as the loveliest, purest volume of poetry to come out of that time. What high hopes there were for the future of this young poet! Then on the 9th October a telegram arrived from the Military Hospital in Crackow to which the poet had been admitted following his mental collapse at the horrors of war. The telegram was touching:

it would give me great pleasure if you could send me a copy of my new book Sebastian in Dream. admitted as patient to military hospital crackow. (georg trakl.)[3]

We could not give him that pleasure. The book wasn't ready. And only three weeks later the poet took his own life with an overdose of drugs.

It was in Spring, 1913 too that the first letters began to arrive from a Swiss writer called Robert Walser, written in a delicate eighteenth-century hand; letters whose contents could not have been simpler and whose tone was absolutely unique. The first letters have been lost. Here are a few lines from a later one:

. . . I have just finished a new book . . . in which I have brought together twenty-seven separate pieces . . . Each piece has been recast and rewritten as far as possible. Particular care and attention have been paid to selection and arrangement of the various pieces. I believe I can safely say the book is an integrated, pleasing whole. There are transitions in it from descriptive to amusingly concrete passages, from comic to deeply serious ones, even sometimes bordering on the tragic . . . Some older pieces are included alongside some that couldn't be newer . . . I regard the work as a modest kind of building, but one which is homely and completely habitable . . .

Who could resist being beguiled by the tone of such letters? And yet there was no doubt that the compilation of prose passages would find no more than one hundred readers. So I published three volumes of Walser stories for the hundred readers, with drawings by his more famous brother, and extremely attractive books they were too. The stories were not so simple as they looked at first sight. Walter Benjamin wrote a very perceptive essay about them,[4] and Robert Musil wrote the following in August, 1914 for the *Neue Rundschau*:

"Walser suddenly bids his characters be silent and lets the story speak as if it were a character. Like a puppet-show, romantic irony; but there is also something about this playfulness that reminds me faintly of Morgenstern's poems in which the gravity of real relationships follows some thread of word-association and suddenly an underground ripple is set up; only with Walser the association is never purely verbal, but always one of meaning as well, so that the line of feeling he happens to be following at any particular moment rises as if to some great sweep, sidesteps and then goes on its way swaying happily in pursuit of some new enticement. Nor do I wish to claim that this is any more than playfulness, but by any reckoning—even disregarding the uncommon linguistic mastery which is completely captivating—it is no mere literary playfulness, but something fundamentally human, with much softness, musing and freedom and the moral richness of one of those apparently useless, lazy days when our firmest convictions relax into comfortable indifference."[5]

But Walser's prose would be practically unknown today if Suhrkamp had not printed thousands of copies of a lovely little selection.

Other authors didn't announce themselves by letter, they just turned up unannounced in the flesh. What or who the driving force was behind Gustav Meyrink's sudden appearance in my Leipzig office from his home down by the Starnberger See near Munich, I do not know. At that time Meyrink had never written anything except short pieces for *Simplicissimus*, which had never been very successful in book form. The other thing he had done was a translation of Dickens in twenty volumes, for which he had had the crazy idea of translating all slang or dialect in

Dickens into Bavarian! His Dickens edition was a fiasco. But Meyrink's fantastically grotesque stories and parodies had—successful or not—great charm and a character all their own.

I remember Meyrink's visit very well: an aristocratic-looking gentleman, with a slight limp. Exquisite manners. He had the honour, he said, to propose that my firm should take on his first novel, which was completed, though a typescript did not as yet exist. He claimed he had dictated it into a dictaphone (which for winter, 1913–14 was unheard of, nay incredible); it would be a few months before he could deliver the manuscript of the novel *The Eternal Jew*. But he had brought the first chapter in long-hand. Could he please have a signed contract for the novel before his departure for Munich next day. He was not asking the usual percentages, could he please have one lump sum of 10,000 marks for all rights and editions in all languages payable immediately. Would I be good enough to read the pages he humbly placed before me and make my decision. The unusual proposition was put in most immaculate form and in deadly earnest (and I had always thought of him as a humourist).

Somewhat taken aback and a bit embarrassed, I read the foolscap pages in long-hand—they have been carefully preserved to this day—and it was up to me when I finished reading them, in other words after ten or fifteen minutes, to say *"yes"* or *"no"*. I had liked the few pages, but I knew nothing of the book as a whole and 10,000 marks was a lot of money. I found the whole situation a bit absurd, wanted to show I could cope with anything—and said *"yes"*. A man of twenty-six is more inclined to, I suppose. The title of the novel *The Eternal Jew* was later changed to *The Golem* and the book sold in hundreds of thousands of copies. Despite that, it is not a bad book at all, in fact it is the only good novel Meyrink wrote. (I could never convince C. G. Jung that *The Green Face* is a bad novel—Jung thought it was wonderful too.)

To set the reader's moral qualms at rest: despite the lump sum payment for the world rights, the author *was* given a share in the profits. Incidentally, I read recently with some interest that Meyrink, who was born in 1868, was an Expressionist. That's what Knaur's Little Encyclopaedia says and it is normally very reliable. Well, perhaps we'll get back to the hot chestnut called Expressionism later. Let's keep to our theme: how do manuscripts and authors find a publisher?

The *Golem* business gives me an opportunity to say this: if a publisher has the good fortune to have one runaway success with a book, this has one pleasant consequence: it attracts authors. In less successful years the stream of new authors was a trickle, in successful years it became a flood. That was our experience with *Golem*, and a little later with Heinrich Mann and Tagore. (No, Tagore is much better than you think: André Gide, William Butler Yeats, Rilke, Ezra Pound, and many more distinguished writers were far more aware of this than all the German Men of Letters of the Twenties who equated success with worthlessness—one could quote countless examples of the traditional snobbishness of the German writing profession . . .)

Though, naturally, it could never be proved in detail, nevertheless there is no doubt that the unusual success the Kurt Wolff company had with Meyrink, Heinrich Mann, Tagore, also with the early volumes of verse by Werfel and his drama *The Trojan Women* brought the firm a mass of manuscripts and business propositions which would otherwise never have come. The fact that there was in existence a new publishing house ready to accept the younger generation, a firm in which Kafka, Werfel, Hasenclever and others were printed, encouraged countless talented and untalented young writers to send in manuscripts. But it is also to the above-mentioned successes, which indicated that the retail side of the business was dynamic, that the Kurt Wolff Company presumably also owed many non-fiction books which I saw as complementing extremely well the *belles-lettres* side of the business. I calculated—in many cases correctly—that these were the titles which would have a longer life. Some examples of these are: the letters and diaries of Paula Modersohn-Becker; Feuerbach's *Bequest and Letters to his Mother*, Mechtilde Lichnowsky's book about Egypt, Georg Simmel's *Rembrandt*, books by Martin Buber and many others.

Nor must those friends be forgotten to whom the firm owed so much, friends who were both authors and colleagues. The first of these was Kurt Pinthus, who worked longer than anybody else as the house's literary and critical adviser. His judgment was impeccable and he was completely reliable; Willy Haas was a reader too, though not for so long; Franz Werfel was a reader in name only—we wanted to leave him in peace for his creative work. Then there was my friend Mardersteig, the now famous printer of the Officina Bodoni and Valdonega in

Verona; at that time he was the man really responsible for the elegance and distinction of all Kurt Wolff book production. Hans Mardersteig brought about the connection with Frans Masereel. The first time we brought out Masereel's *Book of Hours* in 167 wood-cuts, the Belgian's name was completely unknown in Germany. Within a few years Masereel's wood-cut sequences— *Book of Hours, Sun, A Man's Passion, The Idea, Tale without Words*—in cheap editions with forewords by Thomas Mann, Hermann Hesse and others gained an improbably large following and reached publication figures we had never anticipated in view of the uncompromising quality and basic attitude of these books. And it is largely due to Hans Mardersteig and his friend Carl Georg Heise, the art historian and sometime director of the Lübeck Museum and later of the Hamburg Kunsthalle, that the Kurt Wolff publishing firm has expanded its fine-arts list.

I had previously made some amateurish attempts in the field of art books and I am proud to have published in 1913 the first book by and about Kokoschka—*Plays and Pictures*. I had also gone to Paris, visited Rodin and acquired two of his books: the very successful book entitled *Art*, and the much lovelier book about the cathedrals of France. But the firm was also grateful to the friends I mentioned for vital publications which are today of some historical importance: Will Grohmann's great Kirchner book, Sauerlandt's book on Emil Nolde, Gustav Pauli's book on Paula Modersohn-Becker, *Art and Religion* by Gustav Hartlaub and many more. Above all, I am obliged to remind you that the *Genius*, the most attractive and most splendid journal for traditional and modern Art[6] to appear in the German-speaking world after *Pan* and *Insel*, owed its conception and execution to Mardersteig and Heise. These two also acted as editors for the journal which embraced three rich years of publication, from 1919 to 1921.

Finally, it would be a mistake to disregard how often authors bring other authors to their publisher; the writer who finds himself well-looked after and advanced career-wise by his publisher will feel inclined to encourage his friends to send in their manuscripts to the same firm. It is true this is often done out of good fellowship and not out of any conviction about the quality of their work, but sometimes it pays off—I am thinking in particular of Max Brod who often gave me the impression he was sending me anybody in Prague who could put pen to paper but who knew all along that apart from Kafka and Werfel or Czechs like Březina and Bezruč most of the others were very small fry and unimportant.

After all these examples of how author and publisher come together let me finish with one example of how publisher and author did not come together. It is a dadaist example: when from time to time I studied our list as a whole I always felt one element which was very dear to me was missing: something humorous, absurd, comic, gay, grotesque. A few little booklets by Mynona, Mehring and Reimann, amusing as they were, did not strike me as enough. So I showed marked interest when in 1917 the Dadaists made a few tentative approaches about possible publication.

At the time I knew practically nothing about Dada, but I did know that a man I liked and had known as the dramaturg of the Munich Kammerspiele, Hugo Ball, was one of the founder members of Dadaism. I had published a rather conventional tragi-comedy of Ball's called *Michelangelo's Nose*, and also a volume of verse by his friend Emmy Hennings of whom Werfel thought very highly. If Ball is mixed up in Dada, I thought, there must be something to it. But the letters to the Kurt Wolff Verlag discussing a great publication to be called "Dadaco" or "Dadaglobe" came not from Ball but from Huelsenbeck and Tristan Tzara. Even before I was fully conscious of the total imbecility of everything executed and execrated by Dada under the name Dada, the pedantry, the tedium and the dullness of the letters I received had cured me of the illusion that there might be any kind of creative spark in all this. Reading these letters again now I cannot find one single sentence which it would have been interesting or entertaining to quote. The correspondence dragged on from September, 1919 till April, 1921 and in the end I broke it off and gave up any idea of ever publishing Dada or "Dadaco". Instead I published Ringelnatz's *Kuddeldaddeldu* and *Gymnastic Poems*. All the Dada manifestoes, all the Dada gobbledygook could not equal one single stanza by Ringelnatz and certainly not any of Morgenstern's poems.

The Dadaists soon faded away and found their comfortable little middle-class niches: a wealthy psychiatrist's practice in the U.S.A., a rich marriage etc. Only poor little old Tristan Tzara sits sad and lonely over a café crème on the terrace of the Deux Magots. Hugo Ball turned Catholic and wrote a book about

Hermann Hesse, who had never been a Dadaist. The fact that at least six publications in the last few years have been dredging up dead Dada all over again strikes me as astonishing, unless it is taken as a warning to the present-day generation. The most popular of these publications—in the DTV series—includes as one of its illustrations an unpublished hand-bill for the Dada book I never published. To find the name of Kurt Wolff printed in giant capitals as the publisher of the Dada book which never appeared, on this hand-bill which I had never clapped eyes on, before I saw it in this pocket-book I had absolutely nothing to do with, was not a very happy experience for Kurt Wolff. Dada too ought to observe the old maxim: Honesty is the best policy![7]

The only reality which did come to fruition on the periphery of my Dada-associations was the publication of a non-dadaist story with illustrations by George Grosz. The author Huelsenbeck called this work, *Dr. Billig am Ende*, a novel. And in February, 1920, in Munich there was a lecture evening by the same Huelsenbeck in the Kurt Wolff Verlag lecture room which held about 150 people. The topic was: *The Aims and Essence of Dadaism*. The report in the Munich *Neueste Nachrichten* the following morning read as follows:

"Despite pressing enquiries from members of the audience, the lecturer would not or could not give any more than the vaguest general comments on this the latest of the modern movements and these were directed partly against Expressionism, partly against the *bourgeoisie* and partly against reason itself in the broadest sense. He just kept on repeating that Dadaism had had tremendous success and had spread throughout the world with its Cabaret scandals, hoaxes, propaganda methods and riots."

Looking back on this evening forty years later Richard Seewald describes it "as a minor incident which took place in Munich in the main room of the Kurt Wolff Verlag in the Georg Hirth building" . . .

"Huelsenbeck the poet was supposed to talk about Dadaism before a select and invited audience. And he spoke. After about a quarter of an hour paralysing boredom began to spread through the room, and I expressed the general feelings of the audience when I called out to the platform: 'Herr Huelsenbeck, is the rest going to be as boring as what we have heard so far? We can't just sit here and let everybody read from his Ph.D thesis.' Everybody laughed and applauded my dadaistic interruption, incidentally the only thing in this line there had been so far. The unfortunate character of the platform began to stammer, he apologized, said this wasn't a Dada evening, he was dealing with the history of Dadaism etc.! He tried to read his own poems. But he didn't have much luck with them either. It had turned into a Dadaist evening after all. There were shouts of 'Goethe' from one corner, 'Rilke' from another and so on."[8]

So Seewald's experience was the same as my own. The only thing he can remember about this Dada evening was being bored.

But, you may object—there is not much difference between the Dada poets and Johannes R. Becher and the Kurt Wolff Verlag did publish several of his volumes of verse. Well, I believe there *is* a distinction to be made between stammering and stuttering, but I am certainly not proud of having published Becher. Becher was no Dadaist, he was what the literary historians call an Expressionist. And so at last we come back to this ghastly term which pursues me always like a shadow I cannot lose, the word I jokingly used in connection with Meyrink.

I feel very strongly about this Expressionism business and therefore I should like to make one short and very personal comment which, thinking of all the authors of the Kurt Wolff Verlag, strikes me as legitimate:

For years I have seen myself as a publisher of modern poets and also of more traditional authors whom I, rightly or wrongly, thought worth while. I have never followed any slogan or any one movement—but over the years this claim has tended to be contested more and more. It has been my accursed and detested fate to become famous as the publisher of *Expressionism*. Attempts are still being made, now more than ever, to stick one common label on a group of writers publishing between 1910 and 1925 and to call them Expressionists. But they never shared this common label. For thirty-five years I have been fighting this in private conversations with friend and foe alike. To no avail. That is why I should now like publicly to announce my credo:

Expressionism implies a collective. No collective ever produced a single verse, let alone a complete poem. The creative act is something individual.

What are described as Expressionist features are never applicable to the really *great* creative writers of that time. Significant writers and poets whom I am proud to have published never had *anything* in common with so-called Expressionism even if they are included in modern exhibitions on Expressionism and classified as such in the histories of literature. Their names were:

Kafka, who as a writer is closer to Johann Peter Hebel and as a thinker closer to Kierkegaard than to any writer of the twentieth century.

Heym, the German-speaking brother of Baudelaire.

Trakl, who takes up the great tradition of Hölderlin.

Stadler, the Alsatian who loves Francis Jammes and Péguy, not Johannes R. Becher.

Werfel, whose *Friend to the World* derives from his love of Walt Whitman.

Ernst Blass, who does not really belong in such august company, but who deserves to be mentioned because this "Expressionist" wrote to me in 1915: "Stefan George and I carry on the great German tradition."

Sternheim, whose ambition it was to become a German Molière.

Schickele, the nature-lover who paints landscapes and women in the manner of Renoir, not Kirchner.

Heinrich Mann, whom to my astonishment and incredulity many still rank higher than his brother Thomas.

Karl Kraus, who made the Expressionists the object of his satire and in an elegy addressed to Kurt Wolff bewailed the fact that I published them.

Enough said. These are pretty well the only Kurt Wolff Verlag authors who have survived. I think few names could be added to the list of survivors. I hope the dead ones—buried or not—will forgive me.

At least none of the names I have listed wanted to be called an Expressionist. So why talk of Expressionism when the rest is silence?

If Döblin, Georg Kaiser and various other names have not been mentioned here, this is only because I have confined myself to the Kurt Wolff Verlag.

Did somebody say what about Benn? But isn't it the later Benn who is the great poet? He has claimed (and in writing) that he doesn't know what Expressionism is and I have a letter Benn wrote me in 1917 in which he writes of a poem I had asked about from the early cycle Morgue: "It is a very inferior poem!" Unfortunately I did publish only the volume of his early prose Brains; I felt I couldn't mention the Benn who wrote that in the same breath with Kafka and Trakl.

What about Ehrenstein's famous "talc and arse-hole's mucous growth" poetry? I just cannot find it in me to think of him as still vital even if attempts should be made to resurrect him with new editions etc.

With these remarks and sallies against so-called Expressionism, for which I myself bore part, or even a great deal of the blame, the publisher takes his leave, knowing that all his many bad books—Expressionistic and non-Expressionistic—will take him to purgatory if not straight to hell. I hope some of his books will make you think well of him still—till your children and grandchildren find even the good ones remote and distant and consign them to their last resting-place in the grave-yard of literary history.

C. F. W. Behl
Encounters with Expressionism

From my Memoirs

It was in the year 1910 that I first heard the young poet Georg Heym reading from his works, barely two years before he was drowned in the icy black waters of the Havel. This man from Hirschberg had an elemental air about him and the impact he made on his friends, who were mostly city men of letters, was quite extraordinary. This impression has been modified since his death with the publication of his diaries which reveal burning personal ambition and great psychological insecurity for which he compensated by deliberately thrusting behaviour. At the time, however—and this is the impression one has every time one re-reads his poetry—the demonic possession of his terrifying visions and the dark, foreboding rhythms of his verses echoing like hammer blows had the effect of an electric storm. This was my first encounter with Expressionism.

This term had first cropped up in Paris at the beginning of the century in the visual arts, but now it has long since fallen into the hands of literary historians to be used and abused by them. When it was first applied to literature I do not know. At any rate it was then for the first time in the new pathos of Heym's stanzas—New Pathos Cabaret was the name Kurt Hiller gave to the evenings he organized in the New Club started in 1909 —that I became aware of a decisive turning point. A revolution and new beginning were now discernible, along with the other distant portents for the future which only very few far-sighted people could see coming. *Fin de siècle* with the last flowering of Impressionism (Herman Bang, Eduard von Keyserling, the early Thomas Mann etc.) was finished. People were sick of the "Neo-Romantic" kind of realism deriving from Art Nouveau.

With eruptive force the new art of Expressionism burst forth with an explosive ecstasy that smashed all the old rules and melted language down to new harder forms, in some cases even stripping all the flesh off completely.

In the many journals, pamphlets and other publications of the four years preceding the outbreak of the First World War in which one can discern the first stirrings of Expressionism or, for example, in the programmes put on by the various groups —at the Gnu[1] in Reuss and Pollack's book-shop in the Potsdamer Strasse or in the back-room of the Café Austria or Alfred Wolfenstein's Warring Brothers[2] at the Cassirer Art Gallery—the movement demonstrated such a multiplicity of personal manifestations that inevitably the term Expressionism appeared problematic when used as a collective. After all it embraced both the emotional and the intellectual prophets, the dramatists writing in idiosyncratic, dialectically tempered linguistic forms and the intellectual activists like Kurt Hiller. And yet they did all have something in common, as Kurt Pinthus indicated in his preface to the 1919 edition of his *Twilight of Mankind*, namely: "The intensity and the radical nature of feeling, basic attitude, expression and form," which compel them to "fight against the type of humanity characteristic of the departing age and prepare the way for the new and better humanity they long for."

The playful *épatez le bourgeois!* of the Bohemians had now developed into the bitter conflict adumbrated in the apocalyptic poem *End of the World* by Jakob van Hoddis: "The bourgeois' hat flies off his pointed head . . ."

It must have been about the end of 1913 or even the beginning of 1914 at one of the many shows put on by the modern art movement that I saw the poet Max Herrmann on the platform for the first time. Physically he was mis-shapen, but otherwise he was a man, whose spirit and simple, almost naïve humanity, seemed to radiate some secret beauty. We later became very good friends and in the Twenties he wrote brilliant Cabaret reviews for my journal *The Critic*.[3] I should think he was then still living in Neisse, the home-town with which he had a love-hate relationship and which made him suffer as long as he lived there. For all his friendly contacts with all sorts of Expressionists, he himself was never an Expressionist in any real sense and yet there were some Expressionist notes discernible in the music of his verses. I realized this when I heard him read with great

288

venom his poem of hatred for Neisse and the philistines of that city who tormented him so much. This poem comes at the end of his novel *Cajetan Schaltermann*.⁴ The last line, uttered with tremendous explosive power, goes: "The township swells up like a poisonous fungus and bursts."

Among Alfred Richard Meyer's *Lyrical Pamphlets*, which had introduced many an Expressionist to the reading public, including among other things Gottfried Benn's *Morgue*, there appeared in 1912 a booklet of *Futurist Poems* by F. T. Marinetti and almost at the same time Herwarth Walden's *Sturm* printed a special supplement with *The Futurist Manifesto*, whose hyper-ecstatically inflated language struck us as a dehumanized parody and distortion of Expressionism of a terrifying kind: "Set fire to the libraries! Divert the canals to flood the art galleries! . . . We sing the praise of war, the only true cleanser in the world . . ." The ghostly shadow of the impending war was long since with us. Georg Heym had prophesied it in his famous poem: "He who has slept long is now arisen . . ." Truly a prophetic vision whose last two stanzas cast their black shadows even as far as the horrors of the night bombing raids during the Second World War in which whole cities were destroyed. The visionary courage with which Heym had personally confronted the image of horror had never failed to move me every time I read that poem until I was brought up short by a passage in his diary: "July 1910. If only something would happen . . . Even if somebody were to start a war, that would suit me fine. Peace-time existence is as mouldy, sticky and slimy as the wax-polish on old furniture."⁵

The war Heym had longed for, but which he did not live to see, came in 1914, and because people at first confused it with the Wars of Liberation and the 1870–71 Campaign its outbreak was accompanied by a shower of war-poems in the traditional style. But in the *Weisse Blätter*, founded just one year before, the Expressionists gathered. And when the gay mask of "Up and at 'em lads" had soon slipped, revealing the fearful Medusa's head of global war and pain, suffering, annihilation, demoralization and when the nightmare of no escape had transformed initial enthusiasm into despair and hatred and rebellion against the world-wide slaughter, then voices were raised in René Schickele's courageous journal opposing and denouncing the war. I shall never forget that time in 1917 when I read Leonhard

K

289

Frank's story *The Waiter*[6] about the man who loses his only son, the apple of his eye, in the war and how he progresses from his own individual suffering to the recognition of the culpability of the age, hence to a revolutionary indignation which gives him the strength to fight for the "Triumph of Freedom and Love". Frank, who had had to go into exile early, because he had publicly slapped the face of a writer in the Café des Westens for rejoicing at the news of the sinking of the *Lusitania*,[7] proclaimed in our side of the trenches the revolution of the heart—while on the other side Barbusse was shaking up the conscience of mankind and Rolland was getting ready to write *Clérambault*, the "story of a free conscience in war-time". With four more stories in which the waiter's revolt gradually sweeps the masses of suffering mankind into an "ecstasy of freedom and brotherly love" Frank rounded off the whole cycle under the collective title, clearly meant as a challenge, *Man is Good*. That this work, quite apart from its contents, basic attitudes and impetus, should also inevitably be a document of literary Expressionism by reason of its form, was a sign that Expressionism had received from the experience of war new impulses both consistent with its own nature and heightening it even more. Above the chaotic din of a World War clanking to an end and the ensuing German catastrophe, the voice of the French poet Marcel Martinet with his "Poètes allemands, o frères inconnus" had been heard and taken to our hearts. As if echoing this voice came the appeal to French youth drawn up by Kasimir Edschmid (at that time an Expressionist leader) and signed by important personalities from the intellectual and artistic life of Germany. It appeared in Carlo Mierendorff's *Tribunal*[8] in autumn, 1919: "Union must come soon and must last. Nothing divides us. Our aim, path and goal are the same . . ." This was the kind of language with which Expressionism sought to exercise some influence on the cultural and political life of the time.

Following the example of the *Free Stage* theatre club, an earlier device for evading censorship, *Young Germany* had been conceived in Berlin in 1918 at the Reinhardtbühnen with the intention of serving the cause of modern dramatists with productions for club members only—and also, as Heinz Herald the society's producer expressly proclaimed, in order to further the cause of Expressionist drama in general on the stage. And it was here at these theatre matinées in the Schumannstrasse that I experienced my most impressive encounters with Expressionism. Walter Hasenclever's *Son*[9] already looked a little dated and pre-war. The young man obsessed with his parricide complex is saved from the final step when his father has a stroke, etc. However, the inflammatory dialogue interspersed with lyrical diction brought out the true Expressionist actor in Ernst Deutsch: expressive power burning like a bright flame from within, intellect combined with pathos in the original sense of the word, a master of his voice in suffering and angry protest. But shortly before there had been what was perhaps the most powerful event for the *Young Germany* theatre club: Reinhard Goering's *Naval Encounter*,[10] the tragedy of seven sailors in the gun-turret during the battle of Jutland, beginning with a cry followed by dialogue in free verse rhythms with every-day speech and lyrical language intermixed, mounting to a climax in: "Fatherland, fatherland, oh dear fatherland, we are as swine waiting for the slaughter!" Everybody left the theatre in silence, shaken to the core. That was Expressionist art driven to the limit of what was bearable: Expression, still white hot from the experience only just lived through. And then as the year drew to a close and defeat had already developed into the November Revolution Fritz von Unruh's tragedy *The Family*,[11] conceived as the first part of a trilogy of victory over the idea of force, in powerfully eruptive verses, still twitching from the bloody pangs of birth, proclaiming the destruction of brazen force: "O warm breath of motherhood! Melted by you let the avalanche roll / crushing the barracks of naked force beneath it / and whatever has raised its head too blatantly into the blue sky / shall crumble . . ." People in this play are nameless, symbolic cyphers of human suffering, experience and protest. This was the only time Unruh produced a work so successful in building up his revolutionary pathos into truly monumental dimensions: in this play he was giving expression to a humanity transformed by war, and I thought the performance of the great tragic actress Rosa Bertens who imbued the rôle of the mother with the kind of compassion, which the symbolic nature of the part lacked, was one of the almost unsurpassable successes of the Expressionist theatre.

Probably only survivors from the years after the First World War will remember the compulsive awareness of new beginnings, a feeling which whipped up a whole generation of writers into a state of creative unrest, calling for expressive form. It was as if the language had run hot, as if it were feverish, as if the age were breathing down its neck, the age which would soon seem threatened by counter-currents of disappointment and disillusionment. Nowadays if I flick through the pages of the slim volume of verse called *The New Day*, which I published in 1919 with a revolutionary cover drawing by Walter Mehring, the Expressionistic language strikes me as both foreign and familiar at the same time because it brings back what I lived through at that time so intensely:

Pamphlets wet and sticky with printer's ink,
Dog-eared already fly around people's heads,
... Storm is roused and raging.
One man hangs darkly between the masses and the stars
On the edge of the pillar
And reads: proclamation!

Yes, that's what it was like! Once when I was returning from a turbulent rally at which Hellmut von Gerlach had demanded the abdication of the Kaiser, I found myself jammed in the heaving mass of people on the Alexanderplatz. A tattered and torn pamphlet was thrust into my hand, I was pushed up onto a raised surface of some kind and I had to shout the proclamation out over the heads of the multitude. Naturally when I recorded this in verse-form it had to be in breathless, expressively condensed language! So this bundle of poems, some of which had been published previously by the journal called *Young Germany*[12] became the humble part I played in the Expressionist movement.

Ludwig Marcuse
Something of a deluge

Expressionism like politics lived loudest on the stage. It's poetry, which was to prove of more lasting value than its plays, was read at the time, but it was secondary—it was only occasionally recited in public and then always by Fränze Roloff looking . . . like a torture victim . . . which was what she looked like all the time : like one of Lehmbruck's figures. To this was added the shrill screaming voice of the then newly imported jazz; only Valeska Gert was more Expressionistic; compared with her the rainbow was a monotonous sequence of colours. Ludwig Hardt the *récitateur* drummed out Kleist and Börne pieces in the Expressionist manner; hacked them to bits and flung the fragments in the audience's face. Occasionally he did uncover the machine-like rhythm concealed in a classical author; when that happened our own age shone forth from the past. There was also contemporary Expressionist prose : Sternheim's grotesquely distorted serving-girls and cooks; Sternheim twisted grammar the way Valeska Gert twisted her arms and legs.

But Expressionism really came to life on the stage; the stage made it into a cult. The well-known lyrical anthologies were widely read; but the real impact came from the comedies of Sternheim, the tragedies, platonic dialogues and tragi-comic farces of Georg Kaiser, the rhetorical creations of Toller and Hasenclever with their impassioned lyricism in five acts. What were they impassioned about? In days of yore the bards would gather an audience and get them to nod their agreement perhaps even at court and festive occasions . . . perhaps the more political these old bards were, the more significant was the rôle they had to play. Was Expressionism political?

Rather the opposite, I should say. Theirs was more of a lamentation and a gospel of salvation. A revolution, aimed not like that of the Young Germans at bringing about changes in the institutions of society, but at a new view of the world; in that respect related to the Mystics. A breakthrough of timeless values, and in that respect related to Romanticism, only much more vital. What fascinated many of us was precisely the kind of thing the present-day generation (which ought to be called the Cool Generation) despises, namely the exclamatory "Oh-Mankind" type of verse. I should like to advance an outspoken defence of the "Oh-Mankind" poetry of Werfel and Wolfenstein and their friends. This represented the first attempt since the Romantics to break the chains of historical pressures—and to make humanitarian demands not for tomorrow or the next day but for right now! It represented a faith in the ahistorical, a temporal revolt in favour of timeless values. This was ecstatic militancy with vaguely anarchic tendencies.

Werfel wrote:

> The status quo cracks
> Primeval chaos rises to the surface.[1]

Against this there was but one form of protection:

> Neither hope for the future, nor the Gods
> Can take the terror out of death,
> One thing only can do this:
> The thought of what was and can be
> In human relationships.
>
> (Goering)[2]

So Expressionism was also an escape from "primeval chaos" into the arms of one's fellow men.

Eastern religions and philosophies came into it. Tagore imported Asia, and it swamped the reader; this being pre-Nehru, it was still a kind of holy narcotic. Arno Nadel, the rosy-cheeked little Polish Jew with the gentle smile, was influenced in his poetry by Lao-tse; in the circle of writers, painters and musicians which he had gathered round him, works of the

Chinese and Indian mystics were regularly read and commented on.

Expressionism was essentially apolitical, as is any faith which is breaking new ground—and any that believed seven-league boots will take one straight to one's goal. The scream drowned out the word; the scream made the eternal new order and the eternal old disorder sound like one and the same thing. Unamuno who called upon his contemporaries to cry out in the wilderness . . . was one of the most powerful voices in this apolitical earthquake. The fractured syntax (and not only in the linguistic arts) mirrored the fracturing of the materialistic world which the Romantics had proclaimed more idyllically and elegiacally. This new inter-relationship was mirrored most comprehensively on the stage, that old complex of poetry, plasticity, sound and colour, that total work of art.

The non-recognition of the empirical world became very apparent when in Jessner's production of *William Tell* Switzerland was indicated merely by raked steps. Where the infinity of cosmic space becomes of prime importance the particular milieu disappears. Man was seen against the vastness of the firmament and not within three walls; Jessner's *Othello* opened with the back view of some heads silhouetted against the distant horizon, the borderline was still a compromise with good taste as is also the term firmament. Mostly the figures were plunged into darkness, in front of black curtains, picked out by a magic beam of light; never at any price, in front of the family portraits and the ancestral furniture. Stars (not the ones that rule our destinies but jack-o'-lanterns), clouds and dark of night—are all eminently unpolitical back-drops. They provide no occasion for social criticism.

But even the theatre-goers who thought the stage was a place reserved for timeless utterances only set aside the hours between dinner and supper to this; the rest of the time they expected something more substantial; and besides, the war could not be forgotten so quickly. So Expressionism took on an extremely political colouring, in a kind of mystical union with politics. Anybody who did not share this delusion was quickly pushed into the background. Who had ever heard of Arno Nadel? Ernst Deutsch and Johanna Hofer gave a reading from his works in the Fritz Gurlitt Art Gallery; but his quiet, gentle whispering did not have the same impact as theatre revolutions which gave themselves such pacifistic and socialistic airs, even though they were really eschatological. These showed no way ahead, instead they merely swamped the audience in alternating waves of hatred and longing (in a kind of theatrical switch-bath); but they did pretend (at least the critics of Expressionism did) that as a result of Goering's *Naval Encounter* criminal and property law had improved. The actors just could not help rushing out on to the apron-stage to engage the public directly: to implore, to goad, to ridicule. Richard Révy told me that he had the greatest difficulty in restraining his actors in Grillparzer's *Life is a Dream*; the habit of thundering at the stalls had become instinctive. And we contemptuously rejected the theatre of Otto Brahm and Max Reinhardt with the slur: "Peep-Show" theatre.

Georg Kaiser's *Gas* and Toller's *Transformation* were as far removed from politics really as the mystic exaltations of the medieval nun Hildegard von Bingen. The past years had been steeped in blood, besides, the war had been lost, so there was a double reason for getting into a state . . . in every sense. This ecstatic state was called political because rage caused a foaming at the mouth. There were four types which especially produced this sense of indignation: Raffke (the name coined about this time for profiteers), chauvinists, generals and statesmen en bloc; the Expressionists loved type-classifications like the ones "phenomenology" goes in for; they loved the grand gesture and were not too worried about details. They set up these "types" as Aunt Sallies and flung the word "peace" in their teeth; and probably seriously imagined peace would come if only these ugly species of mankind could be eradicated. They also thought they were political because Ernst Toller (a magnificent orator when he gave full rein to his emotions) took a trip to Moscow; and because Fritz von Unruh, a true aristocrat and General's son, had turned democrat and became their pin-up, the crown jewel in the new democratic Imperial crown fostered by the *Frankfurter Zeitung* and the *Berliner Tageblatt*. There was a great deal of goodwill in all this. The Expressionists penetrated into the political sphere and thereby turned it into a tribunal: Hitler, too, was part of its heritage—yes, Hitler too; they shared the same tendency to scream, the tendency to get into a state. The Expressionists wanted paradise, the Hitlerites wanted hell and an even more sickening heaven.

Politics is either a very dry, methodical business (the noble goal so passionately desired must be ever-present yet non-obtrusive)—or it is a lot of hot air, the great sin of the "political" (unpolitical—irresponsible) intellectuals. But human happiness is advanced by poetic excess too; it gave the theatre-goer the bliss of sensing something he deeply longed for. That is not to be despised, as long as poetic flight does not upset serious political actions. Where Expressionism did attempt something concrete in the political sphere (for example in Kaiser's *Gas* or in Toller's *Luddites*) it was childish. Expressionistic drama was only really political when it stopped being Expressionistic and became propaganda. For example, in some plays by Friedrich Wolf, the most legitimate of Sudermann's successors, who had also used the theatre for political conflicts; and in some of Brecht's didactic pieces, imparting ideas of party discipline. Here the theatre was a practical instrument for political purposes. Brecht's theatrical ethic that drama should not appeal to feelings but should instil political behaviour had been successfully practised by the theatre of the Jesuits in the seventeenth century. Their dramatic theory teaches something practical: subjugation by means of the theatre.

In every stream it is possible to isolate the original sources from the secondary waters carried along by them. The ones swept along are either of the same type themselves or they are interested or overwhelmed parties or one or the other or all at once. That's how a stream grows. It all began with those who no longer took the life they were born into for granted. There had been too much death, too much suffering and too much falsehood in it. The roof one had had over one's head had become faulty. Hence voices were suddenly heard which for some time had been proclaiming that mankind was living under a faulty roof: Kierkegaard, Nietzsche and Strindberg.

For twenty years I had been living under a solid, middle-class roof at No. 10 Bachstrasse,[10] in the Hansa Quarter of Berlin; today this house is a hole in the ground, the only reason one is not particularly aware of it is that there are too many other holes beside it, so all in all the place looks more like a wasteland than anything else. In 1919 I began to see the stars—ever since Kant "the stars in their heavens" have been standard middle-class equipment. But I also began to see what is not there beyond them. Expressionism attracted me—by its negation of tables and chairs and all that stuff, by its liberation of vision for what is only obscured by all the rubbish, large and small. I heard the naked truth in Däubler's *Northern Lights* and saw it in Meidner's portraits and both saw and heard it most clearly in the powerful Strindberg piece in which somebody is a young man one second, a grown man the next and then an old man—and the play is still far from over.

You start off by being a tiny part of the general experience. Then you are swept off your feet, unable to stand up to the swelling tide any more. One Sunday matinée some silly people sat in the Deutsches Theater watching Kokoschka's *Murderer, Hope of Womankind*, and of course they understood not one word—and still they applauded at the end till their hands were raw; and what was worst of all, they genuinely meant it. They were full of enthusiasm for Kokoschka the great painter and Max Reinhardt the great producer and for all the high society which had turned out in full war-paint to salute and support this "Modern Germany". Who ever really knows what he likes or does not like? At least, in the theatre you know more quickly than you do with a book in your lonely room : too quickly.

And there is the third group that swells the intellectual flood —the interested parties : publishers, theatre-directors, actors, critics and hangers-on . . . Many invested in Expressionism, only very few coldly and calculatedly, many speculatively, many were just swept along. The greater the enthusiasm, the higher the shares rose on the market—and only a simple-minded person believes that the enthusiastic interested parties act purely out of calculation, or that they are not genuinely enthusiastic; even with more concrete objects, enthusiasm for business and enthusiasm for what is good for business is a very artificial division. This whole idea of "business" is in itself a conglomeration of power, money, prestige and all sorts of other sources of personal gratification. Partisans are generally interested parties, interested parties are generally partisan : that's human nature; for man does not live on longing alone. And the commercially useful and at the same time genuine desire is the mortar which turns individuals into an ideological body.

This, being a non-organized party, is best described as a clique; it is strongest when its ties are both idealistic and commercial. The clique has still not been properly examined by the sociologists because the term "clique" is pejorative and conceals the fact that there is a great deal more to what holds it together than that. Since the caste-system has broken up into sub-castes the clique has become one of the basic elements of society. Without it the complex called literature cannot be understood; that curious compound of productive individuals, editors, art-gallery directors, publishers, publishers' readers, theatre directors . . . joined together by a bond which is intangible but still very strong. The Germans are alone in thinking of "literature" solely in terms of works of art. In this misconception, too, they are that other-worldly nation which even in its campaigns of conquest is as blind as the bard of ancient times.

Like any god of this kind Expressionism is not to be photographed and not to be defined. It was a hotch-potch of tendencies, names and associates. It was—in the field of drama—occasionally what is meant by "modern drama". Somebody young like Zuckmayer, who had been accepted into the ranks of the Expressionists with his *Crossroads* and *Pankrace Awakes,* was awarded the Kleist Prize for his fresh farce *The Merry Vineyard*[3]—and to show my partisanship at the time I put at the top of my review : "*For* modern drama"; as if I were using this old-fashioned modern farce to throw down the gauntlet to all non-modern dramatists from Schiller to Hauptmann.

Max Krell
Expressionism–glory and decline

To talk about the first half of the twentieth century without mentioning Expressionism would not only be unjust, it would mean leaving a gaping hole. For Expressionism has played a decisive part in the history of German literature which only the violence of political events has kept from the present-day reading public.

It was born everywhere and nowhere; its coming was in the air. It had many progenitors. It was to be met with first in the aggressive modern journals of Berlin (*Sturm, Aktion, Die Weissen Blätter*); of Darmstadt (*Das Tribunal*); of Innsbruck (*Der Brenner*), in the cabarets of Zurich, in the lecture-rooms of Vienna and Frankfurt, in the theatres of Hamburg and Prague. Everywhere German was spoken it came to the fore; its books appeared first of all with unknown publishing houses, then quickly conquered the big ones.

By the time the temporary hermetic isolation brought about by the war of 1914–18 was over and countries outside Germany realized that something was happening in German literature that Paris and London did not have, at least as such an elemental phenomenon, it had already passed its peak. For its recorded life-span was short, the historians tend to restrict it to fifteen years; and what are fifteen years in the mainstream of a literature that has lasted a thousand years!

You can set a cross against it and against nearly all its exponents; and yet—it has passed away, but it has not died.

Expressionism has not gone through the development normal for a movement like Impressionism and Naturalism, Futurism or more recently Existentialism. These grew out of an evolutionary process. Expressionism sprang up everywhere at once on a broad front and spontaneously tore the chain of development asunder instead of adapting to it organically. It reacted against the prevailing aesthetic prejudices and found the justification for its existence in politics, in the widespread laxness of the age and its indifference to social questions, but most of all in the dictates of its belief in human rights.

There were no general lines agreed upon by certain individuals or groups. Expressionism possessed no ingeniously devised programme. Challenging statements about the meaning of Expressionism of the kind made by Kurt Hiller, René Schickele, Kasimir Edschmid etc. were protests as much as proclamations: declarations of total war on politics.

Their protest was directed against that kind of conventional *laissez-faire* and illusory white-washing, which, even as late as the first decade of the century, still meant acting as if everything in our world were well-ordered and well cared for "under the army's protective wing". Literature especially was deeply ensconced in the thick plush of high society.

But everything was not all right. Young writers could see with eyes as yet undimmed just what was going on all around them. They spoke not as socialists or liberals or nationalists. They spoke as man to man. They wanted to force people's eyes open, because, whether from indolence or thoughtlessness, the "older generation"—good, solid citizens all and splendid in their own sphere—were simply incapable of coping with the catastrophe which they, the young people, could plainly see was about to engulf them.

If poets are seers as the Ancients believed, then this is exactly what these young poets were. This is what made them capable of such Cassandra-like utterances in forms of extreme emotion.

First to appear on the scene were verses, sizzling white-hot verses, often not very polished, which appealed straight to the heart. Revolutionaries, even intellectual ones, do not write with kid gloves. Theirs was a cry from the heart; the poets dealt openly with realities which till then had been at the hidden core of all poetry. The naked throbbing heart. They were not understood. The heart only gets a hearing when it concerns Eros. But the Expressionists wrote no love poems to lovely ladies. They were ridiculed until, with drum-roll and howitzer shells, the bloody horror of war burst upon the world.

And now, when it was too late, these young men *were* understood. In the success they enjoyed after the war there is some measure of remorse from those who had not been prepared to listen before.

And now the dramatists came on the scene, often in works which began with fiery monologues, later gaining more and more dramatic intensity. Following the example of Walter Hasenclever, they declared war on their fathers, on father figures of every kind, screaming at them, that they were the ones who were guilty of the wrong direction things had taken and of the rigidity and stagnation of their society; fathers who had put business before the demands of the heart as in Sternheim's *1913*. The state had not been prepared to admit this before the 1914–18 war and so the censor had stepped in.

And then came Expressionist prose. Here the statement of things as they were and the demand for change could be put on a broad basis, barriers were torn down and the new man sought out in as far away places as China (cf. Döblin's *The Three Leaps of Wang Lun*). Edschmid's stories were dazzling sorties into all possible regions and all possible ages. Leonhard Frank's stories destroyed the illusion of military glory and Heinrich Mann's novels stripped off the deceitful masks of the epoch.

But the Expressionists' ideals had probably been set too high for the age to grasp. Hardly had the experience of war settled when the normal citizens fell back into their former indolence. The call of the young poets echoed in vain. Past mistakes had to be paid for and appeals to the heart just got in the way again.

The Expressionists themselves stopped making their appeals. Only in youth can appeals be as violent as theirs had been. In the years of manhood the storm abated. Some betrayed their convictions, Hanns Johst and Arnolt Bronnen were caught in the snares of National Socialism, Bert Brecht, unquestionably a great writer, opted for Communism, which Johannes R. Becher also served as a Minister for Cultural Affairs; both paid the penalty and ended in desiccating didacticism. For a spell Gottfried Benn also wavered, but he stopped himself in time and entered on a period of maturity.

A totalitarian régime then flung the works of literary Expressionism on the pyre as "debased art" and forced its writers into concentration camps, exile or suicide.

But the spirit cannot be destroyed or exiled or driven to suicide. In our own days Karl Otten, himself one of the most convinced partisans of the Expressionist era and one of its three or four survivors, has literally raked all the buried and forgotten material out of the ashes and made it all available again, and Kurt Pinthus has brought out a new edition of his anthology *Twilight of Mankind.*[1]

Two generations which have had no knowledge of the existence of these works are confronted with the amazing discovery that for once in our century the poet did arise among our people and proclaim the rights of the heart.

APPENDIX

COMMENTARY

Preamble

Some commentary on the texts included in this volume is given wherever necessary for better historical appreciation. The commentary is in two sections. The first section consists of additional information on particular texts. This includes essential data, e.g. date of writing or date of publication plus some indication of any subsequent printings or variants, then brief biographical details where required in this context. Parallel passages from other sources then follow if they have anything additional to contribute to the extract concerned. Finally, particular passages or references are explained, book-titles identified, sources given for quotations etc. For journals, etc., the references given are to the reference book by the editor of the present volume: *Die Zeitschriften und Sammlungen des literarischen Expressionismus*. Stuttgart, Metzler, 1964 [= Raabe, No. . . .]. The editor has given the reference number in the text.

To avoid a maze of cross-references an alphabetical list of all persons mentioned in this book with brief comments on each name, has been compiled. Naturally, very well-known names especially from German literary history (e.g. Lessing, Goethe, Heine) are not included.

In the index at the end of the book all personal names are listed and page references given.

1 Textual Commentary

HEINRICH EDUARD JACOB

Berlin-Vorkriegsdichtung und Lebensgefühl. Written in 1961, published in: *Imprimatur. Ein Jahrbuch für Bücherfreunde*, New Series, Vol. 3 (1961-62), pp. 186–89. The author (b. October 7th, 1889, died October 25th, 1967) studied in Berlin before World War I. Since 1910 belonged to the New Club circle and so was early acquainted with Kurt Hiller, Georg Heym and his friends. Contributor to *Aktion, Pan, Sturm*, etc. At the time J. was working on his novel *Der Zwanzigjährige* (publ. 1918).

1 In 1908 Paul Cassirer put on a Van Gogh Exhibition in his Show Room.
2 U. Gaday was Franz Pfemfert's *nom de plume*.
3 After the title-poem *An Gladys* in Ernst Blass' volume of verse, *Die*

Strassen komme ich entlang geweht. Heidelberg, Richard Weissbach, 1912, p. 11.

4 From Kasimir Edschmid's manifesto: *Expressionismus in der Dichtung.* In: *Die Neue Rundschau.* No. 29, I (1918), p. 364.

5 Heym's dream-diaries are published in the collected works ed. Karl Ludwig Schneider, Vol. 3: Tagebücher, Träume, Briefe. 1960.

6 From Heym's poem *Berlin I.*

7 Cf. also H. E. Jacob, *Georg Heym. Erinnerung und Gestalt.* In: *Der Feuerreiter.* Vol. I (1922), pp. 52–65. This essay complements the passage printed here. On the New Club it has the following comment:

> The young emissaries of the neo-aristocratic trend are to be found every Wednesday evening in the back-room of a west-end hostelry, the Nollendorf Kasino in the Kleiststrasse. Who are they? Amid all the clouds of smoke and the gaseous discussions the blood-red covers of the *Fackel* and the *Schaubühne* are easier to spot than the human faces, but some who can be identified are Erwin Loewenson the student of philosophy, John Wolfson the student of art history, Jakob van Hoddis the poet, Schulze and Baumgardt the lawyers, occasionally also Ernst Blass the poet and Robert Jentzsch who was later killed in the war. But the real central figure of the group clearly seems to be Kurt Hiller, the charming and engaging orator, logical debater and fiery pamphleteer—also the proud possessor of a Ph.D. and a bald head which is why, among all these extremely young men, he is the Club's spokesman. It is his bald pate which at public functions becomes the focus of popular vexation and the centre of attention. A few years later the poetess Else Lasker-Schüler was to write the line: "The light bulb is mirrored on his brow . . ." (p. 58).

8 The first line of Heym's poem *Der Krieg.*

9 The first *Aktion* "Revolution Ball" took place on February 4th, 1913 and was repeated on February 13th. The second "Revolution Ball" was one year later on February 4th, 1914, its sequel on February 23rd.

ARMIN T. WEGNER

Aufbruch. Berlin 1910. Appeared under the title: *Mahnmal der Dichtung. Ein Blatt der Erinnerung an das Geschlecht von 1910.* In: *Deutsche Zeitung* (Cologne), October 16th, 1961. The ending referred to the occasion for the piece, namely the visit of the Marbach Expressionism Exhibition to Berlin, and has been changed here. Wegner (b. October 15th, 1886 in Elberfeld) studied law and graduated in Berlin in 1913. His earlier volumes of verse were: *Zwischen zwei Städten.* 1909; *Gedichte in Prosa.* 1910; *Höre mich reden, Anna-Maria.* 1912; *Das Antlitz der Städte.* 1917; *Die Strasse mit den tausend Zielen.* 1924. Wegner was an *Aktion* contributor from 1917 on. Lives in Rome since leaving Germany.

1 Hiller had graduated in 1907 with a thesis on criminal law (*Die krimi-nalistische Bedeutung des Selbstmordes*). In 1910 Wegner was still a student.

2 The term first cropped up in Germany about 1911 and was then applied to literature.

3 The first two stanzas of Heym's poem *War*, which first appeared in 1912 in: Heym, *Umbra vitae. Nachgelassene Gedichte.*

4 *Revolution.* Bi-weekly. Ed. Hans Leybold [No. 5 ed. Franz Jung]. Vol. I, No. 1–5. Munich, H. F. S. Bachmair 1913 [cf. Raabe, No. 16].

5 On the "Revolution Ball", *see* Jacob, note 9.

ERNST BLASS

Das alte Café des Westens. Published in: *Die literarische Welt.* Vol. 4 (1928), No. 35, pp. 3–4. Blass (1890–1939) was the author of the once well-known book of verse *Die Strassen komme ich entlang geweht*, which on its appearance in 1912 made him famous in the Café des Westens circle in Berlin. In spring, 1913 he detached himself from this circle, and became associated in Heidelberg with a classicistic school of formal poetry; but he came back to Berlin during the war and later even found his way back to the Café life.

1 Much has been written about the Café des Westens, especially by the *habitués* themselves. John Höxter, for example, gives the following description (*So lebten wir. 25 Jahre Berliner Bohème.* Berlin, Biko-Verlag, 1929, pp. 38–43):

"Good-day, Herr Höxter!"

In the door-way stands Red Richard presenting arms with a wooden newspaper holder. "There's a letter for you at the bar." A nod of welcome from a plaster cast of Emperor Wilhelm II placed with unintentional symbolism on top of the squawk-box, in other words, the telephone kiosk. From the niche by the newspaper-stand the circle gathered round its leader, Dr. Kurt Hiller, calls to me with a gusto corresponding to its youth and advanced slogans, they are the Neo-Rhetoricals, the inventors of what Kerr called "Advanced Lyric Poetry": Jakob van Hoddis who shares my two-roomed flat, Georg Heym who had presented me with a flowery Biedermeier sofa for it, on condition that he could have the room and this piece of furniture for appropriate use once a week, Ernst Blass, Walter Mehring etc.; the youngest of the bunch, and the best among them were so soon to be lost. Van Hoddis, the never-satisfied brooder, disappeared in the darkness of insanity; Heym, a kind of German Rimbaud, drowned in the wintry waters of the Havel.

I stop for a couple of minutes to sort out door-key problems with Hoddis (he loses about one a week), then I have to move on to fetch my letter. But I am caught up at the very next table. Herwarth Walden's *Sturm* associates, Else Lasker-Schüler, Dr. Döblin, Peter Baum, Dr. S. Friedlaender-Mynona and Carl Einstein have visitors from Vienna; Karl Kraus and Adolf Loos are introducing their latest discovery to the Berliners—Oskar Kokoschka, the painter. Portrait sketches consisting of unusual lines and curly scratches are handed round and Koko enjoys himself making the incomprehensible even more difficult with obscure comments. For instance, when somebody fails to make out a vein on a head he has drawn he says: "It's a beastly worm."

Mynona, unsociable and desperately nervous, suddenly feels uncomfortable; his hands shake, beads of perspiration break out on his forehead. Suddenly I see him take his old heirloom of a time-piece out of his pocket, reach for a glass of water and then slowly slip the chronometer on the end of its chain into the cold water. "Ah," he sighs contentedly, conscious of my enquiring glance, "that *is* refreshing." And then slips his watch back into his pocket as if nothing unusual had occurred. *Probatum est!*

Anton, the placid waiter who always looks so pale, has meanwhile brought me my letter. There is no *billet-doux* in the envelope, just two theatre tickets; the *Comédie Française* is doing a season at Kroll's under Monnet-Sully, and Dr. Karl Ludwig Schröder's *Deutsche Theater-Zeitung* and its editorial staff of Gustav Hartung and Dr. Richard Bermann-Höllriegel have given me the job of using it for my weekly theatre review and caricature.

Now a few tables along, among the faces of my real day- and night-time friends, Erich Mühsam, Ferdinand Hardekopf, René Schickele, Rudolf Kurtz, Ali Hubert, Benno Berneis, Lotte Pritzel, Emmy Hennings etc. I notice a new face; Max Oppenheimer [Mopp] the artist from Prague is the newcomer who, for the time being, is trying to get himself known, liked and appreciated by telling funny stories. Quietly I sit down beside them and join in the gales of laughter. Mopp is reaping great triumphs. In the end he notices me: "Well now, Herr Höxter," he says, "from what we hear in Prague you're supposed to be such a funny man and you're sitting there not saying anything?" "What do you expect in your presence, Herr Oppenheimer? How could I a piece-worker in the joke business compete with a whole department-store of jokes like you? No, no my dear fellow. I know when I'm beaten! What a gigantic stock of jokes and all so astonishingly cheap!"

Meanwhile Mühsam has decided to accompany me to the *Comédie*; but for the moment he can't pay for his coffee. Dr. von Rosenberg, the always helpful Russian Privy Councillor, whispers to him: "I've just remembered I owe you ten Marks; do you mind if I let you have them now . . ." "You're wrong," Mühsam interrupts him coldly, "it was twenty marks!" Exploiter? Anarchist? Bohemian? To find the answer consult Mühsam's own book "On the morality of borrowing money".

Besides, the Privy Councillor thought nothing of it, or at most took it as a joke. He was never mean; every day he used to go to the office of his investment consultant Hugo Karo and so as not to lose a moment he would take Hans Braun with him in a taxi. But he never had any idea whether his accounts were in the red or not.

The following little episode is typical of the way he handled money. Herr von Rosenberg could not stand being alone. Braun, his legal adviser, is late; so he asks me to accompany him to town. He tells the taxi driver to stop outside the new three-tiered shopping arcade in the Friedrichstrasse: "This we must see!" "Right!" We stroll through the gigantic building; through the first floor, the second and the third. The taxi waits outside. In front of a counter on which there are 5, 10 and 20 Mark tickets for the first demonstration flight by the Wright brothers, organized by the Berliner Zeitung, he stops. "Lucky we came this way, otherwise I'd have forgotten all about this! Now, miss, give me . . . let me see, Höxter, who do you think would like to go along? My friend Braun, Miss Schnor, you, me . . . Yes, and maybe Begas! That's . . . let me see . . . five, yes five tickets at 20 marks each, if you please!" I say thank you, he pays with a 100 mark note and we go. We're hardly back in the taxi when the Councillor turns to me: "Oh, my dear Höxter, how embarrassing . . . would you do me a favour and pay the taxi? I've just remembered that 100 mark note was all the money I had!" Yes, life is hard, but there are always some things that are really essential.

2 The New Club was founded in 1909 by Kurt Hiller as a literary secession from the Free Academic Society of Berlin. The first members, apart from Kurt Hiller himself were Erwin Loewenson, Jakob van Hoddis, Erich Unger, John Wolfson, and W. S. Ghuttmann. A collection of documents on the New Club is being prepared for the present *Literature of Expressionism* series by Karl Ludwig Schneider.

3 Blass' poem appeared in the *Fackel*. Vol. 12 (1910–11), No. 313–14, p. 29.

4 *Schloss Nornepygge* appeared in 1908. Hiller's enthusiastic review can be found in: Hiller, *Die Weisheit der Langenweile*. Vol. I. Leipzig 1913, pp. 143–51.

5 Presumably this refers to the Max Brod evening organized by the *Aktion* on December 15th, 1911 in the Harmoniumsaal in Berlin. Brod read the still unpublished *Weltfreund* poems. Werfel himself was not present.

6 *Herder-Blätter* (Ed. Willy Haas and Norbert Eisler, Vol. 4/5 together with Otto Pick.) Vol. I, No. 1–4/5. Prague, Publisher J. G. Herder-Vereinigung 1911–12. [Cf. Raabe, No. 6.]

7 The journals mentioned are: *Hyperion*. A Bimonthly Journal. Ed. Franz Blei and Carl Sternheim. Series 1–3. Munich, Hans v. Weber 1908–10. *Der lose Vogel*. A monthly magazine. Ed. Franz Blei. Vol. I. Leipzig, Demeter Verlag 1912–13. *Pan*. A Fortnightly Journal. Ed. Wilhelm Herzog and Paul Cassirer [later by Alfred Kerr]. Vols. 1–4. Berlin, Paul Cassirer [etc.] 1910–15. [Cf. Raabe No. 3.]

ALEXANDRA PFEMFERT

[*Die Gründung der "Aktion"*.] Extract from the Commemoration programme *Die Aktion*. *Stimmen der Freunde* broadcast by the Westdeutsche Rundfunk, Cologne in February, 1961. Research, recordings and commentary by Roland H. Wiegenstein. Alexandra Pfemfert *née* Ramm (1883–1963), who came to Germany with her sister Maria [Schaefer] in 1908, married Pfemfert and shared in the work of the *Aktion* from first to last.

1 *Der Demokrat*. Journal for liberal politics and literature. Ed. Georg Zepler. (Editor in Chief: Franz Pfemfert.) Vols. 2–3. Berlin 1910–11. Continued under the new name: *Der Weg*. Vols. 4–6. 1912–14.

2 The first number of the *Aktion* appeared on February 20th, 1911.

CLAIRE JUNG

Erinnerung an Georg Heym und seine Freunde. Extract from the unpublished memoirs: *Leuchtet die Zukunft*. A Statement of Accounts. Claire Jung *née* Otto (b. February 23rd, 1892) was the girlhood friend of Hildegard Krohn, Georg Heym's girl-friend. It was for her he wrote the famous poem *To Hildegard K*. Claire Otto was first married to Richard Oehring the writer, and then to Franz Jung from whom she was later separated. Now living in Berlin.

JOHANNES R. BECHER

[*On Jakob van Hoddis*.] Extract from Becher, *Das poetische Prinzip*. Berlin, Aufbau-Verlag 1957. pp. 102–8. Becher (1891–1958) born and bred in Munich, studied in Berlin in the winter semester 1911–12, then in Munich; it was here Jakob van Hoddis often visited him. Becher's earlier publications are listed here for ease of reference: *Der Ringende*. *Kleist-Hymne*. 1911; *Die Gnade eines Frühlings*. Poetic works 1912; *Erde*, a novel 1912; *De Profundis Domine* 1913; *Verfall und Triumph*. 2 vols. 1914. The first contribution to the *Aktion*: Vol. 1912, col. 355: *Auf die März-gefallenen 1848*. Later in his theoretical but very confessional books

312

Becher was often passionately and positively critical of his early literary beginnings. (Cf. *Verteidigung der Poesie.* 1952; *Poetische Konfession.* 1954; *Macht der Poesie.* 1955; *Das poetische Prinzip.* 1957.)

1 As already mentioned, Hoddis' *Weltende* was first published in the Berlin weekly *Der Demokrat* of January 11th, 1911, but was soon the talk of the town. Van Hoddis' impact on Becher lasted a long time (cf. Becher, *Ein Mensch unserer Zeit*, 1929, p. 9). In the sequel to his novel *Der Abschied* Becher calls Hoddis the "Founder of the Neopathetic School", and the poem *Weltende* "The Marseillaise of the Expressionist Revolution". Kurt Hiller, Franz Pfemfert, Kurt Pinthus and others also saw this poem as the beginning of the Expressionist movement. Richard Seewald, on the other hand (in: *Der Mann von gegenüber*, 1963, p. 273), says this:

A poem by Klabund seems to me to express better than any other the spirit of all those who started this revolution in 1910.

> *What a rotten business!*
> *At the fruitful moment for my parental pair,*
> *I was not even there.*

These three lines contain the whole thing *ab ovo*: the revolt not only against our fathers, but even the protest at being born at all; and to that extent it surpasses the Jakob van Hoddis poem *End of the World* which is generally taken as the beginning of Expressionism.

> *The bourgeois' hat flies off his pointed head,*
> *The air re-echoes with a cry.*
> *Roofers plunge and hit the ground.*
> *And at the coast—one reads—seas are rising.*

At the same time it must be admitted the situation at that time could not have been expressed in more concise symbols: the bourgeois, a figure of ridicule, loses his (top) hat, i.e. his dignity, which flies off his head, the general shouting, accorded no further explanation (is it fear or protest?), fills the air everywhere, the misfortune of those who attempt to patch up the faulty roof of the (ancestral) home, the mounting flood-tide of "barbarians" along the shores of Europe.

ALFRED RICHARD MEYER

[*Über Alfred Lichtenstein und Gottfried Benn.*] Extract from the extremely autobiographical book: *Die maer von der musa expressionistica.* Düsseldorf, Die Fähre 1948. pp. 12-16. A. R. Meyer (1882-1956) was the publisher of the Lyrische Flugblätter which appeared between 1907 and 1924. This was a collection of Expressionist poetry. He was also involved in Expressionism as author and critic. In his book he gives his personal slant on Early Expressionist poetry. The chapter printed here continues where Becher leaves off and is intended to characterize the atmospheric impact of the modern poetry of the time.

1 Lichtenstein's poem Die Dämmerung was published in: Der Sturm, Vol. I (1910-11), No. 55, March 18th, 1911, p. 439, also in: Simplicissimus, No. 16 (1911-12), p. 450. When Lichtenstein published the poem with his own commentary (Die Aktion, No. 3, 1913, Section 942 ff.), Pfemfert made the following remark: "Remember the fine poem: Weltende . . . by Jakob van Hoddis published in the first year of the Aktion. The fact is that Alfred Lichtenstein had read this poem before he ever wrote anything like it himself. So it is my belief that it is to van Hoddis the credit goes for having found this 'style', to Lichtenstein goes the lesser credit for having developed, enriched and helped it along."

2 Schickele in an article Freischärler (Die Bücherei Maiandros. Book 4/5. Supplement, May 1st, 1913, p. 4).

3 Zwiebelfisch. Vol. 4 (1912), 2, p. 75 f. The quotation is the conclusion of the brief review.

4 In a collective review Gedichtbände by Hans Friedrich. In: Janus. Münchener Halbmonatsschrift für Literatur, Kultur, Kritik. Nr. 1 (1911-12), 15, April 1st, 1912, p. 358. The reviewer continues, with Georg Heym's Ewiger Tag in mind: "The latest literature of the Imperial Capital (for it is only in its air that such abortions can thrive and only there that a publisher can be found tasteless enough to print them) is bringing forth strange blossoms, but they have a nasty smell of decay."

MAX BROD

[Der junge Werfel und die Prager Dichter.] Extracts from his autobiography: Streitbares Leben, Munich, Kindler 1960, pp. 12-18, 21-24, 27-29. Brod (b. on May 27th, 1884, died December 20th, 1968, in Prague) is associated with the history of Expressionist literature in Prague both by personal friendships and by his own literary activities. The passages included here from his Autobiography are intended to give an impression of the personality of the young Franz Werfel and his friends. The whole of Brod's book is strongly recommended. Further information in the memoirs of Willy Haas, though he does not give references: Die literarische Welt. Munich, List 1957.

1 Brod's early books: Tod den Toten. 1906; Experimente. Four stories

1907; *Schloss Nornepygge*. The novel of the indifferent man. 1908; *Der Weg des Verliebten*. 1908; *Die Erziehung zur Hetäre*. 1909; *Ein tschechisches Dienstmädchen*. 1909; *Tagebuch in Versen*. 1910.

2 Cf. Kurt Hiller, *Die Weisheit der Langenweile*. Vol. I. Leipzig, Wolff, 1913, pp. 143–51.

3 There it says: "Brod's *adlatus* became the early Werfel . . . Werfel owes the new language he developed in his *Weltfreund* to the preliminary work done by Brod."

4 Willy Haas also write on the publication of this poem (*Die literarische Welt*, 1957, p. 19).

JOHANNES URZIDIL

Im Prag des Expressionismus. Written 1961, first version in : *Imprimatur*, New Series, Vol. 3 (1961–62), pp. 202–4; printed here from the revised and extended text, which forms the introductory chapter to : Johannes Urzidil, *Da geht Kafka*. Zurich, Artemis 1965. Urzidil (b. February 3rd, 1896 in Prague, died November 2nd, 1970) published his first poems in the *Aktion* 1916. His volume of Expressionistic verse appeared 1919 : *Sturz der Verdammten*. The present summary survey is expanded in Urzidil's *Prager Triptychon* (1960). There memories of the Expressionist period were turned into stories.

1 *Der Mensch*. Cultural monthly. Ed. Leo Reiss. Vol. I. Brünn, Verlag der Zeitschrift *Der Mensch*, 1918. [Cf. Raabe, No. 38.]

KURT PINTHUS

Leipzig und der frühe Expressionismus. Written in the autumn of 1964 in Marbach a. N. for publication in this volume. The author used the appropriate paragraphs from his story of the Ernst Rowohlt Verlag (In : *Rowohlt Almanach*, 1902-1962. Reinbek, Rowohlt, 1962, pp. 9–40) some of which he was able to use unaltered. He also used his works on Walter Hasenclever (In : Hasenclever, *Gedichte—Dramen—Prosa*. Ed. by Kurt Pinthus. Reinbek, Rowohlt, 1963, pp. 6–62, and on Kurt Wolff (Epitaph in : *Jahresring* 64–65, pp. 298–301). Pinthus (b. April 29th, 1886 in Erfurt) was reader with Rowohlt from 1919 on, then with Kurt Wolff in Leipzig. 1919 saw the publication of his epoch-making anthology *Menschheitsdämmerung*. From 1919 he was mainly critic and writer in Berlin. On leaving Germany he went to live in New York.

1 On the printing of Georg Heym's poems cf. Georg Heym, *Dichtungen und Schriften* ed. by Karl Ludwig Schneider. Vol. 3 (1960), p. 222 ff.

2 On the history of the Kurt Wolff Verlag see the picture presented by Karl H. Salzmann, *Kurt Wolff, der Verleger. Ein Beitrag zur Verlags-*

und Literaturgeschichte. In: *Archiv für Geschichte des Buchwesens.* Vol. 2 (1958–60), pp. 375–403; Kurt Wolff, *Autoren, Bücher, Abenteuer. Betrachtungen und Erinnerungen eines Verlegers.* Berlin, Wagenbach 1965; also the memoirs of Arthur Seiffhart, *Inter folia fructus.* Berlin, Fundament Verl. 1948.

3 On the whole series cf. Ludwig Dietz, *Kurt Wolffs Bücherei "Der jüngste Tag". Seine Geschichte und Bibliographie.* In: *Philobiblon* 7 (1963), pp. 96–118.

RICHARD SEEWALD

[*Im Café Stefanie.*] Extract from Seewald autobiography: *Der Mann von gegenüber.* Reflection of a life. Munich, List, 1963, pp. 137–143. Seewald (b. May 4th, 1889 in Arnswalde), painter, graphic artist and writer in Ronco, lived in Munich until 1924, during his early life he was in close contact with the Munich Bohemians. To supplement and expand the present description we include here a passage from Franz Jung's autobiography *Der Weg nach unten* (Neuwied, Luchterhand, 1962, pp. 69–72):

> *Bohemianism disintegrates*: In 1911 I was already too late for the Schwabing Bohemianism which put its stamp on nearly a decade of German literature and art. There may possibly have been some common bond earlier holding the Schwabingers together that resulted in their being characterized as Bohemians—their deliberate affront to anything conventional or to bourgeois traditions perhaps, the *élan* of their "épatez le bourgeois" which they had taken over from Paris. In this climate of deliberate affront to the bourgeoisie there must have been a deeper purposefulness than I ever came across. There was a certain residue of this left over isolated and almost timeless already . . . the habit of borrowing from artists who had "arrived" and whose pictures sold readily, and of making sure never to pay the landlady her rent on time; that's about all it came to.
>
> The new secession which had formed out of scattered groups was already falling apart. Their literary equivalent had not yet acquired any particular profile or character. The painters left were completely outside the original Bohemian circle and already making the breakthrough to Expressionism, that provocatively independent art form not influenced by Paris or Milan. In the sphere of literature, on the other hand, I came across nothing but business as usual. The older types who probably thought of themselves as Bohemians in the old days met outside Schwabing in the Torgelstube—the Wedekinds, Halbes, Bierbaums, Bleibtreus etc., the contributors and editors of the journals *Simplicissimus* and *Jugend* and all the other literary gentlemen who had been accepted there, Herr Piper and Herr Langen and the patrons of the arts who were already calling themselves

essay writers; this circle was very exclusive. It was really more of a skittle club.

In the Café Stefanie there was a splendid man, Dr. Franz Blei, endowed with vast critical acumen—it gives me special satisfaction to say that because Blei treated me with a contempt he never tried to conceal—the *Trottelbuch* had just been published—he always dismissed me completely as a writer. He had his own circle of young people, scions of well-to-do parents, with aesthetically attuned and beautiful manners. They had come to Munich to learn the business of writing, that's to say, how to write novels and assemble poems . . . as a hobby. Blei introduced these people to the literary game, brought them to the notice of the journals he was associated with and made them buy from the Munich publishers. This circle too considered itself very exclusive and Margot felt very much at home in it.

And in the Café Stefanie itself Erich Mühsam and Roda Roda, both really Torgelstube types, still sat playing chess every day at the same time. Attraction for visitors. Julius, the head-waiter, used to show them off to tourists as sights worth seeing—Mühsam because of his revolutionary's beard, Roda Roda because of his red waist-coat.

Among the Bohemians who had changed over from the Café Dôme in Paris to the Stefanie in Munich Henri Bing, the Simplicissimus cartoonist, put on the biggest show. He, too, was always surrounded by a circle of like-minded disciples—like-minded in conceit, loud-mouthed in their behaviour and lavish in throwing money about even when they had none; Julius, the waiter, had to put up the money and then see that he got it all back again. I assume that the majority of the Bing-disciples later all became commercial travellers. In this circle too Margot was a very welcome guest.

The Bohemian way of life had already been drawn into the maelstrom of the general economic crisis which was to put its mark on the century more and more as time passed. The most important rôle in the socially critical destruction of the "good old days" was played by Sigmund Freud's concept of psychoanalysis. The fight over the correct interpretation of the master's principles between the disciples who had abandoned Freud the master was over. Otto Gross, assistant under Kräpelin at the Munich University Psychiatric Clinic, had already left Munich for Ascona and was carrying on his studies independently there.

In his Munich period Otto Gross had gathered a circle of followers who for the most part went to Ascona with him; the ones I knew were Leonhard Frank, Karl Otten, Frick and Schiemann whom I was to meet again ten years later in Moscow. The Ascona crowd often came to Munich, and Otto Gross himself with whom I became better acquainted on one of these visits.

I myself was not in a position to observe the effect of this group

317

in undermining traditional cultural and social concepts. The better I got to know Gross later, the more I grew to regret the years I wasted as a commercial correspondent in Berlin. In all the years to come I was never to make up for all the time I lost.

For further autobiographical descriptions see: Erich Mühsam, *Namen und Menschen*. Unpolitical memories. Leipzig, Volk und Buch 1949; Oskar Maria Graf, *Wir sind Gefangene*. München, Drei Masken-Verl. 1927.

1 *Kain*. Journal for humanity. Ed. by Erich Mühsam. Vol. 1–5. Munich, Kain-Verl. 1911–14, 1919. [Cf. Raabe, No. 5.]

2 Klabund and Richard Seewald: *Kleines Bilderbuch vom Krieg*. Munich, Goltz-Verl, 1914. 26 illustrations.

3 Frank's story *Die Ursache* was published in 1916 by Georg Müller, Munich.

MARIETTA

Klabund. Chapter from a book of Marietta di Monaco, *Ich kam—ich geh*. Travel-scenes, memories, portraits. With silhouettes by Ernst Moritz Engert. Munich, Süddeutscher Verlag, 1962, pp. 80–88. The ending has been omitted. Marietta, real name Marie Kirndörfer, was a friend of all the Schwabing Bohemians. In Munich in May, 1914 Klabund wrote a prose piece about her which was a mixture of truth and fiction: *Marietta. A love-story from Schwabing*. The story was probably first published about the end of 1914 in a daily paper [cf. Klabund in a letter to Walter Heinrich, February 23rd, 1914: "Have you read the Marietta story?"], in book-form 1920 as Vol. 79 of the *Silbergäule*. On the cover it says: "This is no *roman à clé*: laughing at life and death the artists explode into the action of this Romantic Schwabing love-story under their own names: Marietta, Klabund, J. R. Becher, Emmy Hennings, Dorka, Theodor Etzel and Heinrich F. S. Bachmair the publishers. And all the goings on at the Simplicissimus, the artists' pub. And Munich." As Marietta's text follows the Klabund one very closely, especially in two paragraphs—though with notable departures—the Klabund text is here included in full:

I have no father-land.
I have no mother-land.
Every foreign language reminds me of home.
I am a Polish princess: pretty but sloppy.
I squint.
That's how I see the world.
I really ought to wear a monocle.
I win a cow-bell from the Munich Welfare Lottery.

I tie it round my neck and let it tinkle.
Everybody would like to be my cow-boy.
I am Marietta.

But I am not quite Marietta yet.
I am still working up to it.
I am still undecided.
Sparkling fire.
And lots of smoke.
I wear an orange blouse all wrongly buttoned up and I tell blue
fairy-tales and grey anecdotes by Klabund every night at the
Simplicissimus.
Some of them are faintly pink and taste of raspberry jam.
I earn 4 Marks a show and not even my dinner thrown in.
I'm looking for an extra job.
Yesterday a very young, beardless youth came into the Simplicissimus
with Etzel.
Etzel said: "This gentleman wants a manuscript typed!"
I can type, because I used to work in the office of Lese, a paper near
the Cattle Mart.
I said: "I'll be glad to do it."
The young man ordered me a glass of punch.
I sat down beside him.
We didn't say much.
He shyly put his arm round my waist once.
Emmy Hennings sang her song about "little legs".
She screeched like a Danish sea-gull, rising from the waters of the
Kattegatt.
"Come round tomorrow morning about eleven and collect the manu-
script," said the young man and left.
He moved like an athlete and had eyes like a pirate.
He was wearing a suit of pale sail-cloth.
He smelled of seaweed and swayed like a sailor.

The young man lives at Kaulbachstrasse 56, ground floor.
The door was open when I arrived and he said: "Like to come part
of the way with me? Here is the manuscript!"
On the table lay a cheque from the Jugend.
I took the manuscript.
It was verse.
I asked him: "Did you write this?"
"Oh no," he smiled, "certainly not."
But I was sure he had.
—We walked along the Kaulbachstrasse.
In the sun.

He took his hat off and the sun descended on him like a golden bird.

"I'm lovely in the nude," I said.

I had to say something. "Habermann has painted me."

He looked down my blouse and said:

"Maybe!"

There was an Italian flower-seller on the corner of Kaulbach- and Veterinärstrasse.

He bought a red carnation from her and made me a present of it.

I felt he was making me a present of it.

He is proud.

I don't like him.

He said good-bye.

To get a typewriter I climbed through a ground-floor window into the office of Heinrich F. S. Bachmair whose maid I had once been.

I typed the poems on the office paper of Heinrich F. S. Bachmair Publishers because I could not find any other kind of paper.

Becher came in with Dorka and caught me.

He wanted to give me a thrashing. "What the hell are you doing here?"

But Dorka quietened him down.

They headed for the sofa in the next room.

The young man was not in Munich.

I brought the manuscript to a man he had written me about.

I got 8 Marks.

I cried.

I hated the young man who had gone away.

Who was a stranger to me.

So far "above" me.

Like an airman.

I had to get away.

I was sick of Munich.

Major Hoffman spoke to me in the Café Stefanie:

"How would you like to model for Princess von Thurn und Taxis?"

I said: "Love to." (. . . I look lovely in the nude. Habermann did a picture of me . . .)

I was cabled the fare and went.

Princess von Thurn und Taxis' photograph always hangs above my bed.

She is a regal woman. Her presents are regal. But the hands she bestows them with are those of a dethroned bourgeoise.

While she is modelling me I read aloud from a book: *The Japanese Nightingale*.
Or I tell her all sorts of stories.
All sorts fondle me and I am like stone.
I tell her I have slept on landings and on a bench in the gardens of the Pinakothek.
I opened my eyes about 4 a.m. and the soldier on guard stood over me.
With shouldered arms he smiles: "Had a good sleep?"
He says he is a baker and used to getting up early.
He likes all-night guard duty when the stars pass across the sky like golden children, hand in hand. He likes being a soldier.
There were lovely roses in the gardens: light red and dark red. The guard told me to pick some. He'll watch out for the police.

The weather turns cold.
I have no coat.
I sleep with a business man called Hirsch.
He looks like a dusty book nobody likes to touch.
He is anonymous.
He splutters with excitement.
He has a brother and a friend who are both painters.
They make fun of him: "You have not got a chance with Marietta, She is a Bohemian. She doesn't do it for money!"
Hirsch has given me 50 Marks.
He asks me to marry him.
He is very concerned about me.
He makes the waiter bring me a foot-stool.
I put my feet under it so that no one will see the holes in my shoes.
He is very unhappy.
He thinks his brother and his friend have the ideal profession.
While all he does is make money.
What could he have to offer me?
I'm an ideal girl in his eyes. (He must have read Murger's *Bohème* before he tried to sleep with me.)
I said I was nothing like the ideal girl he took me for.
For I would never sleep with him again.
Despite the 50 Marks.

I don't let it get me down.
We are sitting in the Café Stefanie.
The young man is there too.
He has just got back.
While I was in Paris he was in Switzerland.

In Paris I passed through the Red Sea with dry feet the waves arched before me.

He still thinks he can ignore me as if I were a pebble.

But now I am a rock.

He is taken aback.

His forehead bleeds from beating against the stone.

I love him.

His blood runs into my womb.

I tell him about Paris.

We drink Samos in the "Gay Bird".

About nine o'clock in the evening we take a cab to the Isar valley.

It rains.

We run over a hare.

It was a female carrying three young.

The driver will have it for tea.

His wife will serve it up with cucumber salad.

We conceive the idea of founding a club and all buying green scarves.

It is five o'clock in the morning.

The new day waves its yellow hat.

From behind clouds.

We stroll along the Leopoldstrasse.

The poplars stand erect like male organs, but in full foliage.

I tell him about Paris.

He is as silent as a dictaphone faithfully recording everything you speak into it.

Oh if only he would keep all of me!

Not just what I say: my hair too.

My tiny breasts.

My obscene slanted eyes and my slender feet.

And my thirsty mouth.

I am his child.

I lie curled up in his belly.

My fists clenched before my blind eyes.

Whom will they hit when my eyes can see?

He will give birth to me.

Next morning he tells his landlady to bring breakfast.

Eggs, cocoa and ham.

His room is very small.

On the walls hang pictures he has bought at the fair.

At about 1,25 Mark a piece.

He says they are by Veronese, Habermann (whom I know), Paolo Francese and Anton von Werner. There's a nude among them with breasts swirling to her knees.

The postman knocks.
I pull the cover over my head.
The young man gives me 10 Marks.
He smiles says he is going to write a feature about me.
For the *Berliner Tageblatt*.
The 10 Marks are my share of the fee.
Maybe I could help him make a lot of money if I would go to Monte Carlo with him next spring, he says.
I'd be his capital.
He would pay for my wardrobe.
And shares in me would soar away up over the 500 mark . . .

I tell the young man (who now hangs over my bed beside Princess von Thurn and Taxis: a laughing face in hat and coat)—that I keep a diary.
I keep it like you'd keep a mountain mule guiding it along stony paths past turbulent chasms and patina green pastures.
But away in the distance the white Jungfrau gleams with her silver horn and Grindelwald rests in sun-lit silence.
He thinks this is marvellous.
Says I must bring him the diary some time.
Maybe he could show it to his publisher.
Maybe he would publish it.

When I left him there was a bunch of crushed carnations on the stairs.
Did he ever love me?
My head is forced round.
He is not human.
He is a forest with a thousand trees.
Mountain forest.
Reaching for a different sun.
With winds blowing from Uruguay.

"Marietta," the young man said, "I shall consult the heads of the hangman's victims about my fate. . ."
I was scared, laughed nervously.
For the hangman's victims know everybody's dark future.
"If they tell me the truth I shall offer up a gold coin to you, Marietta."
He disappeared behind the curtain.
Suddenly a scream rang out.
Not one scream: millions of horrible screams.
It came from outside and from the window where I was standing I was flung dazed back into the room.

I drew back the curtain.
The young man was hanging from the hook over the stove.
His eyes crept from their sockets like two snails.
On the ground by his feet lay a mint-new coin.

I shall never consult the heads of the hangman's victims about myself.
(And that terrible scream on the death of the young man. I have
a natural explanation for it: it came from the nearby slaughter-house.
It was the scream of thousands of dying oxen, calves, pigs.)
When I die the oxen will not scream . . .
I yearn for the electrifying intoxication of the boulevards.
For Paris.
For the little prostitutes who gleam like porcelain in the dusk. For
the thin flower-girls who will masturbate with you for a franc in the
dim lobbies.
My head feels as if I've been hanged.
The young man has hanged me.
My head hangs perpendicular like a chandelier from the ceiling.
My eyes burn like wax candles.
They are fragrant.
Like Christmas.
I am Maria.
I shall conceive the Holy Ghost.
Immaculate.

1 Mistakenly for 1912 as the context shows.
2 Klabund lived in Munich, Kaulbachstrasse 56 during the winter semester
  1912–13.
3 Klabund's *Morgenrot! Klabund! Die Tage dämmern!* was published by
  Erich Reiss in Berlin, September, 1913.
4 No trace of this in Becher's early works.
5 On his association with Max Halbe, Klabund writes to Walter Heinrich
  on November 18th, 1912: "Herr Henckell has been good enough to
  introduce me to Halbe's Bowling Club and the Young Crocodile." On
  December 30th, 1912, he writes: "I spent Christmas Eve with Mühsam
  at Halbe's house. Halbe is a charming person—and he can tell stories
  better than he writes them—but his daughter is even more charming.
  What I found delightfully unliterary, as I already saw Dietrich Stobäus
  hanging over my head, was the fact that he gave me some *pâté de foie
  gras* and a bottle of Danziger Goldwasser." (Klabund, *Briefe an einen
  Freund.* Ed. by Ernst Heinrich. Cologne 1963, p. 62f.) This incident
  turns up again in Klabund's extremely autobiographical novel *Roman
  eines jungen Mannes*, though much caricatured.
6 Berlin, Erich Reiss 1916, p. 62.

7 This refers to the trilogy of one-acters *Russland marschiert, Der feiste Kapaun, Tommy Atkins*, which were performed in Munich, autumn, 1914.

HEINRICH F. S. BACHMAIR

Bericht eines Verlegers 1911–1914. Published in the second Johannes R. Becher supplement of the journal *Sinn und Form*, 1960, pp. 97–110, under the title: *Bericht des ersten Verlegers 1911–1914*. However, as this excellent essay is more than a study of Becher alone the title was changed for the present collection of texts. Bachmair (1889–1960), pseudonym Sebastian Scharnagl, was involved in Early Expressionism in Munich both as publisher and author.

By way of additional commentary two passages from Johannes R. Becher's *Tagebuch 1950: Auf andere Art so grosse Hoffnung* (Berlin, Aufbau-Verlag, 1951) are included here in the notes, referring to the first section:

—Berlin: September 30th: Saturday.

Spent a considerable time in the Warsaw Bridge district: there in the Memeler Strasse was where I started my discovery of Berlin in 1911. The tall tenement building in which I had a scantily furnished room thrust out like a three-cornered rock into the surf of the big city; on the first floor was the Café Komet, whose band provided my enchanted lullaby, whenever I did happen to sleep at home, which was rare. For night and day I was making voyages of discovery the length and breadth of Berlin. A Polish widow was my landlady; she had a wastrel of a son who used to beat her if she didn't give him money for the cinema. (When I think back I can still recall the wonderful taste of breakfast on my tongue, *very* yellow, rather runny butter and warm newly-baked rolls—indifferent coffee.) A few houses further along the Memeler Strasse lived Bachmair. At his place we founded our publishing house; the *Kleist-Hymme*, that misbegotten opus, was published right there in the Memeler Strasse. Why did we decide to live there when we had an adequate allowance? Because we wanted to go and live among the people, to get away from our well-to-do parental background. Of course, whenever we went out and about we did so with an adequate monthly cheque. Our regular haunt of paradise became the "Aschinger" whose mounds of free bread-rolls we found particularly attractive. Then Bachmair drummed up an author of "best-sellers" for his publishing firm in the shape of Frances Külpe, a Baltic-German lady; this grandmother of a star-attraction helped us to get our *Kleist-Hymne* off the ground. Her shocker of a book was called *On the Volga* . . . From the Warsaw Bridge area I timidly moved into the Café des Westens, and at once I got to know Franz Pfemfert, the editor of the *Aktion*. Getting to know him meant real contact with the world of literature. The Bonsels Circle in Munich, into which I had been accepted, had no further hold over me, although my first attempts had been strongly influenced by Bonsels, Brandenburg, Isemann and Dehmel of course . . . When I came back in 1945 I happened to meet Alois the waiter in the re-opened Café Vienna and he promptly presented me with a bill from 1913 for a lunch I had once had in the Café des Westens and never paid for. This bill which he had saved up over forty years was a remarkably grotesque welcome. (p. 522f.)

May 9th–12th: Tuesday to Friday.
Stood outside the house in Nassauische Strasse 17: the *Aktion* office (at the back of the building). How anxious I was the first time I went in there and climbed the steps, held my breath and rang the bell, until I stood in front of the desk at which sat Franz Pfemfert, and waiting for the life-and-death decision heard that the poem I had sent in would be published in the next number. No other publication ever gave me such a feeling of tension and joy as the sight of a poem published in the *Aktion*: it seemed to confirm me as a poet and as a revolutionary [. . .]. The house with the boarded-up church looked just as I remembered it. I tried to conjure up the atmosphere of those years, Kaiserallee, Spessartstrasse, Emserstrasse, Kurfürstendamm, Café des Westens, Olivaer Platz, Paulsborner Strasse, Uhlandstrasse, Halensee—but wherever I roamed, starting in the Memeler Strasse by the Warsaw Bridge where the publishing business was launched with H. F. S. Bachmair—only a very remote trace of the atmosphere of that wonderful, passionately-ecstatic and crazy youth still remained—it was gone for ever . . . This gone-for-ever-feeling was in itself a feature of my own home-coming. Incidentally my first poem published in the *Aktion* was called "Auf die Märzgefallenen (1848)" (p. 266f.)

1 Becher's poem *Christine* is in his verse-collection *München in meinem Gedicht*. Starnberg, Bachmair 1946, p. 22f.
2 Richard Dehmel read in the Neuer Verein, end of November, 1909. Becher describes his visit to the poet in his novel *Der Abschied*. This visit is also mentioned in Becher's letters to Dehmel (Hamburg, Staatsbibliothek: Dehmel-Archiv) most of which are still unpublished.
3 Reviewed by Hans Brandenburg in: *Deutsches Literaturblatt*. Ed. Michael Georg Conrad. Vol. 2 (1912), No. 5 of May 1st, p. 4.
4 Reviewed by Hans von Hülsen in: *Janus*. Vol. I (1912), No. 14, p. 332f.
5 Reviewed by Alfred Richard Meyer in: *Die Aktion*. Vol. I (1911), col. 1397.
6 Albert Michel's book of verse *Frühling* was published in 1914, in the same year as another: *Bergtod und andere Gedichte*.
7 Contributions by Michel in the *Aktion* 1914 and 1915. To him Becher dedicates his poem *Getötetem Freund. Vermächtnis des sterbenden*

Soldaten. (Becher, *Verbrüderung*. Poems. Leipzig, Kurt Wolff, 1916, p. 29–31.)

8 Included here, pp. 322–327.

9 Becher writes about his friend Emmy Hennings, to whom various of his poems are dedicated, in this *Tagebuch* 1950 (Berlin, Aufbau-Verlag, 1951, p. 237f.):

> Found one of Emmy Hemmings' poems too in the *Aktion*. She was my first poetic venture, my passionate adventure, whirling me right into the heart of the literary world and introducing me to Leonhard Frank, van Hoddis, Hardekopf etc. She is portrayed in *Abschied*. Later as Hugo Ball's wife she became a devout Catholic, saw her for the last time in 1934 near Lugano in a forgotten Tessin village—half old woman, half little girl—I owe her a lot, a whole lot for my first attempts. It's often been said of me I always paid in cash: this is is not true . . . On the contrary, for most of what I have accomplished I still owe a lot to this day. I have left gigantic unpaid debts all over the place.

One characteristic passage from Becher's novel *Abschied* (Berlin, Aufbau-Verlag, 1945, p. 359f.) is quoted here:

> Magda invited me into the Castle gardens. We sat outside in the open air in the Arcade Café. In the little pavilion a military band was playing. I was standing in the tobacco shop on the Kosttor, puffing out the smoke from a cigarette, because yesterday the case against Kunik for robbery and murder had begun in camera.
>
> "You know," Magda sought me out with her eyes: "You used to write good poems. I still know one of them by heart! Listen to it:
>
>> At night, now and then,
>> You tell yourself yet again:
>> Time seems to be in spate.
>> 'Must make ready, at this rate!'
>>
>> Time is always in spate.
>> Soon it will be late.
>> Soon all shall be still.
>> If that is time's will.
>>
>> Till the message at the door
>> Reads: Never more.
>
> That's the real thing . . . But the stuff you are scribbling nowadays . . . Well, better not think about it . . . Doctor Hoch has condemned me to death for incurable complexes . . . That would just suit him! No thanks, I won't let him send me to the dogs, no sir . . . You soul-

searchers, you human tin-openers! Nobody could put up with you for long! How I'd like to just love somebody, just love somebody . . . Real corny with lace doilies and lucky porcelain figures: that would be really living, wonderful, eh? . . . That's what you drive a person to with all your *outré* behaviour . . . Stop thinking about how dangerous you are: You're harmless, a bunch of bourgeois gone hay-wire . . . You can't kid me, I'm from the country, from Holstein, my mother took in washing . . . What use are you to anybody, none, not even to yourselves . . . Something will have to bring you to your senses . . . Sack is the only one among you who's worth anything. He just pretends to go along with you. He writes about hunger and the poor. And about making something of yourself . . . Why am I telling you all this? I don't know either. You miserable fool you . . ."

I poked about in my ear again.

Bourgeois gone hay-wire, she had said. She looked across to the the military band, and turned away:

"To be hanged . . ."

"You still at school?" She asked casually in a different voice.

"Upper sixth. Leaving certificate exams are in three days."

"Interesting. Have you done any work for them?"

"Yes, I've done all the work."

"Studying is hard, isn't it?"

"Grammar school boys like us have no easy time of it."

"Does learning come easy to you?"

"For somebody like me it's not easy to . . ."

"Oh, I understand. I have a hard time of it too. You see, I have to bring up a child into the bargain."

"You sing at the 'Wasp', don't you? . . ."

10 *Das Verhältnis*. Novelle. In: *Die Neue Kunst*. Vol. I (1913–14), pp. 31–56; a different version under the title: *Das kleine Leben*. In: Becher, *Verfall und Triumph*, Vol. 2. Berlin. Hyperion-Verlag, 1914.

11 Published by Bachmair, 1913.

12 *Die neue Zeit*. Contributions to the History of Modern Literature. Ed. H. F. Bachmair. 1st Book. Munich, H. F. S. Bachmair, 1912 [Cf. Raabe, No. 133].

13 *Die Neue Kunst*. Bimonthly. Ed. Heinrich F. S. Bachmair in association with Josef Amberger, Johannes R. Becher and Karl Otten. Vol. I. Munich, Bachmair, 1913–14 [Cf. Raabe, No. 14].

14 Josef Amberger, *Der unendliche Weg*. Poems. Munich, Bachmair, 1914. 64 pages; Karl Otten, *Die Reise durch Albanien*, 1912. With 7 drawings by Franz Henseler. Munich, Bachmair 1913. 71 pages.

15 Franz Blei, *Die Welle*. Play in 3 acts. Producer: Hugo Ball; designer Richard Seewald. *Première* in the Munich Kammerspiele on December 10th, 1913. First show put on by the journal *Die Neue Kunst*. Pro-

gramme (8 pages) with short commentaries by Franz Blei, Hans Leybold, Robert Gournay, Friedrich Markus Huebner, Robert Musil.
16 Fortnightly. Ed. Hans Leybold [No. 5 ed. by Franz Jung]. Vol. 1,
No. 1–5. Munich, H. F. S. Bachmair, 1913 [Cf. Raabe, No. 16].

FRITZ MAX CAHÉN

Der Alfred Richard Meyer-Kreis. Written in 1961, published in: (*Imprimatur.*) New Series Vol. 3 (1961–62), pp. 190–193. Cahén writes in greater detail of his time with the Alfred Richard Meyer Circle in his memoirs, *Der Weg nach Versailles.* Memories of 1912–1919. Boppard, Boldt, 1963, p. 24ff. The author, later a political commentator (b. December 8th, 1891 in Saarlouis, died August 29th, 1966) studied for a few semesters at Paris among other places, was in Berlin from 1913 and published in A. R. Meyer's series *Die Bücherei Maiandros* 1913–14. On A. R. Meyer and his *Lyrische Flugblätter* see his book referred to above: *Die maer von der musa expressionistica.* Düsseldorf. Verlag Die Fähre 1948. Further material in George G. Kobbe, *Munkepunke-Bio-Bibliographie.* Berlin 1933; Catalogue Fa. Edelmann No. 69, 1962. A complete list of the *Lyrische Flugblätter* in: Raabe: *Die Zeitschriften und Sammlungen des literarischen Expressionismus,* 1964, pp. 163–68.
1 The *Paris* pamphlet cannot be traced.
2 Rudolf Leonhard, *Angelische Strophen.* Berlin, A. R. Meyer, 1913; *Beate und der grosse Pan,* written at that time, not published till 1918 (Munich, Roland Verl.)
3 *Morgue und andere Gedichte* published by A. R. Meyer in May, 1912, Benn's second pamphlet *Söhne.* New Poems in October, 1913.
4 *Ballhaus.* A lyrical Pamphlet. Published 1912 [Cf. Raabe, No. 110].
5 *Die Bücherei Maiandros.* A Periodical of 60 to 60 Days. Ed. Heinrich Lautensack, Alfred Richard Meyer, Anselm Ruest. Book 1–6 with supplements. Berlin-Wilmersdorf, Paul Knorr 1912–14 [Cf. Raabe, No. 11].
6 *Der Mistral.* A lyrical anthology [Ed. A. R. Meyer]. Berlin-Wilmersdorf, Paul Knorr 1913. (Die Bücherei Maiandros. IV–V Book.) [Cf. Raabe, No. No. 114].

WALTER MEHRING

Berlin Avant-garde. Published in: *Als das Jahrhundert jung war.* By Theodor Heuss. Ed. Josef Halperin. Zurich and Stuttgart, Artemis, 1961, pp. 31–40. Mehring (b. April 29th, 1896 in Berlin), writer and poet, was actively involved in Dada during the Expressionist period. The sketches included here are youthful impressions which mirror the atmosphere in

Berlin 1912–14. In addition cf. Mehring *Die verlorene Bibliothek.* Autobiography of a Culture. Hamburg, Rowohlt 1952 [2nd ed. Munich, Kreisselmeier 1964]; *Berlin Dada.* A Chronicle with photos and documents. Zurich, Verl. Die Arche, 1959.

1 *Der blaue Reiter* is meant. Ed. Kandinsky and Marc—Munich, Piper 1912.

2 Cf. the description in Mehring, *Die verlorene Bibliothek*, 1952, p. 107f.

3 Mehring is referring to the French Special Supplement of the *Aktion*, Vol. 5 (1915), No. 49/50 of December 4th. The dedication in italics in the first column of this number goes: "This special 'France' number is dedicated to Charles Péguy, the poet and André Derain, the painter who died in the war. F. P."

RUDOLF LEONHARD

Marinetti [in Berlin 1913]—published in: *Rudolf Leonhard erzählt.* Selected and introduced by Maximilian Scheer. Berlin. Verlag der Nation 1955. pp. 229–233. The passage is from the last years of the Expressionist and later Socialist writer Rudolf Leonhard (1889–1953). His most important early works are: *Angelische Strophen.* 1913; *Der Weg durch den Wald.* Poems. 1913; *Barbaren.* Ballads. 1914; *Über den Schlachten.* 1914; *Aeonen des Fegefeuers.* Aphorisms. 1917; *Polnische Gedichte.* 1918; *Beate und der grosse Pan.* 1918; *Katilinarische Pilgerschaft.* 1919; *Alles und Nichts!* Aphorisms. 1920 etc.

1 The first time Marinetti was in Berlin was April, 1912, for the *Sturm* Futurist Exhibition. Walden's journal *Der Sturm* published Marinetti's Futurist manifestos translated by Jean-Jacques [i.e. Hans Jacob in 1912. The latter writes about this in his memoirs *Kind meiner Zeit.* Cologne, Kiepenheuer-Verlag, 1962, p. 30–32]. In spring, 1913 Marinetti held a reading in Berlin. It was then that Alfred Döblin wrote his open anti-Marinetti letter *Futuristische Wortkunst* (*Der Sturm*, Vol. 3, March, 1913, No. 150/151, p. 28off.)

2 Marinetti, F. T.: *Futuristische Dichtungen.* Translated by Else Hadwiger. Berlin, A. R. Meyer, 1912. Published in 1912 with a preface by Rudolf Kurtz.

3 Leonhard wrote about the lecture in the *Bücherei Maiandros.* Book 4/5, Supplement for May 1st, 1913, p. 6f. as follows:

In the Choralionsaal a scintillating lecture by F. T. Marinetti, the discoverer, founder and leader of Futurism showed an enthusiastic and generally very appreciative audience yet again, that any—and I mean absolutely any—artistic theory is right for the person who conceives it. In Marinetti's case two theories have to be differentiated: the general and the technical. In the general theory, that is the part concerned with artistic ethics, he explains how literature

which in the past has always been in praise of contemplative immo-
bility, and even slumber, must now move on to sing the praises of
aggressive movement, feverish insomnia, must be in love with danger
and laud ceaseless energy and mad bravery, the dangerous leap, the
slap in the face, the punch in the jaw. And above all the new goddess
that sends us into ecstasies: speed. The racing car, the aeroplane,
war, anarchy, revolutions and electrically flood-lit arsenals are the
tasks the Futurist poet has to master, and to live up to them he must
explode with excessive heat and give his all. The present-day poet,
the Futurist, stands on the pinnacle of the ages; he must not be
backward looking; museums and libraries are to be destroyed. And
all art is war. These are all words which have often been uttered
over the last few centuries in revolutions, ultimatums and critical
heart-searchings. Marinetti too is not talking about a new kind of
poet, the Futurist, he is really talking about the poet as such when
in the battle against the "literary" he demands creativity instead
of passive enjoyment, when in his condemnation of logic he demands
creative energy instead of intellect. When was it not the case that
the poet has to impart warmth and that passion is his only virtue?
That he has to feel and conjure up the very heart of living matter.
For all the passion, ecstasy and intoxication, with which it is proclaimed, there is nothing new in all this; even speed has been exploited in poetry, before the Futurists, for all sorts of voyages in both
dream world and reality.

It is on speed alone, which he pushes even to the point of simultaneity (think of modern painting), that Marinetti bases his technical
suggestions. Their aim is a massive simplification of language which
should have no time to record in well-measured periods the mad
surge of things. Verbs are only permissible in the infinitive, adjectives
and adverbs are banned, punctuation (which should be used more
extensively!) is done away with and is to be replaced from this day
to the next with mathematical symbols, leaving only analogy to
make the connecting link between the remaining nouns (the question
is, though, will it be enough?). As I have said already: the theory
is correct—for Marinetti's own works. His temperament—boom,
boom-ta-ra—simply hurls out the things he wants to say, giving
each equal value, making no distinctions and gradations; meanwhile
the rest of us, call us decadent if you will alongside this new bar-
barian, still must have rhythm and periods, still look for melos and
climax. This technique, the "telegram style" known to our literature
before Marinetti came along our way, can be used successfully for
three themes only: the roaring explosions of a great machine, the
clash of battle, perhaps the height of ecstasy, and the end of the
world. But what about cranking up the engine, Herr Marinetti, and
the preliminaries and blissful aftermaths of love? Marinetti wisely

limits his choice of themes; and in this extract from the *Battle of Tripolis* which he recited, the impetus of his technique combined with his own excitement was effective. That for other things he still uses the same syntax as the rest of us was shown by the Futurist works recited by Resi Langer in Else Hadwiger's excellent translations which contain many lovely lines and many powerful images; just not very new and not really modern ones. This is how they were recited too; they made one think of moonlight and all sorts of things that Marinetti, whose poetic gifts are ruined neither by his theory nor by his propaganda, would like to see killed off or done away with.

FRANZ JUNG

[*Über Franz Pfemfert und die "Aktion".*]—Published in his autobiography: *Der Weg nach unten. Notes from a Great Age*. Neuwied, Luchterhand 1961. pp. 83–87—Jung (1888–1963), writer and commercial journalist, was one of the most influential political thinkers of Expressionism. From 1912 till 1921 he contributed to *Die Aktion*. Early books: *Das Trottelbuch.* 1912; *Kameraden . . . !* 1913; *Sophie. Der Kreuzzug der Demut.* 1915; *Opferung.* 1916; *Saul.* 1916; *Der Sprung aus der Welt.* 1918; *Gnadenreiche, unsere Königin.* 1918; *Jenan,* 1919; *Joe illustriert die Welt.* 1921; *Der Fall Gross.* 1921; *Proletarier.* 1921; *Kanaker. Wie lange noch?* Two plays. 1921; *Technik des Glücks.* 2 vols. 1921–1923 etc.

1 The story *Morenga* appeared in *Aktion*—Vol. 3. (1913) Cols. 1143–1146.
2 Most of the books listed above were published by *Die Aktion* publishers (Franz Pfemfert), Berlin-Wilmersdorf.

NELL WALDEN

Kokoschka und der "Sturm"-Kreis. Published in: J. P. Hodin (Ed.) *Bekenntnis zu Kokoschka. Memories and Meanings.* Berlin and Mainz, Kupferberg, 1963, pp. 74–82. The ending was omitted as it refers to later meetings with Oskar Kokoschka—Nell Walden, Herwarth Walden's second wife—they were married in the Registry Office on November 23rd, 1912—published a book in 1954 with Lothar Schreyer: *Der Sturm. Ein Erinnerungsbuch an Herwarth Walden und die Künstler aus dem Sturmkreis.* Baden-Baden, Woldemar Klein. In 1963 Nell Walden published: *Herwarth Walden. Ein Lebensbild.* Berlin and Mainz, Kupferberg. Both of these detailed studies are strongly recommended. In addition the following contribution is printed here. Incidentally it is noticeable how few authentic records there are of the earliest years of the *Sturm* which was founded in 1910. The autobiographical notes by Lothar Schreyer and Georg Muche do not start until the year 1916.

1 Oskar Kokoschka, the Viennese friend of Karl Kraus and Adolf Loos, was in Berlin from March, 1910 till February, 1911. He became one of the earliest *Sturm* contributors: not only his drawings—his drama, too, *Mörder Hoffnung der Frauen* appeared in it (Vol. I No. 20, July 14th, 1910). Peter Scher talks about this early period in an essay: *Als Kokoschka mich malte* (published in: *Das literarische Deutschland*, Vol. 2, 1951, 4, reprinted in: *Oskar Kokoschka. Ein Lebensbild in zeitgenössischen Dokumenten*. Ed. Hans Maria Wingler. Munich, Langen/ Müller, 1956, pp. 20–24). We print this essay here in the notes because it mirrors the beginnings of the *Sturm*:

Forty years ago about the time the Peter Baum portrait recently rediscovered in Paris was being painted, Kokoschka painted me too and this picture has now been lost just like the other one.

Kokoschka, who at that time looked like a twenty-year old, was in Berlin to paint Tilla Durieux for Paul Cassirer. He and Herwarth Walden (who had just started the *Sturm*) and I often used to meet in a café by the Friedrichstrasse station. Often Else Lasker-Schüler, the "Swan of Israel", was there too. She was married to Herwarth Walden and floated about like a fantastic creature from another world.

I think one is justified in calling Herwarth Walden's bold creation, *Der Sturm*, the cradle of Kokoschka's international fame. All his fabulous portraits, including the one of me, appeared in the *Sturm*. The most impressive of them all was the portrait of Alfred Loos. I had stuck a print of it up on my wall and one day my cleaning woman looked at it closely for some time and then said: "That man looks hard of hearing." And in fact Loos was seriously handicapped by bad hearing and the portrait showed that so clearly that this simple woman saw it at once with no difficulty. So the phrase Adolf Loos had coined about Kokoschka and which Karl Kraus had sanctioned proved correct: he had "the eye of God".

At that time Kokoschka was a lanky young man with a curiously long skull. Also, he used merely to smile mysteriously when Walden, Gottfried Benn, Alfred Döblin and Rudolf Blümner got involved in some really heated debate. But suddenly he would throw in a sentence that would sum up the whole welter of warring opinions and open up new perspectives which were always respectfully treated.

We were all pretty hard up and never had any money; in a sense it was much like the present day. Walden continually worried whether he was going to have sufficient money to buy the paper for the next number of the *Sturm* which was beginning to cause something of a stir as an inflammatory rag. Naturally there was also the other *avant-garde* paper already in existence, published by Franz Pfemfert, Maximilian Harden's opposite number—this was *Die Aktion* for which, to Walden's sorrow I also wrote articles. Both papers

333

snarled at each other constantly of course, as one might expect in such circles. Pfemfert called Walden, who had acquired a mane of blonde hair, the "peroxide Somali" and Walden accused him of letting his Russian wife wear the breeches.

To get back to the working capital for the *Sturm*. When everything went wrong and 20 or 30 marks meant all the difference between life and death they would come to me because they saw me as something of a Croesus, who, being literary editor of a weekly and also on the pay-roll of the *Berliner Tageblatt*, was paid regular fees and even had something approaching a regular salary. But generally I did not have any money either, so what we did was this—I got Walden or Else Lasker-Schüler to write something under the name of some allegedly famous foreigner which I, as editor, accepted for publication and paid for. So the *Sturm* could keep going for another number.

Cassirer made Kokoschka a modest monthly advance for the Durieux portrait, most of which was sent to his parents in Vienna. He often just had sixpenny worth of ice-cream wafers for lunch and we were really living well if we could afford sausages and potato salad at Aschinger's for our main meal (you could eat as many rolls as you liked there free). The coffee to follow was the main thing, because it was always accompanied with the telling of tall tales. Walden, who was always the hungriest, as Lasker-Schüler was not exactly what you might call a good housewife, even had the nerve to eat the larger part of his meal and then noisily call for the manager to complain bitterly about the quality of the food so that they were forced to give him another portion free.

Kokoschka didn't really enjoy the Cassirer contract because Tilla Durieux, the great and famous actress, treated him like dirt, wouldn't receive him if she didn't feel like it and often kept him waiting although he always kept every appointment religiously.

One day he turned up at my place in Karlshorst to do my portrait. I went for a walk with him in the semi-rural surroundings. When we came past some pasture-land he asked me—with his usual mysterious smile—whether they were "meads" or "swards" and if so, did the little lambs graze on the "banks of the babbling brook" like they did in Schiller.

Then he set to work. On a great sheet of normal foolscap paper he began scraping about with a pencil stump then smudging out; then he squeezed on paint out of a tube and scratched around in it with a fingernail. As he said, one shouldn't be afraid to use a hammer or even a jemmy if necessary, because what's the point of "drawing" and "painting" when all that really counts is producing something convincing.

It turned out a crazy picture. He had taken away all my male beauty (truth will out—there's no other word for it; later in America

I was most favoured by the ladies because they said I looked like a genuine redskin); well, he had captured my likeness by lifting off all the top layer revealing the face of a fairly desperate convict underneath. And this was yet another example of "the eye of God", for he had no means of knowing that I had done 20 months in prison some years before for an alleged affront to the Oldenburg M.P. Ruhstraht and had picked hemp till the blood poured from my fingers. But this is by the way and just to give some really concrete example of the fantastic, one might almost say, demonic ability of this artist.

I suppose this portrait will come to light again eventually like the one of Peter Baum, in Paris or Stockholm—maybe even in New York.

If Oskar Kokoschka should ever set eyes on these lines he will remember and perhaps be moved just a little. I send him my greeting across all the chasms of life and death. Kokoschka himself in his *Geschichte von der Tochter Virginia* has cast some memories of these days in poetic form. (O.K. *Spur im Treibsand*, Stories, Zurich, Atlantis, 1956, p. 9ff):

I spent my first Christmas Eve in Berlin with my friend, an unemployed, half-blind actor who organized propaganda lectures on modern painting in the rooms of the Expressionist Art paper *Der Sturm* (Rudolf Blümner, ed.) of which I was a founder member. We both sat huddled up in blankets because we had no fuel for the stove, warming our hands over a teapot standing on a primus stove (. . .)

If anybody had tried to calculate my life chances when I was co-founder with Herwarth Walden of the most modern German art journal, and poet, artist, variété reviewer, publicity agent and delivery boy all in one, no one would have given much for my future. My entire fortune consisted of the clothes I stood up in, an iron bedstead, a wash basin, a towel (. . .)

2 Elsewhere (*Der Sturm. Ein Erinnerungsbuch* . . . 1954, p. 11) Nell Walden writes about how the art exhibitions in the *Sturm* started:

About the beginning of 1912 Herwarth Walden had moved the *Sturm* office and publishing-house out west (Potsdamer Strasse 18). He had leased a two-roomed flat there. A little room covered from floor to ceiling with bookshelves and furnished with a huge desk and a divan bed was his editorial office. He was available there at any time, surrounded by galley proofs and enshrouded in a blue haze of cigarette smoke. The next room was the despatch-room with piles of *Sturm* issues. Here dwelt his secretary. Alt-Westen, Potsdamer Strasse (though not No. 18 for long) was to become the centre of the *Sturm* movement. The burning issue for the time being, however, was whether the *Sturm* should put on art shows or not. I was in favour and Herwarth Walden went looking for suitable showrooms. In the Tiergartenstrasse 34a. he found a distinguished old mansion (the so-called Gilka Mansion, Gilka was a famous brand-name for liqueur), which the family had sold off and which was doomed for demolition. A huge new building was going up on the site. Until that happened the mansion-house could be rented on a short-term basis. They turned out to be ideal exhibition rooms in an excellent location. It was there that the early *Sturm* exhibitions took place: The first in March, 1912: The Blue Rider, Oskar Kokoschka. The second followed in April, 1912: the Futurists with Futurist Manifesto by Marinetti, the poet and spokesman of the Italian Futurist group . . . The third exhibition was shown in the new rooms in the Königin-Augusta-Strasse 51. But this domicile, too, proved temporary. By June, 1913 office, publishing-concern and living-quarters plus the exhibition rooms had already found yet another abode in Potsdamer Strasse 134a. Here the *Sturm* Movement headquarters remained till the very end . . .

HANS FLESCH VON BRUNNINGEN

[*Die "Aktion" in Vienna*]. Taken from the Memorial Broadcast *Die Aktion* arranged by West German Radio, Cologne in February, 1961. Voices of friends, collected, recorded with commentary by Roland H. Wiegenstein. Hans Flesch [von Brunningen] (b. February 5th, 1895 in Brünn) poet, writer, radio commentator had his first publication in 1917 in the series *Der jüngste Tag: Das zerstörte Idyll*. He contributed to the *Aktion* from 1914 on.

1 Published in the *Aktion*, Vol. 4 (1914), No. 9, February 28th Col. 194–97.
2 The special number (No. 30 of July 25th, 1914) contains the following contributions by Hans Flesch: *An den Tod* (A Pamphlet for the Metropolis); *Gedichte; Der Satan*. [*Novelle*]; in addition a short essay by Heinrich Nowak on Flesch and a title page drawing by Egon Schiele.

JACOB PICARD

Ernst Blass, seine Umwelt in Heidelberg und "Die Argonauten". Written 1961, published in *Imprimatur*. New Series. Vol. 3. (1961–62), pp. 194–99. Picard (b. January 11th, 1883 in Wangen/Allgäu, died October 1st, 1967), lyric poet and story-writer, lived, studied and graduated (1913) in Heidelberg. End of 1913 his first volume of verse appeared: *Das Ufer* (Hermann Meister). The second appeared in 1920: *Erschütterung*.

1 *Die Argonauten*. A monthly magazine. Ed. Ernst Blass. 1st Series [1–12] Heidelberg, Richard Weissbach 1914–21. [Cf. Raabe, No. 17].
2 The book was published by Richard Weissbach in December, 1912.

3 Borchardt's speech was published as No. 8 of the *Argonauten* in autumn, 1915. It was also sold separately.

4 Oskar Kokoschka, *Ernst Blass*. Oil painting. Kunsthalle Bremen.

5 *Saturn*. A monthly magazine. Ed. Hermann Meister and Herbert Gross-berger. [No. 3. and 4 by Hermann Meister; No. 5. by Hermann Meister and Robert R. Schmidt.] Nos. 1–5. Heidelberg. Saturn-Verlag, 1911–14, 1919–20 [Cf. Raabe, No. 7].

6 Werfel read on November 25th, 1913 in Heidelberg.

7 The monthly supplement *Literatur und Wissenschaft* appeared in 1910 and 1911, 1911 ed. Richard Weissbach. E.g. Picard wrote on Bruno Frank, *Die Nachtwache* (April, 1910); Emil Strauss (August, 1910); Benno Geiger and Hans Carossa (September, 1910); Dauthendey, *Asiatische Novellen* (October, 1910); Hermann Hesse, *Gertrud* (December, 1910); Platen (April, 1911); J. V. Jensen, *Der Gletscher* (September, 1911).

8 Georg Heym. To the memory of one who died young. In: the *Frankfurter Zeitung* 1912, No. 36.

KARL OTTEN

1914—Sommer ohne Herbst. Erinnerung an August Macke und die Rheinischen Expressionisten. Written 1954, transmitted 1955 by the Nord-westdeutscher Rundfunk, Cologne. The manuscript was kindly made available by Mrs. Ellen Otten (Locarno) for inclusion here. Karl Otten (1889–1963), writer and poet, friendly with the writers of the revolution in Munich, with the modern painters in Bonn, belonged to the Franz Pfemfert circle. Towards the end of his life his great achievement was the rediscovery of literary Expressionism through his activities as editor of anthologies and collections of Expressionist works. (*Ahnung und Aufbruch*. Expressionist Prose. 1957; *Schrei und Bekenntnis*. Expressionist Theatre 1959; *Expressionismus—grotesk*. 1962; *Ego und Eros*. Masterpieces of Expressionist Narrative Prose. 1963).

1 On August Macke and his friends c.f. Elisabeth Erdmann-Macke, *Erinnerung an August Macke*. Stuttgart, Kohlhammer 1962; also the well-documented monograph by Gustav Vriesen, *August Macke*, 2nd enlarged ed. Stuttgart, Kohlhammer, 1957.

2 Karl Otten: *Die Reise durch Albanien, 1912*. With drawings by Franz Henseler. Munich, Bachmair, 1913.

3 The Exhibition of Rhineland Expressionists lasted from July 10th–August 10th, 1913, in the Friedrich Cohen Art Gallery, Bonn, Am Hof 30. Those exhibiting included: Heinrich Campendonk, Ernst Mortiz Engert, Max Ernst, Otto Feldmann, Franz Henseler, Franz M. Jansen, Joseph Kölschbach, August Macke, Helmuth Macke, Carlo Mense, Heinrich Nauen, Marie Nauen, Olga Oppenheimer, Paul Adolf Seehaus, William Straube, Hanns Thuar. Cf. K. F. Ertel, Rheinische Expressionisten. In

337

Köln: Quarterly for the Friends of the City of Cologne. 1963, No. 2.
with eight illustrations.

OTTO FLAKE

Halbfertiges Leben. Epitaph to Ernst Stadler, who was killed on October
30th, 1914 near Ypres. Published in: *Die Neue Rundschau,* No. 26 (1915),
Vol. I, pp. 267–71. The concluding sentences referring to Stadler's work
are omitted. Otto Flake (1880–1963) like Schickele, Stadler and Arp was
one of the leading representatives of the Alsatian literary circle which
first came together in 1901–2 in the *Stürmer.* As an S. Fischer Verlag
author, Flake stood a little apart from Expressionism but the new
currents were not without influence on him. In his chronicle-type autobiography *Es wird Abend,* Report on a Long Life (Gütersloh, Mohn 1960)
Flake keeps coming back to Stadler, whom he calls a "Strassburg Hugo
von Hofmannsthal". This contribution touches upon Strassburg's share
in Expressionist literature, but at the same time coming at the end of this
first section it is something of an epitaph to the writers killed at the
beginning of the war. The whole of Early Expressionism could be
described by the title given to Flake's Essay, *Halbfertiges Leben.*

1 Kasimir Edschmid writes on Stadler's lecturing activities in his epitaph
In memoriam Ernst Stadler (Die Weissen Blätter. Vol. 2, 1915, p. 122f.):
He spent the summer travelling back and forward between Brussels
and Strassburg. The Brussels examinations timed until the last days
of term. Between times he gave two lectures in Strassburg. He was
preparing for the first of September when he was due to leave for
America whose vast distances, now so near, filled him with excitement. Over all these journeyings some now half over, some nearly
completed and some still stretching out before him with boundless
attractions, fell the shadow of war though I laughingly tried to
distract him. He didn't say he didn't believe it would come, but a
horrible tension gripped him and inwardly tortured him. He was
looking forward to his new translations of Francis Jammes which
were about to appear in print, but into this joyful anticipation fell
once again the worry about the military service he still had to face
up to. He talked, simply and nobly of fine things. Nothing was more
foreign to his nature than aestheticism. He could talk with enthusiasm about the Strolling Players of whom he thought particularly
highly: this was an exuberant band of fellow-students, male and
female, who made their way through Alsace in a hay wagon putting
on good solid theatrical fare for the peasants with lots of colour,
youth and gay costumes. How he would have loved to take them
to Gebweiler where his brother was.
There was a crowd of lively young men who worshipped him

with youthful chivalry. Wherever they are, in trenches everywhere, on every front, they will be deeply shocked to learn of his death.

I heard his last lecture on the series of modern poetry from the Naturalists right up to the present day, to which he had devoted the whole summer term. In it he divided up the main stream into three: Heym, Werfel, Schickele, of whom the last was his special favourite. So there arched over his last activities as a scholar the broad fresco of our own day in the art which was his mistress.

2 *Der Aufbruch.* Poems. Leipzig, Verlag der weissen Bücher 1914. Cf. also the edition of Ernst Stadler's *Dichtungen.* Ed. Karl Ludwig Schneider. 2 vol. Hamburg, Ellermann, 1954.

EMIL SZITTYA

Die Künstler in Zürich während des Krieges. Published in: Szittya, *Das Kuriositäten—Kabinett.* Encounters with Happenings. Hoboes, Crooks, Artistes, Religious Maniacs, Sexual Curiosities, Social Democrats, Syndicalists, Communists, Anarchists, Politicians and Artists. Constance, See Verlag, 1923 pp. 277–84. Szittya (1886–1964) who lived in Paris from 1906, was an *homme de lettres* and an art-writer. This work from which we include an extract was a curious source-book for the history of twentieth century literature, a mixture of fact, hearsay and gossip.

1 Kurt Münzer, *Verirrte Bürger*, München, Georg Müller, 1918.
2 *Wissen und Leben.* Swiss Fortnightly. Ed. Ernst Bovet. No. 1–15. Zurich 1907–8 to 1921–22. Continued as the *Neue Schweizer Rundschau.*
3 *Die Ähre.* Weekly for Literature, Concerts, Theatre and Entertainment. Vols. 1–4. Zurich 1913–16.
4 *Der Mistral.* Ed. Hugo Kersten and Emil Szittya. [No. 3 by Walter Serner]. Vol. 1. [No: 1–3] Zurich 1915. [Cf. Raabe No. 23].
5 This is not quite accurate. Hugo Ball was not the founder of the Munich Journal *Revolution* (1913), but the friend of the editor Hans Leybold and one of his closest collaborators.
6 No journal with this title could be traced.
7 Henri Barbusse, *Feuer.* Translated by Leo von Meyenburg. Zurich, Rascher 1918. Ball's review could not be traced.

CHRISTIAN SCHAD

Zürich/Genf: Dada. Written 1961, published in: *Imprimatur.* New Series. Vol. 3 (1961–62), pp. 215–18. Schad (b. August 21st, 1894 in Miesbach) lives as a painter and graphic artist in the vicinity of Aschaffenburg. In the Twenties he painted portraits in the New Objectivity style. He recounts his part in Expressionism and Dadaism in the present contribution. One general comment must be made at this point. It is not the intention of this book to document exhaustively the development of Dada, but to show by means of a few autobiographical documents selected from masses of material how deeply anchored Dadaism is in so-called Expressionism. The sources are listed in the bibliography.

1 *Sirius*. Monthly magazine for literature and art. Ed. Walter Serner. 1915–16 (Nos. 1–8]. Zurich, Sirius-Verlag, 1915–16 (Cf. Raabe, No. 25).

2 The same story is told by Hans Arp in his contribution, *Dadaland*. (See below).

RICHARD HUELSENBECK

Zürich 1916, wie es wirklich war. Published in *Die Neue Bücherschau*, Vol. 6 (1928), 12, pp. 611–17. This is a reply to Hugo Ball's diary published 1927 called *Die Flucht aus der Zeit*, inspired by Kurt Kersten, who in the same journal, Vol. 6, 1928, 10, pp. 538–40, reviewed Ball's work and wrote: "The high-light [in Zürich] was a literary cabaret. Ball, whose creation it essentially was talks about it. The basic message was defeatism, but it was also destructive and subversive in every respect. Ball has a lot to say about it. It would be nice if Huelsenbeck would talk freely about this period sometime. He would possibly be able to add something to Ball, probably even put him right." Huelsenbeck (b. April 23rd, 1892 in Frankenau/Hessen) studied medicine in the winter semester 1913–14 and in the summer semester 1914 in Munich. In Zurich along with Hugo Ball, Hans Arp, Tristan Tzara and Marcel Janco he became the co-founder of the Cabaret Voltaire. He brought Dada to Berlin. Early Expressionistic and Dadaistic publications: *Phantastische Gebete. 1916; Schalaben, Schalomai, Schalamezomai. 1916; Verwandlungen. Novella. 1918; Azteken oder Die Knallbude. 1918; Dada siegt. 1920 Deutschland muss untergehen! 1920; Doctor Billig am Ende. 1921*. In 1920 he edited the *Dada-Almanach*. Huelsenbeck has written variously about his association with Dada (see Bibliography). In addition to the present passage in which Huelsenbeck, writing from the situation of 1928, passionately swears allegiance to Dada, the corresponding passages from his essay *Die dadaistische Bewegung (Die neue Rundschau.* Vol. 31, 1926, pp. 972–79) are given as follows:

> In the year 1916 in a gloomy little alley in Zürich, Hugo Ball and Emmy Hennings founded the Cabaret Voltaire which was to become the cradle of Dadaism. The Cabaret Voltaire soon became the literary centre for all those whom the war had flung outside the frontiers of their own country. Here poems were recited, there was singing and dancing, and discussions on the possibilities of modern art. The Cabaret Voltaire became an experimental theatre for all problems of modern aesthetics. Among the intimate associates of the Cabaret

Voltaire, apart from the author of these lines, were the Roumanians Marcel Janco and Tristan Tzara, and the German painter Hans Arp. Arp had come from Paris and brought from there a precise knowledge of those ideas of Picasso and Braque which have since become world-famous under the heading of Cubism.

Tzara was very well-versed in international art and literature and had connections with all parts of the world. We corresponded with the Futurists in Italy and knew Boccioni's *Pittura e Scultura futuriste*. In Munich, Ball had been very close friends with Kandinsky and his circle with whom he had been on the point of starting an "Expressionist Theatre" when war broke out. In the Cabaret Voltaire pieces and impressions from various countries became the object of intensive discussions. In general the tendency was to favour abstract, non-representational art. Kandinsky and Picasso were recognized as outstanding personalities, while Marinetti with his Futurism and his furious Nationalism was not so much in accord with the whole radically pacifistic atmosphere of the Cabaret Voltaire. Arp, in particular, was an opponent of the Futurist concept which he said was like a little dog sitting up to beg. We were quite overwhelmed by the thought that a tree was not a living object with trunk, leaves and blossoms, but was really only the realisation of an idea to which one had to relate. The Cubists solved the practical problem of representation by simply abandoning perspective; they simply brought the picture forward out of space as it were, made it into a relief and reduced it to mathematical symbols, which were supposed to be immediately expressive.

1 The *Revolution* was ed. 1913 by Hans Leybold (one number by Franz Jung). Among the contributors were Hugo Ball, Richard Huelsenbeck etc. [Cf. Raabe, No. 16].

2 The poem *Der Henker* by Hugo Ball appeared in the first number of the *Revolution* October 15th, 1913 and caused the number to be confiscated.

3 Ball worked temporarily in the editorial office of *Zeit im Bild*.

4 *Die Freie Zeitung* in Berne was ed. by Ball 1917–20. A selection was published under the title: *Almanach der Freien Zeitung*. Ed. Hugo Ball. Berne 1918.

5 Hugo Ball's *Die Flucht aus der Zeit* (Munich, Duncker and Humblot 1927) p. 77 ff. can be taken as a reliable source for the course of events in Zurich 1916–17. Also his letters: *Briefe* (Zurich, Bentiger 1957).

HANS ARP

Dadaland. First published with the sub-title: Zurich Memories from the Time of the First World War. In: *Atlantis*, Vol. 20, pp. 275–77; reprinted in: *Unsern täglichen Traum* . . . Memoirs, Works and Thoughts from the Years 1914–54. Zurich, Die Arche, 1955, pp. 51–61. Hans Arp (b. September 16th, 1887 in Strassburg, died June 7th, 1966). Sculptor, painter and poet lived in Zurich during the First World War and so was involved in Zurich Dada. Hans Arp has published various reminiscences of the period (cf. bibliography).

ERWIN PISCATOR

Die politische Bedeutung der "Aktion". Transmitted on February 26th, 1961 by the Westdeutsche Rundfunk, Cologne, as part of the feature programme *Die Aktion*, organized by Roland H. Wiegenstein; printed in: *Imprimatur*, New Series, Vol. 3 (1961–62), pp. 211–14. Piscator (b. December 17th, 1893 in Ulm/Kreis Wetzlar, died March 30th, 1966), actor, producer and theatre director, was a contributor to the *Aktion* in the First World War. In his well-known book *Das politische Theater* (Berlin, A. Schultz, 1929. p. 15f.) he writes about Pfemfert and his journal as follows:

Art, real, absolute art must show itself equal to any occasion. I have lived through more and worse bombardments than this since, in the trenches outside Ypres, but this one flattened my "private vocation" as it did the trenches we were occupying and killed it as dead as the bodies that lay all around us. That despite this, there is no need for art to shrink from reality was proved to me once and for all by the journal called *Die Aktion*, on which a group of men were working, who even if they were not completely clear in their minds about the ultimate causes nevertheless scratched the real face of war onto the walls of our dug-outs, and screamed the truth out loud. But their cries were swallowed up by the detonations of the grenades in whose smoke their figures disappeared. Through my poems I had already established contact with the *Aktion* which at that time was directed by Pfemfert, the only man in Germany openly opposed to the obligatory war hysteria. (And here I must pay my belated thanks to Franz Pfemfert, the confused and embittered man who was subsequently to destroy his own work.) Though gagged by the Censor, Pfemfert gathered these voices together and tried with them at least to indicate what things were really like. An anthology of *Poems Written in the Field* closed with these words: "This book, last refuge of a homeless idea, I set up against the age we live in . . ." A tentative start to waging political warfare with literary means.

1 Poems by Piscator under the heading *Verse vom Schlachtfeld* in the 1915 and 1916 numbers.

2 The poems of Kurd Adler (1892–1916) appeared in collected form in the series *Der rote Hahn* under the title: *Wiederkehr*. 1918. Erwin Piscator dedicated a poem *Kurd Adler getötet* to this poet killed in action,

whom he did not know personally!, it was included in Pfemfert's anthology *1914-1916* (Berlin 1916) in which Adler is also represented with some contributions.

SYLVIA VON HARDEN

Erinnerungen an einst . . . Written 1961, published in: *Imprimatur*, New Series, Vol. 3 (1961-62), pp. 219-22. Sylvia von Harden (1893-1963), friendly with Ferdinand Hardekopf, the secret king of Expressionism, published works in Expressionist journals. Her volume of verse: *Verworrene Städte.* 1920. The memories included here are to be understood as atmospheric scenes from Expressionism. They warrant closer examination as to their reliability in particular cases. The book mentioned at the end has not yet appeared.

1 *Die Bücherkiste* Monthly magazine for literature, graphic art and book reviews. Ed. Leo Scherpenbach [the last number by Sylvia von Harden]. Vols. 1-2. Munich, H. F. S. Bachmair 1919-21 [Cf. Raabe, No. 67].

LOTHAR SCHREYER

"Was ist der Sturm?" Extract from his autobiography *Erinnerungen an Sturm und Bauhaus.* Munich, Langen/Müller, 1956, pp. 7-17. Schreyer (b. August 19th, 1886 in Dresden, died June 18th, 1966) painter and writer, was friendly with Herwarth Walden from 1916 and from 1916-26, managing editor of *Sturm,* 1917-20 director of the Sturm Expressionist Theatre. Published plays at the time: *Jungfrau,* 1917; *Meer. Sehnte. Mann.* 1918; *Nacht.* 1919; *Kreuzigung,* 1920, etc. Schreyer wrote several books and memoirs about Expressionism (cf. bibliography p. 406). An essay of his *Vom Leben des "Sturms"* (*Imprimatur*, New Series, Vol. 3, 1961-62, pp. 223-27) was prefaced by the short statement which follows:

There were always two sides to Herwarth Walden's *Sturm*: an age ending and a new beginning. Our intention was to serve the new beginning and at the same time we helped to end another age. Looking back, the apocalyptic nature of our work, its fruitlessness, but also occasional successes, seem almost uncannily clear. Also clear are the human comfort and the hope, almost surpassing human belief that lay over people and events.

What I owe Herwarth Walden as an artist and a friend cannot be expressed in words. Whenever I try to make particular statements the words seem to fail me somehow. Despite this, in the years since the triumph of the *Sturm* I have twice attempted to express this.

343

First of all in the book *Der Sturm, ein Gedenkbuch an Herwarth Walden und die Künstler des Sturm-Kreises*, which I published in 1954 with the help of Nell Walden, Herwarth Walden's second wife and companion in the battle for modern arts. This is a documentary book. Then I also added another book *Erinnerungen an Sturm und Bauhaus* in 1956.

In these publications—as well as in the one included here—the particular character of the admittedly very esoteric *Sturm* Circle, is clearly expressed. It becomes clear that what the group meant by Expressionism was rather different from the accepted meaning, which Walden dismissed as pseudo-Expressionism. In his very restricted usage it applies more or less exclusively to the artists of the *Sturm*.

1 Schreyer's drama *Nacht* was first published in the *Sturm*, Vol. 7 (1916– 17), pp. 40–44.

2 In addition we include a passage on Herwarth Walden by Georg Muche (*Blickpunkt, Sturm, Dada, Bauhaus, Gegenwart*. Munich Langen/ Müller, 1961, p. 191 f.):

The passage of time modifies things but on looking back Herwarth Walden becomes a sibylline creature. His head was like that of the Sphinx. He set riddles and had the answer ready himself: "What is art?" "Art is chance, but not everybody gets one."—"What is the artist?" "The artist is merely the instrument of his work." "And what is this work?" "Art is as inhuman as God."

Expressionist pathos cannot be explained away merely as the out-bursts and art-forms of talented people of that particular period. They were guided by the voice of the future. This "chance which not every-body gets" did come their way and gave them a heightened self-awareness which freed them from all the forms and rules of art which had been binding them in the past and made their works quite new.

Walden: "The danger is self-awareness without self and without awareness." He knew the spiritual point of departure from which the poets and painters created their works. He placed himself pro-tectively in front of his artists. He fought for them. With biting scorn he mercilessly and ruthlessly lashed his opponents with the empty drivel of their own art-jargon. His artists became famous. He himself was never touched by fame. All his friends left him and he left his friends.

Herwarth Walden was a man of slight frame, quick movements, penetrating understanding, finally balanced sense of order which he looked for in others more than in himself. He was resilient, bold and occasionally, a little bit lost. Then suddenly, as he talked the sentences would come like whiplashes. And then over his face would creep the faintest trace of a grimace which he would try to control with a sharp intake of breath and a snort through the nostrils, while his right arm described a slow circle, bringing the hand holding the cigarette up to his lips.

Herwarth Walden the man has been written about both by friends, and by people he annoyed, insulted, antagonized. None of them proved capable of describing him as he really was, neither his friends nor his foes. Walden was like opaque glass. Any encouragement or assistance he got came from the best of his few friends, from Rudolf Blümner, Lothar Schreyer, August Stramm and from Nell his wife, who helped him in the decisive years with understanding, initiative and good advice and concealed her worries about the success and further life of the *Sturm* with a gentle charm.

3 August Stramm's prophet was Rudolf Blümner. Schreyer writes about him in his *Erinnerungen an Sturm und Bauhaus*, pp. 78–81 :

The conscience of the *Sturm* was Rudolf Blümner. He served the *Sturm* with unswerving honesty and infinite loyalty. He was Herwarth Walden's most faithful friend.

Rudolf Blümner was the first *Sturm* artist Herwarth Walden introduced me to. This was on my second or third visit to the *Sturm* when my future collaboration with Herwarth Walden had been agreed upon. I remember distinctly. It was in Walden's little dining-room. There stood the tall gaunt figure of Rudolf with the intelligent narrow face Kokoschka has painted and drawn so often, looking down at me with his short-sighted eyes. His reserved nature exuded a forthright manliness which appealed to me. We had absolute confidence in each other from the very first minute. Our talk was direct and factual. Within half an hour we had already decided to found a *Sturm* school, the work of which would rest on both Rudolf Blümner's shoulders and mine. A curious conformity in our life patterns seemed to link us together. Our birthday was the same, August 19th. Blümner was thirteen years older than me, it is true, but we never noticed the age difference. He was a lawyer like me and like me had decided not to follow this profession. He had turned to the stage like me, had been a leading producer with Reinhardt and one of his best actors too. As a man and an artist he had been just as disgusted with show business as I was. He had realized the crucial artistic importance of Expressionism as I had done, and was as determined as I was to be both a theoretical and a practical Expressionist. He had been alive to the new artistic trend at a time when I was only dimly aware of it. But right from the start he never considered me as somebody who should be learning from him, but as his equal, seeking out the new artistic principles and putting them into practice. I moved up very quickly in Expressionist circles but he was always completely without envy, always ready to help. He had but one ambition; to get to the bottom of things, to create and to do everything he set out

to do with the best possible intentions and as well and as honestly as
he could. This made his personal life very difficult, but it made his
own artistic work exceptionally great.

Rudolf Blümner's great achievement was the creation of an
Expressionist art of elocution. He—and he alone—could give our
literary works of art the tonal quality appropriate to them, a quality so
unique that it extinguished our literary efforts only to rekindle them
with the declamatory power of his elocutionary art for which there
was no name but which was as much a work of art exploding out
of the revolutionary turn of the times as Franz Marc's pictures or
August Stramm's poems. August Stramm's poetry was what really
sparked off Rudolf Blümner's art. This is why he had greater insight
into the essence of Stramm's work than anyone else. Rudolf Blümner's
underlying principle was voice-control enabling him both to hurl
out word-tone structures of shattering strength and to drop his voice
to the merest whisper, so that the primeval sound of the word was,
as it were, created afresh. Anybody who ever heard him recite
Stramm's *Die Menschheit* or *Weltwehe* had some inkling of just how
pregnant the primeval word could be—other worlds, stars, all the
realms of the Cosmos would rise up out of it in lofty array. Every
week for years on *Sturm* Evenings Rudolf Blümner gave his poetry
readings. The *Sturm* Evening of September 1st, 1916, was a memorial
ceremony for August Stramm. Some poems by the *Sturm* poets that
Rudolf Blümner read in the course of the years were gathered together
by us in the little book *Sturm-Abende* which we published and
dedicated to him.

It was the only logical conclusion of this development that Rudolf
Blümner should, at the height of his powers, conceive the "absolute"
sound-poem consisting entirely of a rhythmical sequence of linguistic
sounds, a verbal art form which was completely abstract in the sense
that the words had no concrete meaning but were pure sound. This
work "*Angolaïna*" was the complete literary parallel to the absolute
painting to be found in the work of Kandinsky. Linguistically it was
a cosmic event, a unique phenomenon of great power and virile
tenderness, a genuinely purifying storm of pure spirit, shattering
the human sphere, an expression of the creative forces which make
order out of chaos—a cosmos even, universe and beauty; yes beauty,
as the term cosmos implies. For this work had the perfection of
beauty. It died with the artist Rudolf Blümner.

Rudolf Blümner gave about three hundred readings on *Sturm* Evenings in the course of the years, in Berlin, in many other German
cities and abroad. In Berlin he always spoke in the little exhibition
hall of the *Sturm*, with the pictures of the *Sturm* artists all around
him. Here there was always only a small circle of listeners, thirty to
one hundred people including a regular band of faithful followers who

always came back for more from this great artist. The *Sturm* Evenings
in other places generally attracted audiences of hundreds; they were
invariably a sensation, involving always a great deal of ridicule and
general lack of comprehension on the part of the public. In Hamburg
Rudolf Blümner read my first dramatic text, *Nacht*.

Rudolf Blümner was a regular and powerful contributor to the
Sturm paper. Here he chose the advancement of Expressionism as
his particular task . . .

4 On the "word artistry of the *Sturm*" Schreyer wrote extensively in his
Erinnerungen an Sturm und Bauhaus pp. 84–94:

We never liked to talk of "Literature" or "Poetry", we preferred
"word artistry", etc.

We tackled every form of word artistry: novels, novellas, short-
stories, letters, dramas, hymns, epics, aphorisms, essays. We published
our works in the *Sturm*, issue by issue, or in the books which *Sturm*
published occasionally.

We altered each of these forms in our own particular way, which
as we saw it, justified the description "word artistry". As with the
Sturm painters so too with *Sturm* "word-artistry", great artistic freedom was essential. Following their example we refused to accept any
rigid form: in "word-art" either. This is what makes novels as different
as those of Paul Scheerbart and Herwarth Walden possible, or dramas
as different as Kokoschka's, August Stramm's or my own, or poems as
different as Else Lasker-Schüler's, Wilhelm Runge's and Otto
Nebel's.

The essay as a form of social and art criticism took up a lot of
space in every number of the journal. But all criticism was given
artistic form. And all criticism had to have its positive side. It served
the cause of artistic change, proper appreciation of particular works,
pictures, literary forms. Men as convinced of their mission as Herwarth
Walden and Rudolf Blümner were, naturally did not resort to kid-
gloves when dealing with opponents of the *Sturm*, who turned against
the modern art movement not only out of lack of understanding but
because they had the temerity to impugn the personal integrity of the
artists. Herwarth Walden's essays are like a rapier duel and easily
demolish the opponent. Rudolf Blümner's essays are impartial in their
quest for the truth and in their proclamation of the verdict.

The *Sturm* essays in criticism were a kind of mopping up operation.
They attacked all contemporary, artistic and literary phenomena which
were no longer in tune with the spirit of the changing times, and
represented mere relics of all the decaying concepts of the nineteenth
century. In the fundamental upheavals in the social strata, the
sciences, in philosophy etc., these rudiments—*Rudimentär* was the
name of a drama by August Stramm—prove to be very tough. The
birth of a new world-view can never be possible without sacrifice,

347

blood and tears; two world wars are proof enough of that. The *Sturm* mopping-up operation was very close to war and revolution. Mopping up often comes close to total destruction. But mopping up is the essential preliminary and the first step to something really new.

The main concern of the *Sturm*, as of World War and World Revolution, was the new image of man. The "new man" was what was really wanted. This meant an even greater reaction against the "old man". We demonstrated this reaction by a curious unmasking of what he had been like. There is no completely satisfactory concept to describe this attitude and the works it produced. Perhaps the concept of humour or the humorist comes closest to this type of thing. But humour implies taking things too seriously. We prefer to talk of irony, excluding, however, its reverse side, namely, painful renunciation. Perhaps this unmasking is best compared with a children's game in which all external reality is exchanged for an internal reality and everything goes through constant transformations all the time according to an agreed "rule"—and everything is laughed at all the time as it were. This is how Paul Scheerbart, Mynona and Kurt Schwitters, for example, go about transforming and unmasking the "old man" until there is nothing left of him, or, as Schwitters says of "Anna Blume": "You look the same from the front and back". In this process nothing is left of the "old man" but an echo and this echo is conciliatory and good, for it is pure. It is on the purity of its sound and the rhythmic harmony of its sound-composition that the prophetic force of *Sturm* "word artistry" rests. Just as the painters and sculptors of the *Sturm* were forced to purify the techniques of painting and sculpture in order to proclaim spiritual reality, and had to start once again from prime forms and prime colours, from the basic relationships of both static and dynamic colour formations, in order to express this relationship in terms of painting or sculpture, so too the "word-artists" of the *Sturm* had to start out from the basic elements of the word, that is from its sound and intonation. The individual word, was taken to be both unit and totality of sense, sound and intonation. Hence the "word-art-work" now becomes a rhythmic-harmonic composition of individual sentences and individual words. These can exist in a logical grammatical relationship; but such a relationship is only one among many possibilities. The essence of the word-art-work is its artistic logic, which consists in the associations of complex values and constantly provides various strata of these values which can be heard either individually or all together. This phenomenon, of which there are earlier traces in Germany as well as in Italy among the Futurists and in France among the Cubists, reached its climax in the works of August Stramm. [. . .]

PAUL WESTHEIM

Wie "Das Kunstblatt" entstand. Written in Mexico, December, 1957, published in: *Vierzig Jahre Kiepenheuer 1910–1950.* An Almanac. Ed. Noa Kiepenheuer. Weimar, Kiepenheuer, 1951, pp. 53–57. As an art critic and writer Westheim (1886–1963) was the complete opposite of Herwarth Walden and the *Sturm.* His great accomplishment was in making Expressionist Art widely known and in making Expressionist literature available by printing it in the *Kunstblatt.*

1 *Das Kunstblatt.* Ed. Paul Westheim. Vols. 1–15. Potsdam, Kiepenheuer (From Vol. 10: Berlin, Hermann Reckendorf) 1917–31.

2 *Die Schaffenden.* Ed. Paul Westheim. Vols. 1–8. Potsdam, Kiepenheuer (from Vol. 3: Berlin, Euphorion-Verlag) 1918–33. In folders.

HERMANN KASACK

Wolf Przygode und "Die Dichtung". First printed in: *Deutsche Zeitung,* July 8–9th, 1961; extended version in: *Imprimatur,* New Series, Vol. 3 (1961–62), pp. 228–34. The epitaph to Wolf Przygode was privately printed in 1927 (reprinted in: Kasack, *Mosaiksteine.* Frankfurt, Suhrkamp, 1956, pp. 207–30). In his Marbach speech *Deutsche Literatur im Zeichen des Expressionismus* (*Merkur* 15, 1961, pp. 353–63) Kasack talked again about Przygode's *Dichtung* at greater length. As the author of the present passage writes extensively about the readings of 1916–17, we include it at this point, although the *Dichtung* appeared after the *Neue Jugend* which is discussed in the next passage. Kasack (1896–1966) poet, writer, publisher's reader; after the last war he was for many years president of the Deutsche Akademie für Sprache und Dichtung, since 1915 a contributor to the *Aktion* and other Expressionist journals. Early books: *Der Mensch.* Verse 1918; *Die Heimsuchung.* Story 1919; *Die tragische Sendung.* Drama 1920; *Die Insel.* Poems 1920; *Die Schwester.* Tragedy 1920; *Der Gesang des Jahres.* 1921; *Stadium.* A cycle of poems 1921. *Vincent.* Play 1924.

1 *Die Dichtung.* Ed. Wolf Przygode. Nos. 1–2 with programme. Munich, Roland-Verlag (From 2 on: Potsdam, Verlag der Dichtung G. Kiepenheuer) 1918–23. [Cf. Raabe, No. 43.]

2 Albert Ehrenstein's piece on Karl Kraus appeared in 1920 as Book Seven of the *Gefährten* with an appendix by Georg Kulka, *Der Götze des Lächelns.*

WIELAND HERZFELDE

Wie ein Verlag entstand. Published in: *Das Wort.* Literary monthly magazine. Ed. Bertolt Brecht, Lion Feuchtwanger, Willi Bredel. Vol. 1

(1936) 2, pp. 97–102. Herzfelde (b. April 11th, 1896 in Weggis/Switzerland), was the founder and for years the director of the Malik-Verlag, which as this passage shows was started in the Expressionist period. He also wrote poems and stories, collected under the title : *Unterwegs. Blätter aus fünfzig Jahren*. Berlin, Aufbau-Verlag, 1961. This also contains the autobiography : *Immergrün. Merkwürdige Erlebnisse und Erfahrungen eines fröhlichen Waisenknaben*. Berlin, Aufbau-Verlag, 1949.

1 Most of these journals have been named elsewhere. *März* came out 1907–1917, partly edited by Wilhelm Herzog. *Der Anfang* was a paper for young people. Vols. 1–2 from May, 1913 till July, 1914 (ed. by Georges Barbizon and Siegfried Bernefeld).

2 Cf. Herzfelde's autobiography : *Immergrün*. There the author does not discuss Expressionism. But the book does contain one chapter on George Grosz : *Ein Kaufmann aus Holland*.

3 The journal which came out in six instalments in 1914 was : *Neue Jugend*. A journal concerned with modern art and new ideas. Ed. Heinz Barger and Friedrich Hollaender. Vol. 1, instalments 1–6. Berlin, Verl. Neue Jugend 1914 [Cf. Raabe, No. 18]. The journal, edited by Wieland Herzfelde, was published under the title : *Neue Jugend*. Monthly journal. Ed. Heinz Barger. Wieland Herzfelde Ed.-in-Chief. Vol. 1 [7–12]. Berlin, Verlag *Neue Jugend*, 1916–17. 7–10 appeared July to October 1916 (pp. 123–210), 11–12—in the newly-established Malik-Verlag—as a double number February/March, 1917.

4 *Der Almanach der Neuen Jugend auf das Jahr 1917*. (Ed. Heinz Barger). Berlin, Verlag Neue Jugend [1916]. [Cf. Raabe, No. 177].

5 *Erste George Grosz-Mappe*. 9 Original Lithographs. Berlin, Barger 1917; *Kleine Grosz-Mappe*, Berlin, Malik-Verlag. 1917.

6 The full programme is given in Raabe, *Die Zeitschriften und Sammlungen des literarischen Expressionismus*. 1964, p. 63.

7 Else Lasker-Schüler's novel, *Der Malik* appeared in instalments in the *Aktion*, in the *Brenner* and finally in the *Neue Jugend*, but always only a few chapters at a time. The complete work only appeared 1919, published by Paul Cassírer.

8 The first weekly number came out May 1st, 1917, the second in June, 1917. Of the last two numbers of the *Neue Jugend* in newspaper format Franz Jung writes as follows (*Der Weg nach unten* 1961, p. 113) :

The real centre for our particular type of provocation was the journal called *Neue Jugend*. Its format was that of a large newspaper, like the London *Times*, which was quite an achievement in an age of paper restrictions and bans on new publications. It was a sight for sore eyes : being in four colours one time, black paper with white lettering the next. In it we issued an appeal for food ration cards for prisoners of war to be sent to a collecting point which was completely fictitious : starving Germany will not forget the suffering of her enemies. In it George Grosz went on at great length about the psychological necessity for cycling: without bicycles no politics.

The life and soul of the whole operation was Jonny Heartfield. Even looking back, what he accomplished seems inconceivable. The text always had to be set up piecemeal and printed at different printers. Naturally we had no licence for the paper and no genuine place of publication. We fooled printer and police alike. And yet Jonny managed to have copies sold by most of the newspaper kiosks. People bought it purely because of its lay-out; besides, there was no mention of peace in it—the only thing the police were on the look-out for. All the same, copies had to be disposed of inside one hour. That was all the time the police needed to procure a confiscation order. All in all only very few copies were ever confiscated. We distributed most of them secretly or sent them by post, safe and sound in naval wrappers.

9 Such shows were not so rare even in war-time. Tilla Durieux writes in her memoirs (*Eine Tür steht offen*. Berlin, Herbig, 1954, p. 201):

In the Viktoriastrasse they started to have readings again. I read poems by Schönlank and Hatzfeld. Our publisher was offered a pacifist story by Leonhard Frank. Paul [Cassirer] and I were enthusiastic about its content, and so I suggested reading it at one of these evenings. Paul had come back hostile towards war and made no secret of his opinions. As usual we had an invited audience for this evening of about 300 people, gathered in our studio, on whose walls hung the finest pictures of great masters. First of all Gertrud Eysoldt read some poems, then I read the story. Being sick of war, the people in the audience were swept off their feet by this story. I read with great feeling and at the end of the reading the whole room rose to its feet as one man and shouted: "Peace! Peace!". Some hot-heads wanted to rush out into the streets and start a demonstration, but fortunately they were restrained by the more level-headed members of the audience. Anyway, the inevitable happened and this gathering came to the notice of the general public and the newspapers published reports under the headlines: "Intellectuals' Pacifism" and "A Haunt of Pacifists". The consequence was a house-search which naturally brought no incriminating evidence to light [. . .]

RAOUL HAUSMANN

Club Dada. Berlin 1918–20. Written in Limoges 1958. Publ. in: *Dada. Dokumente einer Bewegung*. Catalogue arranged by Karl Heinz Hering and Ewald Rathke. Düsseldorf 1958. Hausmann (b. July 12th, 1886 in Vienna, died 1971) was one of the leading representatives of Berlin Dada.

Editor of Dadaist publications, manifestos, author of sound poems. Hausmann has written about this time at some length in *Courrier Dada*. Paris,
Le Terrain vague 1958 [No German Edition].

1 *Die Freie Strasse*. 1–8. Folge der Vorarbeit. Berlin, Verlag Freie Strasse
1915–18 [Cf. Raabe, No. 26].

2 Huelsenbeck writes about his part in Berlin Dada in the essay already
referred to, *Die Dadaistische Bewegung* (In: *Die Neue Rundschau*, Vol.
31, 1920, pp. 972–9):

> I arrived in Berlin in January 1917 and found everywhere the greatest
> possible contrast to conditions in Zurich. Sheer want had driven
> everybody to the end of their tether, the German Empire was cracking
> in all its joints and the most resounding victory communiqués were
> no longer capable of banishing the expression of worry and secret
> fear on everybody's faces. In Zurich, where there was no rationing,
> art could not help going all idyllic and frivolous. There writers could
> express their horror at the cruelties of war in lovely trochees and
> well-rounded novels. In Berlin fear gripped the heart and the horizon
> darkened; there were too many people in mourning about. Right
> from the start Dadaism was placed in quite a different situation. With
> the most transparent logic Expressionism had developed in Germany
> into *the* official art movement. Its tendency to inwardness, its call
> for the mysticism of the Gothic cathedrals, its proclamation of
> humanity was taken as a beneficial reaction against the horrible
> slaughter in the trenches. People took refuge in an art which promised
> its proselytes rich delights through abstract art and withdrawal from
> the real horrors mentioned above. Immediately the Dadaist in Berlin
> was witness of an interesting psychological process, he could observe
> the "spiritual" in life, and its cognates. Art and Literature, acting
> as a kind of usefulness factor. The men who marched off to the front
> with Goethe in their knap-sack, wanted Goethe to be "useful" as
> "recreation". But as the Dadaists saw it, art was no rest-centre and
> ought never to be "used" to justify anything. The Dadaist saw
> Expressionism as a withdrawal, a flight from the hard edginess of
> things. He himself was someone who had waged a bitter battle with
> life and loved looking danger straight in the eye. The first Dadaist
> manifesto which I composed in Germany at the request of my friends
> was directed against Expressionism. [. . . He then includes his
> Dadaist Manifesto.]
>
> [. . . on April 12th, 1918 in the Berliner Sezession we put on our
> first propaganda evening at which I talked at some length about the
> aims of Dadaism. Else Hadwiger read Futurist poems while George
> Grosz read some of his own. Raoul Hausmann talked about the new
> material in paintings. We were determined right from the start to
> abandon our rôle as the onlooker in artistic matters. The Zurich
> programme had changed completely. It was no longer a question of

producing the "right kind of art". Art was now merely a propaganda medium for the revolutionary idea. We tried to destroy the artistic and cultural ideologies of the comfortable classes with their own weapons. In closed phalanx, with all the weapons of wit, satire and the grotesque, we tried to smash the idea of "usefulness" within the mental province of a tired bourgeoisie, because we saw in this an immeasurably unjust classification. As has already been indicated, spirit, as we saw it, was not to be found only in the artistic achievement of a poet, we considered it absurd to want to make people more spiritual and better (meliorism!) as in our opinion the metaphysical value of a "spiritual" person, and that of a watering-can, to take any random example, could never be differentiated by any kind of intellectual manipulation. This has been called *Bolshevism in Art;* we were suspected of being insane iconoclasts. Insanity was all that people could attribute to us; they could not understand what we were driving at—least of all the "clever" people who found Dada at best "quite witty" and tried to assure us we were really being at our most dadaistic when we ourselves laughed at Dada.

The poor fools did not perceive the note of Judgment Day, which—paradoxical as this may seem—was, for the perceptive person, present in Dadaism and could be heard, roaring, screaming and shouting. The extreme relativity of things and ideas, the veiling and death agony of every form of faith—the "Decline of the West". The masses felt stricken to the heart as it were. Our mammoth demonstrations turned into mortally dangerous exercises. In Dresden the audience stormed the platform and tried to attack us with chair legs. In Leipzig we spoke in front of three thousand people from behind a protective cordon of thirty policemen. In Prague only sheer chance enabled us to pacify the enormous mob. How did we set about rousing people to such a frenzy? How did we arrange our evening programmes? We adopted a tactic of direct attack on the public. We worked on the assumption that it was an educational undertaking of great value to show the audience, which had come out of sheer curiosity and just for sensation, how unbelievably utilitarian and vulgar an attitude it was to imagine one can buy ten mark's worth of "art". We wanted to show these people who came along with whistles, trumpets and brass-knuckles, as crudely as possible that their concepts of art and intellect were just an ideological superstructure which they were here trying to acquire for money in order to justify all the crooked deals of their daily life. We wanted to show them a new primitive life, in which intellect has disintegrated leaving room for simple impulsive actions, in which the complicated symbolism of melody has been replaced by noises, and life is an enormous joyful mighty confusion of conflicting wills. One time we would employ the simultaneous poem, another time the bruitist concert. The simultaneous poem is spoken from the stage by several persons at once. It had been discovered theoretically in Paris and then introduced for the first time in practice in Zurich by Tristan Tzara. The noise concert, I believe, goes back to Marinetti, who put on *Le réveil de la capitale* in the La Scala, Milan, with drums, sewing machines and children's rattles. In our shows we read manifestos aimed straight at the audience; we sang and danced but always with that revolutionary impetus which proceeds from total awareness of the psychological value of art. From the outside, it is true, all that people saw was a form of "eccentric behaviour" with which I personally deny any connection.

In the meantime, Dada has made its triumphal march round the world. It has penetrated as far as America and Australia. In Paris it is reaping thunderous triumphs at this moment. Dada will die—but when it dies, it will decide the time and the manner, itself, so as to be able to say with unaccustomed pathos: "I have not lived in vain".

3 Huelsenbeck's Dada Speech is printed in: *Dada Almanach*. Ed. Richard Huelsenbeck. Berlin, Erich Reiss, 1920, pp. 104–8.

4 Franz Jung gives his account of Berlin Dada as follows (*Der Weg nach unten*, 1961, pp. 110–12):

The impulse to direct action with which a revolution must start, very soon lost its driving force and moved over to gimmicks supposedly designed to score off society in another way. At first a detailed form of provocation was directed at individuals by individuals. The kind of movement which seemed about to form in Berlin had hardly more than the name in common with the "Dada" movement which in Zurich had had its centre in the Cabaret Voltaire, because the name proved very useful for our onslaughts. If the Zurich Dadaism of the Arps and Tristan Tzaras was supposed to stand for various aesthetic reforms, none of this reached Berlin. Richard Huelsenbeck, who had emigrated back to Berlin from the Cabaret Voltaire, was received as one who had actually seen what the artist emigrés in Switzerland and elsewhere had been up to in their attempts to shake off the yoke of aesthetic tradition, something Futurism had tried but failed to do. But Huelsenbeck, who showed great promise in his early writings had not the slightest influence on us. He remained a foreign body. He was suffered as an appendage, or as a kind of alibi for the name Dada, that was all.

Dada, with which for a time the intellectual élite (or in other words what was on the intellectual surface) was pre-occupied, in reality never penetrated very deeply into the mentality of this stratum and left absolutely no traces of its existence behind. Everything from this transition period to revolution which is called Dadaism, that is readiness for revolution, is wrongly named. When official

Dadaism came on the scene in Germany the revolution was over; it had failed even before the republic was proclaimed. I don't know anything about this Dadaism. I lost touch after the collapse of Germany. I took part neither in their journals nor in their organized gatherings.

Perhaps I may be permitted to add a few remarks about the Dada movement in the last months before the end of the war, as we lived through them before the historians came along; I am not speaking for others, not for any group or movement, just for myself alone, expressing my own personal opinions.

I consider Raoul Hausmann to be the most talented of these intellectual *agents provocateurs*, an exceptional painter and a very facile philosopher who was as seriously concerned with astronomy and mathematics as he was with his attempt to create a new fashion in men's clothes. In the meantime he had discovered a Super Dada in Baader, the architect.

I do not know whether Baader really was an architect who had sold land that did not belong to him, so that he had to join the army to escape the consequences. However, there are witnesses to testify that before a parade of veteran reserve companies in Brussels he did call on Kaiser Wilhelm to step forward, because he had a message from God for him to stop the war immediately. That same day he was shipped back to Germany and probably stuck in a lunatic asylum. He had a wife and four children, though none of us ever set eyes on them.

Hausmann had his studio near Steglitz and came across him one day in some uncultivated hilly country. Baader, the prophet, was surrounded by a variety of elderly men and women to whom he was preaching the idea of a one-man army which would smash all the other armies when the time was ripe and he, Baader himself would be the duty corporal.

Hausmann took him back to his studio and remodelled him into the Super Dada. What means or exercises he may have employed for this I do not know.

This Baader, who was otherwise a harmless and friendly character and the spitting image of the man in the cigar shop on the next corner, was then treated by Hausmann as his dummy, his punch-ball. Baader moved and spoke only as Hausmann directed him.

5 This evening's programme is reproduced in Huelsenbeck, *Dada*. Eine literarische Dokumentation. Reinbek, Rowohlt, 1964, p. 26.

6 Huelsenbeck's *Dadaistisches Manifest* is reprinted in: *Dada-Almanach*. Ed. R. Huelsenbeck. Berlin, Erich Reiss, 1920, pp. 36–41

7 Hausmann's *Pamphlet gegen die Weimarische Lebensauffassung* was printed in: *Der Einzige*, Vol. 1 (1919), pp. 163–64.

8 *Der Dada*. Director: Raoul Hausmann [No. 3. George Grosz, R. Haus-

mann, John Heartfield]. Nos. 1-3, Berlin, Selbstverl. [No. 3: Malik-Verl.] 1919-20 [Cf. Raabe, No. 78].

9 *Erste Internationale Dada Messe*. Organized by marshal George Grosz, Dadasoph Raoul Hausmann, Dada Mechanic John Heartfield. Catalogue. Art dealer Dr. Otto Burchard 1920.

10 *Dada-Almanach*. Ed. on behalf of the Head Office of the German Dada Movement by Richard Huelsenbeck, Berlin, Erich Reiss, 1920 [Cf. Raabe, No. 141]; *En avant dada*. A History of Dadaism. Hanover, Steegemann, 1920. (*Die Silbergäule*, Vol. 50-51).

KARL JAKOB HIRSCH

[*Revolution in Berlin*]. Extract from the autobiography in letter form: *Heimkehr zu Gott*, Munich, Desch, 1946, pp. 64-69. Hirsch (1892-1952), painter, graphic artist and writer was a contributor to the *Aktion* and a founder-member of the November group. The passage is included to indicate the significance of the Revolution of November 9th, 1918.

HANS ROTHE

Theater. Es begann mit Sorge und endete mit Unruh. Written in autumn, 1964 for this volume—Rothe (b. August 14th, 1894 in Meissen), the leading Shakespeare translator of our time was dramaturg at the Leipzig theatre 1920-25, then at the Deutsche Theater in Berlin 1926-30. Wrote dramas, radio plays, novels. Left Germany, now lives in Florence.

1 By an oversight the *première* of *Seeschlacht* was not mentioned in the book *Die Spielpläne Max Reinhardts* which was published by the Piper-Verlag, Munich in 1930. The editor Franz Horch was always inconsolable about this oversight which appears to be the only one in his vast compilation.

2 To appreciate Goering's work today is virtually impossible because for reasons of economy, *Seeschlacht* appears as a prose play in the reprints by Langen-Müller Verlag:

3 To complete the picture we give here a list of all the Expressionist plays produced during the 1917-18 season at the Deutsche Theater. Franz Horch's book is the source.

23.12.1917: Reinhard Sorge, *Der Bettler*. Producer: Max Reinhardt.

17. 1.1918: Georg Kaiser, *Die Koralle*. Producer: Felix Hollaender.

3. 3.1918: Reinhard Goering, *Seeschlacht*. Producer: Max Reinhardt.

6. 9.1918: Franz Werfel, *Der Besuch aus dem Elysium*. Producer: Heinz Herald.

6. 9.1918: Friedrich Koffka, *Kain*. Producer: Heinz Herald.

25.10.1918: Reinhard Goering, *Der Erste*. Producer: Erwin von Busse.

22.11.1918: Walter Hasenclever, *Der Sohn*. Producer: Erwin von Busse.

26.11.1918: Georg Kaiser, *Der Brand im Opernhaus*. Producer: Georg Kaiser.

22.12.1918: Fritz von Unruh, *Ein Geschlecht*. Producer: Heinz Herald.

26. 1.1919: Rolf Lauckner, *Der Sturz des Apostels Paulus*. Producer: Felix Hollaender.

31. 1.1919: Georg Kaiser, *Von morgens bis mitternachts*. Producer: Felix Hollaender.

27. 4.1919: Else Lasker-Schüler. *Die Wupper*. Producer: Heinz Herald.

25. 5.1919: Oskar Kokoschka, *Hiob*. Producer: Oskar Kokoschka.

25. 5.1919: Oskar Kokoschka, *Der brennende Dornbusch*. Producer: Oskar Kokoschka.

25. 1.1920: Arnold Zweig, *Die Sendung Semaels*. Producer: Heinz Herald.

21. 4.1920: Paul Kornfeld, *Himmel und Hölle*. Producer: Ludwig Berger.

24. 2.1921: Walter Hasenclever, *Jenseits*. Producer: Stefan Grossmann.

12. 4.1921: August Stramm, *Kräfte*. Producer: Max Reinhardt.

24. 8.1921: Kasimir Edschmid, *Kean*. Producer: Gustav Hartung.

19.10.1921: Fritz von Unruh *Louis Ferdinand Prinz von Preussen*. Producer: Gustav Hartung.

9. 4.1922: Alfred Brust, *Der singende Fisch*. Producer: Bernhard Reich.

14. 5.1922: Arnolt Bronnen, *Vatermord*. Producer: Berthold Viertel.

30. 6.1922: Ernst Toller, *Die Maschinenstürmer*. Producer: Karlheinz Martin.

20.12.1922: Bertolt Brecht. *Trommeln in der Nacht*. Producer: Otto Falckenberg.

ALFRED GÜNTHER

Dresden im Expressionismus. Written end of 1964 in Stuttgart for inclusion in this volume. The author (b. March 5th, 1885 in Dresden, died December 17th, 1969) published his first volume of verse in 1908, was then active as a journalist, from 1914 on the literary section of the *Dresdener Neueste Nachricten*. Later also publisher's reader. Lived in Stuttgart. In addition to his memoirs attention is drawn to Fritz Löffler's *Expressionismus in Dresden*. In: *Imprimatur*, New Series, Vol. 3. (1961–62), pp. 235–39.

1 On Hellerau cf. Paul Adler, *Hellerau*. In: *Das Literarische Echo* 15 (1912–13), col. 1687–1691.

2 *Neue Blätter*. Ed. Carl Einstein (from No. 7 by Jakob Hegner i.a.) Series 1–3. Berlin, Baron (etc) 1912–13 [Cf. Raabe, No. 10].

3 On these journals cf. Raabe, Nos. 39, 44, 58.

FRIEDRICH WOLF

Felixmüller. Published in *Dramaturgische Blätter*, Vol. 2. (1948), 3; reprinted in: *Austellungskatalog Conrad Felixmüller*, Halle, 1949. The ending of this essay has been omitted. Friedrich Wolf (1888–1953), Socialist dramatist and story-writer, began his career in Expressionism. His play *Das bist du*— one of the many Late Expressionist dramas—had its *première* on October 9th, 1919 in the Dresden Schauspielhaus. It appeared in book-form in the series *Die Dramen der Neuen Schaubühne* (Vol. 4, 1919, 74 pp.) with Felixmüller's stage designs. The latter (b. May 21st, 1897 in Dresden) returned the compliment with an essay written in 1957: *Erinnerungen an Friedrich Wolf*, publ. in *Neue Texte*. Almanach für deutsche Literatur, Vol. 3, Berlin, Aufbau-Verlag, 1963, pp. 375–81. The first part is as follows:

We first met in Dresden, in 1918. About the beginning of 1919 the members of the Workers' and Soldiers' Council went on from one of their sessions to meet writers and artists in Dresden's Italian Village. Friedrich Wolf was a thin, long-legged character. He wore an ill-fitting field-grey uniform and had puttees round his thin legs. As he wore no insignia of rank, one would never have guessed that he had been an officer in the medical corps, and in charge of the 12th Army Corps military hospitals, nor would one have guessed from his austerely clinical demeanour that he was a poet, except that he insisted on my listening to a play he had just finished. He said he wanted to read it to me because he had read an essay I had written about the "modern stage" in the *Zwinger*, the journal of the Saxon State Theatre. The State Theatre had returned his new play with the comment that the production indicated by the author was impossible.

So Friedrich Wolf came to my studio and read *Das bist du*. He read with enthusiasm; indicated the stage effects: the star on which beings appear out of the air, from inside it, with thunder and lightning, fire and smoke. There was much leaping about, rushing hither and thither, gesturing, declaiming, hammering points home, standing still, running up and down, sitting.

Quickly I sketched the chaotic setting with a few crayon strokes. The second setting was in nature: in the gardener's garden, the sun, the flowers, the bee-hive; the people—the gardener, the black-smith; the man and the woman. Then the next setting; night: the room with the young lovers in the moonlight. And the world of objects that speak: axe, bench, crucifix. The demonic nature of things as they come to life and are transformed. Again and again the artistic power rose to a climax of dramatic expression. In my stage-sketches the play began to assume theatrical form. The characters began to take shape, with their costumes, colours and attitudes. Friedrich Wolf's enthusiasm swept me off my feet. His play and the ideas in it were uncharted country for me, but by the time he had finished reading I could clearly visualize how the staging would be possible. The movement of his work with its constant series of transformations (Tat wam asi—that is you) demanded a constantly changing stage design, which would develop as the play developed and whose expressiveness would be constantly mounting with the play. It all seemed to me to be eminently feasible. Friedrich Wolf gathered up my crayon drawings, and was gone in a flash. Two days later I received a telegram: *"Das bist du* accepted for production, if *you* do the stage design."

What could be better than collaboration with Friedrich Wolf on this production? Berthold Viertel joined us as director. And being filled with the youthful *élan* of the revolutionary storms of our time we worked on the stage design with utter dedication down to the very last detail. First we discussed all the drawings thoroughly and I then built little models for each scene to show how flexible each of the structures was. I had a completely free hand, we were carried along on a wave of excitement and we had all the modern stage machinery and the great props-department under the direction of Linnebach, at our disposal. I painted all the flies, back-drops, scenery etc., myself using buckets of paint as a mobile palette and big brooms as paint brushes. Otto Altenkirch who was normally responsible for all the stage settings for the State Theatre and who was himself a very highly regarded Naturalist landscape painter and stage designer gave us the run of his theatre workshop. We tried lots of experiments; much had to be done more than once. From spring to autumn 1919 we worked and filed away at our set before we ever tried it out on the stage. For there were lots of difficulties to be overcome—and not merely shortage of materials. When we did start rehearsals our ideas met with obstacles of yet another kind. At first the actors refused to appear in the admittedly shapeless costumes of the "beings" (in the first and last scenes): and it certainly was very uncomfortable to have to wear thick flax wigs and voluminous sack-like costumes of starched material. Some of the other older actors were afraid of the hoist into which they had to ascend and descend for the first scene, in order to appear suddenly on the tip of the star as "beings". Then there were scene painters who would insist on painting naturalistic little flowers, etc., for the garden scene, while I had to come along with a barrow-load of colours and paint them all out, substituting huge shapes with my large brush.

Friedrich Wolf, nervously excited, was here, there and everywhere, soothing one person, encouraging another, doing everything in his power to persuade the actors to discard their usual sentimental style and change it into a lofty and tragic vein. In order to remodel their language into something that sounded precise and new and far removed from court theatre diction, Wolf read his work to them himself. Time and again he would protest against the way they always modified and toned down the poetic power of his language; and he often quarrelled with Berthold Viertel, the director over this; in their anger each would rush from the stage in different directions.

However, Friedrich Wolf did manage in the end to get his play produced; the first Expressionist play to be put on without any concessions to popular taste, and it was a resounding success for the Royal Court Theatre—as it then still was—for the poet, the producer and the designer.

The public was won over, all three artists were called forward again and again with wild enthusiasm. Expressionism had been shown to be feasible on the stage. The play became part of the regular repertoire, sustained by revolutionary enthusiasm, anti-convention, pro-regeneration in human relationships—and in the artistic life of Dresden at that time it represented a victory for the new age. The generation back from the war, especially the young poets and painters, brought their enthusiasm into the theatre and drew some more from it. The liberal middle-class of the old princely city of Dresden was seized with revolutionary fervour and paid homage to the poet Friedrich Wolf. [. . .]

FRIEDRICH BURSCHELL

"Revolution" und "Neue Erde". München 1918-19. Written 1961, published in: *Imprimatur*, New Series, Vol. 3 (1961–62), pp. 244–48. Burschell's memoirs, which will include the passages given here, are to be published in book form. Burschell (b. August 9th, 1889 in Ludwigshafen, died April 4th, 1970) studied in Heidelberg before the war, after World War II worked as a writer and translator in Munich. As additional material we include here Richard Seewald's memories of Munich 1918–19 from *Der Mann von Gegenüber*, 1963, p. 42f.:

How did we really live in those days? Most of us carried on as before gossiping endlessly about literature, art and politics. Very few attempted to salvage genuine values out of the collapse or carry our heritage over into the future. Some Activists behaved as if the future had already arrived and denying their heritage leapt into the political arena. They joined the Artists' Council which had sprung up alongside the Workers' and Soldiers' Councils. They closed the academy, organised rallies and made speeches. But that comes under the heading of civic responsibility to be discussed elsewhere. Among the ambitious there are generally many fools and only a handful of idealists. The last two categories generally have to do the paying. Wachelmaier, the painter who produced Expressionist wood-cuts under the nickname "Wach" for the revolutionary number of the *Münchner Neueste Nachrichten* was probably shot and buried somewhere. He was never seen again. Landauer, who had once produced a modern version of Meister Eckhardt the mystic, was murdered by the White Guards. Toller was in hiding for weeks not far from me.

In an overgrown garden on the Werneckstrasse there stood a house which was slowly falling down, a regular haunted house like something out of Kubin. It was called "Suresne Castle". On the first floor lived a musician called Harburger; the son of the well-known cartoonist from the *Fliegende Blätter*, who was a day-dreamer. Amid the wild disorder of his large room stood an organ, a grand piano, a spinet and a Bach clavier. For the last-mentioned instrument he had composed charming, rather old-fashioned pieces. He was one of our friends. Beneath him lived Lahusen, who composed Jazz music, and next door to him Reichel, the first man to imitate Klee. And that was where Toller was hiding. When there was a raid—they were looking for him and suspected he was hiding here—he disappeared behind a concealed door and nobody ever betrayed him.

That was how he lived. According to one story, the great David sent the gold coins he received for painting the Oath of the Horatians skimming across the river Seine like flat stones. But we didn't have any gold coins—just paper money. That's what the defeat was like. No more war! was the battle cry of the intellectuals.

1 *Revolution*. Weekly. For All and One. (Ed. Friedrich Burschell with the help of friends.), Vol. 1 [1–2]. Munich, Verlag Wochenschrift Revolution, 1918 [Cf. Raabe, No. 52].

2 *Die Pforte*. A Book Series. Vols. 1–6 Munich, Dreiländerverlag, 1919 [Cf. Raabe, No. 160].

3 *Dokumente der Menschlichkeit*. A literary – historical – political series. Vols. 1–20, Munich, Dreiländerverlag, 1919–20.

4 *Neue Erde*. Half-Monthly Magazine. Ed. Friedrich Burschell. Vol. 1 [1–3], Munich, Dreiländerverlag, 1919 [Raabe, No. 57].

KASIMIR EDSCHMID

In memoriam Carlo Mierendorff. Published as introduction to Carlo Mierendorff, *Literarische Schriften*, Darmstadt, Darmstädter Verlag, 1947, pp. v–xiii. This appreciation is printed here because of the particularly realistic picture of the Darmstadt Circle. Edschmid (1890–1966) was the most successful of the Expressionist prose-writers and also an influential theoretician for the movement. His most important Expressionist publications are: *Die sechs Mündungen*. Stories 1915; *Das rasende Leben*. Two stories 1916; *Timur*. Stories 1917; *Die Fürstin*. 1919; *Stehe von Lichtern gestreichelt*. Poems 1919; *Die achatnen Kugeln*. Novel 1920; *Die*

M*   361 *doppelköpfige Nymphe.* 1920. As additional material to the rather inaccessible essay on Mierendorff and his friends attention is drawn to Edschmid's book of memoirs: *Lebendiger Expressionismus.* Discussions, Portraits, Reminiscences. Munich. Desch 1961. In his *Tagebuch 1958–1960,* Desch 1961, p. 397f. Edschmid recapitulates:

Occasionally in the year 1913, a schoolboy called F. C. Lehr would visit me in the attic room of my father's house where I used to work. He told me that he and his friends dabbled in literature. There was something defenceless but by no means shamefaced about the way he put this. A nice lad called Haubach, who later shot himself, lived a few houses away and had been acquainted with me for years. He and Mierendorff were only six or seven years younger than me but at that age this meant a lot. They were still at school, while I had studied at four different universities and graduated from Giessen in 1914. I got to know Mierendorff through Haubach on the barrack square when we all volunteered for the infantry. And in the meantime I had also met Pepy Würth, who was about two years younger than the others.

Even as a fifteen-year-old Pepy had made a name for himself in some famous advertising competition and was just school leaving-age when the war began. I happened to meet him standing on the corner of Wilhelminen and Rheinstrasse the day the results came out. He just straightened his pork-pie hat on to the back of his head a bit and transferred his cigarette to the other corner of his mouth. He was wearing a green polo-neck pullover and no collar. Very cool, very superior, silent, the born revolutionary who ended up boss of all his friends. That was what he was like, always.

At the age of sixteen Pepy was already writing his *Dachstube* Pamphlets which were duplicated and distributed gratis. That same year he bought some type and went into print. He printed like other men wage war or serve as priests. Gritting his teeth, full of vehemence and with the coolness of the professional. Once, on the occasion of the twenty-fifth anniversary of his publishing concern he wrote ironically about himself in the *Preisgesang.* This two-tone jubilee issue with coloured illustrations contained not only a solemn compilation of his entire *oeuvre* to date—there was also a duet from two grateful authors.

One of these, *Kakau*, was in reality Hans Schiebelhuth, and the other FU, was Fritz Usinger. Pepy summed himself up in the preface as follows: "So I was everything at once, not just publisher, but typesetter and printer too, reader, agent and factotum, colourist and illustrator, packer and despatch-man, shorthand-typist, book-keeper, warehouse clerk and printer's devil, all in one person."

Then came the first books by Haubach, by Mierendorff, by Usinger, whose entire lyrical and essayist output he published and also the curious verse of Wilhelm Merck, a friend of Hasenclever's, in 1918. Then the series called *Die kleine Republik*. This was followed by the *Swasticrusade* by Hans Schiebelhuth, who died twenty years later in America. This was 1920. He was far ahead of his time. He saw the approach of anti-Semitism.

> There's a thing called a swastika around!
> Watch out for names like Brown!
> Polish your opinions with the appropriate chrome
> Approach the world-pogrom.

> There's a thing called a swastika around:
> And I've
> Instructed all Christian cabbies in town
> To stop employing Jewish-looking mares
> And I've
> Asked the Pope
> To join the Communist Party
> And back something beautifully Modern Arty.

And then Pepy started the *Tribunal*. As publisher of this spectacular journal, one of the most interesting of this whole period, Pepy was entering the first stage of world notoriety. Mierendorff's impetuous temper and Pepy's coolness produced between them a paper of intellectual and revolutionary standing characterized by an unspoiled youthfulness.

1 *Die Dachstube* (Ed. F. C. Lehr; artistic ed. Joseph Würth). Nos. 1–4. Darmstadt, Verlag, Die Dachstube, 1915–18 [Cf. Raabe, No. 24].

2 Carlo Mierendorff, *Der Gnom*. With four drawings by Joseph Würth, 1917; Fritz Usinger, *Der ewige Kampf* [Poems]. With original lithographs by Carl Gunschmann, 1918; Theodor Haubach, *Jacques Prince*. With original lithographs by Ludwig Breitwieser. 1918. The books are in the series: *Bücher der Dachstube*.

3 *Die kleine Republik*. A Pamphlet series. Nos. 1–15. Darmstadt, Verlag. Die Dachstube, 1918–24 [Cf. Raabe No. 156].

4 Reproduced in the Marbach Expressionism Catalogue.

5 *Das Tribunal*. Hessische radikale Blätter. Ed. Carlo Mierendorff Nos. 1–2. Darmstadt, Verlag Die Dachstube, 1919–21 [Cf. Raabe No. 59].

6 On Colin's speech in Darmstadt, Edschmid writes as follows in his *Lebendiger Expressionismus*, 1961, p. 364:

When we reached the hall there were three or four hundred youths standing outside demonstrating—against Colin. The room was packed and electric. On the platform I introduced him as an advocate for Germany. Boos. I said we intended to throw out anybody who caused a disturbance. Colin started. He spoke a few sentences in broken German. As soon as he started to speak French a youth got up in the front row and protested. I leapt from the platform, grabbed him by the scruff of the neck and threw him out a side door. Colin was able to continue. But his voice could hardly be heard for outside the youths who now filled the whole street, had started to sing the "Wacht am Rhein". Followed by "Deutschland über alles", then the "Wacht am Rhein" again.

We ourselves were all very young. But it did not matter a bit to those young people out there that the Belgian was speaking against a French Government's wild desire to annex the Rhineland, that he spoke passionately in favour of setting free the countless German soldiers still held prisoner of war, and that he clearly and obstinately demanded negotiation. The fact that he did this in French as he did not speak German fluently enough was sufficient to trigger off a riot. The exasperated youths outside screamed: "Smash the Belgian, the damned French-speaking swine", just as they were later to cry: "Shoot Walter Rathenau, the damned Jewish pig". All the same, Colin did manage to have his say. A few hundred followers accompanied him to his hotel, followed by as many nationalists eager to string him up. [. . .]

7 *Hessenborn.* Hessische Blätter für sittliche Kultur, Vol. 1, April 1st, 1919, 16pp. [Cf. Raabe, No. 59].

8 On the Darmstadt production of Alexandre Dumas' *Kean* in Kasimir Edschmid's adaptation cf. Edschmid, *Lebendiger Expressionismus*, 1961, p. 367ff.

9 *Tribüne der Kunst und Zeit.* A series, ed. by Kasimir Edschmid. Vols. 1–29. Berlin, Erich Reiss 1919–23. [Cf. Raabe, No. 159]. Edschmid writes about the series in: *Lebendiger Expressionismus* 1961. p. 345ff.

10 Carlo Mierendorff, *Hätte ich das Kino!!* 1920, 56pp. (*Tribüne der Kunst und der Zeit,* Vol. 15).

11 Hans Schiebelhuth, *Der Hakenkreuzzug.* Neo-dadaistic anti-poetry. With original wood-cuts by Victor Joseph Kuron. 1920. 20pp. (Die kleine Republik. No. 9).

PAUL STEEGEMANN

Fünf Jahre Verleger (in Hanover). Published in: *Das Stachelschwein.* Ed. Hans Reimann. Vol. 1 (1924) 6, pp. 3–5; reprinted in: *Imprimatur,* New Series, Vol. 3 (1961–62), pp. 258–59. Steegemann (1894–1956) was one of the courageous publishers of Late Expressionism in Hanover.

1 The series meant is *Die Silbergäule* which began to appear in October, 1919 and was Steegemann's main venture. By 1922 sixty-two books had appeared. [Cf. Raabe, No. 163].

2 Titles and dates of the publications mentioned are: Hans Reimann

[Arthur Sünder], *Die Dinte wider das Blut*. 1921; Hans Reimann, *Ewers*. A guaranteed depraved and trashy Novel. 1922; Hans Reimann, *Hedwig Courths-Mahler*. Simple Stories for the Happy Home. 1922; Kurt Hiller, *175, die Schmach des Jahrhunderts*. A polemic. 1922; Richard Huelsen-beck, *En avant Dada*. A History of Dadaism. 1920; Wilhelm Michel, *Der abendländische Zeus*. Essays on Rudolf Steiner, Oswald Spengler, *Hölder-lin* . . . 1923; *Der intime Balzac*. Anecdotes translated Ossip Kalenter. 1922; Dési Stinnes, *Die Söhne*. Eight political scenes. 1923; Arthur Landsberger, *Raffke & Cie*. The New Society, 1923.
3 Paul Verlaine, *Frauen*. German trans. by Curt Moreck. 1920; Verlaine, *Männer*. Trans. Curt Moreck and Hans Schiebelhuth, 1920; Aubrey Beardsley, *Venus und Tannhäuser*. A romantic story. With nine additional chapters by Franz Blei. 1921.

HANS HARBECK

Expressionismus in Hamburg. Written in 1961, publ. in: *Imprimatur*, New Series, Vol. 3 (1961–62), pp. 249–52. Harbeck (1887–1968) graduated in Munich in 1910, then lived as writer and critic in Hamburg. His early verse collections are: *Revolution*. 1918: *Der Vorhang*. 1920; *Rund um den Hund*. 1921; *Die Jungfrau*. 1923.
1 *Die rote Erde*. Monthly Magazine for Art and Culture. [No. 2. without sub-title]. Ed. Karl Lorenz. No. 1 and Folge 2 [1st and 2nd Book]. Hamburg (various publishers) 1919–23. [Cf. Raabe, No. 80].
2 Hans Leip, *Der Pfuhl*. Novel. Munich. A. Langen, 1923.
3 *Der Freihafen*. Newsheet of the Hamburg Kammerspiel Theatre, ed. Erich Ziegel. Vols. 1–4, Hamburg, 1918–21.
4 Johannes R. Becher has given a poetic version of this occasion in one of the chapters from the sequel to his autobiographical novel *Abschied*. It is quoted here although from the context it belongs in another part of the book:
The 'scandal' came about because Anders received an invitation from the theatre-manager of the Munich Kammerspiele to take part in a matinée performance devoted to the patriotic mission of modern German literature. Other participants named were Frank Wedekind and Klabund.
Anders at once sent his acceptance from Berlin. The moment he agreed to go he had conceived the plan for the kind of work of contemporary patriotic character *he* wanted to read.
The title just had to be "The Battle".
"*Die Schlacht! Die Schlacht!*" he said over and over again. That was better than "The War". The German word for battle had echoes of shambles, slaughter-house, being slain and slaughtered etc., it also

reminded him of battle-pictures and the famous panorama *Die Schlacht bei Sedan* and all the hundreds of similar pictures that appeared daily in all the papers.

But the *Schlacht* he wanted to write would have to be quite different . . .

"Make no mistake, Gentlemen, I'm not one of your Felix Dahn's or Wildenbruch's."

"And no Herr von Possart either," he added, thinking of the way he would read his poem . . .

This poem *Die Schlacht* had to be twenty-five stanzas long and written in iambics. In this poem a battle would be fought *against* all the usual battle descriptions, it had to be the most modern and most fearful of battles, the battle to end all battles. Needless to say even Homer's descriptions of battle would appear trivial beside it . . .

His "Battle" took place and in a few days Anders had finished his work. It was such an accumulation of gruesome horrors, one bestiality piled on top of another—that the last line seemed to Anders exceptionally appropriate, it was a variation of Horace's "Dulce et decorum est pro patria mori", which now read "And that is why it is sweet and honourable to be slaughtered like fat-stock on the field of slaughter".

He meant to take this last line, which he saw as summing up the whole thesis of the poem, and fling it into the audience's smug face . . .

He treated the poem as Top Secret, it would shatter the world soon enough.

And the battle grew.

It was soon twice the size. It kept growing like a land-slide. It could not just be restricted to the battlefield, it had to leave its bloody traces on the home-front too. Houses went up in flames, whole streets collapsed, rivers rose up and even the sea took part in the battle, not just devouring ships by the hundred, but rolling over the coast-line sweeping far inland, swallowing up villages and turning fields and pasture-land into swamps. The battle had even spread to the air, air-ships rained down fire . . . There was no stopping it.

Even as he was standing waiting in the theatre, Anders was adding another stanza, but nobody tried to stop him from reading his enormous poem.

The first stanza was supposed to be spoken as the curtain was going up:

> *Curtains up . . . Oh, you shall see the slaughter*
> *For what it really is—and die yourselves.*
> *All you sitting here expecting the usual guff*
> *We've had enough of that, enough . . .*

And then the battle was to be unleashed, in a monotone, hummed, purred, murmured with hoarse, croaking voice and not till the end was the poem to rise to a kind of cynical apotheosis . . .

But first Frank Wedekind welcomed the German invasion of Holland and Belgium and pointed out how this military operation would be of great economic advantage especially, because it opened up a rich field of activity for the German Civil Service. The German Civil Servant was lauded by Wedekind as a new type of human being, far surpassing the English Colonial Official, who would see his calling in spreading efficiency and reliability throughout the world. The Age of the German Civil Servant had arrived. In his lofty ethical mission only the Christian missionary was in any way comparable to him.

The public, at first not sure whether Frank Wedekind was being serious or facetious, was slow to applaud—but in fact Wedekind was in deadly earnest about everything he had said and he complained bitterly in the wings that, once again, he had not been taken seriously.

There were a few jolly soldiers' songs by Klabund which were heartily applauded.

Then the announcer boomed "The Battle" into the microphone and gave the poet a sign to step up to the lectern.

Anders had never been on a stage before and so he thought the theatre was dark because the curtain had not gone up yet. So he passed the time waiting for the curtain to go up, doing all sorts of silly things; he made faces, stuck his tongue out at the audience, then turned his behind in that direction and he tapped his forehead in the direction of the wings where the theatre-manager was sitting with some of the stage-hands.

He thought the theatre-manager was just joking when he leapt up in horror, wringing his hands and shaking his head in desperation . . .

The darkness of the theatre began to come to life. There was whispering, a babble of voices—threatening voices began to reach the lectern, which Anders held on to in terror, for his hands began to shake when he realized the curtain had been up all the time and that none of his vulgar display could have escaped the audience . . .

"Get off the stage!"

This cry shattered him so completely that he was incapable of moving and stood as if nailed to the spot . . .

When there was another cry of "Curtain!" Anders was as white as a sheet but now he was ready for anything. He had to do something no matter what happened.

So he left the lectern and advanced to the edge of the stage, put his finger to his lips as if appealing for silence and raised his hands in entreaty.

Breathless silence.

The public was as tense as he was, ready for something ghastly, the absolute limit.

And now he was screaming out, gesticulating wildly:

> Curtains up! Oh you shall see the slaughter,
> For what it really is—and die yourselves.

A deafening roar rose up to meet him, while Anders repeated over and over again:

> And die yourselves, and die yourselves,
> Kick the bucket . . . yes, kick the bucket!

He could see some people starting to rush the stage. Objects rained down on him. The theatre-manager had leapt out from the wings and was trying to drag Anders away from the furious audience.

Once again Anders commanded silence.

And again breathless silence, as if the height of scandal had not yet been reached.

"With your permission, ladies and gentlemen, I should like to offer a modern translation of the famous line by Horace:

"Dulce et decorum est pro patria mori".

A few people nodded appeasingly, apparently people were prepared to stop the scandal there and let the poet make some sort of honourable retreat.

Anders stood motionless as if himself etched in bronze like the classical saying, "In my modern contemporary translation, the saying now goes like this—"

You could hear the breathless hush—

And then—with clenched fists and flailing arms—he thundered out the verses:

> And this is why it is sweet and honourable
> To be slaughtered like fat-stock on the field of slaughter.

Anders had no idea how he got to the waiting-room of the Central Station in Munich, ready to take the next train to Berlin. In the train, people were talking about how the patriotic matinée at the Munich Kammerspiele had finished up with an unbelievable scandal. He had somehow lost the manuscript of his poem. He was tired and fell asleep carried along on a gentle rocking roar. When he woke up it was Jena already.

"Dulce et decorum est," he hummed to himself.

"Pro? Pro? Pro?" he asked.

And he smiled proudly, "What a scandal!"

KURT WOLFF

Vom Verlegen im allgemeinen und von der Frage: wie kommen Verleger und Autoren zusammen. Manuscript of a radio broadcast by the Westdeutscher Rundfunk, Cologne, first printed in: *Sprache im technischen Zeitalter*, Vol. 3 (1964), pp. 894–904; printed here from Kurt Wolff, *Autoren, Bücher, Abenteuer. Betrachtungen und Erinnerungen eines Verlegers.* Berlin, Klaus Wagenbach, 1965, pp. 13–25. Looking back from the perspective of old age, the publisher Kurt Wolff (1887–1963) gives in this talk an evaluation of his own activity as a publisher which in its beginnings was closely associated with Expressionism even if Wolff reacts against the idea of Expressionist Literature. On the history of the firm, cf. Karl H. Salzmann, *Kurt Wolff der Verleger.* A contribution to the history of publishing and letters. In: *Archiv für Geschichte des Buchwesens*, Vol. 2 (1958–60), pp. 375–403.

1 The early period of the Ernst Rowohlt Publishing House has been written up more extensively by Kurt Pinthus using his own recollections of events in: *Rowohlt Almanach 1908–1962.* Ed. Mara Hintermeier and Fritz J. Raddatz. With a preface by Kurt Pinthus and the complete bibliography from 1908–61. Reinbek, Rowohlt, 1962, p. 9ff.

2 Walter Hasenclever, *Der Sohn.* A drama in 5 Acts. Leipzig. Kurt Wolff, 1914.

3 Trakl's letters to Kurt Wolff are not yet published in full.

4 Walter Benjamin on Robert Walser cf. Benjamin, *Schriften.* Vol. 2, Frankfurt, Suhrkamp, 1955, pp. 148–151.

5 In Musil's literary chronicle. In: *Die Neue Rundschau.* No. 25 (1914), pp. 1167–69.

6 *Genius.* Journal for traditional and modern art. Ed. Carl Georg Heise, Hans Mardersteig [Vol. 1, and Kurt Pinthus]. Vols. 1–3, Munich, Kurt Wolff, 1919–21 [Cf. Raabe, No. 74].

7 *Dadaco. Dadaistischer Handatlas.* To appear 1920 in the Kurt Wolff Verlag. This handbill for a book that never appeared has often been reproduced, as e.g. in the dtv—pocket book: *Das war Dada.* Writings and Documents. Ed. Peter Schifferli. Munich, 1963, p. 156

8 Quoted from Richard Seewald, *Der Mann von gegenüber.* Munich. List, 1963, p. 277.

C. F. W. BEHL

Begegnungen mit dem Expressionismus. Written in 1961, published in *Imprimatur*, New Series, Vol 3 (1961–62), pp. 240–43. This chapter will be included in Behl's book of memoirs to appear under the title, *Es war erst gestern. Ein Leben zwischen Themis and Thespis*, by the Nymphenburger Verlag, Munich. Behl (b. March 3rd, 1889 in Berlin, died February

28th, 1968), retired county judge, lived for many years in Berlin as lawyer, writer and critic, later lived in Munich.

1 Kurt Hiller's literary cabaret *Gnu* was founded in 1911, after a disagreement with the writers of the *Neuer Club* which he had also started. In the *Gnu* many Early Expressionists read from their works before 1914.

2 Little is known about Wolfenstein's cabaret. On March 24th, 1914, there were readings by Paul Boldt, Leo Matthias, Gottfried Benn, Alfred Wolfenstein, Egmont Seyerlen. The gathering was held in the Cassirer Gallery.

3 *Der Kritiker*. Weekly Journal for Politics, Arts and Sciences. Ed. C. F. W. Behl and Dr. Neulaender. Vols. 2–9, Berlin, 1920–27 [Cf. Raabe, No. 95].

4 Max Herrmann-Neisse's novel *Cajetan Schaltermann* was published by the Dreiländerverlag in Munich, 1920.

5 Quoted from Georg Heym, *Dichtungen und Schriften. Gesamtausgabe.* Ed. K. L. Schneider. Vol. 3, Hamburg, Ellermann, 1960, p. 139.

6 Leonhard Frank's famous story *Der Kellner* was published first in: *Die Weissen Blätter*, Vol. 3, No. 4 (1916), pp. 149–59. It was included as the introductory story to the volume: *Der Mensch ist gut*, Zurich, Rascher, 1918.

7 Frank gives an account of this in his autobiographical novel *Links, wo das Herz ist* (Munich, Nymphenburger Verlagshandlung, 1952, p. 92f.):

> Michael was already working on the end of his book *Die Ursache*. Dürr, the teacher, has been strangled. The murderer has explained in front of a jury why he strangled his teacher and has been condemned to death. Michael was sitting in the Café des Westens trying to visualize the last hour before the execution. Nearby were four customers, among them the journalist who had given Michael the old oak table. They had been talking enthusiastically about the war for half an hour. Michael's facial muscles were quivering with agitation and scarcely suppressed rage. But his furious looks had no effect on the four war supporters.
>
> Down by the door where the stock-market reports hung alongside the army communiqués he suddenly saw grey-haired stockbrokers embracing each other with shouts of joy. He thought the war was over. It was May 7th, 1915.
>
> The journalist, a well-meaning man who later became the editor of a Socialist paper—after the war—hurried down to see the news bulletins. When he came back he was beside himself with enthusiasm: "We've sunk the *Lusitania* with 1,198 passengers." He said: "The sinking of the *Lusitania* is the greatest act of heroism in the history of mankind."
>
> Michael, who had enough imagination to be able to visualize what happens when 1,198 human beings have to fight for their

lives in the sea at dead of night and drown helplessly, lost his last remnant of self-control. He stood up and without a word struck the journalist in the face. All around people sprang to their feet.

Michael left the Café between a row of hostile customers. He went home at once, packed a bag and left for Switzerland.

The following morning two plain-clothes policemen called at his flat. They asked Lisa about Michael and showed her the warrant for his arrest.

8 *Das Tribunal*—Hessian Radical News Letter. Ed. Carlo Mierendorff. Vol. 1, H.1. Darmstadt, 1919. From *Worte zum Beginn* by Kasimir Edschmid.

9 The *première* of Hasenclever's *Sohn*, was in the Albert-Theater in Dresden on October 8th, 1916, the first production in Berlin was on November 22nd, 1918.

10 The first Berlin production of Reinhard Goering's *Seeschlacht* was in the Deutsches Theater on March 3rd, 1918. The *première* had been on February 10th, 1918 in Dresden.

11 The first Berlin production of Fritz von Unruh's *Ein Geschlecht* was in the Deutsches Theater on December 22nd, 1918. The first performance had been in the Frankfurter Schauspielhaus on June 16th, 1918.

12 *Aus den Zeitgedichten*. In: *Das junge Deutschland*. Vol. 2 (1919), p. 205; *Niederbruch und Aufschwung*. ditto. Vol. 3 (1920), p. 122.

LUDWIG MARCUSE

Ein bisschen Sintflut. Extract from his memoirs: *Mein zwanzigstes Jahrhundert. Auf dem Weg zu einer Autobiographie*. Munich, List, 1960, pp. 69–72. Marcuse (1894–1971) was one of the writers and critics of the so-called Twenties who saw Expressionism in the light of what came after it. This is how he must be read. (Cf. also Marcuse's comments on Bruno Wener's review, *Literatur und Theater der Zwanziger Jahre*. In: *Die Zeit ohne Eigenschaft*—An Account of the Twenties. Stuttgart, Kohlhammer, 1961, pp. 181–94).

1 Franz Werfel, *Bocksgesang*. In 5 Acts. Munich, Kurt Wolff, 1921, p. 131.
2 Reinhard Goering, *Seeschlacht*. Berlin, S. Fischer, 1917, p. 68.
3 Carl Zuckmayer. *Kreuzweg*. Drama. 1919; *Der fröhliche Weinberg*. Comedy. 1925; *Pankraz erwacht*. 1925.

MAX KRELL

Expressionismus—Glück und Ende. Extract from Krell's memoirs: *Das alles gab es einmal*. Frankfurt, Scheffler, 1961, pp. 206–9. Krell (1887–1962), poet, writer and critic, has tackled the phenomenon of Expressionism theoretically several times: *Über neue Prosa*, 1919. (*Tribüne der Kunst und Zeit*, Vol. 7); *Bilanz der Dichtung*. In: *Die neue Dichtung. Jahrbuch*, 1922–23, pp. 257–68.

1 This refers to the first two anthologies by Karl Otten: *Ahnung und Aufbruch*. Expressionistic Prose, 1957; *Schrei und Bekenntnis*. Expressionistic Theatre, 1959; in addition Kurt Pinthus, *Menschheitsdämmerung. Ein Dokument des Expressionismus*, 1959; 51–58,000, 1964.

Biographical Index

If the normal procedure had been followed whereby names occurring in the various documents are explained as they occur, the countless repetitions of the same names and the resulting cross-references would have made the footnotes unnecessarily unwieldy. We have therefore decided to adopt an unusual solution: names already generally familiar from literary and cultural history are not included and only names of contemporaries mentioned in the text or related to Expressionism are listed in the following alphabetical index. This saves space and makes reference easier. Of course, a separate reference work would have been the result if *every* author, artist, philosopher etc. had been given an extensive commentary. So once again a compromise seemed the best solution: in order to leave room for as many texts as possible in the book itself, this index gives only dates of birth and death and bare essentials. For additional information references to specialist works are given. (To date no reference work specializing in Expressionism exists.) The following abbreviations are used:

Aktion — Die Aktion. ed. Franz Pfemfert. Vols. 1–4. Photo copy reprint. Stuttgart, Cotta 1961. Vol. 1 contains a commentary by Paul Raabe. This has also appeared separately.

Brockhaus — Der Grosse Brockhaus. 16th ed. Vols. 1–12. Wiesbaden, 1952–57 [Used only in exceptional cases].

Expr.-Katalog — Expressionismus. Literatur und Kunst 1910–23. An exhibition organized by the German Literature Archive, Marbach. (Catalogue arranged by Paul Raabe and Ludwig Greve.) Marbach 1960; 2nd edition 1961.

Gel.-Kürschner — Kürschners Deutscher Gelehrten-Kalender. 9th edition. Vols. 1–2, Berlin, De Gruyter, 1961.

Giebisch-Gugitz — Hans Giebisch and Gustav Gugitz: Bio-bibliographisches. Literaturlexikon Österreichs. Vienna, Hollinek 1964.

Kosch — Wilhelm Kosch: Deutsches Literatur–Lexikon. Biographical and Bibliographical hand-book. 2nd ed. Vols. 1–4. Bern, Francke, 1949 till 1958. [Only used in exceptional cases.]

Lit.-Kürschner   Kürschners Deutscher Literatur-Kalender. Vol. 1ff. Berlin, de Gruyter 1877 ff. Last ed.: 54. 1963.

NDB   Neue Deutsche Biographie. Published by the Historical Commission of the Bavarian Academy of Sciences. [To date] Vols. 1–6 Berlin, Duncker & Humblot 1953–1964. To Grassmann.

Osterroth   Franz Osterroth: Biographisches Lexikon des Sozialismus. Vol. 1. Hanover, Dietz 1960.

Pinthus   Menschheitsdämmerung. Ein Dokument des Expressionismus ed. by Kurt Pinthus. Hamburg, Rowohlt 1959.

Th.-Kürschner   Kürschners biographisches Theater-Handbuch. ed. by Herbert A. Frenzel and Hans Joachim Moser. Berlin, de Gruyter 1956.

Vollmer   Hans Vollmer, Allgemeines Lexikon der bildenden Künstler des 20. Jahrhunderts. Vols. 1–5. Leipzig, Seemann 1953–1962.

Wilpert   Gero von Wilpert: Lexikon der Weltliteratur. Bio-bibliographical encyclopaedia of authors and anonymous works. Various hands. Published Stuttgart, Kröner 1963.

No page numbers are given in the following list. These can be found in the final index which contains the key to all parts, (text, commentary and bibliography) and includes all names occurring in this volume.

ACHMANN, JOSEPH (b. 1885). Painter and graphic artist. From 1919–21 joint editor of *Sichel* with Georg Britting. Lives in Schliersee. Vollmer.

ADLER, PAUL (1878–1946). Born in Prague, writer in Hellerau. Wrote mystic tales. Contributor to the *Aktion*. Activistic-socialistic tendencies. Expr.-Katalog.

ALTENBERG, PETER (1859–1919). Viennese writer at the turn of the century. Master of short prose. Famous coffee-house habitué. NDB.; Giebisch-Gugitz; Wilpert.

ALTHERR, PAUL (b. 1887). Zurich writer. Author of dramas and radio plays. Lit.-Kürschner '63.

ALTMANN, BRUNO Munich Bohemian. No further details.

AMBERGER, JOSEF Munich man of letters. Co-editor of H. F. S. Bachmair's journal *Neue Kunst* (1913–14). Poetry: *Der unendliche Weg*. 1914.

ANDERSEN-NEXÖ, MARTIN (1869–1954). Danish Storywriter. Lived a long time in Germany, ultimately in Dresden. Wilpert.

ANDRIAN-WERBURG, LEOPOLD BARON VON (1875–1951). Austrian diplomat and writer, friend of Hofmannsthal. Wilpert; Giebisch-Gugitz.

ANNUNZIO, GABRIELE D' (1863–1938). Italian poet of symbolism and decadence. Wilpert.

APOLLINAIRE, GUILLAUME (1880–1918). French poet. Friend and patron of modern French painters. Wilpert.

ARCHIPENKO, ALEXANDER (1887–1964). Sculptor and painter. Sponsored in Germany by the *Sturm*. Vollmer.

ARP, HANS (1887–1966). Modern sculptor, painter and poet. Co-founder of Dada in Zurich, then in Cologne. Lived in Meudon. Wilpert, Vollmer; Lit.-Kürschner '63.

AUSLEGER, GERHARD (1891–1968). Literary works during Expressionism. Editor of the literary journal *Die schöne Rarität* (1917–19). Lived as a book-seller in Offenbach/Main.

BAADER, JOHANNES (1875–1955). Architect from Stuttgart. Joined Dada in Berlin, and has gone down in history as Super Dada.

BACHMAIR, HEINRICH F. S. (1889–1960). Publisher and writer from Munich (pseud. Sebastian Scharnagl). Friend of Johannes R. Becher. Aktion.

BÄUMER, LUDWIG (1888–1928). Writer in the *Aktion* circle. Lived in Worpswede. Politically active in the 20's. Aktion.

BALL, HUGO (1886–1927). Writer, social-critic and philosopher. Till 1914 dramaturg at the Münchener Kammerspiele. 1916 co-founder of Dada in Zurich (Cabaret Voltaire). NDB very faulty; Wilpert; Aktion; Expr.-Katalog.

BALLA, GIACOMO (1874–1958). Italian painter; representative of Futurism. Wilpert.

BARBUSSE, HENRI (1873–1935). French. Radical political writer. Wilpert.

BARLACH, ERNST (1870–1938). Sculptor, graphic artist. Played a vital role as dramatist in the history of Expressionist theatre. Otherwise a loner, like his friend Theodor Däubler. NDB; Vollmer; Wilpert.

BASSERMANN, ALBERT (1869–1952). Famous German actor in Berlin. NDB.

BASSEWITZ, GERDT VON (1878–1923). Writer. Wrote plays, fairytales and essays. Belonged to the young Ernst Rowohlt's circle of friends. Lit.-Kürschner '22.

BAUDISCH, PAUL (b. 1899). Austrian writer, dramatist and translator. Wrote Express. novels and plays. Lives in Munich. Lit.-Kürschner '63; Expr.-Katalog.

BAUM, OSKAR (1883–1941). Blind Prague poet. Friendly with the Prague Expressionists. Aktion; Expr.-Katalog.

BAUM, PETER (1869–1916). Berlin poet and writer, friend of Else Lasker-Schüler's. Contributor to the *Sturm*. Aktion.

BAUMEISTER, WILLI (1889–1955). Painter and graphic artist. Representative of abstract art. Vollmer.

BAUMGARDT, DAVID (1890–1963). Philosopher and philosophical journalist.

375

In his youth belonged to the Berlin circle of Neopathetiker. Gel.-Kürschner '61.

BECHER, JOHANNES R. (1891–1958). Expressionist, later socialist, poet and writer. Voluminous early writings. Later theoretical essays very significant for an understanding of Expressionism. Wilpert; Aktion; Pinthus; Expr.-Katalog.

BEHL, C. F. W. (1889–1968). Lawyer, writer and theatre-critic. Friend of Gerhart Hauptmann. Lit.-Kürschner '63.

BENJAMIN, WALTER (1892–1940). Essayist, literary critic and art historian. Author of very important prose. Aktion; [not NDB, Wilpert!].

BENN, GOTTFRIED (1886–1956). Important lyric poet, writer of narrative prose and essays. Expressionist beginnings. Wilpert; Pinthus; Aktion.

BENNDORF, FRIEDRICH KURT (1871–1945). Dresden writer and journalist. Friend and interpreter of Albert Mombert. Kosch.

BERGNER, ELISABETH (b. 1897). Actress. Express. beginning to her great career. Lives in New York when not travelling. Th.-Kürschner.

BERGSON, HENRI (1859–1941). French philosopher, also important for the theory of Expressionism. Brockhaus.

BERTENS, ROSA. Actress.

BILLINGER, RICHARD (1889–1965). Austrian regional poet. Lived in Starnberg. Wilpert; Lit.-Kürschner '63; Giebisch-Gugitz.

BING, ELLEN. Wife of the following.

BING, HENRI (b. 1888). French painter and graphic artist. Before the First World War he moved in bohemian circles, in Munich. Vollmer.

BLASS, ERNST (1890–1939). Berlin poet and writer, friend of Kurt Hiller, editor of the journal Die Argonauten (1914–1921). Wilpert; Aktion; Expr.-Katalog.

BLEI, FRANZ (1871–1942). Versatile writer, critic and essayist, very influential in the literary life of the turn of the century and of Expressionism. Founder of literary journals. Intermediary for French literature. NDB; Wilpert; Aktion.

BLEIBTREU, KARL (1859–1928). Naturalist dramatist, story-writer and theoretician. NDB; Wilpert.

BLOCH, ALBERT (1882–1961). American painter and designer. Vollmer.

BLOCH, ERNST (b. 1885). Philosopher and writer. Now living in Tübingen. Gel.-Kürschner '61.

BLÜMNER, RUDOLF (1873–1945). Friend and assistant of Herwarth Walden. Organized countless Sturm lecture-evenings all over Germany. Expr.-Katalog.

BOCCIONI, UMBERTO (1882–1916). Italian painter and sculptor. Leading representative and propagator of Futurism. Vollmer.

BODMAN, EMANUEL, Baron von (1874–1946). Neo-Romantic poet. NDB; Wilpert.

BOLDT, PAUL (1886–1919). Early Expressionist poet in Berlin. Aktion; Expr.-Katalog.

BOLZ, HANS (1887–1918). Painter and wood-carver. Encouraged by Herwarth Walden. Vollmer.

BONSELS, WALDEMAR (1880–1952). Poet and writer, for some time, also publisher. Friendly with the Munich poets. NDB, Wilpert.

BORCHARDT, RUDOLF (1877–1945). Poet and writer, author of exceptional essays and speeches. Friend of Hofmannsthal and of R. A. Schröder. NDB, Wilpert.

BOVET, ERNST (1870–1941). Professor at the University of Zurich 1901–21. For years editor of the Swiss monthly *Wissen und Leben* (forerunner of the *Neue Schweizer Rundschau*).

BRAND, KARL (1894?–1917). Prague poet, friend of Johannes Urzidil, but for whom he would have been forgotten. Aktion.

BRAQUE, GEORGES (1882–1963). French painter and graphic artist. Vollmer.

BRAUN, FELIX (b. 1885). Conservative Austrian writer and poet. Wilpert; Lit.-Kürschner '63; Giebisch.-Gugitz.

BRECHT, BERTOLT (1898–1956). Dramatist and poet. Creator of "epic theatre". Wilpert.

BREINLINGER, HANS (1888–1961). Painter and graphic artist. Lived in Constance. Vollmer.

BRITTING, GEORG (1891–1964). Poet and story-teller. Significant Expressionist Novellas. Co-editor of the literary journal *Die Sichel* (1919–21). Wilpert; Lit.-Kürschner '63.

BROD, MAX (1884–1968). Prague writer and poet. Voluminous writings. Friend and patron of Kafka, Werfel and other Prague writers. Lived in Tel-Aviv. Wilpert; Lit.-Kürschner '63; Aktion; Expr.-Katalog.

BRONNEN, ARNOLT (1895–1959). Writer and poet. First dramatic successes towards the decline of Expressionism. Friendship with Brecht. Wilpert.

BRUANT, ARISTIDE (1851–1925). French poet and cabaret artiste. Author of songs and satirical pieces. Wilpert.

BUBER, MARTIN (1878–1965). Jewish writer and philosopher. Works on the politics and philosophy of society. Lived in Jerusalem. Wilpert; Gel.-Kürschner '61; Lit.-Kürschner '63.

BUCHET, GUSTAVE (b. 1888). Swiss painter and wood-carver. Lives in Geneva. Vollmer.

BUEK, OTTO (b. 1873). Philosophical writer and translator. Friend of Franz Pfemfert. Lived in Paris. Aktion.

BURSCHELL, FRIEDRICH (1889–1970). Writer and translator, Editor of Expressionist journals. Lived in Munich. Lit.-Kürschner '63.

BUSCH, FRITZ (1890–1951). Conductor. 1918–1922 conductor of the Stuttgart Opera. 1922–33 the Dresden Opera. Brockhaus.

BUSCHBECK, ERHARD (1889–1960). Austrian novelist and critic. Friend of Georg Trakl and Theodor Däubler. Dramaturg of the Burgtheater in Vienna after 1918. Giebisch-Gugitz.

BUSONI, FERRUCCIO (1866–1924). Piano virtuoso and composer. Creator of Expressionist music. Lived in Berlin from 1894 on.

CAHÉN, FRITZ MAX (1891-1966). Political journalist. Belonged in his youth to the A. R. Meyer circle. Lived in Bonn. Aktion.

CAMPENDONK, HEINRICH (1889–1957). Modern painter and wood-carver. Associated with the Sturm-circle. Vollmer.

ČAPEK, JOSEF (1887–1945). Czech painter and writer. Brother of Karel Čapek. Wilpert; Vollmer.

CAROSSA, HANS (1878–1956). Novelist and poet. No connections with Expressionism. Wilpert.

CARSTENS, LINA (b. 1892). Actress. 1915–1926 at the Leipzig Schauspielhaus. Countless film parts. Lives in Munich. Kürschner.

CASSIRER, PAUL (1871–1926). Art dealer and publisher, art-patron and collector. In the Cassirer Art Gallery many modern art shows and countless readings and performances were held. NDB.

CHAGALL, MARC (b. 1889). One of the great painters of the 20th century. Lives in Vence. Vollmer.

CLAUDEL, PAUL (1868–1955). French poet. Representative of the "renouveau catholique". Wilpert.

CONRAD, MICHAEL GEORG (1846–1927). Naturalist novelist and critic. 1885–1901 editor of the journal *Die Gesellschaft*. NDB; Wilpert.

CONRADI, HERMANN (1862–1890). Brief career as naturalist poet. Author of the novel *Adam Mensch* (1889). Wilpert.

DÄUBLER, THEODOR (1876–1934). Representative poet of Expressionism. Author of the *Nordlicht*. Propagator of modern art. NDB; Wilpert; Pinthus; Expr.-Katalog.

DAUTHENDEY, MAX (1867–1918). Impressionist poet of the turn of the century. Published poems, dramas, stories, travel-books and also his autobiography. Wilpert.

DAVRINGHAUSEN, HEINRICH (b. 1894). Rhineland painter and graphic artist. Began as collaborator on the *Neue Jugend*. Lives in Cagnes-sur-Mer. Vollmer.

DEHMEL, RICHARD (1863–1920). Writer of the turn of the century, especially lyrical poetry. Many public readings. Understanding patron of the young talents among the new generation of poets. NDB; Wilpert; Aktion.

DELAUNAY, ROBERT (1885–1941). French painter. His "Eiffel Tower" was a picture much admired in the "Blue Rider" and *Sturm* circles. Vollmer.

DESSOIR, MAX (1867–1947). Philosopher, psychologist and aesthetician. NDB.

DEUTSCH, ERNST (1890–1969). Actor, born in Prague. Friendly with Hasenclever and Werfel. Lived in Berlin. Th.-Kürschner.

DIETERLE, WILHELM (1893–1972). Actor, since 1921 mainly in films. Since 1926 film director in U.S.A. Lived in Hollywood. Th.-Kürschner.

DIETRICH, RUDOLF ADRIAN (1894–1969). Poet of Late Expressionism, nicknamed Gothic Dietrich. Lived in Hamburg. Lit.-Kürschner; Aktion.

DILTHEY, WILHELM (1833–1911). Philosopher. NDB.

DIX, OTTO (1891–1969). Painter and graphic artist. Leading representative of "New Objectivity" in the 20's. Vollmer.

DÖBLIN, ALFRED (1878–1957). Writer and poet. Some Expressionist prose works, though he became critical of Expressionism. His famous novel *Berlin Alexanderplatz* came out in 1929. Wilpert; Expr.-Katalog.

DOHRN, WOLF (1878–1913). Son of Anton Dohrn the Zoologist. Dr. Phil., friend of Theodor Heuss, follower of Friedrich Naumann. Co-founder of the Deutsche Werkstätten in Hellerau.

EBERZ, JOSEF (1880–1942). Painter and graphic artist. Member of the November Group. Collaborator in countless Expressionist journals. Associated with the Darmstadt circle. Vollmer.

EDSCHMID, KASIMIR (1890–1967). Writer and poet. Spokesman for Expressionism (prose and theoretical writings). Countless books. Lived in Darmstadt. Wilpert; Lit.-Kürschner; Aktion; Expr.-Katalog.

EGGELING, VIKING (1886–1925). Swedish painter. In Switzerland during First World War. Creator of the abstract film. Vollmer.

EHRENBAUM-DEGELE, HANS (1889–1914). Lyrical poet of Early Expressionism in Berlin. Friendly with Paul Zech and Else Lasker-Schüler.

EHRENFELS, CHRISTIAN Baron von (1859–1932). Professor of Philosophy in Prague. Dramatist. NDB.; Giebisch-Gugitz.

EHRENSTEIN, ALBERT (1886–1950). Expressionist poet and prose-writer. Author of the famous *Tubutsch*. NDB.; Wilpert; Pinthus; Giebisch-Gugitz; Expr.-Katalog.

EHRLER, HANS HEINRICH (1872–1951). Suabian writer and poet. NDB.; Wilpert.

EINSTEIN, ALBERT (1879–1955). Physicist and philosopher. Founder of the theory of relativity. NDB.

EINSTEIN, CARL (1885–1940). Writer of narrative prose and art criticism. Powerful influence on the Expressionist generation. Author of the prose book *Bebuquin*. Aktion; [Not in NDB; Wilpert!]; Expr.-Katalog.

EISNER, KURT (1867–1919). Writer and Socialist politician. 1918–19 President of Bavarian Republic. NDB.

ENGEL, ERICH (b. 1891). Actor, theatre producer (1918–21 with the Kammerspiele in Hamburg). Film producer. Lives in Berlin. Th.-Kürschner.

ENGERT, ERNST MORITZ (b. 1892). Silhouette and graphic artist. Moved in Bohemian circles in Schwabing. Lives in Hadamar. Vollmer.

ENSOR, JAMES (1860–1949). Significant Belgian painter and graphic artist. Also composer and writer. Vollmer.

ERNST, MAX (b. 1891). Surrealist painter and graphic artist. Took part in Cologne Dada.

ERNST, OTTO (1862–1926). Petit bourgeois writer of the turn of the century. Often ridiculed by the Expressionist generation. Wilpert.

ESSIG, HERMANN (1878–1918). Dramatist. Friend of Herwarth Walden and the *Sturm*, about which he wrote a *roman à clé*: *Der Taifun*. NDB.; Wilpert; Expr.-Katalog.

ETZEL, THEODOR (1873–1930). Prose writer, journalist and editor of popular literary journals. Kosch.

EULENBERG, HERBERT (1876–1949). Neo-Romantic writer and poet. Round 1910 the Rowohlt-Verlag standard author. Wilpert.

EVOLA, JULES. Italian Dadaist. Co-editor of the journal *Bleu* in Mantua.

EYSOLDT, GERTRUD (1870–1957). For years a famous actress at the Deutsches Theater in Berlin. Many public poetry readings. NDB.

FALCKENBERG, OTTO (1873–1947). Important theatre producer at the Munich Kammerspiele. NDB.

FEHLING, JÜRGEN (1885–1968). Actor and producer. Many years in Berlin. Significant productions. Th.-Kürschner.

FEININGER, LYONEL (1871–1956). Painter and graphic artist. One of the leading exponents of modern painting. 1908–1919 in Berlin, then active with the Bauhaus. Vollmer.

FELIXMÜLLER, CONRAD (b. 1897). Expressionist, later Realist painter and graphic artist in Dresden. Now lives in Berlin. Vollmer.

FICKER, LUDWIG VON (1880–1967). For years editor of the Innsbruck literary journal *Der Brenner* (1910–54). Friend of Georg Trakl, Karl Kraus, Theodor Däubler. Lived in Innsbruck. Giebisch-Gugitz; Expr.-Katalog.

FISCHER, SAMUEL (1839–1934). Founder and Director of the S. Fischer Verlag in Berlin. Thereby played a leading part in the literature of the turn of the century.

FLAKE, OTTO (1880–1963). Novelist and essayist. Friendly in his youth in Alsace with René Schickele and Ernst Stadler. Marginally involved in Expressionism. Important work in later life. Wilpert; Lit.-Kürschner.

FLESCH-BRUNNINGEN, HANS (1895–1969). Prose writer and radio commentator. Lived in Vienna. Giebisch-Gugitz; Aktion.

FONTANA, OSKAR MAURUS (1889–1969). Austrian writer and theatre-critic. Lived in Vienna. Wilpert; Lit.-Kürschner; Giebisch-Gugitz.

FÖRSTE, JOHN [OR JOMAR]. Dates of birth etc. not ascertainable. Contributor to the *Aktion* during the war. Aktion.

FORSTER, RUDOLF (1889–1968). Austrian actor, lived in Berlin 1920–1932. Th.-Kürschner.

FORT, PAUL (1872–1960). French poet. Wilpert.

FRANK, LEONHARD (1882–1961). Writer and poet, originally painter. During Expressionist period a writer of pacifist narrative prose (*Der Mensch ist gut*. 1918 etc.) which had considerable influence. Wilpart; Lit.-Kürschner '63; Expr.-Katalog.

FREUD, SIGMUND (1856–1939). Doctor, founder of psycho-analysis. NDB.

FRIEDLAENDER, SALOMO (1871–1946). Philosophical exponent of a philosophy of polarity. Used the *nom de plume* Mynona (=anonym[ous] backwards) to publish "grotesque" stories. Aktion; Expr.-Katalog.

FRITSCH, ERNST (b. 1892). Berlin painter. Began as Expressionist. Vollmer.

FUCHS, RUDOLF (1890–1942). Prague poet, translator and journalist. Belonged to the circle of modern Prague writers. Giebisch-Gugitz.

GEIGER, WILLI (1878–1970). Painter and etcher in Munich. Friendly with many writers of the time. Voluminous work as an illustrator. Vollmer.

GEORGE, STEFAN (1868–1933). Poet and leader of the George Circle. NDB.; Wilpert.

GERT, VALESKA (b. 1900). Dancer and Cabaret artiste, famous particularly in the 20's. Lives in Berlin. Th.-Kürschner.

GEYER, EMIL. Actor in Vienna.

GIACOMETTI, AUGUSTO (1877–1947). Swiss painter. Vollmer.

GIDE, ANDRÉ (1869–1951). French writer and poet. Wilpert.

GIELEN, JOSEPH (1890–1968). Actor and theatre-producer. Active 1924–34 at the State Theatre in Dresden. From 1948 Director of the Burgtheater in Vienna. Th.-Kürschner.

GILLES, WERNER (1894–1961). German painter and graphic artist. Vollmer.

GLAU, LUISE. Actress. Now living in Kassel.

GOERING, REINHARD (1887–1936). Expressionist poet and dramatist. NDB.; Wilpert.

GÖSCH, DOCTOR. Munich Bohemian.

GÖTZKE, BERNHARD (b. 1884). Actor and theatre-director, countless film parts.

GOLDSCHMIED, LEONOR. Naturalist writer.

GOLL, IVAN (1891–1950). Expressionist writer from Lorraine. Co-founder of surrealism in Paris. Wrote in German and French. NDB.; Wilpert; Pinthus; Aktion; Expr.-Katalog.

GOTHEIN, EBERHARD (1853–1923). Leading social historian and economist in Heidelberg. NDB.

GRAF, OSKAR MARIA (1894–1967). Prose-writer, author of numerous novels, stories and essays. Lived in New York. Lit.-Kürschner.

GRAMATTÉ, WALTER (1897–1929). Painter, graphic artist and book illustrator. Vollmer.

GRANACH, ALEXANDER (1890–1945). Actor, with Max Reinhardt at the Deutsches Theater for many years.

GROHMANN, WILL (1887–1972). Art historian and art critic. Propagandist for modern art. Numerous monographs on modern painters. 1926–33 Director of the State Art Gallery in Dresden. Lived in Berlin. Gel.-Kürschner '61.

GROPIUS, WALTER (1883–1969). Architect. 1918 founder and director of the Bauhaus in Weimar, later in Dessau. Numerous modern buildings in Germany, England and America. Lived in U.S.A. Brockhaus.

GROSS, OTTO (1877–1919). Psychoanalyst, disciple of Freud. Lived in Ascona and Munich. Associated with Franz Jung, Oskar Maria Graf, Johannes R. Becher and others. Aktion.

GROSZ, GEORGE (1893–1959). Paintings and drawings. Countless collections of socially critical pictures and drawings. Vollmer.

GÜTERSLOH, ALBERT PARIS (1887–1973). Austrian painter, professor at the Academy of Liberal Arts in Vienna. Also lyric poet, short-story writer and essayist. Aktion; Lit.-Kürschner; Giebisch-Gugitz.

GUILBEAUX, HENRI (1884–1938). French political writer. Edited *Anthologie des lyriques allemands contemporains depuis Nietzsche*.

GUMBEL, EMIL, J. (1891–1966). Mathematician and statistician. Lived as scientist in New York. Gel.-Kürschner.

GUMPERT, MARTIN (1897–1955). Expressionist poet, doctor and later author of biographical novels. Wilpert; Expr.-Katalog.

GUNDOLF, FRIEDRICH (1880–1931). Literary historian in Heidelberg, disciple of Stefan George. Author of famous monographs on German writers. Kosch.

GUNSCHMANN, CARL (b. 1895). Painter and wood-carver. Lives in Darmstadt. Vollmer.

GURLITT, FRITZ. Berlin art business. Owner was Wolfgang G. (b. 1888). Now lives in Munich.

GUTTMANN [GHUTTMANN], SIMON (b. 1890). Friend of Georg Heym. Journalist. Lives in London. Aktion.

HAAS, WILLY (b. 1891). Writer, theatre-critic and reviewer. 1912–13 co-editor of the *Herder-Blätter* in Prague, in the 20's editor of the *Literarische Welt*. Lit.-Kürschner.

HACK. Second-hand book dealer in Zurich.

HADWIGER, ELSE (1877–?). Writer and translator (of Marinetti) wife of the following.

HADWIGER, VICTOR (1878–1911). Fore-runner of Expressionism. Came to Berlin from Prague. Died young. Wilpert; Aktion.

HALBE, MAX (1865–1944). Naturalistic dramatist, later author of realistic narratives. Wilpert.

HARBECK, HANS (1887–1968). Writer and critic in Hamburg. Worked on various Expressionist journals. Lit.-Kürschner '63.

HARDEKOPF, FERDINAND (1876–1954). Writer in the *Aktion*-Circle. Slim literary *oeuvre* inspired by *Art Nouveau*. Important translator. Wilpert; Aktion; Expr.-Katalog.

HARDEN, MAXIMILLIAN (1861–1927). Publicist, social critic. Editor of *Zukunft* (1892–1922). Wilpert.

HARDT, LUDWIG (1896–1947). Reciter in Berlin. Lived in New York. Remembered for his *Vortragsbuch [Selected Readings]* 1924.

HARINGER, JAKOB (1883–1948). Expressionist writer. Tramp and poet. Wilpert; Expr.-Katalog.

HARTA, FELIX ALBRECHT (1884–1967). Painter and graphic artist. Professor in Vienna. Vollmer.

HARTUNG, GUSTAV (1887–1946). Important theatre-producer. Active 1914–

1920 at the Frankfurt Schauspielhaus, 1920–1924. General Director of the State Theatre in Darmstadt. Ultimately Director of the Kammerspiele in Heidelberg.

HASENCLEVER, WALTER (1890–1940). Expressionist writer and poet. His best known early drama *The Son* appeared in 1914. Friend of Werfel and Pinthus. Wilpert; Aktion; Expr.-Kalalog.

HATZFELD, ADOLF von (1892–1957). Poet and short story-writer, with Expressionist beginnings. Wilpert; Expr.-Katalog.

HAUBACH, THEODOR (1896–1945). Socialist politician. Friend of Carlo Mierendorff in Darmstadt. Chosen by Goerdeler to be his Minister of Information. Executed by the Nazis. Osterroth.

HAUBRICH, JOSEPH (1889–1963). Lawyer and art collector in Cologne. Leading patron of the arts: in 1946 he gave his vast collection of modern art to the Wallraf-Richartz-Museum.

HAUPTMANN, CARL (1858–1921). Dramatist, story-teller and lyric poet. Gerhart Hauptmann's brother. Literary works in the tradition of the Silesian mystics. Wilpert.

HAUPTMANN, GERHART (1862–1946). One of the greatest German writers of the twentieth century. Wilpert.

HAUSMANN, RAOUL (1886–1971). Painter, writer. Co-founder and head of the Berlin Dada Group. Lived in Limoges. Lit.-Kürschner '63.

HEARTFIELD, JOHN (1891–1968). Real name Helmut Herzfeld. Painter and graphic artist. Creator and master of photomontage. Brother of Wieland Herzfelde. Vollmer.

HECKEL, ERICH (1883–1970). Painter and graphic artist. Co-founder of the *Brücke* in Dresden. Lived in Hemmenhofen on Lake Constance. Vollmer.

HEEMSKERK, JACOBA van (1876–1923). Dutch painter and graphic artist. Active in the *Sturm* Circle. Vollmer.

HEGNER, JACOB (1882–1962). Publisher and writer. In 1912 established the Hellerau Publishing House and the Hellerau Printing Works. Brilliant typographer. Translated and published the modern French Catholic authors. After the last war established new publishing concerns in Olten and Cologne. Lit.-Kürschner '63.

HEIMANN, MORITZ (1868–1925). For years publisher's reader with S. Fischer in Berlin. Dramatist and Essayist. Wilpert.

HELD, FRANZ (1862–1908). Father of Wieland Herzfelde and John Heartfield. Author of socially critical novels, stories and dramas. Aktion.

HENNINGS, EMMY (1885–1948). *Soubrette* and Cabaret artiste before the First World War, especially in Munich. Friendly with many modern poets. Married to Hugo Ball, lived in Switzerland. Poetry and memoirs. Aktion; Expr.-Katalog.

HENSCHKE, ALFRED. *See* Klabund.

HENSELER, FRANZ (1885–1918). Rhineland Expressionist painter and graphic artist.

HERRMANN-NEISSE, MAX (1886–1941). Expressionist poet. Lived as writer and critic in Berlin. Wilpert; Aktion; Expr.-Katalog.

HERZFELDE, WIELAND (b. 1896). Writer and publisher. Founder and director of the Malik-Verlag. Aktion.

HERZOG, RUDOLF (1869–1943). Popular writer of the turn of the century. Wilpert.

HERZOG, WILHELM (1884–1960). Writer and editor of journals (*Pan; Forum*). Author of numerous successful dramas of the 20's. Settled in Munich. Aktion.

HESSE, HERMANN (1877–1962). Started off as a writer in Neo-Romanticism Vast literary *oeuvre*. Wilpert.

HETTNER, OTTO (1875–1931). Dresden painter and graphic artist, son of the literary historian Hermann Hettner. From 1919 on professor at the Art Academy in Dresden. Brockhaus.

HEUBERGER, JULIUS. Printer in Zurich. Publisher of Dada publications.

HEYM, GEORG (1887–1912). Poet of Early Expressionism in Berlin. Wilpert; Pinthus; Aktion; Expr.-Katalog.

HEYMEL, ALFRED WALTER (1878–1914). Munich poet and patron of modern literature and fine book production. Co-founder of the *Insel*. Friend of Hofmannsthal. Wilpert.

HEYNICKE, KURT (b. 1891). Poet of the *Sturm* Circle. Later author of novels, radio plays, film scenarios. Lives in Merzhausen near Freiburg. Wilpert; Pinthus; Expr.-Katalog.

HILLE, PETER (1854–1904). Poet and tramp at the turn of the century. Worshipped by Else Lasker-Schüler. Wilpert.

HILLER, KURT (1885–1973). Writer and publicist. In younger years an important *homme de lettres*, later activist and political writer. Aktion; Expr.-Katalog.

HIRSCH, KARL JAKOB (1892–1952). Expressionist painter and graphic artist. Co-founder of the November Group in Berlin. Ultimately free-lance writer. Vollmer.

HODDIS, JACOB VAN (1887–1942). Poet of Early Expressionism of considerable influence. Insane from 1914 on. Wilpert; Pinthus; Aktion; Expr.-Katalog.

HÖCH, HANNAH (b. 1889). Painter in Berlin. Member of the November Group. Lives in Berlin. Vollmer.

HOERSCHELMANN, ROLF VON (1885–1947). Swabian painter, writer, collector. Friend of Alfred Kubin. Vollmer.

HOETGER, BERNHARD (1874–1949). Expressionist sculptor, also architect and painter. Lived 1911–1919 in Darmstadt. Till 1933 in Worpswede. Vollmer.

HÖXTER, JOHN (d. 1938). Designer and graphic artist. Unforgettable character in Berlin Bohemian circles. Aktion; Vollmer.

HOFER, JOHANNA. Actress at the Munich Kammerspiele. Th.-Kürschner.

HOFER, KARL (1878–1955). Modern painter and graphic artist. 1919–1933 Professor at the Berlin Art Academy. Vollmer.

HOFFMANN, CAMILL (1878–1944). Writer, Cultural Attaché to the Czechoslovakian Embassy in Berlin. Published several volumes of poetry, wrote countless reviews. Also translator and editor. Giebisch-Gugitz.

HOFMANN, LUDWIG von (1861–1945). Painter and graphic artist. Exponent of *art nouveau*. Taught 1903–08 in Weimar, 1916–1928 in Dresden. Vollmer.

HOFMANNSTHAL, HUGO von (1874–1929). Austrian poet. One of the greatest figures in German Twentieth century literature. Wilpert.

HOFMILLER, JOSEF (1872–1933). Essay writer and critic. Translator. For many years editor of *Süddeutsche Monatshefte*. Wilpert.

HOLITSCHER, ARTHUR (1869–1941). Story-teller and travel writer. Lived a very nomadic existence. Wilpert; Aktion.

HOLLAENDER, FELIX (1867–1931). Naturalist novelist (*Der Weg des Thomas Truck*. 1902), from 1908 on dramaturg at the Deutsches Theater in Berlin, assistant to Max Reinhardt. From 1920 director of the Grosses Schauspielhaus. Wilpert.

HOLZ, ARNO (1863–1929). Writer and theoretician of a radical form of Naturalism. Wilpert.

HOY, SENNA (1884?–1914). Anarchist writer at the turn of the century. 1904–05 editor of the literary-political journal called *Kampf*. Friend of Else Lasker-Schüler. Aktion.

HUBERMANN, ANGELA. Writer in Zurich. Aktion.

HUELSENBECK, RICHARD (b. 1892). Psychiatrist and writer. Co-founder of Dadaism in Zurich and Berlin. Travel-books in the Twenties. Author of various books about Dada. Wilpert; Lit.-Kürschner; Aktion; Expr.-Katalog.

JACOB, HEINRICH EDUARD (1889–1967). Poet, writer, author of important reference works and biographies of musicians. Associated with Early Expressionism in Berlin. Wilpert; Lit.-Kürschner; Aktion.

JACQUES, NORBERT (1880–1954). Best-seller writer. Author of novels, stories, travel-books. Kosch.

JAHNN, HANS HENNY (1894–1959). Poet and organ-builder. Lived in Hamburg. Important author with Expressionist connections. Wilpert; Expr.-Katalog.

JAMMES, FRANCIS (1868–1939). French writer much admired by the Expressionists. Wilpert.

JANCO, MARCEL (b. 1895). Painter and architect. Co-founder of Zurich Dada. Now living in Tel-Aviv. Vollmer.

JANNINGS, EMIL (1884–1950). Important actor. Began his great career in Berlin 1910, from 1925–34 mainly active in films. Brockhaus.

JANOWITZ, FRANZ (1892–1917). Poet from Bohemia, killed in the war. First discovered by Max Brod. Poetry: *Auf der Erde*. 1919. Giebisch-Gugitz.

JANOWITZ, HANS (1890–1954). Writer and film producer. Giebisch-Gugitz.

JAURÈS, JEAN (1859-1914). French socialist and writer. Pacifist assassinated on the day before the outbreak of hostilities.

JAWLENSKY, ALEXEJ VON (1864-1941). Modern painter originally from Russia. From 1896 in Munich. Close to the Blue Rider group of artists. Ultimately lived in Wiesbaden. Vollmer.

ICHAK, FRIDA (1879-1952). Wife of Ludwig Rubiner. Translator, Communist journalist and editor, founder-member of the German Communist Party. Lived from 1930-45 in the Soviet Union.

JENTZSCH, ROBERT (1890-1918). Mathematician and writer. Belonged to Georg Heym's circle of friends. Aktion.

JOUVE, PIERRE JEAN (b. 1887). French writer and critic. Wrote pacifist poetry during the First World War. Wilpert.

JOYCE, JAMES (1882-1941). Leading Irish writer. Author of *Ulysses*.

JUNCKER, AXEL. Book-seller, originally from Denmark. From 1902 on published numerous pre-expressionistic works.

JUNG, FRANZ (1888-1963). Writer and business journalist. In his early years an influential prose-writer. Aktion; Wilpert; Expr.-Katalog.

KÄSTNER, ERICH (b. 1899). Poet and story-teller. One of the most outstanding literary figures of the 20's. Wilpert; Lit.-Kürschner '63.

KAFKA, FRANZ (1883-1924). Prague writer. Significant exponent of narrative prose with world-wide influence. Wilpert.

KAHN, JAKOB (1899-1923). Darmstadt painter, died young. Vollmer.

KAISER, GEORG (1878-1945). One of the great German Expressionist dramatists. Wilpert.

KALÉKO, MASCHA (b. 1912). Poet and writer of radio-plays. Lives in Jerusalem. Lit.-Kürschner '63.

KALENTER, OSSIP (b. 1900). As poet, story-teller and essay-writer a master of the shorter form. Translator. Lives in Zurich. Wilpert; Lit.-Kürschner.

KALSER, ERWIN (b. 1889). Actor and theatre-producer. From 1910 in Munich, from 1923 on in Berlin, active again there on his return from exile. Th.-Kürschner.

KALTNEKER, HANS (1895-1919). Expressionist dramatist and story-teller. Wilpert.

KANDINSKY, WASSILIJ (1866-1944). Painter. Founder and master of abstract art. Belonged to the Blue Rider circle. 1922-33 teacher at the Bauhaus. Also wrote verse and plays. Vollmer.

KANEHL, OSKAR (1888-1929). Expressionist, later Communist poet. 1913-14 editor of the literary journal *Wiecker Bote*. Ultimately dramatist and producer. Aktion.

KASACK, HERMANN (1896-1966). Late Expressionist poet, later novelist. Publisher's reader, after World War II President of the German Academy for Language and Literature. Lived in Stuttgart. Wilpert; Lit.-Kürschner; Expr.-Katalog.

KAYSER, RUDOLF (1889-1964). Critic, biographer, editor. In his youth moved in Berlin Expressionist circles. For many years chief editor of the *Neue Rundschau*. Aktion.

KAYSSLER, FRIEDRICH (1874–1945). Actor for many years at the Deutsches Theater in Berlin. Author of Impressionistic dramas. Wilpert.

KEIL, HERMANN (b. 1889). Book illustrator and graphic artist from the "Dachstube" circle in Darmstadt. Later architect.

KELLER, JULIUS TALBOT (?–1946). Rhineland writer. Associate of Karl Otten, contributor to the *Aktion* and the *Weisse Blätter*.

KELLER, PHILIPP (b. 1891). Compatriot and friend of Walter Hasenclever and Karl Otten. Author of a novel: *Gemischte Gefühle (Mixed Feelings)* 1913. Professor of Medicine living in Aachen.

KERR, ALFRED (1867–1948). Berlin theatre-critic. 1911–14 editor of the literary-political journal *Pan*. Wilpert; Aktion.

KERSTEN, HUGO (1892–1919). Berlin *homme de lettres*. Contributor to *Aktion*. During the war co-editor of the short-lived journal *Mistral*. Aktion.

KIRCHNER, ERNST LUDWIG (1880–1938). Modern painter and graphic artist. Co-founder of the Dresden "Brücke". In Berlin also associated with writers. Vollmer.

KISCH, EGON ERWIN (1885–1948). Prague writer. Wrote famous reportages and travel-books. Wilpert.

KLABUND (1890–1928). Real name Alfred Henschke. Poet, story-teller, dramatist. Most influential Expressionist work his volume of verse: *Morgenrot! Klabund! Die Tage dämmern!* (1913). Wilpert; Expr.-Katalog.

KLAGES, LUDWIG (1872–1956). Philosopher, graphologist and social-critic. At first associated with the George Circle. Brockhaus.

KLEE, PAUL (1879–1940). One of the great German painters of the 20th century. Taught 1922–33 at the Bauhaus. Vollmer.

KLIMT, GUSTAV (1862–1918). Austrian painter, professor at the Art Academy in Vienna. Leading exponent of *art nouveau* in Austria. Thieme-Becker.

KNOBLAUCH, ADOLF (1882–1951). Writer and director of a publishing concern. At first associated with the "Neue Gemeinschaft" Circle, 1914–18 he belonged to the *Sturm*-Circle. Expr.-Katalog.

KOBUS, KATHI. (1856–1929). Well-known owner of the "Simplicissimus" cabaret in Munich. Schwabing.

KÖNIG, LEO von (1871–1944). Painter, exponent of Impressionism. Portrait painter. Vollmer.

KÖPPEN, EDLEF (1893–1939). Writer and publisher's reader. Friend of Hermann Kasack. Contributor to Wolf Przygode's *Dichtung*.

KÖSTER, ALBERT (1862–1924). Professor of German Literary History in Leipzig. Research in 18th century literature.

KOKOSCHKA, OSKAR (b. 1886). Austrian painter, graphic artist and poet of great influence. Wilpert; Vollmer.

KOLLWITZ, KÄTHE (1867–1945). Painter and sculptor. Vollmer.

KORNFELD, PAUL (1889–1942). Expressionist dramatist and story-teller. Wilpert; Expr.-Katalog.

KRAPOTKIN, PETER (1842–1921). Russian revolutionary. Exponent of Communist anarchism. Aktion; Brockhaus.

KRAUS, KARL (1874–1936). Journalist, writer and poet. Editor of *Die Fackel* (1899–1936) most of which he wrote himself. Feared satirist and polemicist. Wilpert.

KRAUSS, KRISTIAN (b. 1880). Writer. Lived in Bad Neuenahr. Lit.-Kürschner. '63.

KRAUSS, WERNER (1884–1959). One of the great actors of the twentieth century. For many years at the Deutsches Theater in Berlin. Th.-Kürschner.

KRELL, MAX (1887–1962). Story-teller and translator. At first associated with Expressionism. Lived for many years in Florence. Wilpert; Lit.-Kürschner '63.

KRONACHER, ALWIN (1883–1951). Theatre-producer and writer. Important theatre productions in Leipzig. Emigrated to America after 1933.

KRONBERG, SIMON (1891–1947). Youth leader and choir conductor in the Young Jewish Ramblers. Author of numerous plays most of which are forgotten. Expr.-Katalog.

KRONFELD, ARTHUR (1886–1942). Psychiatrist. Wrote numerous scientific works and features. Friend of Ernst Blass. Aktion.

KUBIN, ALFRED (1877–1959). Austrian artist and writer. Considerable amount of book-illustrations etc. Vollmer.

KÜLPE, FRANCES (1862–1946). Novelist, born in Russia, lived in Munich. Kosch.

KUHLEMANN, JOHANNES THEODOR. Rhineland writer.

KULKA, GEORG (1897–1929). Late Expressionist Austrian writer. Active in the Kiepenheuer Verlag. Expr.-Katalog.

KURTZ, RUDOLF (1884–1960). Writer, film-director for many years. Ultimately editor-in-chief in Berlin. Aktion.

KUTSCHER, ARTUR (1878–1960). Lecturer and professor of theatre history in Munich. Promoter of new talent (Kutscher Prize). Aktion.

LABAN, RUDOLF (1879–1958). Dancer and dance teacher. Founder of the art of modern dancing. Brockhaus.

LAFORGUE, JULES (1860–1887). French Symbolist poet. Wilpert.

LANDAUER, GUSTAV (1870–1919). Socialist writer, social critic and translator. Important influence on political Expressionism. Wilpert.

LANDSBERGER, ARTUR (1876–1933). Writer. Wrote novels about the Berlin *demi-monde* mainly. Wilpert.

LANGER, RESI. Berlin *diseuse*. Wife of A. R. Meyer.

LASK, EMIL (1875–1915). Professor of Philosophy in Heidelberg. Logician. Brockhaus.

LASKER-SCHÜLER, ELSE (1869–1945). Famous poetess of Expressionism.

Wrote poetry, prose, dramas. Worshipped by the younger generation. Wilpert; Expr.-Katalog.

LASSON, GEORG (1862–1932). Theologian and philosophical historian. Great editor of Hegel's works.

LATZKO, ANDREAS (1876–1943). Austrian writer and poet, mainly stories. Connections with Expressionism. Giebisch-Gugitz.

LAUTENSACK, HEINRICH (1881–1919). Munich dramatist and poet. Friend of Frank Wedekind and Franz Blei. Wilpert; Aktion.

LAUTRÉAMONT, COMTE DE (1847–1870). French writer. Fore-runner of modernism. Wilpert.

LEER, SOPHIE van. Expressionist painter and poet. Friendly with Herwarth and Nell Walden. 1915–18 secretary to the *Sturm*.

LÉGER, FERNAND (1881–1955). French painter. Leading exponent of Cubism. Vollmer.

LEHMBRUCK, WILHELM (1881–1919). The most important Expressionist sculptor. 1910–14 in Paris, after 1914 in Zurich and Berlin. Vollmer.

LEIP, HANS (b. 1893). From Hamburg, a story-teller and poet with Northern connections. Lives in Fruthwilen/Switzerland. Wilpert; Lit.-Kürschner '63.

LENIN, W. I. (1870–1924). Russian revolutionary statesman. Came to power with the October Revolution 1917 and built up the Soviet Union. Brockhaus.

LEONHARD, RUDOLF (1889–1953). Socialist and pacifist writer and poet. Friend of J. R. Becher, Hasenclever, Meidner. Wilpert; Aktion; Expr.-Katalog.

LEPPIN, PAUL (1878–1945). Writer and poet, the "uncrowned king of the Prague Bohemians". His early novel *Daniel Jesus* (1905) is one of the books which influenced Early Expressionism. Expr.-Katalog.

LEUPPI, LEO (b. 1893). Swiss painter and wood-carver. Lives in Zurich. Vollmer.

LEWIS, SINCLAIR (1885–1951). American novelist and Nobel Prize winner. One of the leading American writers of the twentieth century. Wilpert.

LEYBOLD, HANS (1892–1914). Young Munich writer. Friend of Hugo Ball and Klabund. 1913, editor of the literary journal *Revolution* in Munich. Aktion.

LICHNOWSKY, MECHTILDE (1879–1958). Poetess very close to Expressionism, descendant of the Empress Maria Theresa. Married to a diplomat. Lived in England for years. Wilpert.

LICHTENSTEIN, ALFRED (1889–1914). Early Expressionist poet. Aktion; Wilpert; Expr.-Katalog.

LICHTENSTEIN, ERICH. Publisher and writer. Now living in Berlin as a critic.

LIEBKNECHT, KARL (1871–1919). Left-wing politician. Founder-member of the German Communist Party. Osterroth.

LILIENCRON, DETLEV von (1844–1909). Leading poet of the turn of the century. Naturalistic and Impressionistic stories and poems. Friendly with Richard Dehmel and the Naturalists. Wilpert.

LOERKE, OSKAR (1884–1941). Important poet and essayist. Friend of Moritz

Heimann and Wilhelm Lehmann. Also outstanding critic of Expression
ist literature. Wilpert.

LÖWENGARD, KURT (b. 1895). Hamburg painter and graphic artist. 1919–20
active at the Bauhaus. Vollmer.

LOEWENSON, ERWIN (1888–1963). Friend of Georg Heym. Founder-member
of the Neue Club. Exponent of "Neopathos". Later philosopher, active
as teacher in Israel.

LOOS, ADOLF (1870–1933). Viennese architect. Fore-runner of modern architecture. Friend of Karl Kraus and Ludwig von Ficker. Vollmer.

LORENZ, FELIX (1875–1930). Berlin writer. Wrote novels, stories, cabaret
songs, satires, etc. Kosch.

LORENZ, KARL (1888–1961). Late Expressionist writer in Hamburg. Author
of extensive Expressionistic works in verse. Editor of the *Rote Erde*
(1919–23).

LOTZ, ERNST WILHELM (1890–1914). Significant Early Expressionist poet
influenced by Stadler. Educated as a Prussian military cadet, from 1912
on, free-lance writer. Pinthus; Expr.-Katalog.

LOUYS, PIERRE (1870–1925). French novelist and poet. Friend of Mallarmé,
Gide, Valéry. Wrote extremely erotic novels and poetry. Wilpert.

LUBASCH, KURT (1891–1956). Berlin *litterateur*. Friend and literary executor
of Alfred Lichtenstein.

LÜCKEN, IVAR VON (1874–?). Dresden writer. Friend of Kokoschka. Wrote
poems and stories.

LUKÁCS, GEORG (1885–1971). Leading Marxist literary critic. Lived in Budapest. Brockhaus.

LUXEMBURG, ROSA (1870–1919). Left-wing politician and writer. She was
a founder-member of the German Communist Party and drafted its first
programme. Osterroth.

MACKE, AUGUST (1887–1914). Important painter associated with the "Blue
Rider" group. Vollmer.

MAETERLINCK, MAURICE (1862–1949). Belgian writer. Symbolist poet and
dramatist. Wilpert.

MAKART, HANS (1840–1884). Austrian painter. Leading exponent of Neo-
Baroque in the nineteenth century. Brockhaus.

MALLARMÉ, STÉPHANE (1842–1898). The most important French Symbolist
poet. Wilpert.

MANN, HEINRICH (1871–1950). Important twentieth-century novelist, dramatist, essayist. A politically committed writer, pacifist and social critic
much admired as such by the Expressionists. Wilpert.

MANN, THOMAS (1875–1955). The greatest German novelist of the twentieth
century. Wilpert.

MARC, FRANZ (1880–1916). Painter. Along with Kandinsky the spokesman
for the "Blue Rider". Close associations with *Sturm* and with Else
Lasker-Schüler. Vollmer.

MEYER, ALFRED RICHARD (1882–1956). Publisher of Early Expressionism in Berlin. Editor of the *Lyrische Flugblätter*. Also writer and poet (under the *nom de plume* Munkepunke), *gourmet* and bibliophile. Aktion; Wilpert.

MEYER, RICHARD M. (1860–1914). Berlin literary historian. Protégé of Wilhelm Scherer. Among other things wrote several surveys of German literature, especially of the nineteenth century. Kosch.

MEYERHOF, OTTO (1884–1951). Doctor and physiologist. For many years director of the Kaiser-Wilhelm-Institute for Physiology in Heidelberg. Nobel Prize winner. Brockhaus.

MEYRINK, GUSTAV (1868–1932). Writer of fantastic tales in the tradition of E. T. A. Hoffmann. His famous novel *Der Golem* (1915) is a masterpiece of the fantastic genre. Wilpert.

MICHEL, ALBERT (1895–1915). Young Munich poet, friend of J. R. Becher and H. F. S. Bachmair. Killed in the war. Aktion.

MICHEL, WILHELM (1877–1942). Writer, essayist and social critic. Lived in Darmstadt. Kosch.

MIERENDORFF, CARLO (1897–1943). Writer associated with the Darmstadt "Dachstube" Circle. Socialist politician, member of the Reichstag till 1933. Resistance worker. Osterroth; Expr.-Katalog.

MILIC, VINKO. Serbian sculptor.

MITSCHKE-COLLANDE, CONSTANTIN von (1884–1956). Dresden painter. With Dix and Kokoschka founded the "New Secession" in Dresden. Vollmer.

MOISSI, ALEXANDER (1880–1935). Actor discovered by Kainz. Acted for many years with great success at the Deutsches Theater in Berlin. Brockhaus.

MOMBERT, ALFRED (1872–1942). Leading Neo-Romantic poet. Author of cosmic hymns and myths. Fore-runner of Expressionism. Wilpert.

MONDRIAN, PIET (1872–1944). Dutch painter. Exponent of a kind of constructivism in modern art. Vollmer.

MÜHSAM, ERICH (1878–1934). Anarchist and socialist writer. Publisher and editor of literary-political journals. Wilpert; Aktion; Expr.-Katalog.

MÜLLER, ROBERT (1887–1924). Austrian writer and publisher much admired by Musil. Wrote novels, travel-books, essays and treatises. Giebisch-Gugitz.

MÜNTER, GABRIELE (1877–1962). Painter in Munich. Belonged to the Blue Rider Circle. Friend of Kandinsky. Vollmer.

MÜNZENBERG, WILLY (1889–1940). Communist politician. 1920 leader of the Communist Youth Internationale. 1924 member of the Reichstag.

MUNCH, EDVARD (1863–1944). Norwegian painter and graphic artist. Important pioneer of modern art. Vollmer.

MUSIL, ROBERT (1880–1942). Austrian writer. One of the great novelists of the twentieth century. Wilpert.

MYNONA see S. FRIEDLAENDER.

NADEL, ARNO (1878–1943). Jewish religious poet and dramatist. Wilpert.

NAUEN, HEINRICH (1880–1941). Rhineland Expressionist painter. 1920–36 professor at the Art Academy in Düsseldorf. Vollmer.

NAY, ERNST WILHELM (1902–1968). One of the best-known abstract painters of the present day. Lived in Cologne. Vollmer.

NELSON, LEONHARD (1882–1927). Philosopher. Founder of the Neo-Friesian School. Moralist. Taught in Heidelberg. Brockhaus; Osterroth.

NEUMANN, CARL (1860–1934). Art-historian in Heidelberg. Among other things wrote an important book on Rembrandt. Brockhaus.

NEUMANN, I. B. (1887–1961). Art-dealer and collector in Vienna, Berlin; ultimately in New York.

NOLDE, EMIL (1867–1956). Real name Emil Hansen. Expressionist painter and graphic artist. Member of the "Brücke" in Dresden. Vollmer.

NOWAK, HEINRICH (1890–after 1939). Austrian writer. Contributor to Expressionist journals. Aktion.

OEHRING, RICHARD (1889–1940). Writer and journalist on economic subjects. During the First World War was associated with Franz Jung, Oskar Maria Graf, Georg Schrimpf and others. Aktion.

OPFERMANN, KARL (1891–1960). Hamburg sculptor, influenced by Expressionism. Vollmer.

OPPENHEIMER, MAX (1885–1954). Painter and graphic artist, born in Vienna. Nick-named Mopp. Well-known portrait artist. Contributor to the Aktion. Aktion.

ORSKA, MARIA (1893–1930). Actress in Mannheim, Hamburg, Berlin and Vienna. Unforgettable leading lady in plays by Oscar Wilde and Wedekind.

OTTEN, KARL (1889–1963). Writer, at first with the Munich Circle, then with the Aktion in Berlin. Wrote novels, stories, poetry, biographies and travel-books. Towards the end of his life editor of Expressionist anthologies and collections. Pinthus; Aktion; Lit.-Kürschner '63.

PALLENBERG, MAX (1877–1934). Vienna-born actor. In Berlin in the 20's played character parts with unsurpassable wit. Brockhaus.

PALUCCA, GRET (b. 1902). Dancer and dance-teacher. Disciple of Mary Wigman. Founder and director of the Palucca School in Dresden. Numerous first prizes at International Dancing Contests. Th.-Kürschner.

PANIZZA, OSKAR (1853–1921). Doctor, author of fantastic, decadent works. From 1904 in an asylum. Wilpert.

PECHSTEIN, MAX (1881–1955). Expressionist painter and graphic artist. Member of the "Brücke". Lived in Berlin. Wilpert.

PÉGUY, CHARLES (1873–1914). French writer and poet of the renouveau catholique. 1900–14 editor of the Cahiers de la Quinzaine. Wilpert; Aktion.

PERTRENZ, ADOLF (1873–1915). Editor of the *Tägliche Rundschau* in Berlin. Killed in the war.

PFEMFERT, ALEXANDRA (1883–1963), née Ramm. Wife and business associate of Franz Pfemfert. Also a translator. Aktion.

PFEMFERT, FRANZ (1879–1954). Founder and editor of the *Aktion* (1910–32). Great patron of modern art and literature. Later left-wing propagandist. Aktion.

PHILIPPE, CHARLES-LOUIS (1874–1909). French novelist in the Naturalist tradition. Portrayed the living conditions of the lower classes. Wilpert.

PICABIA, FRANCIS (1879–1953). French painter. One of the leading representatives of French Dadaism. Vollmer.

PICARD, JACOB (1883–1967). Poet and story-teller. At first quite close to Expressionism. Lived at The Hague. Lit.-Kürschner '63.

PICASSO, PABLO (1881–1973). One of the great artists of the twentieth century. Vollmer.

PICK, OTTO (1887–1940). Writer, poet, editor and translator. From Prague. Friend of Werfel, Brod, Kafka. Intermediary between German and Czech literature. Aktion.

PINTHUS, KURT (b. 1886). Writer; for many years publisher's reader (with Ernst Rowohlt and Kurt Wolff). Editor of the Expressionist Anthology *Menschheitsdämmerung* (1919). Important theatre critic. Lit.-Kürschner '63.

PISCATOR, ERWIN (1893–1966). Actor, producer, theatre-director. Creator of Political Theatre. Th.-Kürschner.

POELZIG, HANS (1869–1936). Leading twentieth-century architect. 1903–16 director of the Art Academy in Breslau, 1916–19 City Engineer and Professor at the Technical University in Dresden, then active in Berlin. Numerous famous modern buildings. Brockhaus.

POPPER, ERNST. Prague writer. Contributor to the *Herder-Blätter*.

PRAMPOLINI, ENRICO (1894–1956). Italian painter and sculptor. 1912 became associated with the Futurists. Later created abstract works. Vollmer.

PREETORIUS, EMIL (b. 1885). Painter, graphic artist, illustrator, book-designer and collector in Munich. Vollmer.

PRITZEL, LOTTE (1887–1952). Well-known puppeteer, admired and loved by the young poets of the time. Later married to Dr. Pagel in Berlin. Vollmer.

PRZYGODE, WOLF (1895–1926). Founder and editor of the journal *Die Dichtung* (1918–23). Friend of Hermann Kasack. Expr.-Katalog.

RADBRUCH, GUSTAV (1878–1949). Famous professor of Law and politician. Professor in Heidelberg. Apart from specialist works also wrote brilliant essays. Brockhaus.

RAMIN, GÜNTHER (1898–1956). Organist and choir master. 1934, he succeeded Karl Straube as Thomaskantor in Leipzig.

ROWOHLT, ERNST (1887–1960). One of the most praise-worthy publishers of the twentieth century. Founded his first publishing concern in 1908, his second in 1919. Interpreter of modern movements in literature.

RUBINER, LUDWIG (1881–1920). Writer and translator. Exponent of political activism. Wrote literary works and manifestos. Aktion; Wilpert; Expr.-Katalog.

RUEST, ANSELM (1878–1943). Writer in Berlin. Critic and editor. Also wrote philosophical books and essays. Aktion.

RUNGE, WILHELM (1894–1918). Poet of the *Sturm*-Circle. Killed towards the end of the war. Expr.-Katalog.

SACHAROFF, ALEXANDER. Well-known modern Russian dancer.

SACK, GUSTAV (1885–1916). Munich poet killed in the war. His novels, stories and poems were posthumously published by his wife, Paula Sack.

SAGAN, LEONTINE. Munich actress.

SCHAD, CHRISTIAN (b. 1894). Painter and graphic artist. In Zurich Dadaist and friend of Walter Serner. In the 20's important portraits in the "New Objectivity" manner. Lives near Aschaffenburg. Vollmer.

SCHAEFER, HEINRICH (1889–1945). Writer and teacher in Berlin. Contributor to the *Aktion* and brother-in-law of Pfemfert. Aktion.

SCHAEFFER, ALBRECHT (1885–1950). Formalist poet not associated with Expressionism. Countless volumes of verse, novels, stories, essays etc. Wilpert.

SCHEERBART, PAUL (1863–1915). Turn of the century Neo-Romantic author of fantastic tales. Much admired by the Expressionists. Wilpert.

SCHELER, MAX (1874–1928). Philosopher and writer. In his early writings exponent of Husserl's phenomenology, founder of a new philosophical anthropology. Brockhaus.

SCHER, PETER (1884–1953). Real name Fritz Schweynert. Munich writer, editor of *Simplicissimus*. Author of satirical pieces, anecdotes, stories. Aktion; Kosch.

SCHERPENBACH, LEO. Munich book-seller and publisher. Editor of the *Bücherkiste* (1919–21).

SCHICKELE, RENÉ (1883–1940). Poet, writer, and editor. Great work as editor of the *Weisse Blätter* (1914–20). Poetic development from *Art Nouveau* through Expressionism to a new Realism. Wilpert; Pinthus; Aktion; Expr.-Katalog.

SCHIEBELHUTH, HANS (1895–1944). Poet of Late Expressionism. Belonged to the Darmstadt "Dachstube" circle. Later the brilliant translator of Thomas Wolfe. Wilpert.

SCHIELE, EGON (1890–1918). Austrian Expressionist painter and graphic artist. Vollmer; Aktion.

SCHILDKRAUT, RUDOLF (1862–1930). Leading Berlin actor.

SCHILLING, HEINAR (1894–1955). Dresden. Expressionist poet. Later numerous books on the German race. Expr.-Katalog.

SCHLAF, JOHANNES (1862–1941). Prose-writer and dramatist. With Holz the founder of "out-and-out" Naturalism. Wilpert.

SCHLEMMER, OSKAR (1888–1943). Modern painter and designer. 1920–29 professor at the Bauhaus. Vollmer.

SCHMIDKUNZ, WALTER (b. 1887). Popular writer. Writes novels, stories, anecdotes. Collaborates with Louis Trenker. Lives in Neuhaus near Schliersee (Upper Bavaria). Lit.-Kürschner '63.

SCHMIDT, ERICH (1853–1913). The most famous German literary historian about the turn of the century. Disciple of Wilhelm Scherer. From 1887 on Professor of German Literature at the University of Berlin. Kosch.

SCHMIDT-ROTTLUFF, KARL (b. 1884). Expressionist painter and graphic artist. 1905 founder-member of the Brücke in Dresden. Living in Berlin since 1911. Vollmer.

SCHNACK, FRIEDRICH (b. 1888). Writer and poet. Published poems, novels, children's books, travel-books, animal-books, etc. Wilpert; Lit.-Kürschner '63.

SCHNEIDER, OTTO. Viennese *Littérateur*. Contributor to Expressionist journals.

SCHÖNBERG, ARNOLD (1874–1951). Composer. Inventor of twelve-tone music. Involved as a painter in "Blue Rider". Brockhaus.

SCHOLZ, GEORG (1890–1945). Modern painter and graphic artist. 1923–33 professor at the Art Academy in Karlsruhe. Vollmer.

SCHREYER, LOTHAR (1886–1966). Writer and painter. Friend and associate of Herwarth Walden. Chief editor of the *Sturm*; producer for the *Sturm* theatre. Later specialized in writing Art Books. Wilpert; Lit.-Kürschner '63; Expr.-Katalog.

SCHRIMPF, GEORG (1889–1938). Painter. Friend of Oskar Maria Graf. Development from Cubism to New Objectivity. Vollmer.

SCHUCH, ERNST von (1846–1914). Conductor, from 1872 Musical Director, from 1889 General Musical Director of the Dresden Opera. Brockhaus.

SCHÜLEIN, JULIUS WOLFGANG (1881–1970). Landscape-painter and graphic artist, also book-illustrator. Vollmer.

SCHWABACH, ERIK ERNST (1891–after 1933). Writer and patron of the arts Leipzig, later in Berlin. Financed the *Weisse Bücher* series in Leipzig. Aktion.

SEEBACH, NIKOLAUS GRAF von (1854–1930). Director of the Dresden Court Theatre 1894–1919. Encouraged the modern dramatists of the turn of the century. Brockhaus.

SEEHAUS, PAUL ADOLF (1891–1919). Expressionist painter, etcher and artwriter. Belonged to August Macke's circle of friends. Vollmer.

SEEWALD, RICHARD (b. 1889). Painter, designer and writer. Began as an Expressionist. Lives in Ronco. Vollmer; Lit.-Kürschner '63.

SEGALL, LASAR (1889–1957). Russian-Brazilian painter and graphic artist. Lived in Berlin and Dresden till 1923, then went to Brazil. Vollmer.

SERNER, WALTER (1889–after 1927). Poet and art-writer. During the war fore-runner of Dada in Zurich. Author of hair-raising crime-stories. Aktion.

SEVERINI, GINO (1883–1966). Italian painter. Founder-member of the Futurist movement. Later Classicist. Vollmer.

SIEBURG, FRIEDRICH (1893–1964). Writer and poet. Important literary critic and essay-writer. Author of successful travel-books and biographies. Began as a writer of Expressionist poetry. Wilpert; Lit.-Kürschner '63.

SIMMEL, GEORG (1858–1918). Professor of philosophy in Berlin. Sociologist and moralist. Influence on Kurt Hiller and his friends. Brockhaus.

SINSHEIMER, HERMANN (1884–1950). Important producer, editor and theatre-critic. Kosch.

SLODKI, MARCEL (1892–1943). Polish painter, graphic artist, illustrator. During World War I in Switzerland; connections with the Dadaists. Vollmer.

SOENNECKEN, FRIEDRICH S. (1848–1919). Industrialist. 1875 founded his now famous office equipment firm. Patron of the arts. Brockhaus.

SOERGEL, ALBERT (1880–1958). Literary historian. Author of the best-known history of Expressionism. Kosch.

SOLOGUB, FJODOR (1863–1927). Russian Symbolist poet. Wilpert.

SOMMERFELD, MARTIN (1894–1939). Literary historian. Ultimately lived in America. Kosch.

SORGE, REINHARD JOHANNES (1892–1916). Dramatist and lyric poet. *Der Bettler* (*The Beggar*) 1912 is generally accepted as the first Expressionist drama. After his conversion wrote religious mystery plays. Wilpert.

SOUPAULT, PHILIPPE (b. 1897). French writer and poet. Dadaist and Surrealist. Wilpert.

SPELA. Well-known *chansonette* in Munich Bohemian circles.

ŠRAMEK, FRÁŇA (1877–1952). Czech lyric poet. Much translated during the Expressionist period. Wilpert.

STADLER, ERNST (1883–1914). Expressionist poet and literary historian. Exponent of so-called Early Expressionism. Wilpert; Aktion; Expr.-Katalog, Pinthus.

STEEGEMAN, PAUL (1894–1956). Publisher in Hanover. In the publishing firm he founded in 1919 numerous Expressionist works appeared in the *Silbergäule* series.

STEGEMANN, HEINRICH (1888–1945). Hamburg Expressionist painter and graphic artist. Vollmer.

STEINRÜCK, ALBERT (1872–1929). Leading actor. 1908–20 in Munich, then in Berlin. Also famous parts in films. Brockhaus.

STERNBERG, LEO (1876–1937). Turn of the century writer. Especially lyric poetry. Later regional tales and dramas. Aktion; Kosch.

STERNHEIM, CARL (1878–1942). One of the best-known dramatists of the

20th century. Inventor of a very aggressive prose style. Wilpert; Aktion; Expr.-Katalog.

STIEMER, FELIX. Dresden publisher and writer. Founder of the Dresden publishing house, 1917. Friend of Felixmüller.

STINNES, DÉSI. Daughter of the great industrialist Hugo Stinnes. Wrote *avant-garde* prose in the 20's.

STRAMM, AUGUST (1874–1915). Early Expressionist poet and dramatist. The most consistent and *ultra* of the *Sturm* Circle poets. Friend of Herwarth Walden, who became his prophet. Wilpert; Pinthus; Expr.-Katalog.

STRAUB, AGNES (1890–1941). Leading actress, in Berlin from 1916 on. Brockhaus.

STRAUBE, KARL (1873–1950). Composer of Church music. From 1918 on Thomaskantor in Leipzig and then conductor of the Gewandhaus choral concerts. Brockhaus.

STRICH, BROTHERS. Fritz Str. (1882–1963). Literary historian. 1910 Lecturer in Munich, later professor in Berne. Walter Str. (1885–1956). Psychologist.

STRINDBERG, AUGUST (1849–1912). Swedish Naturalist writer. Powerful influence on German literature. Wilpert.

SUARÈS, ANDRÉ (1868–1948). French writer, author of outstanding essays. Wilpert.

SUDERMANN, HERMANN (1857–1928). Much performed and widely read naturalist dramatist and novelist. Wilpert.

SUERMONDT, EDWIN. Art-historian. Discoverer of Henri Rousseau.

TAEUBER, SOPHIE (1889–1943). Swiss painter. Wife of Hans Arp. Involved in Swiss Dada. Many-sided outside activity. Vollmer.

TAGGER, THEODOR (1891–1958). Pseudonym Ferdinand Bruckner. Successful dramatist of the 20's. Exponent of New Objectivity in drama. During the Expressionist Period editor of the journal Marsyas, also wrote stories. Wilpert.

TAGORE, RABINDRANĀTH (1861–1941). Indian poet and philosopher. Nobel Prize Winner. Wilpert.

TEGTMEIER, WILLI (b. 1895). Painter and graphic artist. In his initial stages active in the Hamburg circle of artists. Vollmer.

TESSENOW, HEINRICH (1876–1950). Architect. From 1903 professor in Vienna. 1920–26 in Dresden. Among his famous buildings the Festival Hall in Dresden-Hellerau. Brockhaus.

THIMIG, HERMANN (b. 1890). Actor in Vienna, son of Hugo Thimig. 1916–24 at the Deutsches Theater in Berlin. Th.-Kürschner.

THOM, ANDREAS (1884–1943). Real name Rudolf Csmarisch. Austrian writer, published novels and stories during the Expressionist period. Giebisch-Gugitz.

TOLLER, ERNST (1893–1939). Expressionist dramatist. Involved in the revolution in Munich. Wilpert; Expr.-Katalog.

399

APPENDIX

TOLSTOY, LEO (1828–1910). Russian novelist of the nineteenth century. Wilpert.

TRAKL, GEORG (1887–1914). Early Expressionist lyric poet. Wilpert.

TREUGE, LOTHAR (1879–1919). Poet in the Stefan George Circle. Published poetry in the *Blätter für die Kunst*. Kosch.

TROTSKY, LEO (1879–1940). Russian revolutionary politician. Leading part in the October Revolution 1917, exiled by Stalin. Brockhaus.

TUCHOLSKY, KURT (1890–1935). Berlin writer of the 20's. Satirist, short-story writer and poet. Wilpert.

TWARDOWSKI, HANS HEINRICH von (b. 1898). Actor and writer. Author of several famous parodies (*Der rasende Pegasus*. 1918)

TZARA, TRISTAN (1896–1964). Rumanian. Writer. Founder-member of Dada in Zurich. The most important propagandist for the movement. Later moved over to Surrealism. Wilpert.

UEXKÜLL, JAKOB JOHANN von (1864–1944). Biologist. Professor in Heidelberg and Hamburg. Important environmental researches. Brockhaus.

ULLMAN, LUDWIG (1887–d. after 1955). Austrian writer. Contributor to the *Fackel* and other Expressionist journals.

ULLMANN, REGINA (1884–1961). Swiss religious writer. Friendly with Rilke and other poets of the time. Wilpert.

UNOLD, MAX (b. 1885). Munich painter, graphic artist, illustrator, writer. Vollmer.

UNAMUNO, MIGUEL DE (1864–1936). Spanish philosopher and writer. Brockhaus.

UNRUH, FRITZ von (1885–1970). Expressionist dramatist and prose-writer. Representative figure of German literature during the Weimar Republic. Wilpert; Expr.-Katalog.

URZIDIL, JOHANNES (1896–1970). Writer and editor originally from Prague. Wrote Expressionist poems in long lines, later books of prose. Lived in New York. Wilpert.

USINGER, FRITZ (b. 1895). Writer and essayist. Belonged to the Darmstadt "Dachstube" Circle. His poetry follows classical models. Lives in Friedberg. Wilpert.

VEIDT, CONRAD (1893–1943). Popular filmstar. Trained by Max Reinhardt.

VELDE, HENRY van de (1863–1957). Belgian architect, craftsman, book-designer and writer. One of the first artists in *Art Nouveau*. Vollmer.

VENNER, JOHANNES VINCENT (1883–1951). Swiss editor and writer. Lived in Locarno. Lit.-Kürschner '28.

VERHAEREN, EMILE (1855–1916). Belgian writer. Wrote ecstatic hymns, influenced by Walt Whitman. Wilpert.

VIERTEL, BERTHOLD (1885–1953). Austrian writer, theatre and film-producer. Involved with Expressionism. Wilpert.

VIOLLIS, JEAN. Swiss painter. Vollmer.

VISCHER, MELCHIOR (b. 1895). Editor in his youth wrote dadaistic works for Paul Steegemann. Lives in Berlin. Lit.-Kürschner '63.

WAGNER, FRIEDRICH WILHELM (1892–d. after 1920). Expressionist poet and writer. Nomadic existence. Editor in Hanover after World War I. Since disappeared. Aktion.

WALDEN, HERWARTH (1878–1941?). Invaluable work for the cause of Expressionism in literature and art. 1910 founding of his *avant-garde* journal *Der Sturm*, which he carried on till 1923. In his art-gallery he organized exhibitions, reading from new works, lectures. Also poet and composer. Wilpert; Expr.-Katalog.

WALDEN, NELL (b. 1887). Wife and business-associate of Herwarth Walden. Took part in *Sturm* as poet and painter. Lives in Switzerland.

WALDOFF, CLAIRE (1884–1957). Popular actress and cabaret performer. Lived in Bayrisch Gmain/Upper Bavaria. Th.-Kürschner.

WALLIS, ALFONS. Austrian author. With O. M. Fontana, editor of the *Flugblatt* (1917–18).

WALZEL, OSKAR (1864–1944). Literary historian. In Dresden from 1907–21. Numerous works and editions, specialist in German Romanticism. Brockhaus.

WAUER, WILLIAM (1866–1962). Sculptor, painter, theatre reformer and critic. Friend of Herwarth Walden. Contributor to the *Sturm* and to theory of Expressionism. Vollmer.

WEBER, HANS von (1872–1924). Munich publisher and bibliophile. Editor of the book review paper *Der Zwiebelfisch* (1910ff).

WEBER, MAX (1864–1920). Leading economist and sociologist. Brockhaus.

WEDEKIND, FRANK (1864–1918). Dramatist at the turn of the century. Forerunner of Expressionism. Wilpert; Aktion.

WEGENER, PAUL (1878–1948). Actor and producer. Leading roles in theatre and film. Friendly with Expressionist writers. Brockhaus.

WEINREICH, OTTO (b. 1886). Classical scholar and student of religions. Living as professor emeritus in Tübingen. Gel.-Kürschner '61.

WEISGERBER, ALBERT (1878–1915). Munich painter at the turn of the century. Development from *Art Nouveau* to Expressionism. Killed in the war. Vollmer.

WEISS, ERNST (1884–1940). Prague writer and dramatist. Wilpert; Expr.-Katalog.

WEISSBACH, RICHARD (1882–1950). Heidelberg publisher, founded his own little firm in 1910. There several important Early Expressionist works appeared. Later publication of bibliophile prints.

WEIZSÄCKER, VIKTOR Baron von (1886–1957). Neurologist in Heidelberg. Founder of a general anthropological medicine. Brockhaus.

WELTSCH, FELIX (1884–1964). Prague writer. Philosophical publications. Lived in Jerusalem.

WEREFKIN, MARIANNE von (1870–1938). Russian painter, came to Munich in 1896 with Jawlensky. Member of the Blue Rider Circle. Vollmer.

WERFEL, FRANZ (1890–1945). Prague poet. Extensive early lyrical work. Launched the "Oh-Mankind" type of Expressionist poetry. Later wrote novels. Wilpert; Aktion; Pinthus; Expr.-Katalog.

WERTHEIMER, MAX (1880–1943). Prague psychologist. Gestalt-theory.

WIGMAN, MARY (1880–1973). Dancer. Leading exponent of modern dance. Taught at her own school from 1921 on. Brockhaus.

WINDER, LUDWIG (1889–1946). Writer and poet from Moravia. Kosch.

WINTERSTEIN, EDUARD VON (1871–1961). Famous Berlin actor. At the Deutsches Theater for many years. Th.-Kürschner.

WOLF, FRIEDRICH (1888–1953). Socialist writer and poet. Medical profession. Expressionistic beginnings with his first plays in Dresden. His later play *Professor Mamlock* was a world-wide success. Wilpert.

WOLFENSTEIN, ALFRED (1883–1945). Expressionist poet and story-teller. Exponent of activism. Wilpert; Aktion; Pinthus; Expr.-Katalog.

WOLFF, KURT (1887–1963). German publisher of the twentieth century. All the leading Expressionists were published by him. Later specialized in publishing art-books.

WOLFSOHN, JOHN. Friend of Georg Heym. No further details.

WÜRTH, JOSEF (1900–48). Founder owner of the Darmstadt publishing house "Die Dachstube". Focal point for a circle of friends. Brilliant printer.

ZECH, PAUL (1881–1946). Expressionist poet, story-teller and dramatist. Friendly with Else Lasker-Schüler, Richard Dehmel, Stefan Zweig. Wilpert; Pinthus; Expr.-Katalog.

ZEHDER, HUGO (1881–1961). Dresden journalist. Editor of theatre journals. Ultimately settled in Berlin.

ZEMLINSKY, ALEXANDER VON (1872–1942). Composer. Director of the Academy of Music in Prague. Brother-in-law of Arnold Schönberg.

ZEPLER, GEORG (1859–1925). Doctor, editor, writer in Berlin. Social-political writings and conventional poetry. Editor of the *Demokrat* (1909–14). Fell out with Franz Pfemfert. Kosch.

ZIEGEL, ERICH (1876–1950). Actor and producer.

ZOLA, EMILE (1840–1902). French novelist. Leading representative of the Naturalist School. Wilpert.

ZUCKMAYER, CARL (b. 1896). Successful contemporary German dramatist. Expressionist beginnings. Also writes prose, stories, novels, essays. Wilpert; Lit.-Kürschner '63.

ZWEIG, ARNOLD (1887–1968). Story-teller, essayist, dramatist. Vast *oeuvre*. Lived in Berlin. Wilpert; Lit.-Kürschner '63.

ZWEIG, STEFAN (1881–1942). Austrian writer and poet. Neo-Romantic beginnings. Important biographies and essays. Wilpert.

BIBLIOGRAPHY

Preamble

The first section of this bibliography gives a survey of all memoirs of literary Expressionism which have been published either as books or as contributions to journals and anthologies. A selection from the extremely numerous memoirs of Dadaism is also included. Passages from those sources which have been used in the present volume are indicated in this alphabetical index with our page references.

This bibliography comprises only those works which were published in German up to 1965.

In the second section various key novels and short-stories which give some idea of Expressionist literary life are listed. It need hardly be stressed at this point that this bibliography lays no claim to be complete, for memoirs of this period have been published in an incredibly wide range of places. Hence the present list is provisional. The editor invites the specialist reader to inform him of any omissions.

ARP, HANS: Dadaland. Zürcher Erinnerungen aus der Zeit des Ersten Weltkrieges. In: Atlantis, 20 (1948), H. 6, pp. 275–77; reprinted in the following, extract pp. **175–9**.

ARP, HANS: Unsern täglichen Traum . . . Erinnerungen, Dichtungen und Betrachtungen aus den Jahren 1914–54. Zurich, Verl. der Arche, 1955. 128 pp. Includes Sophie Taeuber (pp. 9–19); Dada war kein Rüpelspiel (pp. 20–28); Dadaland (pp. 51–61); Francis Picabia (pp. 62–65); Miszellen (pp. 73–78); Konkrete Kunst (pp. 79–83).

ARP, HANS: Dadakonzil. In: Die Geburt des Dada. Dichtung und Chronik der Gründer. (Ed. by Peter Schifferli.) Zurich, Verl. der Arche, 1957, pp. 8–12 (written July, 1957); reprinted in: Als Dada begann. Bildchronik und Erinnerungen der Gründer. Ed. Peter Schifferli (Zurich), Sanssouci Verl., 1957, pp. 66–70.

ARP, HANS: Dada: In: Dada. Dokumente einer Bewegung. (Catalogue arranged by Karl Heinz Hering und Ewald Rathke.) Düsseldorf, 1958, 3 pp. (written July, 1958.)

BACHMAIR, HEINRICH F. S.: Bericht des ersten Verlegers (von Johannes R. Becher), 1911–14. In: *Sinn und Form*, 2. Sonderheft Johannes R. Becher, Berlin, 1960, pp. 97–110; our pp. **89–102**.

BALL, HUGO: Die Flucht aus der Zeit. Munich und Leipzig. Duncker und Humblot, 1927, 330 pp. with Index; New Edition: Luzern, Stocker, 1946, 311 pp. A later re-written diary for the years 1914–21 with an introduction on 1911–14.

BARLACH, ERNST: Ein selbsterzähltes Leben. Berlin, Cassirer, 1928, 73 pp. Various reprints.

BECHER, JOHANNES R.: Auf andere Art so grosse Hoffnung. Tagebuch 1950. Berlin, Aufbau-Verlag, 1951. 695 pp. With various memories of Expressionism. Our extract pp. **325–6.**

BECHER, JOHANNES R.: (Bemühungen. Bd. 1–4) Verteidigung der Poesie. Berlin, Aufbau-Verlag, 1952; Poetische Konfession, 1954; Macht der Poesie, 1955; Das poetische Prinzip, 1957. These works contain scattered remembrances. Our chapter on Jacob van Hoddis pp. **43–7.**

BEHL, C. F. W.: Begegnungen mit dem Expressionismus. In: *Imprimatur. Ein Jahrbuch für Bücherfreunde.* Neue Folge, Vol. 3 (1961–62), pp. 240–43. Our pp. **287–92.**

BENN, GOTTFRIED: Doppelleben. Zwei Selbstdarstellungen. Wiesbaden, Limes-Verlag, 1950, 213 pp.

BERGER, LUDWIG: Wir sind vom gleichen Stoff aus dem die Träume sind. Summe eines Lebens. Tübingen, Wunderlich, 1953, 404 pp.

BERGER, LUDWIG: Theatermenschen. So sah ich sie. (Velber bei Hanover.) Friedrich, 1962, 107 pp.

BERSTL, JULIUS: Odyssee eines Theatermenschen. Erinnerungen aus sieben Jahrzehnten. Berlin-Grunewald, Arani, 1963, 238 pp.

BLASS, ERNST: Das alte Café des Westens. In: *Die literarische Welt,* 4 (1928), Nr. 35, pp. 3–4; our pp. **27–33.**

BLEI, FRANZ: Erzählung eines Lebens. Leipzig, List, 1930, 496 pp.

BLÜHER, HANS: Werke und Tage. Geschichte eines Denkers. Munich, List, 1953, 457 pp.

BROD, MAX: Streitbares Leben. Autobiographie. Munich, Kindler, 1960, 543 pp. with index. Our extracts on pp. **53–9.**

BROD, MAX: Prag 1920–30 und seine Schriftsteller. In: *Tribüne,* Vol. 3 (1964), pp. 969–74.

BRONNEN, ARNOLT: gibt zu Protokoll. Beiträge zur Geschichte des modernen Schriftstellers. Hamburg, Rowohlt; 1954, 494 pp.

BURSCHELL, FRIEDRICH: *Revolution* and *Neue Erde.* Munich 1918–19. Aus meinen Erinnerungen. In: *Imprimatur,* Neue Folge, Vol. 3 (1961–62), pp. 244–248; our pp. **247–53.**

BURSCHELL, FRIEDRICH: Zwischen München und Berlin. In: *Deutsche Rundschau.* No. 89 (1963), H. 5, pp. 31–39.

CAHÉN, FRITZ MAX: Der Alfred Richard Meyer-Kreis. In: *Imprimatur,* Neue Folge, Vol. 3 (1961–62), pp. 190–93; our pp. **103–8.**

CAHÉN, FRITZ MAX: Der Weg nach Versailles. Erinnerungen 1912–19. Schicksalsepoche einer Generation. Boppard, Boldt, 1963, 383 pp.

DIETRICH, RUDOLF ADRIAN: Konstanz 1919. In: *Imprimatur*, Neue Folge, Vol. 3 (1961–62), pp. 253–57.

DURIEUX, TILLA: Eine Tür steht offen. Erinnerungen. Berlin-Grunewald, Gerbig, 1954, 342 pp.

EDSCHMID, KASIMIR: In memoriam Carlo Mierendorff. In: Carlo Mierendorff, Literarische Schriften. Darmstadt, Darmstädter Verlag, 1947, pp. v–xiii; our pp. **255–64**.

EDSCHMID, KASIMIR: Tagebuch, 1958–60. München, Desch, 1960, 411 pp. Includes various reminiscences about Expressionism. Cf. our pp. **363–4**.

EDSCHMID, KASIMIR: Lebendiger Expressionismus. Auseinandersetzungen, Gestalten, Erinnerungen. Mit 31 Dichterporträts von Künstlern der Zeit. München, Desch, 1961, 410 pp. with index—cf. here pp. **362–3**.

FELIXMÜLLER, CONRAD: Erinnerungen an Friedrich Wolf. In: Neue Texte, Almanach für deutsche Literatur, Vol. 3. Berlin, Aufbau-Verlag, 1963, pp. 375–81; our pp. **358–60**.

FLAKE, OTTO: Es wird Abend. Bericht aus einem langen Leben. Gütersloh, Mohn, 1960, 629 pp. with index. Our pp. **145–9**.

FLESCH-BRUNNINGEN, HANS: (Die Aktion in Wien.) Transcript from a broadcast by WDR Cologne. Unpublished. Our extract on pp. **129–30**.

FONTANA, OSKAR MAURUS: Der Expressionismus in Wien. Erinnerungen. In: *Imprimatur*. Neue Folge, Vol. 3 (1961–62), pp. 207–10.

GLAUSER, FRITZ: Dada-Erinnerungen. In: Schweizer-Spiegel. October, 1931; Reprinted in: Die Geburt des Dada. Dichtung und Chronik der Gründer. (Ed. Peter Schifferli.) Zurich, Verlag der Arche 1957. pp. 147–55; Das war Dada. Ed. Peter Schifferli. München, dtv. 1963, pp. 125–33.

GRAF, OSKAR MARIA: Wir sind Gefangene. Ein Bekenntnis aus diesem Jahrzehnt. München, Drei Masken-Verlag, 1927, 530 pp. Comments on the years between 1905 and 1919.

GROSZ, GEORGE: Ein kleines Ja und ein grosse Nein. Sein Leben von ihm selbst erzählt. Hamburg, Rowohlt, 1955, 291 pp.

HAAS, WILLY: Die literarische Welt. Erinnerungen. München, List, 1957, 316 pp.

HARBECK, HANS: Expressionismus in Hamburg. In: *Imprimatur*, Vol. 3 (1961–62), pp. 249–52; our pp. **269–72**.

HARDEN, SYLVIA VON: Erinnerungen an einst . . . In: *Imprimatur*, Vol. 3 (1961–62), pp. 219–22; here pp. **187–91**.

HAUSENSTEIN, WILHELM: Lux perpetua. Summe eines Lebens aus dieser Zeit. Vol. 1. München, Alber, 1947.

HAUSMANN, RAOUL: Club Dada. Berlin (1918–20). In: Dada. Dokumente einer Bewegung. (Catalogue arranged by Karl Heinz Hering and Ewald Rathke.) Düsseldorf, 1958, 3 pp.; our pp. **225–7**.

APPENDIX

HAUSMANN, RAOUL: Courrier Dada. Paris, Le Terrain Vague, 1958, 159 pp. with illustrations.

HENNINGS, EMMY: Das Cabaret Voltaire und die Galerie Dada. In: Neue Zürcher Zeitung, May, 1934; reprinted in: Die Geburt des Dada. Dichtung und Chronik der Gründer. (Ed. Peter Schifferli.) Zürich, Verlag. der Arche, 1957, pp. 156–60. Das war Dada. Ed. Peter Schifferli. Munich, dtv. 1963, pp. 117f. (abridged).

HENNINGS, EMMY: Blume und Flamme. Geschichte einer Jugend. Einsiedeln, Benziger, 1938, 320 pp. For the early period.

HENNINGS, EMMY: Das flüchtige Spiel. Wege und Umwege einer Frau. Einsiedeln, Benziger, 1940, 288 pp. Poetic diary up to the war.

HENNINGS, EMMY: Ruf und Echo. Mein Leben mit Hugo Ball. Einsiedeln, Benziger 1953, 291 pp. The most important of E.H.'s books of memoirs.

HERZFELDE, WIELAND: Immergrün. Merkwürdige Erlebnisse und Erfahrungen eines fröhlichen Waisenknaben. Berlin, Aufbau-Verlag, 1949, 255 pp.; also in: Herzfelde, Unterwegs. Blätter aus fünfzig Jahren. Berlin, Aufbau-Verlag, 1961, pp. 5–246.

HERZFELDE, WIELAND: Wie ein Verlag entstand. In: Das Wort. Literarische Monatsschrift. Vol. 1 (1936), H. 2, pp. 97–102; our pp. **217–23**.

HERZOG, WILHELM: Menschen, denen ich begegnete. Munich, Francke, 1959, 494 pp.

HIRSCH, KARL JAKOB: Heimkehr zu Gott. Briefe an meinen Sohn. Munich, Desch, 1946, 191 pp.; our extract pp. **229–32**.

HÖXTER, JOHN: "So lebten wir." 25 Jahre Berliner Bohème. Erinnerungen. Berlin, Biko-Verlag. 1929; 69 pp.; our extract pp. **309–11**.

HUELSENBECK, RICHARD: En avant Dada. Eine Geschichte des Dadaismus. Hanover, Steegemann, 1920. 44 pp. (Die Silbergäule. Vol. 50–51).

HUELSENBECK, RICHARD: Die dadaistische Bewegung. Eine Selbstbiographie. In: Die neue Rundschau. No. 31 (1920), pp. 972–79; our extracts pp. **340–1**.

HUELSENBECK, RICHARD: Das Cabaret Voltaire. In: Der Querschnitt. No. 7 (1927), pp. 137–38.

HUELSENBECK, RICHARD: Zurich 1916, wie es wirklich war. In: Die neue Bücherschau. Jg. 6 (1928), pp. 611–17; our pp. **167–73**.

HUELSENBECK, RICHARD: Mit Witz, Licht und Grütze. Auf den Spuren des Dadaismus. Wiesbaden, Limes-Verlag, 1957, 152 pp.

HUELSENBECK, RICHARD: Dada als Literatur. In: Dada. Dokumente einer Bewegung. (Catalogue arranged by Karl Heinz Hering and Ewald Rathke.) Düsseldorf, 1958.

HUELSENBECK, RICHARD: Dada oder Der Sinn im Chaos. In: Dada. Eine literarische Dokumentation. Ed. Richard Huelsenbeck. Reinbek bei Hamburg, Rowohlt, 1964, pp. 7–23.

IHERING, HERBERT: Begegnungen mit Zeit und Menschen. Berlin, Aufbau-Verlag, 1963, 228 pp. First section of memoirs up to 1918.

JACOB, HANS : Kind meiner Zeit. Lebenserinnerungen. Cologne, Kiepenheuer & Witsch 1962. 285 pp. pp. 18–45 : In Berlin 1910–14; pp. 56ff. In München, 1919.

JACOB, HEINRICH EDUARD : Berlin. Vorkriegsdichtung und Lebensgefühl. In : *Imprimatur*, Vol. 3 (1961–62), pp. 186–89; our pp. **17–21**.

JACQUES, NORBERT : Mit Lust gelebt. Roman meines Lebens, Hamburg, Hoffmann & Campe, 1950, 463 pp.

JUNG, CLAIRE : Leuchtet die Zukunft. Ein Rechenschaftsbericht. Unpublished. Our extract pp. **37–42**.

JUNG, FRANZ : Der Weg nach unten. Aufzeichnungen aus einer grossen Zeit. Neuwied, Luchterhand, 1961, 482 pp.; our extracts on pp. **119–22**.

KASACK, HERMANN : Wolf Przygode und *Die Dichtung* (1918–23). In : *Imprimatur*, Vol. 3 (1961–62), pp. 228–34; our pp. **207–16**.

KESTENBERG, LEO : Bewegte Zeiten. Musisch-musikalische Lebenserinnerungen. Wolfenbüttel, Zurich, Möseler, 1961, 134 pp.

KOBER, A. H. : Einst in Berlin. Rhapsodie 14. Ed. Richard Kirn. Hamburg, Hoffmann & Campe, 1956, 257 pp.

KORTNER, FRITZ : Aller Tage Abend. Munich, Kindler, 1959, 570 pp.

KRELL, MAX : Das alles gab es einmal. Frankfurt/Main, Scheffler 1961, 361 pp.; our extract on pp. **301–4**.

KUTSCHER, ARTUR : Der Theaterprofessor. Ein Leben für die Wissenschaft vom Theater. Munich, Ehrenwirth, 1960, 268 pp.

LEONHARD, RUDOLF erzählt. Selected and introduced by Maximilian Scheer. Berlin, Verlag der Nation, 1955. Also contains some early memories; our pp. **115–18**.

LOEWENSON, ERWIN : Georg Heym oder Vom Geist des Schicksals. Munich, Ellermann, 1962, 159 pp. Also contains some personal comments.

MAHLER-WERFEL, ALMA : And the Bridge is love. In coll. with E. B. Ashton. New York, Harcourt Brace, 1958, 312 pp. German version : Mein Leben. (Pref. by Willy Haas.) Frankfurt a. M., S. Fischer, 1960, 456 pp.

MARCUSE, LUDWIG : Mein zwanzigstes Jahrhundert. Auf dem Weg zu einer Autobiographie. Munich, List, 1960, 389 pp.; one section our pp. **293–9**.

MARIETTA DI MONACO : Ich kam—ich geh. Reisebilder, Erinnerungen, Porträts. Mit Silhouetten von Ernst Moritz Engert. Munich, Süddeutscher Verlag. 1962, 113 pp.; Section on Klabund and his friends; our pp. **83–8**.

MEHRING, WALTER : Die verlorene Bibliothek. Autobiographie einer Kultur. Hamburg, Rowohlt, 1952; 2. ed. Munich, Kreisselmeier, 1964.

MEHRING, WALTER : Berlin Dada. Eine Chronik mit Fotos und Dokumenten. Zurich, Verlag der Arche, 1959, 100 pp.

MEHRING, WALTER : Berlin Avantgarde. In : Als das Jahrhundert jung war. Ed. Josef Halperin. Zurich, Artemis, 1961, pp. 31–40; our pp. **109–14**.

MEIDNER, LUDWIG: Erinnerung an Dresden. In: 1918. Neue Blätter für Kunst und Dichtung. Jg. 1 (1918), No. 2, pp. 36–38; reprinted in: Meidner, Septemberschrei. Hymnen, Gebete, Lästerungen. Berlin, Paul Cassirer, 1920, pp. 11–14.

MEYER, ALFRED RICHARD: die maer von der musa expressionistica. Zugleich eine quasi-literaturgeschicte mit über 130 praktischen beispielen. Düsseldorf, Die Fähre, 1948, 130 pp.; one extract on our pp. 49–51.

MUCHE, GEORG: Blickpunkt. Sturm, Dada, Bauhaus, Gegenwart. Munich, Langen/Müller, 1961, 233 pp.; one section on our pp. 344–5.

MÜHSAM, ERICH: Namen und Menschen. Unpolitische Erinnerungen. Leipzig. Verlag Buch und Volk, 1949, 256 pp.

OTTEN, KARL: 1914 – Sommer ohne Herbst. Erinnerungen an August Macke und die Rheinischen Expressionisten. Radio transcript 1954. First published here pp. 139–43.

PAULY, ERNST: 20 Jahre Café des Westens. Erinnerungen am Kurfürstendamm. Berlin-Charlottenburg, 1913–14, 61 pp.

PECSTEIN, MAX: Erinnerungen. Mit 105 Zeichnungen des Künstlers. Ed. Leopold Reidemeister. Wiesbaden, Limes Verlag, 1960, 127 pp.

PFEMFERT, ALEXANDRA: Die Gründung der Aktion. From a WDR Cologne broadcast. Our pp. 35–6.

PICARD, JACOB: Ernst Blass, seine Umwelt in Heidelberg und Die Argonauten. Biographisches Fragment. In: Imprimatur, Vol. 3 (1961–62), pp. 194–99; our pp. 131–8.

PICK, OTTO: Erinnerungen an den Winter 1911–12. In: Die Aktion. Jg. 6 (1916), Sp. 605.

PINTHUS, KURT: Walter Hasenclever. Leben und Werk. In: Hasenclever. Gedichte—Dramen—Prosa. Ed. Kurt Pinthus. Hamburg, Rowohlt, 1963, pp. 6–62. Also contains personal reminiscences of the Leipzig circle they both knew.

PINTHUS, KURT: Ernst Rowohlt und sein Verlag. In: Rowohlt Almanach, 1908 bis 1962. Hamburg, Rowohlt, 1962, pp. 9–40. Also contains memories of Early Expressionism in Leipzig; our pp. 67–76.

PISCATOR, ERWIN: Die politische Bedeutung der Aktion. In: Imprimatur, Neue Folge, Vol. 3 (1961–62), pp. 211–14; our pp. 181–5.

PULVER, MAX: Erinnerungen an eine europäische Zeit. Zurich, Orell-Füssli, 1953, 94 pp.

REIMANN, HANS: Mein blaues Wunder. Lebenschronik eines Humoristen. Munich, List, 1959, 570 pp.

RICHTER, HANS: Dada-Profile. Mit Zeichnungen, Fotos, Dokumenten. Zurich, Verlag der Arche, 1961, 115 pp.

SCHAD, CHRISTIAN: Zurich/Genf: Dada. In: *Imprimatur*, Vol. 3 (1961–62), pp. 215–18; our pp. **161–6**.

SCHREYER, LOTHAR: Expressionistisches Theater. Erinnerungen. Hamburg, Toth, 1948, 239 pp. (Hamburger Theaterbücherei, Vol. 4).

SCHREYER, LOTHAR: Der Sturm, Ein Gedenktag, *see* Der Sturm.

SCHREYER, LOTHAR: Das war *Der Sturm* in: Minotaurus. Dichtung unter den Hufen von Staat und Industrie. Ed. Alfred Döblin. Wiesbaden, Steiner, 1955, pp. 112–30.

SCHREYER, LOTHAR: Erinnerungen an Sturm und Bauhaus. Was ist das Bild des Menschen? Munich, Langer/Müller, 1965, 295 pp., with numerous illustrations; our pp. **193–9**.

SCHREYER, LOTHAR: Vom Leben des *Sturm*. In: *Imprimatur*, Vol. 3 (1961–62), pp. 223–27.

SCHULZE-MAIZIER, FRIEDRICH: Frühexistentialist unter Frühexpressionisten. Erlebnisse im *Neuen Club*. In: Deutsche Rundschau. Jg. 88 (1962), pp. 331–38.

SEEWALD, RICHARD: Der Mann von gegenüber. Spiegelbild eines Lebens. Munich, List, 1963, 347 pp.; extracts on our pp. **77–81**.

SEIFFHART, ARTHUR: Inter folia fructus. Aus den Erinnerungen eines Verlegers. Berlin, Fundament Verlag, 1948, 51 pp.

SINSHEIMER, HERMANN: Gelebt im Paradies. Erinnerungen und Begegnungen. Munich, Pflaum, 1953, 344 pp. with illustrations.

STARKE, OTTOMAR: Was mein Leben anlangt. Erinnerungen. Berlin-Grunewald, Herbig, 1956, 252 pp.

STEEGEMANN, PAUL: Fünf Jahre Verleger. In: Das Stachelschwein. Ed. Hans Reimann. Jg. I (1924), H. 6 pp. 3–5; reprinted in: *Imprimatur*, Vol. 3 (1961–62), pp. 258–59; our pp. **265–7**.

STERNHEIM, CARL: Vorkriegseuropa im Gleichnis meines Lebens. Amsterdam, Querido-Verlag, 1936, 222 pp.

STURM, DER: Ein Erinnerungsbuch an Herwarth Walden und die Künstler aus dem Sturmkreis. Ed. Nell Walden and Lothar Schreyer. Baden-Baden, Klein, 1954, 276 pp. with numerous illustrations and documents.

SUSMAN, MARGARETE: Ich habe viele Leben gelebt. Erinnerungen Stuttgart, Deutsche Verlags-Anstalt, 1964, 187 pp.

SZITTYA, EMIL: Das Kuriositäten-Kabinett. Begegnungen mit seltsamen Begebenheiten, Landstreichern, Verbrechern, Artisten . . . Constanz, See-Verlag, 1923, 317 pp.; our extract on pp. **153–9**.

TOLLER, ERNST: Eine Jugend in Deutschland. Amsterdam, Querido-Verlag, 1933, 293 pp.

URZIDIL, JOHANNES: Im Prag des Expressionismus. In: *Imprimatur*, Vol. 3 (1961–62), pp. 202–4; different version in: Urzidil, Da geht Kafka. Zurich, Artemis, 1965; our pp. **61–6**.

VIERTEL, BERTHOLD: Dichtungen und Dokumente. Gedichte, Prosa, Auto-biographische Fragmente. (Selected and ed. Ernst Ginsberg.) Munich, Kösel, 1956, 426 pp.

VOGELER, HEINRICH: Erinnerungen. Ed. Erich Weinert. Berlin, Rütten & Loening, 1952, 375 pp.; 27 illustrations.

WALDEN, NELL: Der Sturm. Ein Erinnerungsbuch, see Der Sturm.

WALDEN, NELL: Herwarth Walden. Ein Lebensbild. Mainz, Kupferber, 1963, 132 pp. with 48 illustrations. With documents and comments by his contemporaries.

WALDEN, NELL: Kokoschka und der Sturm-Kreis. In: J. P. Hodin, Bek-enntnis zu Kokoschka. Mainz Kupferberg, 1963, pp. 74–85; extract on our pp. **123–8**.

WESTHEIM, PAUL: Wie *Das Kunstblatt* entstand. In: Vierzig Jahre Kiepen-heuer, 1910–50. Ein Almanach. Ed. Noa Kiepenheuer. Weimar, Kiepen-heuer, 1951, pp. 53–57; our pp. **201–5**.

WOLF, FRIEDRICH: Felixmüller. In: Dramaturgische Blätter. Jg. 2 (1948), H. 3; reprinted in: Ausstellungskatalog Conrad Felixmüller. Halle, 1949; our pp. **243–6**.

WOLF, KURT: Vom Verlegen im allgemeinen und von der Frage: wie kommen Verleger und Autoren zusammen. In: Sprache im technischen Zeitalter. Jg. 3 (1964), pp. 894–904; included in: Wolff, Autoren, Bücher, Abenteuer. Berlin, Wagenbach, 1965, pp. 13–25; our pp. **273–85**.

Novels and Stories

BALL, HUGO: Flametti oder vom Dandysmus der Armen. Novel. Berlin, Erich Reiss, 1918, 224 pp.

BECHER, JOHANNES R.: Abschied. Einer deutschen Tragödie erster Teil. 1900–14. Berlin, Aufbau-Verlag, 1945, 429 pp.; our extract pp. **325–6**.

BECHER, JOHANNES R.: Wiederanders. Sequel to the novel Abschied. Frag-ment. In: Sinn und Form. 2. Sonderheft Johannes R. Becher. Berlin, 1960, pp. 511–51; our extract pp. **325–6**.

ESSIG, HERMANN: Der Taifun. Novel. Leipzig, Kurt Wolff, 1919, 367 pp.

FLAKE, OTTO: Nein und Ja. Roman des Jahres 1917. Berlin, Verlag Die Schmiede, 1923, 254 pp.

FRANK, LEONHARD: Links wo das Herz ist. Novel. Munich, Nymphen-burger Verlagsanstalt, 1952, 260 pp.; our extract pp. **370–1**.

KLABUND: Marietta. Ein Liebesroman aus Schwabing. Hannover, Steege-mann, 1920. (Die Silbergäule. Bd. 79); our extract pp. **318–24**.

KLABUND: Roman eines jungen Mannes. (Der Rubin.) (Published

posthumously.) In: Klabund: Gesammelte Werke in Einzelausgaben. Bd. 6. Romane der Sehnsucht. Vienna, Phaidon-Verlag, 1930.

LASKER-SCHÜLER, ELSE: Mein Herz. Ein Liebesroman mit Bildern und wirklich lebenden Menschen. Munich, Bachmair, 1912, 167 pp.

LICHTENSTEIN, ALFRED: Café Klösschen. Two fragments from the 1st version of the story: Café Klösschen. In: Lichtenstein, Gedichte und Geschichten. (Ed. Kurt Lubasch.) Vol. 2. Munich, Georg Müller, 1919, pp. 40–53.

MYNONA: Graue Magie. Berliner Nachschlüsselroman. Mit 6 Zeichnungen von Lothar Homeyer. Dresden, Kaemmerer, 1922, 374 pp.

SIEMSEN, HANS: Wo hast du dich denn herumgetrieben? Erlebnisse. Munich, Kurt Wolff, 1920, 11 pp.

URZIDIL, JOHANNES: Prager Triptychon. Munich, Langen/Müller, 1960, 230 pp.

WERFEL, FRANZ: Barbara oder die Frömmigkeit. Vienna, Paul Zsolnay, 1929, 809 pp.

INDEX OF NAMES

413